WITHDRAWN

# PAGANISM

IN

# ARTHURIAN ROMANCE

# PAGANISM

## IN

# ARTHURIAN ROMANCE

John Darrah

THE BOYDELL PRESS

First published 1994
The Boydell Press, Woodbridge


ISBN 0 85115 350 X


The Boydell Press is an imprint of Boydell & Brewer Ltd
PO Box 9, Woodbridge, Suffolk IP12 3DF, UK
and of Boydell & Brewer Inc.
PO Box 41026, Rochester, NY 14604, USA


British Library Cataloguing-in-Publication Data
Darrah, John
    Paganism in Arthurian Romance
    I. Title
    398.22
    ISBN 0–85115–350–X

    Library of Congress Cataloging-in-Publication Data
Darrah, John.
    Paganism in Arthurian romance / John Darrah.
        p.    cm.
    Includes bibliographical references (p.) and index.
    ISBN 0–85115–350–X (alk. paper)
    1. Arthur, King. 2. Britons – Kings and rulers – Biography.
3. Great Britain – Antiquities, Celtic. 4. Paganism – Great Britain –
History. 5. Great Britain – History – To 1066. 6. Arthurian
romances – Sources. 7. Paganism in literature. I. Title.
DA152.5.A7D358 1994
942.01'4–dc20
[B]                                                          93–37182

The paper used in this publication meets the minimum requirements
of American National Standard for Information Sciences –
Permanence of Paper for Printed Library Materials, ANSI Z39.48–1984

Printed in Great Britain by
St Edmundsbury Press Ltd, Bury St Edmunds, Suffolk

# CONTENTS

# FOREWORD

Cervantes was well aware how slender is the link between Arthurian Romance and reality. 'What are we to say of the ease with which a hereditary Queen or Empress throws herself into the arms of an unknown wandering knight' he asked?[1] The answer to his question did not become apparent until, about a century ago, Sir James Frazer made known the significance of the rule of the priest-king of Nemi (described in more detail below). It was then noticed that something rather similar to the events at Nemi occurred in the earliest French versions of the romances, and it is to them we must turn, with some help from the ancient Celtic tradition, to find how Cervantes' question is to be answered, and how a great many other instances of apparently irrational behaviour are to be explained.

The strangeness of the Arthurian story is there for all to see. Arthur's life began when Merlin transformed Uther Pendragon's appearance so that he could sleep with another man's wife; and it ended with the mortally wounded king expending his last remaining energies in getting his sword thrown into a pool. In between there are many strange incidents, such as: the sword drawn from a stone; Lancelot's upbringing at the bottom of a lake; Gawain's increase in strength with the waxing of the sun; and Morgan le Fay's 'Valley of No Return'. And there are many other instances of behaviour in which the laws of nature seem to be disregarded. The Arthurian legends, in respect of their strangeness, can only be compared with ancient mythologies and with those epics in which the course of the lives of heroes is regulated by interfering deities. I propose to show that the romances look like mythology because they are influenced to a considerable degree by recollections of pagan thought-patterns.

To do this it is necessary to go far behind the familiar presentations of Malory and Tennyson, to the ultimate roots of the Arthurian legends (as we know them now) eight hundred or more years ago. Arthur is a Celtic hero, and the most primitive accounts of his actions are preserved in the most ancient Welsh tradition. What that tells us bears no resemblance to the chivalry of the

---

[1] *King Arthur in Legend and History*, R.W. Barber, p. 101.

Arthurian court in more familiar versions. In the early Welsh tales, Arthur and his men are usually depicted as in conflict with the powers of the Otherworld. For instance, one of the few exploits in this tradition, in which Arthur himself participates, is a fight against a hag (a supernatural being). 'Then Arthur sprang to the cave entrance and threw his knife Carnwennan at the hag, so that it struck her down the centre and made two vats of her, and Caw of Scotland took the blood and kept it with him.'[2] In spite of the great difference from the well-known activities at Camelot, the Welsh stories contain information which is just as important as the French in understanding the Arthurian phenomenon.

Camelot, strange to say, is absent from the early Welsh tradition. Stories about Arthur's court there, with the Round Table and the individuals and adventures associated with it, first appeared in written form in France in the twelfth century. These French romances tell the familiar story of Arthur and his court, including the sword in the stone, the love of Lancelot and Guenever and the mysterious achievement of the Holy Grail by Galahad. The difference between the two traditions is so great that it has sometimes been suggested that the romances are wholly invented, like a modern novel. Yet, in spite of the differences, it is generally acknowledged that the French versions had Celtic origins. Perhaps, it is said, Breton story-tellers, who followed Norman lords to Wales, picked up local folk-tales there. In whatever way the transfer from Wales to France came about, the French Arthurian stories are deeply imbued with recollections of Celtic pagan activities and Celtic mythological personages; the courtly behaviour barely conceals a primitive scene which overlaps the Welsh tradition in some of its most interesting characters and activities.

All this has been said before, at least in part.[3] Here I go much further and as a result of careful consideration of the French romances put forward the view that a significant proportion of the distinctive features of the Arthurian legend can best be explained as the shadowy projection of half-forgotten pagan places, personages and behaviour on to a twelfth century screen. These features, the core of the legend, include, as already mentioned, the sword drawn from the stone and returned to the pool, the doings of the Damsel of the Lake, Gawain and Morgan le Fay; the Round Table, the loves of Lancelot and Guenever and of Tristan and Yseult, and also, and by no means the least interesting, the various acts of Merlin, particularly the stones he moved and erected, and his changes of shape into, for instance, a shaggy herdsman exercising power over the wild animals of the forest.

2  *Mabinogion*, tr. J. Ganz, Penguin, p. 175.
3  For Welsh origins see R.S. Loomis in *Arthurian Legend in the Middle Ages*, pp. 274–294 and also *Wales and the Arthurian Legend*; H. Newstead, *Bran the Blessed in Arthurian Romance*; P. Mac Cana for an ancient Celtic theme receiving 'its ultimate and classical statement in the romances of Lancelot and Guenivere and of Tristan and Iseult.' *Celtic Mythology*, p. 112. For pagan origins: J. Weston in *Ritual to Romance*; Loomis, *The Grail: from Celtic Myth to Christian Symbol*; and the works of Goetinck, Markale and Cavendish.

How is paganism[4] to be recognized? As I have hinted above, its recognition marks are strange behaviour and an uncanny atmosphere. These are the result of a belief in the superiority of the spiritual over the material: a belief in the ability of, for instance, an Irish high priest to raise a storm to scatter an invading fleet, or of a Breton priestess to fly through the air in the form of a bird, or of a Welsh king to suffer transformation into a boar. However, in spite of the air of lack of reality which characterizes many of the principal themes of the Arthurian legends, an origin in pre-Christian religion is by no means obvious on reading even the earliest romances. Long before the time the stories came to the notice of French-speaking court poets their content had been altered accidentally by the many repetitions of story-tellers, who continued to tell their tales after the pagan significance of the original myth had been forgotten. The time-honoured tales were also embellished and deliberately twisted to make them acceptable to a new courtly audience. It is probably true to say that the changes in the Arthurian legend have been so great that there is now no logical trail back to any original, pagan or otherwise.

To take an example, in recent years archaeologists, among others, have noticed that the myth of the sword thrown into water – to be specific, the sword Excalibur thrown into a lake at King Arthur's command – corresponds to the real-life deposition of offerings, including weapons, into watery places; a custom which continued over a period of many thousands of years up to the first few centuries AD. If, as has been suggested, the myth really is a recollection of an ancient pagan practice the implications are interesting in several ways. From the point of view of archaeology an analysis of the Arthurian legends could (and as the following pages will show, does) reveal the ownership of the hand which is supposed to have seized the sword, and hence by further study the name and characteristics of the deity to whom the prehistoric offerings were made; and for students of the romances there would be a comment on the antecedents of these tales, an indication that their roots were in remembered paganism. It is to be noted that the casting of a sword into water is an act which occurs only in the French romances and is completely missing from the earliest Welsh literature.[5] So if the myth is to be taken as a recollection of a pagan past, its presence in the French tales and its absence in the Welsh leads to an unexpected conclusion. A link with the remote past would be provided for a set of tales which came to be preserved in a foreign tongue and appeared later than their British counterparts; in short, in a literature in which it has generally been thought that a recognizable residue of remembered paganism is less likely to be found than in the earlier indigenous traditions.

In spite of the close resemblance between myth and fact in this instance, it is

4 In the context of the romances, the religion of the pre-Christian inhabitants of Britain and France.
5 In the *Mabinogion* the spirit of the waters is represented by the Lady of the Fountain; nothing in that story is thrown into the spring, but food was offered in lakes in the Middle Ages.

impossible to prove that the sword thrown into the pool is anything other than the creation of a poet's imagination, and the same view will be appropriate when we come to examine other episodes which sound as if they have a pagan origin. For one thing, there are obvious possibilities of contamination of the native tradition from outside sources. As an instance, a certain giant called Asue[6] required a tribute of six youths and six maidens on May 1st, and, in another tale, Arthur is said to have ordered all children born to noble families on that same date, May 1st, to be destroyed, in a vain attempt to encompass the death of Mordred, who it had been prophesied would kill him.[7] Who is to say that the first is not imported from the classical tradition of the tribute given by Athens to the Minotaur, and the second imported from the Biblical account of Herod and the Innocents? For the sword thrown in the pool there is no obvious alternative source in any other tradition, but the invention of the writer might supply what sounds like a pagan motif, particularly if he is an exponent of a genre in which such motifs are included, much as a writer of science fiction might casually propose a fundamental principle which had previously been unknown.

The impossibility of arriving at absolute proof is not necessarily a bar to further enquiry. Scientists cope with this difficulty by constructing a model in the form of a set of hypothetical circumstances and asking if the reality which can be observed (and in the case of scientists, measured) corresponds to what might be expected as the outcome of the operation of the model. The explanation of some facet of the natural world so arrived at will only survive until some better model is constructed, which more accurately mimics the real world as it is perceived through observable phenomena. Another way of describing this approach is 'fit'. The author of a recent paper explaining some palaeolithic rock art as drawings of hallucinations perceived in trance states comments that, in the absence of proof, he has stressed the complexity of the 'fit'.[8] To use this approach to investigate the possibility that there are traces of paganism in the romances obviously presents difficulties, but here is an example of how it might work. As I have said, certain incidents in the romances are well-known to correspond to the actions of the priest-king at Nemi, a place in the Alban Hills not far from Rome. Reliable Roman authors describe how, from the most remote times until well after the time of Christ, each successive holder of this strange religious office retained his high-sounding title of 'King of the Woodland Clearing' only for as long as he could defend himself against a murderous attack from a challenger for his position, who would kill him if he could. The attacker if successful took over the defence of the sacred site, marked by a particular tree, until he too met the same fate, and so on.[9] Although Nemi is the only place at which this custom is

---

6  *Guiron le Courtois*, ed. Lathullière para. 253.
7  *Morte Darthur*, bk I ch. 27.
8  'Wrestling with Analogy', J. D. Lewis-Williams, *Proc. Prehistoric Society*, 1991, pt. 1, p. 155.
9  *The Golden Bough*, Sir J. G. Frazer, pt. I ch. 1. See Introduction below, p. 6, for more detail.

recorded, sacred woodland clearings were once widespread in Europe, including Britain, judging by the survival of the place-name element 'Nemet-', representing nemeton – a sacred site in woodland.[10] The religious views of the prehistoric inhabitants of Britain are likely to have been subjected to influences from many quarters. Just as many prehistoric styles of construction and of manufactured articles are not confined to this country, so those manifestations of religious activity which I suggest to have been remembered in the British legends will not have been unique to Britain but will also have been familiar in varying degrees to the inhabitants of other parts of Europe.

The nub of the system at Nemi is the replacement, by a successful challenger, of the defender of a site containing a special tree. The replacement of a defender by his murderer is a circumstance so different from the normal course of human behaviour that, when the same sequence of events occurs not once but many times in the romances, suspicions are bound to be aroused that it is derived from the actual practice of this strange activity. If so how has the recollection of it fared in the course of oral transmission over the centuries? If Malory had included the story of Clochidés, the system might have been more familiar. To fight this doughty defender of a mound, Sir Bors had to swear that if victorious he would defend the hill all his life, until he too should be defeated. The continuation of the custom is the best touchstone for the rite of Nemi, but not the only one. Analysis suggests that the many versions of the 'challenge' system which appear in the romances can be recognized because they are composed of six easily recognized elements.

If we suppose this system to have been in force many centuries before the romances came to be written down, and the memory of it to have been preserved by repetition in many different places by story-tellers who had no idea of the original significance of the stories they repeated, we can speculate that the end result, the oral tradition which was available to twelfth century writers, would have in some cases been eroded, so that only a few of the elements were included, and in others would have embodied distortions either by the accidents of an inexact form of transmission, or deliberately to incorporate the tradition into a story-teller's standard formula. So for all six elements to appear in one episode would be comparatively rare but less complete versions and altered versions would be comparatively common. This is in fact what is to be found in a general survey of the legends and will be discussed in detail in the chapter on the 'challenge' which follows later. The point is, that the end-product conforms to the supposition that the model proposed was in operation. I will draw attention to many instances in which pagan motifs appear to be present in traditional tales, but can never claim proof of pagan origins, only that the supposition of pagan origins best fits the observations of a reader of the earliest French texts. For example, the explanation,

---

[10] *Pagan Celtic Britain*, A. Ross, p. 63; *Roman Place-names in Britain*, Rivet and Smith, under Aquae Arnemetiae; see Gazetteer under Nemus for British examples, and for a note on the meaning of the word nemus.

that it was some aspect of pre-Christian religion that accounts for the strange behaviour of those queens who offer their bodies and their fortunes to the winners of tournaments, will only survive until such time as, like the sacred king at Nemi, it is superseded by a better.

The question now arises as to what purpose is served by imagining a model with a limited shelf-life. There is, of course, no doubt about the usefulness of this system in explaining natural phenomena. There are many examples of untestable assumptions providing a satisfactory framework for the advancement of knowledge until such times as they are replaced by a more accurate representation of reality. The 'indivisible' atom and the 'immutable' element provided the background for enormous advances in natural science. But when the system is applied to literary themes an essential second step is missing. A scientific hypothesis is only useful in so far as it results in predictions which can be tested by experiment. Without the possibility of verification, I suggest that the value of this approach as it is used here is the possibility that it may reveal links between traditional tales and the prehistoric monuments of Britain. Unlike the monuments of Greece, our own are not enlivened by such dramatic events as occurred in, say, the house of Atreus. If we are ever to have anything comparable to the traditions of Agamemnon at Mycenae or Nestor at Pylos, it will have to be sought in the indigenous British mythology, in, that is to say, the Arthurian Legend; and since the prehistoric monuments of the west are for the most part likely to have had a religious significance, any link with them is likely to be in the general field of paganism.

Most people would think it unlikely that the recollection of any activity from such a distant past could survive in a clear enough form to be recognized today. But to demonstrate the possibilities, consider for a moment a passage from a late French romance, *Perceforest*. A round stone temple is described, and through the doorway a ray of light from the setting sun fell on a throne, in which was ensconced the desiccated corpse of the last high-priest, wrapped in a sheepskin. There is not only a possibility of 'fit' here, the romance has also some interesting suggestions to make: that it was what the light fell on that mattered (as at, for example, New Grange); that the setting sun was important on some occasions, rather than the rising; and that the light fell on a corpse (what else, indeed, would have been at the end of the passage at New Grange?). The same author also describes a temple of the Goddess of Dreams, where couches are set out for visitors and their dreams explained, a somewhat similar set up to what is supposed to have taken place at the Romano-Celtic temple at Lydney in Gloucestershire. These are only two of many potential correspondences between myth and fact which taken together will provide a complex 'fit' between Arthurian tradition and prehistory.

As I have said, the scientific method depends for its success on its ability to make predictions which can be verified. The only way in which this could be done using traditional material is if any sites are sufficiently clearly described to be pinpointed on a modern map, in which case excavation might confirm the traditional description. Arthurian geography is so confused that it would be safest not to place too much reliance on this possibility. Nevertheless, there are many pointers in tradition, not all in the romances, towards various cult-sites. To illustrate the possibilities, there are two or three places mentioned in the following story, from the earliest stratum of Welsh legend, which sounds like a picture of paganism seen out of focus through a millennium of repetition by word of mouth:

A Celtic king of Britain called Bran the Blessed was wounded in the foot by a poisoned spear during the course of a battle. He commanded that his head should be cut off and taken first to Harlech in North Wales where his seven companions would spend seven years feasting, with the head proving as pleasant company as ever it was when alive and the birds of Rhiannon singing to them. Then they were to go to the island of Grassholm, ten miles off the south west peninsula of Wales, where they would spend eighty years in joy and delight with the head, in a great hall with three doors, without being aware of the passage of time. And finally they were to take the head to London and bury it in the White Mount, facing France, as a protection against invasion and infection.[11]

Of course the head did not speak; nor did the companions live another eighty seven years; nor did the buried head have any military or therapeutic value. But we have an indication of the belief that these things could happen. Pre-historians regard the talismanic head as a pagan motif, and this motif clinging to the memory of Bran[12] reinforces the widely accepted conclusion that Bran was a god. And once the essentially pagan nature of the antecedents to this episode are clear, the presence in it of the birds of Rhiannon fits very well the prehistorians view[13] that Rhiannon displays the characteristic features of a goddess.

To turn for a moment to the material basis of the tale, three potential cult sites are revealed: Harlech in North Wales, the isolated island of Grassholm off South-West Wales, and the White Mount in London. Though the actual location of the places mentioned in traditional tales is often subject to difficulties of identification, one of these sites might provide archaeological evidence of the date and style of the worship of Bran. Grassholm in particular is confirmed as a pagan cult site by a cross-reference from another ancient Welsh source. This source draws attention to the presence of a well on the island. This was hurriedly excavated in 1946, revealing high-class pottery[14] of a kind which would not be expected in such a remote situation. But not all the passages from traditional sources which will be quoted later can be taken at their face value. What seems concrete and real, like the great hall on Grassholm with

---

11 *Mabinogion*, tr. Ganz, Penguin, pp. 79ff. In Geoffrey of Monmouth's *Historia* the body of Vortigern's son Vortimer was supposed to have the same apotropaic capacity.
12 *Pagan Celtic Britain*, A. Ross, p. 163.
13 *Pagan Celtic Britain*, A. Ross, pp. 338f.
14 Personal communication.

three doors, may turn out to be part of the embellishment, and what fails to conform to the laws of nature as we understand them now, like the defensive capability of the buried head, however unreal in a material sense, will be found to be a genuine indication of an origin in prehistoric religion. Although the power of Bran's head is imaginary, there is the possibility of a correspondence between it and the real world of prehistory, for its defensive capacity might suggest an explanation for actual skulls in archaeological contexts; for example, this strange capability might confirm the suspicion of archaeologists that those skulls set in the Neolithic ditch at Hambledon Hill may have been deliberately put there to create a psychologically impassable barrier against the passage of intruders. Bran is by no means unique to Welsh tradition; he is also an important figure in the French Arthurian romances. His presence there serves to confirm that there are Celtic mythological motifs in the French romances, it also provides additional information about him which has not survived in the Welsh stories.

Another link between myth and reality is suggested by a place called Gorsedd Bran ten miles east of Llanwrst in North Wales;[15] Gorsedd means a place of assembly or a throne-mound and since Bran is a god, this might once have been a cult site. The strange events at another 'gorsedd' at Arberth in Dyfed are described in detail in the *Mabinogion*;[16] as this gorsedd is said to be a mound, there might be some physical traces left in the ground there. Yet another site closely linked with a pagan deity is 'Mabon's Stone', that is, the Lochmabenstane; interesting details about the god whose name this monument preserves are to be found in both the Welsh and French traditions and are set out in detail in Who's Who? below. As well as these examples, so far largely from Welsh sources, there are a number of others from the romances, to be described in the body of the book, pointing to pre-Christian cult activity at standing stones, at springs, at the mouths of two Welsh rivers, and, most important of all, on Salisbury Plain.

The Arthurian legend is a notoriously difficult subject because it is built up from many layers of tradition and has been subject to the vicissitudes of repetition, translation and even deliberate alteration. It can thus sustain many different legitimate interpretations. The view taken here is that the activities of many of the personages in the Arthurian legend can be recognized as pagan in origin if we compare their actions with known styles of religious behaviour both in classical times and from the fields of archaeology and anthropology. Other general views may result in entirely different conclusions without necessarily being in conflict. The ideas advanced here would only contradict the theory of Arthur as a historical character in about AD 500 in so far as they provided a better explanation for the same observations; but since arguments in favour of the historical Arthur do not rely at all on either the French romances or the early Welsh traditions represented by the *Mabinogion*, there is

15 NGR SH 9760.
16 *Mabinogion*, tr. Ganz, Penguin, p. 86.

no conflict. Here the legends, particularly the romances, are allowed to tell their own story. Even when they are contradictory or impossible to believe, the information carried should not be disregarded. For instance, Arthur's sword Excalibur was obtained by him in two entirely different ways. He drew it from the stone and he was given it by the Damsel of the Lake, whose arm, clothed in white samite, brandished the sword in the middle of a lake. Does a choice need to be made between two distinct and irreconcilable versions of the origin of the sword, or can other information be found to solve the problem? The solution in this case is to examine all the parallels to these events. Elsewhere in the romances a sword was drawn by Galahad from a stone which mysteriously floated to Camelot; and a sword was drawn by Balin from a magic scabbard, brought to Camelot from the Isle of Avalon. As in the better known instance of Arthur and the sword in the stone, in both of these episodes no other knight was capable of withdrawing the sword from its holder; and some characteristics are common to all three swords, showing they are all of the same type. The extra detail from the two new examples of sword-drawing demonstrates clearly that the three swords are pagan symbols, not real weapons; so the withdrawal looks more like a ceremonial act, made under the auspices of a water-spirit, rather than a trial of strength. From this example it can be seen that any proposed explanation should take account of all the information available.

What is improbable and uncanny can be seen as a touchstone which reveals the presence of pagan thought-patterns in the Arthurian legend, and even occasionally identifies pre-Christian sacred places. Of all the varied expressions of paganism so demonstrated, a constant feature is the attempt to alleviate ill-health and to promote prosperity by magic of one sort or another. It is easy enough for us now to see that such efforts were bound to fail, so how did a manifestly unsatisfactory set of beliefs maintain its hold for so long? The answer seems to be that the priestly caste exploited certain fixed characteristics of humanity, such as the ready acceptance of the principle of sympathetic magic, the search for a scapegoat, and the irresistible attraction of water for objects of value. It is possible that the Arthurian legend has retained its popularity so long because it is constructed from such fundamental building blocks. But time brings change. Each successive age has always selected according to its own scale of values and now, after the scientific revolution, the tendency will inevitably be to reject as being irrelevant what does not fit in with our current concept of the laws of nature. The strange behaviour and uncanny atmosphere encountered in the earliest French romances has been progressively diluted over half a millennium. If a late twentieth century selection were to omit what seems improbable today, a fundamental aspect of British tradition, an aspect which contains clues to ancient beliefs, would be forgotten. I hope that this book will help to prevent that from happening.

I have looked at some themes from several viewpoints, such as mythlogy, location or prehistory, which has inevitably caused some duplication. For names, I have followed the spelling in West's *Prose Index* unless there is a well-established alternative in *Morte Darthur*. For instance, I have used Arthur, not Artu. This procedure may seem to create artificial distinctions dependant on minor difference in spelling (e.g. among the Elaines) but will help readers wishing to refer to this useful index. For Welsh names I have followed Rees and Rees in *Celtic Heritage*.

# INTRODUCTION

In 1984 the well preserved body of a man was found in a peat bog at Lindow in Cheshire. Radio-carbon dating at Oxford showed him to have died about two thousand years ago. Because of the preservative quality of the peaty water in which he had been thrown, not only his bones but also his skin, hair, nails and even his stomach contents were available for examination. Lindow Man, as he is now known, came to an unusual end. His 'triple death' involved three fatal injuries. His skull was knocked in, he had been strangled by a thong twisted round his neck, and his throat had been cut.[1] How are we to explain this bizarre triplication of the means of his death? What was to be gained by his death, or lost by his continuing life, so long ago? Was it punishment? Was it ritual?

These are questions which archaeologists, however meticulous their methods, find difficult to answer. A grain of pollen may show that there was once a field of barley where now there is moorland; a snail shell at the bottom of a prehistoric ditch that the surrounding countryside was once woodland rather than pasture; but the reasons for the behaviour of the people of Lindow two thousand years ago can now only be guessed.

There are several ways in which we can attempt to bridge the gap between on the one hand the human remains and the discarded artifacts of everyday life which are found in the ground and on the other the beliefs and aspirations of the men and women to whom they belonged. To begin with there is the material evidence. For instance, careful disposal of the dead and the provision of grave goods suggest the possibility of a belief in life after death; the placing of ritual structures facing in particular directions shows a link between the religion of the time and the sun and perhaps also the moon; and representations of human beings as hunters or warriors or with exaggerated sexual characteristics lead to conclusions which have been presented by various authors.[2] Next we have eye-witness accounts preserved in the written literature of civilized countries, in our case Greece and Rome. Then there is something to be gleaned from the behaviour of primitive tribes in the present day world. And finally there is a great deal to be learned about our own original circumstances from Celtic literature, first for many centuries

---

1  *Antiquity* 59, pp. 25–9 and 63, pp. 71–9.
2  E.g. H. R. E. Davidson in *Scandinavian Archaeology*.

preserved solely by word of mouth, and from folk practices, such as the fires burnt on ancient holy days including Beltaine (the eve of May 1st), St John's Eve (the eve of Midsummer Day, June 24th) and Samain (Hallowe'en, the eve of November 1st). Once again, all these windows on the past have been looked through by competent modern observers. As far as discovering more about prehistoric beliefs is concerned, the bottom of the barrel seems to have been scraped, with, I believe, one exception. There is still a great deal to be learned from that part of our oral tradition which formed the basis of the Arthurian romances and associated material, and which has for various reasons been neglected recently as a potential source of information about the past.

It is well known that information could be passed from mouth to ear over many centuries in pre-literate societies. This procedure sometimes retained very early material until it was preserved in written form. As Professor Clark says, 'it should not be forgotten that the genesis of much of the world's earliest literature, particularly in the sphere of epic poetry and religious writings, was prehistoric in the sense that it was originally composed during the pre-literate period and transmitted by word of mouth. By the same token this early literature – the Homeric poems are a case in point – can sometimes be made to throw light on the mentality and customs of prehistoric peoples that could hardly be obtained from any other source'.[3] There are many examples of the retention of ancient notions, of which one is illustrated by Lindow Man. 'Threefold death' is mentioned several times in early literature. For instance, according to Geoffrey of Monmouth's *Prophesies of Merlin*, which is clearly derived from Celtic sources, this fate befell a certain Merlin whom N. Tolstoy places about a century later than the historical Arthur, that is to say, this Merlin lived in the sixth century AD.[4] He is just one of the manifestations of a composite character made up of elements from several traditions and historical periods, and is said to have been stoned by shepherds, to have fallen down a steep river bank on to a stake which pierced his heart, and to have hung head down in the water, so drowning. Another example comes from the Arthurian Legend and is preserved in an early stratum in which written romances had least diverged from the underlying oral tradition. The victim was a baron of Arthur's court who unwisely asked Merlin on three occasions how he would die, and was given three different answers – that he would break his neck, be hanged and drown. Even while he was deriding the seer for giving contradictory forecasts, he fell from his horse while riding over a bridge, breaking his neck as he hit the ground, being hung by his reins in his fall, and finally drowning in the river.

In these literary manifestations of the threefold death we have a recollection of a motif which must have once played an important role in people's thoughts. Perhaps, it has been guessed, a victim was made acceptable to three deities at once, each of whom required death by a different means. For what-

---

[3]   *Archaeology and Society*, p. 224.
[4]   *The Quest for Merlin*, p. 281.

ever reason, the tradition, by revealing the high social station of the victims, which corresponds with the well cared for hands of Lindow Man, reinforces a suspicion we may have from other traditions that it was a person of importance in the community whose conspicuous death was required to humour the gods in an attempt to avert some impending calamity.

It is interesting to see that the most complete survey of how Lindow man met his death, in its analysis of sources in the oral tradition which suggest that he was ritually sacrificed,[5] refers to an episode from the Arthurian tradition – *Sir Gawain and the Green Knight*. It is very unusual to find any dependence being placed on Arthurian tradition. This instance is from a poem in English with a Welsh hero, but the French versions of Arthurian tradition remain to some extent unexplored. This is not surprising. Compared with their Welsh equivalents, the traditions picked up by the French in the twelfth century were used as a basis of romances scarcely to be distinguished from invented tales. The primitive content is difficult to discern, particularly in the English versions with which everyone is familiar. These are selections and translations from that first flowering of the Arthurian story which took all Europe by storm, the French 'matière de Bretagne' – the 'matter of Britain' – romances composed for the pleasure of French courts but which had their origin in the Celtic oral tradition of Britain. There is a good deal of internal evidence of this Celtic origin; for example, the names of Welsh gods appear as the names of characters in the romances. But there is no certainty about how the transfer took place. An explanation often offered is that at the time of the Norman conquest the French-speaking barons took Breton retainers with them to Wales. There they would have found professional story-tellers whose repertoire is likely have included mythological themes. These tales could have been picked up by the Bretons, whose language was not very different from Welsh, and introduced to a Norman audience on their return home. Whatever the circumstances, a great deal of information about the past of this country including many other examples of ritual deaths has accidentally been preserved in a foreign medium. Without this fortunate chance almost all of it would have been completely forgotten.

The 'matter of Britain' began with four verse epics by Chrétien de Troyes, the heroes of which were Erec, Lancelot, Yvain and Perceval. After his death in the last decade of the twelfth century, various continuators and imitators wrote tales in the same vein. These successors to Chrétien considerably extended the list of characters and the range of adventures. They did not merely copy him but they seem to have had the same access to the original Celtic tradition as Chrétien himself, and their work contains more obvious episodes of pagan origin than does his own. Much of the source material for this book is to be found in these early romances but lengthy compilations in prose succeeded the verse versions, and items of interest crop up in later works right up

[5]  R. C. Turner in *Lindow Man: the body in the bog*, ed. I. M. Stead, pp. 172/3.

to Malory's *Morte Darthur*, which was compiled about three centuries after Chrétien's death.[6]

Quite apart from the overlaying of pagan themes by fanciful inventions, there are three main reasons for the concealment of pagan themes which has led to the comparative neglect of the French material as an adjunct to British prehistory. The first is that although the advent of Christianity did not result in the complete suppression of the stories of gods and goddesses which were the mainstay of the oral traditions of the time, it forced them into hiding. The narrators went on telling the same tales, but they tended to conceal the pagan character of their material by changing the titles of gods to 'kings' and of goddesses to 'queens' and so on. This new 'royalty', though the original may have had no more substantial a home base than a spring or a forest clearing, was naturally provided with courts, castles and retainers corresponding to the trappings of the royal families familiar to the audience. The real life 'retainers' of the original deities, their human representatives such as sacred kings, became transformed into medieval knights (with medieval weapons and medieval fighting techniques) and their consorts into wives or mistresses; and the original driving force of the great heroes of romance, which later will be shown not to be love but to be the devotion of a sacrificial victim to his goddess, leading him to throw away his life for a short span of glory, was interpreted as romantic love, an unfamiliar concept in the twelfth century. Thus a force which irrevocably altered men's conception of women, and which ensured the survival of the Arthurian legend as romantic love's most powerful medieval exponent, arrived on the literary scene almost as an accident and has nothing whatever to do with the historical Arthur.

The second reason for the accidental concealment of pagan themes also concerns the reaction between Christianity and paganism. It is generally agreed that monkish hands transcribed many of the French romances and in so doing they overlaid the pagan originals with a Christian veneer. In taking this action they accidentally provided a camouflage necessary for their survival – the age would not have tolerated outright pagan themes. To effect this transformation they needed to do surprisingly little. As Weston has remarked in *Ritual to Romance*, 'we cannot refrain from the conclusion that there was something in the legends which not merely made possible but actually invited' a transition to high Christian symbolism.

The third reason is that the most influential English translators and popularisers have concentrated on those aspects of the material which corresponded to the life of their own times. In the case of Malory, whose late fifteenth century translation has dominated every succeeding version, his interests were combat, kingship and knightly behaviour. So, though a faithful translator

---

6    The dating of individual texts is discussed in *Arthurian Literature in the Middle Ages*, ed. R. S. Loomis, and in *The Arthurian Encyclopaedia*, ed. N. J. Lacy.

of the French texts on which he based *Morte Darthur*, as a selector from the large amount of material then available he chose to omit a great deal of what was magic and folklore, just that part which can now be recognised, by comparison with the observations of classical authors, as being of primitive origin. The next stage in the presentation of the legends was when Tennyson went even further than Malory in shaping the Arthurian court to the views of his own times. The knights became anaemic travesties of their lustful originals and the real nature of the underlying themes was almost forgotten.

Fortunately, all was not lost. Even the briefest acquaintance with the pre-Tennysonian Arthurian legend shows that the most prominent feature is combat. Indeed, it is a frequent criticism that the constant fare of battles, jousts and tournaments makes Malory's *Morte Darthur* and similar works difficult to read. After combat, the next most important element is love, with a good deal of emphasis on the physical side. The hero victorious in battle always gets the girl, and Lancelot and Tristan, in particular, enter the world stage as great lovers. Perhaps it would be true to say that these stories became popular and, indeed, stayed popular through many centuries by exploiting a facet of the human mind which finds a source of entertainment in stories of violence and sex.

However, the violence and sex of the Arthurian legend differ from their modern fictional counterparts in a most fundamental way. They follow a track so deeply implanted in the human psyche as to explain the long survival of this group of legends. Analysis will show that they originate in a primitive religious cult of great antiquity in which strong men fought to obtain brief possession of a goddess. The fight was real, bloody and fatal and although the goddess may have been an abstraction, her representative on earth was real enough. Success in joust or tournament conferred on the winner a temporary kingship. He would be replaced by a stronger when his vigour declined. The dogma behind this long continued system was that the sexual potency of rulers was thought vital to the well-being of their subjects. Once the significant features of this system have been identified, it will be recognized as providing some of the most popular topics in the romances. Killing someone to obtain the hand of a princess is one end-product in tradition of this system, and it is a commonplace of the legends. How often the princess accepts the slayer of her father or lover, or else the winner of a tournament – an individual she has never previously met! Accordingly, I put forward as best representing the behaviour of most Arthurian knights that prime British example of prehistoric vigour and sexuality (at whatever period it may have first been cut into the chalk), the Cerne Giant – wielding a great club and explicitly erect. Helis, the name by which the giant seems to have been known in eighteenth century Dorset, is the name of two or three Arthurian heroes and may also be linked with an important god. This identification would surprise Malory and shock Tennyson but it is strictly in accordance with the romances themselves.

The damsel that the Arthurian hero fought for – the term 'damsel' in early

French literature implies an unmarried young woman of high social standing[7] – though often described as beautiful, is unlikely to have conformed to modern standards in this respect. If a chalk-cut picture of her had survived beside that of the Cerne Giant, like his it would probably emphasise her sexual characteristics, whether in voluptuous curves exaggerated to grossness according to one school of prehistoric art or else reduced, as in another, to the most abstract of forms, a mere rectangle with a vertical line in the middle of the lower half and with two small circles horizontally spaced towards the top.

It might be thought that the battle for the hand of a princess was a mere fairy story or else one of those constantly recurring themes which crop up in the literatures of the world. Indeed, it is both of these. But thanks to a classical description of the system in action we know that such events actually took place in real life. The account of the events at Nemi does not read like a fairy tale, and a detailed comparison of the ritual there with the actions of many Arthurian knights will leave no doubt that the latter were following the same cult practice for the same reward – kingship of the Woodland Glade.

## The Priest-King at Nemi

At the time of Christ there had been from time immemorial a sacred grove and sanctuary near the Lake of Nemi in the Alban hills, about fifteen miles southeast of Rome. It was dedicated to Diana *Nemorensis*, which title means 'of a natural clearing in woodland',[8] or, more concisely, 'of the Glade'. The oval lake, a haunted place, as if formed by nature to inspire thoughts of pagan divinities, was then known as Diana's mirror. In the words of Sir J. G. Frazer: 'In the sacred grove there grew a certain tree round which at any time of the day and probably far into the night a grim figure might be seen to prowl. In his hand he carried a drawn sword, and he kept peering warily about him as if at every instant he expected to be set upon by an enemy. He was a priest and a murderer; and the man for whom he looked was sooner or later to murder him and hold the priesthood in his stead. Such was the rule of the sanctuary. A candidate for the priesthood could only succeed to office by slaying the priest, and having slain him, he retained office till he was himself slain by a stronger or a craftier.'[9] The attacker was obliged to make a unique gesture to initiate the proceedings, he had to break a branch from the guarded tree to make known his intention to challenge the incumbent. The post which was held by this precarious tenure carried with it the title of Rex Nemorensis – King of the Glade – and the temporary human occupant of this post was regarded as the consort of the goddess Diana herself.

---

7  The romances use 'pucele' for maiden. The Arthurian 'damoiselles' are characterized by adventurousness, self-confidence, mettle and 'above all by the free disposition of their bodies' tr. from Perrett & Weill, *Le bel inconnu*, note to p. 103.
8  *The Golden Bough*, Sir James Frazer, Bk I, vol. I, p. 2.
9  *The Golden Bough*, Sir James Frazer, Bk I, vol. I, pp. 8/9.

Diana was not the only pagan figure on the site. There was a nymph, Egeria, associated with the spring whose waters, tumbling through the trees into the lake, were an important part of the pagan setting; and there was a minor male divinity called Virbius, a masculine counterpart of Diana in chastity and in his love of hunting and woodland pursuits.[10]

In a later chapter I will show that all the significant elements in this description of an Italian pagan cult occur in the Arthurian romances and most of them occur often. Two points are worthy of comment at this point. One is geographical. There might seem a deep divide between the pagan practices of Italy and those of Britain but this is not necessarily the case. The spread of Nemet-type names,[11] from Asia Minor to the neighbourhood of the Antonine Wall in Britain and to Galicia in Spain,[12] does not necessarily imply that the rule of the priesthood of Nemi was in operation, but it is evidence that a religious practice involving sacred enclosures can bridge a far wider gap than that between Italy and Britain.

The other point is that in the account of the rite of Nemi, the ways of cult figures and divinities are being described. Familiarity with Malory or Tennyson will not prepare the reader for the presence of either of these in the Arthurian legend. Only one well-known personage springs to mind as described in a way which hints at her true 'otherworldly' nature, Morgan le Fay, where Fay means fairy (a far more sinister description than could be guessed from the tinselled doll of Victorian book illustrations) and who is specifically called 'déesse' or 'goddess' on occasion. But there are plenty more, as will be found. When the underlying French romances are examined it will be found that the rational and courtly world of the fifteenth century is exchanged in them for something more like the uncanny atmosphere of the earliest Welsh tales, the *Mabinogion*. Thinly disguised as human beings, deities will appear who are capable of shape-shifting, taking animal form, control of the weather and many other miraculous imaginings of the pagan mind. The irrational is never far below the surface. Here is an example:

[10] In case the figure of a priest-king behaving in the way described seems too far fetched to be taken seriously, there is a record of a cruel joke played by the emperor Caligula (AD 37–41), who ordered the current king of the Glade to be murdered because he thought he had held office too long. Nevertheless, the practice continued and was mentioned by Pausanius a whole century later (*The Making of the Golden Bough*, R. Fraser, p. 9). Frazer reports the finding at Nemi of a stone bust thought to represent the king of the Wood. It was two-faced and covered in leaves (*The Golden Bough*, pt. I, vol. I, p. 41).

[11] Mentioned on p. xi.

[12] E.g. Drunemeton, the oak sanctuary of the Galatians, in Asia Minor; Nemetobriga, in Spanish Galicia; and Nemetodurum, Nemeton, and Nemetacum in Gaul. *Pagan Celtic Britain*, A. Ross, p. 63. Ten British examples are given here in the Gazetteer, under Nemus.

*King Arthur at St Augustine's Chapel*[13]

One Ascension Day at Cardoel, Guenever persuaded Arthur to undertake an adventure, namely to visit a very dangerous place where the most worthy hermit in the land of Wales had a chapel. The supernatural perils were underlined by the dream of a squire who was to accompany him. The young man dreamed he had followed Arthur to the chapel, in a clearing in the forest, in which there was a dead knight. In his dream he took a golden candlestick back from the chapel to the court. Still in his dream he felt a deadly wound. He woke. The wound was real. Dying he handed the candlestick to the king. He had never left the court but the figments of his dream became reality. In spite of this warning of the hazards involved, Arthur set off, his courage being measured by the supernatural perils of the adventure. After meeting a holy hermit who gave him his blessing, he came to a most beautiful clearing with the entrance barred by a swinging gate. Near the entrance a young woman sat below a great leafy tree (described as the 'Oak tree of the Glade' in one version[14]). She directed him to a chapel in the clearing, and warned him that any knight who entered died or returned maimed. He was not at first able to enter the chapel but later spoke with the hermit within. When Arthur left, the hermit warned him that any knight who entered the glade must be prepared for an attack. Soon he was challenged by a black knight, mounted on a black horse, who was armed with a fiery lance with which he wounded Arthur in the arm. The flow of blood quenched the flame from the burning weapon and Arthur was able to overcome his opponent, whom he left dead on the ground. At that moment twenty or more armed knights came out of the forest and converged on the dead knight in the middle of the clearing. Meanwhile, Arthur made his way back to the girl at the entrance. This young woman, who was a complete stranger to him, then asked him to obtain the head of the knight he had just killed. In spite of the odds of twenty to one against him, he agreed to do so. Meanwhile, the twenty knights had dismembered the corpse of the black knight and were each carrying a piece back into the forest. Arthur rode after the last of them, who was carrying the head on his spear-point. There was an exchange, not of blows but of words. Arthur told him, in return for the head, that the name of the slayer of the Black Knight was King Arthur. Now a horn was blown by the knight who had been carrying the head and the other knights galloped back to him, while the king returned in haste to the damsel at the barrier. She told him he need no longer be on his guard. He was quite safe once he was outside the glade and had crossed the barrier. The twenty knights, frustrated in their desire for vengeance, killed the knight who had given Arthur the head, hacked his body into pieces as they had the Black Knight, and departed, each carrying a piece. The damsel now anointed Arthur's wounded arm with warm blood from the head. She told him his

---

[13] A paraphrase of *Perlesvaus*, ed. Nitze and Jenkins, compared with the translation by Bryant.
[14] In Ms 11145 Bib. Royale, see Nitze and Jenkins, note to line 433 on p. 41.

wound could only be cured by the black knight's blood. That was why the knights, realising that Arthur had been wounded, were anxious to dispose of the pieces of flesh to prevent him from being cured. The girl told Arthur that the head would be of use to her in recovering a castle which had been stolen from her by treason, if only she could find Perceval, who would recover it for her. She departed in search of him, carrying the head.

In this single episode there are many elements of pagan tradition: the religious festival on which the episode begins (though Ascension is not a particularly good example); single combat in a forest clearing; the girl under a tree at the entrance; the flaming lance; healing blood; and the severed head. A scene from mythology is full of symbolism. There was no need for the original audience to have the symbols explained. The meanings would have been immediately apparent, just as St Peter's keys or St Catherine's wheel in a stained glass window would have been understood by a medieval viewer. The girl under the oak (the species of tree may not be irrelevant); the barrier at the entrance to the clearing where the combat takes place; and the colour of the guardian knight are the standard properties by which the original listeners would have been expected to recognise the significance of the event or religious figure portrayed. By the twelfth century all this would have been irrelevant but the symbols evidently had enough momentum to keep themselves in the mind's eye of the narrators of romances.

Twelfth century narrators may well have credited Arthur in this episode with links to a tradition that had no time scale for them. It is widely agreed that '. . . Arthur's name is found in connection with a much older group of recognizably mythological figures, the shadows of pagan gods; but he always appears as an intruder . . .'[15] In the adventure in the glade it is a pagan activity which is credited to Arthur, rather than a link with deities, but the principal is the same, in that we can recognize in this incident an aspect of the romances which have nothing to do with the historical Arthur of prosaic, post-Roman times.

To find how Arthurian personages came to acquire floating traditions, it will help to consider the activities of other heroes. Lancelot, for instance, was obviously used by story-tellers as a hook on which to hang a sequence of episodes, in each of which he has probably usurped the position of some different original hero. Thus in *Lanzelet* the hero goes through three or four adventures of a very similar pattern, in each killing the heroine's father or brother to obtain her hand and her possessions.

We may suppose that Arthur, as a literary figure, will also have attracted attributes and actions from other heroes during the course of the proliferation of the French romances. The incident in the glade related above and many others may well have been ascribed to Arthur in that way, but there is a great

---

15 *The Figure of Arthur*, R.W. Barber, p. 79.

difference between him and Lancelot or Guenever or any of the other familiar figures of Arthurian romance. Unlike the rest, Arthur has been widely seen as a historical character of around AD 500, at least by those who are not familiar with D. N. Dumville's strictures on the use of the description 'Arthurian' for this period.[16] Is this 'historical Arthur' the Arthur who has attracted so many pagan themes? It is a difficult question to answer but in the analysis of the 'matter of Britain' which follows it will be seen that a considerable proportion of the Arthurian material from the romances is consistently mythological, that is, concerned with pagan divinities, and not historical. There are no links at all between the Arthur of the pages of this book and the fifth/sixth-century man, unless, indeed, it is the latter who is the shadow, a mere distorted projection into the dark ages of the much earlier Arthur, an insubstantial figure of real power, though not necessarily of flesh and blood.

As it happens, there are other examples of pagan tradition of an earlier age which have become incorporated in the medieval pseudo-history of what is known, with doubtful authenticity, as the Arthurian period, and once again their existence is not widely known because of the way Malory treated his material. When he was writing *Morte Darthur* he was faced with the problem of what to leave out from an enormous range of often repetitive French romances. He seems to have rejected the improbable so, as well as magic and mystery, he left out almost all the detail of the strangely unreal story of Joseph 'of Arimathea'. This purports to describe events taking place some hundreds of years before Arthur's birth, in particular the bringing to this country of the Holy Grail containing, it was thought, Christ's blood. Joseph is said to have come with a party of evangelists from the Holy Land or thereabouts and to have converted the inhabitants of Britain to Christianity a long time before this conversion actually happened. Joseph as a Christian missionary can safely be discounted. Obviously no such person existed. But when his 'history' is examined in more detail, it is found to be deeply imbued with paganism. Sometimes this is explicitly described. For instance, one of his associates, a certain King Evalac (whose name happens to be more or less the same as that of a Welsh ancestor deity), is said to have held court in a magnificent temple to the sun. At night he copulated with a wooden idol in the shape of a woman, which he kept in an underground chamber. Later on he was castrated, like other sacred kings (as will be seen later in this analysis of the romances) and finally, centuries afterwards, his story converged with that of Galahad. It need not be thought that the goddess-dolly was dreamt up by some ingenious monk as a symbol of paganism. There are parallel episodes and a good argument for believing them to be factual.[17] So in this instance, and there are plenty of others, the story of Joseph may be revealing something unexpected about our past. We do not have to discard him because he was not the biblical Joseph of Arimathea, merely to suggest an earlier date for the period of his existence.

[16] *History*, 62, 1977, pp. 173–192.
[17] See p. 169, below.

His adventures, and also those of Evalac, sound like garbled recollections of some earlier religious incursion which has been ineptly assimilated to Christian themes because of the self-sacrificing nature of its hero who, foreshadowing Christ, endured death for the common good.

That a personage from prehistory should have been wrongly dated to the first century is entirely in accord with the medieval attitude to the past, with its foreshortened view of the passage of time. Archbishop Ussher was subject to the same constraint when he dated the creation to 4004 BC in the late seventeenth century, and the ingenious Pepys failed to spot the mistake when told that the Kent megalith, Kit's Coty House, was the burial place of a Saxon king.

This lack of historical perspective seems to have led to that most spectacular of chronological lapses, the dating by Geoffrey of Monmouth, to the period of the Saxon invasions, of the moving of the 'bluestones' of Stonehenge from South West Wales to where they now stand on Salisbury Plain. This actually happened well over two thousand years before the period (the Saxon invasion) assigned to it by Geoffrey. Once it is realized that mistakes like this were being made it is possible to see the legends in a rather different light. They seem to contain the tail end of an oral tradition which in ancient times supplied such information about the past as was available, but the individual episodes were not necessarily remembered in the right sequence. So in the moving of the bluestones, which Geoffrey called the 'Giants Dance', we can clearly discern a recollection of an event in the Bronze Age or earlier – what has been described as 'the only fragment left to us of a native Bronze Age literature'.[18] Other ancient events and activities which are to be found in the legends will not be so easy to date, but there is a natural presumption that they are likely to be from a much later phase of prehistory than the moving of the first stones of Stonehenge. In so far as the subject matter of the romances is affected by pre-Christian religious activity, by far the most dominant influence is likely to be the last phase of paganism, which flourished up to the Roman conquest and probably had a resurgence in the period after the departure of the Romans.

Even though the odds may seem very much against finding more memories of the Bronze Age, there are several references to stones being moved, floated and erected, and there is a surprising concentration of important events on Salisbury Plain. The Giants Dance, as will be seen, is far from being the sole remnant of Bronze Age oral literature. Indeed, why stop at the Bronze Age? Tradition records the introduction of ploughing and of grinding grain, before which men are said to have lived by hunting and fowling. And both the title of a divinity prominent in these pages called the Rich Fisher or Fisher King, and also the associated ritual, suggest an origin in pre-agricultural times.

Religions are very conservative. There are instances of deities or rituals persisting over many thousands of years. And there is a peculiarity of

---

[18] S. Piggott – later Professor – *Antiquity* XV 60, p. 319. Current views on the moving of the bluestones are discussed on p. 209 note 1, below.

religions that they often incorporate, or at least indicate, aspects of earlier competitors. This process gives clues to the position of pagan sacred sites, and from dedications to particular saints we can sometimes glean information about the nature of the original cults. For instance, Bishop Germain of Coutances lists nearly a dozen pagan sites on the summits of pointed hills in France which have been replaced by churches dedicated to St Michael.[19] To those he listed may be added the one on top of the tumulus called La Hougue Bie in Jersey[20] and some English examples including St Michael's tower on the top of Glastonbury Tor and the Cornish Mount St Michael. The French list includes a certain St Michel-Mont-Mercure, suggesting a second layer in the process. Whatever the deity involved, a Celtic cult site had evidently been assimilated to the classical Mercury before being taken over by St Michael. Both Mercury (who is sometimes equated with the deity known in Ireland as Lug) and St Michael (who, from the original name Tombelaine for Mont St Michel, may be guessed replaces the original Celtic god Belenus there) reveal something about the original worship at the site. So do some of the dedications to 'Our Lady', possibly in some instances replacing a goddess, and to St Denis (Dionysus), St Apollinaire (Apollo) and many others.[21]

On an even larger scale, many important festivals can clearly be seen to have persisted from pre-Christian times For instance, it is a commonplace that Christmas includes features of a previous system in which the birth of the year was celebrated at the winter solstice. And the very name of Easter is that of a pagan goddess whose festival fell on the spring equinox. An external observer might observe that of the two principal anniversaries of the Christian church one fell more or less on the winter solstice and the other on the first Sunday after the first full moon after the spring equinox; and that the main day of worship was named after the sun. He could be forgiven for supposing that Christianity had a considerable leaning towards astronomy in its doctrines, yet it has none. So we are given a glimpse of the importance of the sun and moon in some earlier dogma which the early church chose to defuse by incorporating it into its own system. Worship of the sun and moon, though presumably of immemorial age, first had an effect which is still visible today when Neolithic monuments were oriented towards the rising or setting sun at the

[19] *St Michel et le Mont St Michel*, A.A. Germain, Paris 1880, pp. 96f. The list includes, apart from Mont St Michel on the coast of Brittany: Mont Dol, Mont St Michel near Saint-Paul de Léon, the mountain of St Michael at Quimperlé, the chapel to St Michael on the great tumulus at Carnac, one of the mountains of Arrée, Noirmoutier, Saint-Michel-Mont-Mercure, Saint-Michel d'Ai-guilhe, one of the peaks of Mont Blanc, Roc Amadour and others, which would no doubt include St Michel de Brasparts, between Quimper and Morlaix. Germain may go further than modern authors in ascribing these sites to Belenus or some similar Celtic deity, but the association between peaks or tumuli and St Michael must be significant in some way.
[20] Shared with Notre Dame de Lorette, and also known as the chapel of Notre Dame de la Clarté. The unusual ascription of 'brightness' here might shed some light on the original cult.
[21] *Les saints successeurs des dieux*, P. Saintyves, Paris 1907. In Ireland the same tendency has resulted in the replacing of the deities Brigid and Anna (Anu, or Danu) by saints of the same name. *Lives of the Saints*, Baring Gould and Fisher, p. 264.

solstices. This practice remained popular in the Bronze Age but seems largely to have been abandoned in the Iron Age. So any surviving record in the oral tradition of orientation towards the rising or setting sun is likely, if it is taken at its face value, to be of very ancient origin.

The principal themes of this book are first, that many recollections of paganism survive in the Arthurian legends; second, that the pagan practices and figures centred on Arthur and the Round Table have not been gathered together in an entirely random fashion but represent some sort of pantheon with, in the background, a consistent dogma; and third, that there is a possibility of correspondence between legend and fact both in respect of geography and artefacts.

The view that the Arthurian legend consists 'largely of folklore and mythic elements'[22] has been around for a long time.[23] What is different here is a more comprehensive analysis of cult patterns than has previously been attempted and a carefully argued solution to the vexed question of Arthurian geography. These lead to a new appreciation of the sequence of cults in time, and to a localization of the physical background of the legends to a point where it might be possible to see if traces of the system can be recognized on the ground.

During the last half a century or so, the position of a 'historical' Arthur of around AD 500 has become more deeply entrenched. Here, a much less concrete personage is proposed. The two views can scarcely be described as opposed, for their existence depends on two different sets of evidence. To prove the existence of either, if that were possible, would not diminish the arguments in favour of the other, since each depends on entirely different premises. On the one hand we have the Arthur whose main claim to fame was a shadowy campaign over many years against the Saxon invaders, and who is thought, from monastic chronicles written long after the event, to have lived in the aftermath of the Roman withdrawal from Britain, when Christianity was general. To set against the supposed reality of post-Roman times we have a mythological figure around whom gather all the ancient gods of the Celtic pantheon.[24] He will be found to be married to one of those territorial goddesses marriage to whom confers sovereignty. At his court are knights who follow the rule of Nemi even, as in the classical example, breaking a 'garland' from a particular tree to provoke combat, or who annually challenge all comers for a crown and the most beautiful maiden that can be found. This is all in the service of religion, for 'the imitative power of human sexuality'[25] is supposed to influence the fecundity of Nature and so to promote general prosperity. The converse of this supposition is that the impotence of, and in

[22] *The Legend of Sir Lancelot du Lac*, J.L. Weston, p. 86.
[23] E.g. in *Studies in the Arthurian Legend*, Sir J. Rhys, Oxford, 1891.
[24] *Le roi Arthur et la société Celtique*, J. Markale, p. 95.
[25] *Rites of the Gods*, A. Burl, p. 81 for this phrase. Numerous examples are provided by Frazer.

particular the castration of, a sacred king is likely to cause widespread barren-ness.

The contrast between the two Arthurs could scarcely be greater. In a nut-shell, one is before the Roman occupation, the other after. The traces left in the ground should be noticeably different. It seems, therefore, that it should be possible to recognize the real Arthur by excavation at a suitable site, some more carefully chosen Cadbury. Unfortunately Arthurian geography has been extremely confused. It offers 'well-known difficulties which are notorious, owing to the ignorance or capriciousness of some of the writers'.[26] This applies not just to the names of individual places but also to the general setting of the romances. It has been argued that it was largely or wholly in Scotland, or else in Wales, or else in Cornwall, or else in Brittany.[27] When the overall picture is so confused, how will it be possible to identify any site where the scene described in legend can be compared with relics in or on the ground? There is just one line of approach which has not yet been tried, and it may seem an unlikely one. Are there any places which can be identified from internal evi-dence, say the shape of a hill or a position at a river-mouth? The legends will be explored with this possibility in mind, leading to a reasonably consistent interpretation of much of Arthurian geography.

This exercise has been successful enough for me to provide a gazetteer of pagan Britain. It is the complaint of archaeologists that prehistory should really be about more than the broken and discarded possessions of the people they study. In Britain the gap can partly be filled by the Arthurian tradition, which reveals the ritual significance of a number of sites, most of them in the Severn valley and estuary or parts of the country adjacent to them. This is not to say there were no others, just that these are the ones that can be identified. However, a surprisingly large proportion of the pagan practices later to be analysed can be tied to those sites which can be located in general terms, such as at the mouth of a particular river. The unexpected clarity of the traditions preserved in the French romances is due to the strange chance that folk-lore collectors in the twelfth century wrote their romances down and so preserved and stabilized them, while in their native home only a small proportion of the great body of tradition received this treatment. The majority was lost and much of what survived became garbled by repetition after its real meaning had been forgotten.

Speaking of the 'errant deeds' so often related of King Arthur and his companions, the Norman author Wace, one of the earliest writers to introduce Celtic themes to the French and the first to mention the Round Table, said 'by reason of his [the narrator's] embellishments the truth stands hid in the trap-pings of a tale. Thus to make a delectable tune to your ear, history goes masking as fable'. In what follows the unmasking process reveals not so much

[26] *An Index of Proper Names in French Arthurian Prose Romances*, G.D. West, p. xiii.
[27] Curiously this argument of exclusiveness is never made for the land of Logres – that is, modern England or at least the western part of it – which was Arthur's own realm.

history as prehistory. As a result several prehistoric sites or structures are no longer anonymous. They are now cloaked with the vestiges of ancient traditions of power and splendour, and they are enlivened by distant memories of the ritual acts of sacred kings, sorcerers, heroes and heroines. The rain-washed stones of British prehistory now have a mythological dimension reminiscent of that of Greece or Crete or Troy or of Ireland, where the links between myth and place have been preserved.

# PART ONE
# AN ARTHURIAN ADVENTURE ANALYSED

# THE CALENDAR OF ARTHURIAN ROMANCE

Arthur's personal adventure in the glade at St Augustine's chapel introduces several pagan themes. Study of these themes will provide an introduction to pagan beliefs and may help us to understand the mental background which underlies the more material aspects of paganism which are analysed in the third part of this book.

To begin with the first theme to crop up in the story – the adventure began on a festival. This is typical of the legends. Ascension Day is less frequently met in the romances than most other festivals, and an explanation of its relevance to pagan thinking must wait till later in this chapter, but the commencement of the episode on a day of festival prompts consideration of the importance of festivals in the legends as a whole. A useful resumé of some of the more popular dates is provided by a well known event, Arthur's coronation.

## How Arthur was Crowned

'At Candlemas many more great lords came thither for to have won the sword, but there might none prevail. And right as Arthur did at Christmas, he did at Candlemas, and pulled out the sword easily, whereof the barons were sore aggrieved and put it off in delay till the high feast of Easter. And as Arthur sped before, so did he at Easter; yet there were some of the great lords had indignation that Arthur should be king, and put off in a delay till the feast of Pentecost.

And at the feast of Pentecost all manner of men assayed to pull at the sword that would assay; but none might prevail but Arthur, and pulled it out afore all the lords and commons that were there, wherefore all the commons cried out at once, We will have Arthur unto our king, we will put him to no more in delay, for we all see that it is God's will that he shall be our king . . . and so anon was the coronation made.'[1]

---

[1] *Morte Darthur*, Malory, bk I, ch. 7.

When the young Arthur drew the sword from the stone, he did so first at Christmas, then at Candlemas, again at Easter and finally at Pentecost, at which festival he was at last crowned. Sequences like this occur many times in the romances. The progression of time was not then generally recorded by the present day notation of days of the month but as on (which may mean 'about') a particular festival, or so many days before or after such an occasion. This is not a feature peculiar to the romances; the world at large in the Middle Ages, from carpenters to tax-gatherers, expressed dates in the same way.

The medieval sequence of church festivals is to a large extent derived from earlier calendars. The main framework, as still today, followed the Roman system in which the year is divided into twelve months of arbitrary lengths; months, that is, which do not correspond to the interval between full moons or between new moons (which is 29½ days). This system, so familiar to us, had rather different precursors. Take, for example, the Celtic year, which is bound to be important in the context of the Arthurian legend, so much of which is derived from Celtic sources. The Celtic year, as exemplified by the engraved bronze sheet found at Coligny, was based on true months from full moon to full moon, with an extra month thrown in every few years to bring the moon calendar of twelve real months, a total of only about 354 days in each year, back into line with the sun calendar of a little over 365 days. This is the same procedure as we use when we put in an extra day in leap years to reconcile a calendar based on 365 days to a sun-cycle which is not an exact number of days. There are several systems still in use today, some of them by very large numbers of people, which follow the ancient principle of reckoning by the moon rather than the sun. Without the introduction of an intercalary month from time to time the dates of their 'new years' every twelve 'moon' months come at different seasons of the year. The Christian church followed Rome for the most part in having a calendar using the sun-year, based on (if not actually beginning at) the lowest point of the sun in the whole year, the winter solstice.

The sword-drawing days include an example of a festival day derived from the sun calendar, Christmas, which is very close to the winter solstice. Of course, this astronomical event plays no part whatever in Christian dogma, neither do the other main astronomical markers, the spring equinox, the summer solstice and the autumn equinox. Nevertheless, the year-god cycle of prehistoric Europe started with the birth of the divine child long before the time of Christ.[2] As far as the sun is concerned, the cycle may be said to begin with the winter solstice. Since the taking over of the observances and holy places of one religion by another is a common enough occurrence, it is reasonable to suppose that December 25th was chosen by the early church because its close proximity to the solstice links the symbolism of the divine child with the sun cycle.

To illustrate the way in which the different calendar systems play their part

2   *The Goddesses and Gods of Old Europe*, Gimbutas, p. 234.

in the medieval (and indeed the modern) calendar, we may turn to the next occasion on which Arthur drew the sword, Candlemas, February 2nd. This festival also has a pre-Christian origin. The Celts used a system of 'cross'-quarter days (see below) of which February 1st is one. This is the day of St Brigid who had an earlier existence as the goddess Brigid, the daughter of the Dagda, a god of fire in the Irish pantheon which was known as the Tuatha De Danann (the people of the goddess Danann). Brigid was one of three goddesses of the same name (triplication is a feature of Celtic goddesses) and she was a fire goddess. Reflecting this origin, Saint Brigid was reputed to keep a perpetual fire in an enclosure to which men were not allowed access; and Candlemas, though displaced by a day, bears marks of the same origin in its name and the symbolism of the candles which used to be burnt on that occasion. Finally we come to the last two festivals on which the sword was drawn, Easter and Pentecost – Christian 'movable feasts' to be described in more detail shortly.

Other sequences of festival days are given in the romances in two lists of court days. They are as follows:

### Court Festivals

In one of the lists, Uther, Arthur's father, decreed that

Christmas, Pentecost and All Hallows[3]

should be kept at Cardoel in Wales. In the other, Arthur is said to have worn the crown at

Christmas, Easter, Ascension, Pentecost and All Hallows.[4]

Of them all, Easter is described as 'the highest' and Pentecost 'the most joyful'. As well as these more important courts, sometimes referred to as 'compulsory' courts, this second list mentions minor courts at Candlemas and mid-August. With St John's Day, that is, Midsummer Day, which was another occasion on which courts were held, these lists include most of the dates mentioned in Arthurian legend for holding courts or other major dated events except for occasional mentions of St Mary Magdalen's Day (July 22nd) and, rarely, May 1st.

Before examining the part played by festivals in the legends it would be as well to explain in more detail the relationship of these festivals to the movements of the sun and moon, which provide the basis for all calendars.

---

3 *Vulgate*, II, p. 58.
4 *Vulgate*, III, p. 107.

### The Solstices and Equinoxes

Looked at astronomically, the year could be said to begin (or be born) at the winter solstice (the shortest day) – about December 21st – after which the days begin to lengthen and continue to do so for the three months to the spring equinox (when day and night are of equal length) – about March 21st – then go on lengthening for another three months to the summer solstice (longest day) – about June 21st – after which the days begin to shorten through the autumn equinox – about September 21st – and continue to do so until the cycle has returned to the winter solstice. This simple progression provides two of the major Arthurian festival dates: Christmas, (the near coincidence of which to the winter solstice, as explained above, can scarcely be an accident) and St John's Day. It also provides the marker, the spring equinox, for the movable feasts.

### The Civil Calendar

The calendar beginning on January 1st which we use today is related to the astronomical year in a somewhat arbitrary fashion, the interval between the winter solstice and January 1st having been decided by Julius Caesar when, in 45 BC he defined January 1st as the day of the first new moon after the winter solstice of that year.[5] The choice of the new moon rather than the full seems appropriate to the burgeoning year because of its promise of increase, but it may have been chosen because the night of the new moon is clear-cut and unambiguous. Unlike the solstices themselves, when the rising or setting sun stays in roughly the same place for a few days, there could be no argument about which night the new moon fell on.

The English quarter days, when rents become due, follow their astronomical markers rather more closely than do the Julian and the present day Gregorian calendars. Lady Day, March 25th; Midsummer Day, June 24th; and Christmas Day, December 25th; are all within a day or two of solstices or equinoxes.

April 5th as the end of the fiscal year is an interesting survival as it represents Lady Day, Old Style. When the Gregorian calendar was introduced to correct an error in the previous calendar, which was allowing church festivals to get gradually later relative to the seasons, eleven days were deleted from the calendar. So that taxpayers should not pay a whole year's tax on a year shorter than 365 days, the Treasury retained its old year end in 1752 and has done ever since. From March 25th to April 5th is eleven days. Even today some agricultural tenancies in East Anglia still retain the old style quarter days for payments of rent.

---

5  *General Astronomy*, H. Spencer-Jones, p. 62.

The astronomical year provides a basis for two other sets of religious festivals, one Christian and one pagan.

## The Movable Feasts

The Christian movable feasts all depend on Easter, which is nowadays related to the solar cycle by being, in the western tradition, the first Sunday after the first full moon which happens on or after the spring equinox. The dependence of a Christian festival on an earlier pagan festival is disguised here, but Easter, according to Bede[6] takes its name from the goddess Eostre or Eastre whose festival was held at the spring equinox. From Easter, Ascension Day follows forty days later, and Pentecost (or Whitsunday) is fifty days after Easter. Easter thus varies from year to year by the length of time after the equinox for the full moon to appear plus up to another six days because it must be a Sunday. It therefore occurs between the last week in March and the last week in April, and Pentecost roughly between the middle of May and the middle of June.

## The Cross-Quarter Days

The most obviously Celtic contribution to the calendar is more simply related to the astronomical framework provided by the sun. It consists of the 'cross'-quarter days which follow the solstices and equinoxes at an interval of rather over a month. The Celts, and probably also their predecessors for countless generations, divided the year according to the seasons as they appear to mankind. Because the Earth takes time to be warmed by the greater power of the sun in summer, and takes time to cool when its power decreases as winter approaches, the seasons lag a month or more behind the sun. Using these *apparent* seasons, the Celts considered the eve of November 1st, Hallowe'en (in Irish, Samain), to be the beginning of winter and also to be the beginning of their year; and the eve of May 1st (Beltaine), to be the beginning of summer. This scheme neatly divides the year into a half when grass is plentiful and a half in which it is not, and is said to be particularly suited to a pastoral people. The other festivals in this system of cross-quarter days are February 1st (Imbolc), closely linked with Candlemas, and August 1st (Lugnasad). As the present day name for the November festival, Hallowe'en (a contraction of Hallow*even*), makes clear, the celebration was of the 'eve', the evening before, rather than the day. What was important seems to have been the transfer from one period to the next rather than the first day of the new period. The Celts did not divide their day from midnight to midnight but from dusk to dusk. They regarded the twenty four hour period as a night followed by a day, and the year as a winter followed by a summer.

6  *Chambers Dictionary*, 1971.

The gap between the cross-quarter days and their astronomical markers is a whole month plus the interval between the marker and the month-end, the latter being nine or ten days, giving about forty days in all.[7] However, there is no need to suppose that in pre-literate times there was an exact correspondence with a formal calendar. The actual day of celebration may have been arbitrarily selected by the priestly caste, or may have been chosen by reference to some other feature, such as the phases of the moon. In one classical account of a Celtic religious festival it was the sixth day of the waxing moon that was important.

## A Festival Not Directly Linked to the Astronomical Quarter Days

Finally, Mid-August, mentioned above, seems to have a rather different pagan origin. August 15th is now the Assumption of the Blessed Virgin Mary but we may suspect, with Frazer,[8] that this merely replaces the earlier pagan festival of Diana which was celebrated in Roman times on August 13th. We shall later find a link between an Arthurian Mid-August festival and the Arthurian equivalent of the classical Diana.

The purpose of this chapter is to find how the narrators of the Celtic themes of the romances organized their material relative to the calendar. How did significant dates from the pre-Christian era, however loosely specified originally, get translated into the rigid framework of a modern calendar? There are one or two obvious examples. At a certain temple of Venus on the boundary[9] of Cornwall and Loenois[10] her day was celebrated 'according to the Roman fashion' at the kalends of May; and a certain Grimal, returning from hawking to greet his mother Florée, wore a chaplet of flowers on the day of St Philip and St Jake (May 1st).[11] The first example signifies the revival of sexuality in spring; and Grimal's mother's name, Florée, and his garland symbolise the other aspect of May 1st, the return of the productivity of nature. Whatever the 1st of May meant in calendar terms to the Celts, whether it was an arbitrary date chosen by a priestly whim, or whether it was a certain number of days from an inaccurately ascertained equinox, or whether it was chosen by some aspect of the moon, the essential nature of the festival has been transferred to a date which even today we can recognize as representative of the original occasion. St Philip and St Jake (James) are irrelevant in this instance. There are

7    Forty days is a period which often crops up in a religious context.
8    *The Golden Bough*, Frazer, Part I, pp. 14–6.
9    Boundaries had a religious significance in pagan times. At Flag Fen there was an alignment of posts across a shallow lake, some 1000 metres long consisting of 2000 or so posts. Deposition of votive offerings, including ritually broken weapons, was centred on this line of posts which is thought to have been a ritual boundary.
10   *Le Roman en prose de Tristan. . .*, ed. Löseth, p. 11.
11   *Le Saint Graal*, ed. Hucher, vol. III, p. 542.

plenty of events occurring on May 1st, but it is a curious aspect of the legends that, unlike the other major Celtic festival Hallowe'en, although May 1st is one of the most important and durable of pre-Christian festivals it is seldom chosen for a royal court in the romances. On the other hand, Midsummer Day, transformed into St John's Day by Christian usage, though never an important festival of the church, is, as G. D. West points out,[12] 'the most popular date in Arthurian romances.' So what is the style of the events which occur on this popular day. And what has happened to those activities, appropriate to spring ceremonies, which have been transmitted from the underlying oral tradition into the romances?

To answer these questions it is necessary to look at examples, so a list now follows of events said to have taken place at various festivals, excluding items which may be taken for granted as normal for such an occasion, such as attendance at Mass, and items which are of everyday occurrence, such as comings and goings of no special importance. To have included these minor items would have sacrificed clarity without altering the balance between the listed festivals.

**Events at Particular Festivals**

Usually 'adventures' and other interesting events are said to happen on a day of festival. A wide-ranging survey shows that almost all dated events fall on the dates included in the list below or within a day or so of them. Only a few are on other festivals: the Feast of Our Lady in September, St Martin's, St Michael's, St Peter's and St Paul's, St Remi's, or St Samson's.

The list which follows shows events taking place at each festival, taken in sequence from the winter solstice. New Year's Day is shown as following Christmas as it does today, but it must be remembered that with a new year starting at the winter solstice, it would be indistinguishable from Christmas; and also that the new year used to begin on several other dates, notably Hallowe'en in a Celtic context and March 25th at the time the romances were being composed.

It is inevitable that this section should consist of a list of incidents. These have not been chosen to illustrate particular points. They are, with the specific exceptions noted above, all the incidents which could be found in a substantial trawl through numerous texts. The items in the list correspond to the observations of a scientist. Individual incidents may or may not be relevant. It is only when all the information has been gathered together and is available for analysis that one can determine whether the narrators have assembled their material at random with respect to the calendar or whether there is a discernible pattern; and if such a pattern emerges relative to particular dates, how it is to be explained.

---

[12] *Index of Proper Names in French Arthurian Prose Romances*, p. 172.

Items from late or possibly less reliable sources are given a reference in square brackets [ ].

## Christmas

Arthur drew the sword from the stone for the first time.

Gawain cut off the Green Knight's head at Camelot in the English *Sir Gawain and the Green Knight*.

A giant fought annually at Pelles' court for the possession of an island.[13]

Erec was crowned and new knights dubbed.[14]

## New year's Day

## Candlemas  (February 2nd)

Perceval died on the eve of this day.[15]

## Easter  (movable)

Lancelot's grandfather, who was also called Lancelot, had his head cut off and thrown into a well.[16]

The lord of Escalon's daughter made love in church which brought about perpetual darkness to the district around.[17]

A knight was wounded in the thigh at a fountain.[18]

The Holy Grail was recharged annually at Easter by a white dove bearing a mass-wafer in its beak. This alone sustained the Maimed King throughout the year.[19]

Lionel was dubbed.[20]

Uther Pendragon was crowned, and

Uther Pendragon met Ygerne.[21]

## May 1st

On May 1st British nobles were slain by 'Saxons' near the Monastery of Ambrius on Salisbury Plain, at the place which Aurelius Ambrosius was later to mark by erecting the bluestone circle of Stonehenge.[22]

Though the day of the month is not mentioned, Guenever was abducted while 'a-Maying in woods and fields' with a retinue 'all bedashed with herbs,

---

13 *Le Roman en prose de Tristan . . .*, ed. Löseth, p. 211.
14 *Erec and Enid*, ed. Roques, vv. 6636ff.
15 *Perceval le Gallois . . .* Potvin, vol. VI, line 45343.
16 *Vulgate*, I, pp. 294/5.
17 *Vulgate*, VII, p. 136.
18 *Vulgate*, V, p. 225.
19 *Parzival*, tr. Hatto, p. 240.
20 *Vulgate*, IV, p. 392.
21 Geoffrey of Monmouth, *Historia*, ed. Wright, p. 96, sect 137.
22 Geoffrey of Monmouth, *Historia*, ed. Wright, p. 70, sect 103/4 and p. 90, sect 128.

mosses and flowers'.[23] In a Welsh version her abductor was Melwas, dressed entirely in green leaves, and she was willing to be taken. Her maids thought him to be a satyr.[24]

The giant Asue took a tribute of youths and maidens at Dolorous Gard annually on this day.[25]

The sword Arthur was later to withdraw was fixed in the stone [in *Perceforest*].[26]

'Right at the beginning of May' Lamorat defeated the lord of the Castle of Ten Knights, so becoming lord himself and wife of the damsel of the castle.[27]

This was the date of the royal spring marriage [in *Perceforest*], with many unions and conceptions among the members of the royal retinue.[28]

Arthur cast adrift at sea all children of knights and ladies born on this day, in a vain attempt to destroy Mordred.[29]

## Ascension Day (movable)

Arthur's personal adventure in the glade at St Augustine's chapel took place.[30]

Galehot's talismanic body was removed from its resting place among the holy bodies and taken back to Wales on the day following Ascension.[31]

Meleagant abducted Guenever after a challenge to any knight to fight for her.[32]

Lancelot endured the burning lance in the testing bed.[33]

## Pentecost or Whitsuntide (movable)

Coronations:

Arthur was crowned King of Logres.[34] (Logres was Arthur's principal kingdom, the western part of what is now England.)

Baudemagus was crowned King of Gorre in South Wales.[35]

Galahad, son of Joseph of Arimathea, was crowned King of Hoselice (now called Wales).[36]

Ambrosius assumed the crown at Stonehenge.[37]

---

23 *Morte Darthur*, Malory, bk XIX, ch. 2; K. G. T. Webster regards Malory's source as earlier than Chrétien.
24 *Celtic Remains*, Lewis Morris (mid 18th Cent), p. 220.
25 *Guiron le Courtois*, ed. Lathuillère, para. 253.
26 *Perceforest*, ed. Roussineau, part IV, p. 1019, ch. L, line 130.
27 *Folie Lancelot*, ed. Bogdanow, pp. 72f.
28 *Perceforest*, ed. Roussineau, part IV, p. 1129, 'la fut faitte mainte acointise sans convoitise ne trahison, ains par plaisance et amour naturelle, dont maint preudhommes et vaillant dames furent puis engendres qui reemplirent le païs.'
29 *Morte Darthur*, Malory, bk I, ch. 27.
30 Page 8 above.
31 *Roman en Prose de Lancelot du Lac*, ed. G. Hutchings, p. 51 (bottom half).
32 *Roman en Prose de Lancelot du Lac*, ed. G. Hutchings, p. 11 (bottom half); *Vulgate*, IV, pp. 156f.
33 *Roman en Prose de Lancelot du Lac*, ed. G. Hutchings, p. 23 (top half).
34 *Morte Darthur*, Malory, bk I, ch. 7.
35 *Vulgate*, VII, p. 144.
36 *Vulgate*, I, p. 282.
37 Geoffrey of Monmouth, *Historia*, ed. Wright, p. 92, sect 130.

Initiations:

Arthur drew the sword from the stone and was acclaimed as king.[38]

Sir Galahad drew a sword from a stone,[39] foreshadowing his kingship at the holy city of Sarras.

Perceval sat in the Perilous Seat and the stone shrieked under him, a mark of kingship[40] which was later to be have effect when he was crowned Fisher King at Corbierc (i.e. Corbenic).

Sir Galahad sat in the Perilous Seat at the Round Table and the Quest of the Holy Grail began.[41]

An unidentified knight sat in the Perilous Seat, escorted by two supporters, and disappeared.[42]

Brumant sat in the Perilous Seat and was consumed by fire.[43]

Notable Courts:

The inauguration of the Round Table at Cardoel by Uther Pendragon.[44]

Reinauguration of Round Table at Camelot on the octave (a word generally used of an eight-day festival but sometimes implying the festivities accompanying an anniversary) of Pentecost.

Guenever married Arthur at this reinauguration.

Uther Pendragon held a court on Salisbury Plain, prior to the battle against the 'Saxons' at the site where Stonehenge was *later* to be erected.[45]

Lancelot slept with Pelles' daughter at a Pentecost court.[46]

Knights dubbed:

Several individuals, including Arthur himself. Also mass creations of fifty[47] and one hundred companions of the Round Table at Cardoel and Camelot respectively.

Tournaments:

Several. Pentecost was the most popular time for tournaments, and since Arthurian tournaments seem to have been arranged for women to find husbands, marriages also took place then.[48]

Miscellaneous:

The feast of Uther was held on this date.[49] It was a custom for kings to

---

38  E.g. *Morte Darthur*, Malory, bk I, ch. 6/7.
39  *Vulgate*, VI, p. 11.
40  Didot *Perceval*, ed. Roach, p. 149.
41  *Vulgate*, VI, pp. 8 and 57.
42  *Vulgate*, II, p. 57.
43  *Vulgate*, V, pp. 319/20.
44  Huth *Merlin*, I, p. 96.
45  Huth *Merlin*, vol. I, pp. 87/92.
46  *Vulgate*, V, p. 379.
47  Huth *Merlin*, vol. I, p. 96.
48  *Guiron le Courtois*, ed. Lathuillère, paras. 30 and 169.
49  *Le Roman en prose de Tristan . . .*, ed. Löseth, p. 437.

celebrate the anniversaries of their coronations, so his coronation on this date is implied.

The Damsel Cacheresse (that is, the Damsel of the Lake under an alternative name) came to the wedding court of Arthur and Guenever.

*St John's Day   (Midsummer Day, June 24th)*

Coronation:

Fergus, victor at a tournament, was married to Galiane and they were crowned on a Sunday [Fergus].[50]

Fire from heaven:

A 'brandon' – a fiery torch – appeared in the sky above a battle against the 'Saxons' at Trebes in Brittany on a Sunday about St John's Day.[51]

A fiery red dragon appeared in the sky at a battle between Uther Pendragon and the 'Saxons' on Salisbury Plain during the last week in June at the place where Stonehenge was later to be built.[52]

King Arthur went to the thunder-storm fountain in the forest of Broceliande to keep a vigil on St John's eve.[53]

Foundations and dedications to St John:

After a victory over the 'Saxons' near the Severn on St John's day, Arthur built a chapel dedicated to St John.[54]

After Arthur had crushed a rebellion headed by Lot and Ryons, he founded a church at Camelot in Lot's honour. It was dedicated to St John, and Lot was buried there with great splendour. The occasion was celebrated with burning torches.[55]

Arthur built a chapel to St John where Meliadus, Tristan's father, killed a 'Saxon' called Ariohan. Images of the two contestants were engraved on the doors.[56]

Knights dubbed:

Several, including Lancelot, who was presented by the Damsel of the Lake at a St John's day court at Camelot on a Sunday.[57] The Damsel of the Lake will be shown to be a local version of the goddess Diana.[58]

---

50 The Romance of Fergus, tr. D. D. R. Owen in *Arthurian Literature VIII*, ed. R. W. Barber, lines 6942ff.
51 *Vulgate*, II, p. 208, line 17, p. 258, line 27.
52 *Vulgate*, II, p. 49/51; Huth *Merlin*, vol. I, pp. 87/92.
53 *Le Chevalier au Lion* (Yvain), ed. Roques, lines 668/9.
54 *Guiron le Courtois*, ed. Lathuillère, para. 48.
55 Huth *Merlin*, vol. I, pp. 262/4.
56 *Le Roman en prose de Tristan . . .*, ed. Löseth, p. 446.
57 *Vulgate*, III, pp. 118/123.
58 As the Damsel Cacheresse.

Miscellaneous:

A damsel with a cart drawn by stags brought 152 severed heads to Arthur's St John's Day court at Pennevoiseuse. This damsel at other times used to carry the Grail in the procession at the court of the Fisher King.[59]

Perceval, Grail hero and later Fisher King, dedicated his life to God on a St John's day.[60]

Merlin arranged to meet the Damsel of the Lake at a magic fountain on St John's Day.[61]

The ford of the Thorntree was at its most adventurous on this day and single combat took place there with a red defender.[62]

Tribute was demanded.[63] [64]

Mabon (the Celtic god equivalent to the sun god Apollo), here called Nabon, invited King Arthur to a great feast.[65]

Lancelot arrived at Corbenic prior to being cured of madness.

Tristan and Yseult drank the love-potion on the summer solstice.[66]

King Claudas of the Waste Land (Terre Deserte in Brittany) gathered his people together at Gannes (Vannes, see Gazetteer) on a St John's Day.

*St Mary Magdalen's Day   (July 22nd)*

King Claudas was crowned and annually celebrated the day by the most important court of the year.[67]

King Baudemagus of Gorre was crowned and the occasion was celebrated annually.[68]

A tournament took place.[69]

A rendezvous was made for knights to meet at Terrican's castle (Terrican sounds like the Celtic god Teruagant).[70]

Lancelot killed a red knight in single combat.[71]

---

[59] *Perlesvaus,* tr. N. Bryant, pp. 33/6 and p. 54.
[60] Potvin, vol. VI, p. 150, lines 45322f.
[61] *Vulgate,* II, p. 280.
[62] *Lai de l'Espine,* ed. Zenker, ZRP XVII, 1893, p. 246.
[63] Didot *Perceval,* ed. Roach, E 2172.
[64] *Tristan,* tr. Hatto, p. 122. This reference is to 'the solstice' and does not specify which. The reference above to tribute demanded by Rome is to Midsummer Day. If, as may be supposed, this applies also to Tristan and Morholt, their battle was fought on the third day after this reference to the summer solstice. Tristan's involvement with the sun is substantial: the battle with Morholt; drinking the love potion; Yseult likened to the sun; and a famous victory by his father was commemorated by a chapel to St John.
[65] *Le Roman en prose de Tristan . . .,* ed. Löseth, p. 469.
[66] *Love's Masks,* M. R. Blakeslee, p. 51 note.
[67] *Vulgate,* III, p. 48.
[68] *Vulgate,* IV, p. 290; the same event is said to have taken place at Pentecost, *Vulgate,* VII, p. 144.
[69] *Vulgate,* V, p. 147.
[70] *Vulgate,* V, p. 472.
[71] *Vulgate,* IV, p. 290/1.

*Mid-August*

As an 'adventure' before eating at this feast Arthur saw Sir Bors driven past in a cart with his legs tied to the shafts, jeered by the crowd and pelted with filth.[72]

Arthur held his first court after his marriage, which had taken place at Pentecost.

The Queen's knights were inaugurated and Gawain became a companion and master of the Round Table after a battle at the minster of St Stephen's.[73]

*All Hallows   (November 1st)*

Perceval was crowned Fisher King at Corbierc (that is, Corbenic) after the death of the previous Fisher King.[74]

Perceval came to Arthur's court at Cardoel on All Hallows. He was knighted on the next day, a Sunday. He then assumed his position next to the Siege Perilous, marking him out to be one of the three achievers of the Grail.[75]

Merlin summoned contingents from all over Britain and Brittany to meet on this day at the great gathering on Salisbury Plain at the site of the tall, hard rock where the final battle between Arthur and Mordred was later to take place.[76]

Bors and Lionel were crowned kings of Gannes and Benoic respectively.[77]

Gawain left court to seek the Green Knight.[78]

Guerrehes killed the Petit Chevalier in a year-end combat.[79]

Kay, Arthur's foster brother, was knighted.[80]

*Annual events on unspecified dates*

The king was burnt annually at the Burning City.[81]

The king was beheaded annually at the Waste City.[82]

Aristor cut off the heads of his lovers annually after a year.[83]

Galahad perished exactly a year after being crowned.[84]

The Sparrow hawk contest in *Erec* took place annually.[85]

---

[72] *Vulgate*, IV, p. 215.
[73] *Vulgate*, II, p. 319.
[74] *Perceval le Galois . . .*, ed. Potvin, vol. VI, p. 150 lines 45222/3.
[75] *Vulgate*, V, p. 385.
[76] *Vulgate*, II, pp. 372–6 and 383/5.
[77] *Vulgate*, VI, p. 316.
[78] *Sir Gawain and the Green Knight*, Tolkien and Gordon, line 536.
[79] *First Continuation*, ed. Roach, part VI.
[80] Huth *Merlin*, Paris and Ulrich, vol. I, p. 133.
[81] *Perlesvaus*, tr. Bryant, pp. 106f.
[82] *Perlesvaus*, tr. Bryant, pp. 90f.
[83] *Prose Index*, West, under Aristor.
[84] Morte Darthur, bk XVII, ch. 22 'at the year's end, and the self day after' he had borne the crown of gold.
[85] *The Creation of the First Arthurian Romance*, Luttrell, p. 97.

The names of these festivals almost all suggest Christianity, but the activities which take place on them include many that are not remotely connected with the Christian religion. In spite of the natural tendency of that era to look at the world from a Christian viewpoint, little attempt seems to have been made to censor paganism – for instance, Perceval sat on the thoroughly pagan 'stone which shrieked', a symbol exactly paralleled in the pre-Christian tradition of Ireland. To all appearances the most definitely Christian activities portrayed in this list are Galahad's quest of the 'Holy' Grail and Perceval's dedication to God. Here again the narrators seem to have assimilated a pagan theme to Christianity without censoring its pagan antecedents. It will be shown later that the gods of the Grail religion were in fact pagan. Meanwhile, perhaps it is not an accident that Perceval's activities should be associated with three of the festivals most obviously influenced by pagan origins: Midsummer Day, All Hallows and Candlemas, and with the stone that shrieked. If individual festivals are examined, there is a scatter of various activities to be found, such as coronations, tournaments and dubbing of knights, over most of them. They do not have a character of their own, except in the case of Pentecost and St John's Day, in both of which certain themes are repeated several times – at Pentecost, coronations (although 'the connection between Pentecost and coronation was not widespread in medieval theory or practice')[86] and initiations; at Midsummer, 'fire from heaven' and buildings dedicated to St John.

## Midsummer Day

St John's Day in particular is notable for the consistency of the activities recorded as having taken place on it. There are no less than five battles, all but one against 'Saxons', at which there are signs of fire in the sky or the dedication of a building to St John. The celestial fire, the thunderstorm and the burning torches are all symbolically appropriate to Midsummer Day as the time when the sun is at its highest point in the sky; but have they, or the buildings made at this time, anything to do with Christianity? A closer look at the buildings will provide a clue. The three religious foundations dedicated to St John after victories in battles can be extended to four, for although the reference to the battle between Uther Pendragon and the 'Saxons' does not mention the foundation afterwards of a chapel to St John, it does say that the bluestones circle of Stonehenge was later built where the battle took place. They were the first stones to be erected on the site of what was to become the most conspicuous construction dedicated to Midsummer that there could possibly be. So at least one of these battles has a strong link with paganism, and several other aspects of St John's Day will be shown to have pagan

86 *The Character of Arthur in Medieval Literature*, R. Morris, p. 44.

origins: the Thunderstorm Fountains, the Ford of the Thorntree and the macabre cartload of heads.

Midsummer Day was a most important religious occasion at least as early as the erection of the bluestone circle, about two thousand years BC, for this circle and also the sarsen circle which succeeded it were both constructed with an axis of symmetry that pointed to the position of the rising sun on Midsummer Day; and its memory lingered on in popular tradition until recent times. As late as 1830 a participant in the celebration of this day in the backward fen country wore ram's horns on his head – the sort of gesture to the gods his predecessors might have made from time immemorial – wore a green veil over his face and offended his neighbours by making strange noises. He was evidently a traditionalist, for he was celebrating on July 5th, that is, Midsummer Day Old Style.[87]

## Pentecost

Perhaps it is not unexpected that St John's Day, to which Christianity only clings by a thread, should attract pagan activities. The same cannot be said for the other prominent festival, Pentecost, which has no obvious pagan original. Yet the events taking place on it include sitting in the accurately named Perilous Seat, which called down celestial fire on any unauthorized occupant. A closer look at this supposed occurrence may indicate what kind of activity narrators allocated to Pentecost. When Galahad was presented at the Pentecost court at which he took his place in the Perilous Seat, he was dressed in red. The French text explains that, 'just as our Lord came in the semblance of fire, so the knight came in red armour which resembles the colour of fire.' There seems to have been some aspect of pagan dogma or ritual which medieval narrators identified with Pentecost because it reminded them of the 'cloven tongues as of fire' which descended on the disciples at that season. The act of sitting in the seat is presented in three versions. For Perceval the stone shrieked, like the pagan Stone of Destiny in Ireland; for Galahad there is the analogy of 'fire from heaven'; and for anyone else, divine vengeance in the form of being burnt alive. At whatever calendar date the pre-Christian original was enacted, some pagan belief or activity has coloured the twelfth century narrator's view of Pentecost so that he allocated to that day the incident in which Brumant the Proud sat in the Perilous Seat and was immediately struck by fire from heaven and reduced to a heap of ashes; and he also commented on the symbolic meaning of Galahad's apparel.

In case it should be thought that Perceval and Galahad both represent Christian ideals, a brief glance at their careers suggests otherwise. The full details must await a more detailed examination of the pagan antecedents of the Grail religion later, but Galahad was engendered deliberately to promote

---

[87] *Pagan Gods and Shrines of the Roman Empire*, ed. Henig and King, p. 51.

prosperity in his mother's land; toward the end of his life he was chosen to be King of Sarras, a place noted for pagan temples and activities; he reigned exactly for a year; and he died at the altar in a scorching blast of flame. Perceval sat on the stone that shrieked; he too became a king; he wore the crown at Corbenic, the Grail Castle, scene of numerous deaths and maimings in association with the Grail;[88] and his title was King Fisher, often used of the castrated sacred kings who go under the name 'Maimed Kings'.

Apart from the Perilous Seat, Pentecost was also a time for coronations and for the Round Table, which was originally inaugurated on this date at Cardoel and later reinaugurated on the same day of festival at Camelot. Both these aspects of Pentecost occur in the incident in which Galahad re-enacts the coronation ritual of drawing the sword from the stone followed by the assumption of office by sitting in the Perilous Seat, the first stage in his progress towards kingship at Sarras. Pentecost is also linked with the Grail Quest and with Uther Pendragon. These links, and that with the Round Table, will later be shown to have pagan antecedents. So although Pentecost is to all appearances a thoroughly Christian festival, the narrators of the romances have allocated to it certain pagan themes. This is to some extent paralleled by popular tradition, where a number of customs celebrating the advent of spring take place at Pentecost in much the same way as they do on May 1st.

The beneficent tongues of flame of the New Testament have been replaced in the romances by destructive fire from heaven in the case of Brumant, a feature which is constantly repeated in the affairs of personages connected with the Grail. Kalafes, Evalac and Joseph 'of Arimathea', for example, were wounded by supernatural fire or fiery beings.[89] If Pentecost owes this link to pagan thinking, it may be because it roughly corresponds in date to two pagan festivals. Pentecost falls on average roughly half way between Beltaine, May 1st, and Midsummer Day, June 24th, two of the festivals at which bonfires used to be lit all over Europe in pagan times, the second of which is noted for the presence in the romances of symbolic fire in the sky. Either or both of these festivals may have contributed towards the composite Pentecost of medieval narrators, which seems partly to have usurped the position of the pagan spring festival, and partly that of midsummer.

Whether the destruction of unauthorised sitters by fire was real or imaginary in the pagan original is an interesting question. The fire would certainly have been real for the disposal of the annual king at the Burning City whose death marked the beginning of a new year.[90]

A less obvious but still important aspect of Pentecost, though of course not confined to it, is marriage and love-making. The presence in the romances of royal marriages in spring will later be found to be representative of the pagan

---

[88] Many knights wished to spend a night in the Adventurous Palace but were invariably found dead next morning. *Vulgate*, I, p. 289.
[89] See chapter on Fire from Heaven for references.
[90] See page 125 below.

sacred marriage with its implication of having been carried out to improve general fertility and prosperity.

At this stage in the review of events at various festivals there are two general points to be made to clarify issues of history and geography. The first is that the apparent presence of the Saxons can be disregarded. As has already been suggested, some traditional material has been misplaced into the post-Roman era because of a general lack of historical perspective until quite recent times.[91] As a consequence, Saxon, the name of the principal enemy of the post-Roman Celts, has been allocated to the antagonists of their ancestors. There is a suggestion in the tradition that these enemies of the prehistoric British were really called Sarrassins, a name which is interchanged with Saxons in some contexts. Since the general term for Saxon in medieval French was Sesne it is easy enough to see how the misconception arose. It was corrected by Malory, who may have had access to a local tradition unavailable to his French precursors. So in *Morte Darthur* the Saxons play little part, and their place as the common enemy is taken by Sarrassins, with no diminution in the effect of the story.

To make matters worse, the Sarrassins were inevitably confused by medieval narrators with the Saracens of the Middle East (in spite of the fact that the latter achieved prominence much later than even the 'historical' Arthur), leading to obvious geographical errors. However, in one instance the 'matter of Britain' does make it clear that its Sarrassins were distinct from the Saracens of the Middle East, the locals taking their name from a place, the pagan city of Sarras which is so prominent in the romances, and not from Abraham's wife, Sarah,[92] as the eastern Saracens were supposed to have done. In reality they seem to have been the aboriginal inhabitants of Britain, who shared the land with 'giants' before the arrival of the evangeliser Joseph of 'Arimathea', which will be argued to have been before even the era of the erection of the bluestones.

The second point which may usefully be made here is that the list of battles against the 'Saxons' and of chapels dedicated to St John does not necessarily imply five separate original battles and four 'chapels' or other religious foundations. If the original event was a battle on Midsummer Day which was followed by the erection of the bluestone circle, it would be so famous that the story would be repeated countless times and in the process degraded into unrecognisable fragments. Even though the place and the personages may be different in some of these survivors, it is quite possible that they all stem from one original event or statement of dogma, and that as far as these chapels to St John are concerned, there was only one solstice oriented temple, the obvious one, but recollected in five separate channels which have diverged until a common original cannot be recognized.

---

[91] See above page 11.
[92] *Vulgate*, I, p. 21.

**May 1st**

An unexpected feature of the festival scene, considering the penetration of Celtic themes into the romances, is the comparative absence of the best known aspect of May 1st, the May Queen, whose royal status reflects an attenuated memory of the ancient pagan concept of the royal marriage intended, as Frazer has it: 'to promote the growth of vegetation by homoeopathic magic'. With him we may also 'assume with a high degree of probability that the profligacy which once attended these [spring marriage] ceremonies was at one time not an accidental excess but an essential part of the rites, and that in the opinion of those who performed them the marriage of trees and plants could not be fertile without the real union of the human sexes'.[93] The only memorable incident which calls to mind this aspect of behaviour is the Maying of Guenever (see above) which had far reaching effects. What has happened is clear enough. Spring ceremonies were not restricted in the European tradition to May 1st. They were also performed in some districts at Pentecost, in others on St George's Day (April 23rd) and in Scandinavia on Midsummer Day. So Lancelot sleeping with Pelles' daughter, an action described as stimulating the prosperity of her country, though reported to have taken place at Pentecost on the second occasion that it happened, probably belongs to a tradition which nowadays would more commonly be associated with May 1st though it was originally spread over a month or two in late spring and early summer. There is a suggestion, though not a substantial one, that the initiation ceremonies of Pentecost in the romances may also have been taken over from May 1st, if we may draw an inference from the sword which was later to be withdrawn from the floated stone at Pentecost having been inserted into it on May 1st [in *Perceforest*].[94]

**All Hallows**

The lists of court festivals with which this chapter began are somewhat similar to those of pagan Ireland. There there were three pre-eminent assemblies: the Feast of Tara, which was held every seven years 'on All-hallowtide – for that was the Easter of the heathen, and all the men of Erin were at that meeting, helping the king to hold it; the fair of Tailtu (now Teltown in East Meath) at Lammas (August 1st): and the Great Gathering of Uisnech (the North East road from Tara) on Mayday.'[95] The emphasis is not the same as in the romances, as the Irish list is confined to cross-quarter days and the solstices are absent. However, the importance of All Hallows is emphasized. Although in the list of events at particular festivals All Hallows does not have a uniform character, some of the individual items are interesting. The link here between

---

[93] *The Golden Bough*, Frazer, pt. I, vol. II, p. 97.
[94] *Perceforest*, ed. Roussineau, bk IV, p. 1019, Chap L, line 130.
[95] Stokes and Windisch, vol. III, heft I, para. 55, p. 216/7.

Perceval and one of the prime pagan festivals is very strong; and the Arthurian great gathering on Salisbury Plain, at the site on which the last battle would be fought, must be rated as one of the more important events in the Arthurian chronicle.

As usual, nothing in this traditional material is absolutely clear cut. For instance, different manuscripts speaking of a demand for tribute confuse Pentecost and St John's day. But even if the edges are a little blurred, there is an impression that the Pentecost of the narrators of romance incorporates information about an important pagan festival in late spring with its own particular characteristics and there is an even clearer and equally distinctive one at midsummer. The pagan nature of both this and of the other Arthurian festivals, at present no more than hinted at, will become clearer as this investigation proceeds.

This analysis of festivals was prompted by Arthur's adventure in the glade which began on Ascension Day. On this particular day, Ascension, there were courts on various occasions at Camelot, Cardoel, Carlion and Talebre, and, as well as the visit to St Augustine's chapel, it was the day on which Meleagant (in the French version) abducted Guenever,[96] the starting point of Lancelot's adventure which involved him with the demeaning cart. So it was by no means an unimportant festival. All there is to say to explain Ascension in terms of the pagan calendar is that it is forty days after Easter. Since the original date for Easter was the spring equinox, this would make Ascension Day equivalent to May 1st. There is support for this identification from the abduction of Guenever on Ascension Day. In other contexts this is described as taking place during 'maying' and the green clothes and floral decorations of the participants suggest that this episode belongs to the spring rituals appropriate to May 1st, which are otherwise unemphasized in the Arthurian record. For the position of May 1st as the prime representation of spring to have been usurped by Ascension Day and also to a certain extent by Pentecost would explain the unexpectedly low profile of May 1st in the romances relative to, say, Hallowe'en.

[96] *Vulgate*, IV, p. 157f.

# THE CHALLENGE

King Arthur's adventure at St Augustine's chapel has been chosen to introduce the reader to paganism because the narrator has constructed this episode from several distinct pagan themes. One feature of this composite story is single combat to the death in a forest clearing. Single combat in a glade is one element of the rite of Nemi, here called 'The Challenge'. One element on its own is not enough to identify the episode with certainty as conforming to this rite. However, as the details of the Challenge are described more resemblances between it and Arthur's adventure will become apparent.

As mentioned in the foreword, to have a complete correspondence with Nemi the elements which should be expected are:[1]

   (1)  A sacred site
   (2)  which contains a significant natural feature,
   (3)  is defended by a particular individual with his life.
   (4)  An opponent may by a specific act challenge the defender to fight.
   (5)  The challenger,[2] if successful, takes over the defence of the site,
   (6)  and takes the defender's title and possessions, including in many cases his wife or daughter.

In the romances there are many examples of the theme which contain most of these elements, and some which contain them all. Probably the best known native version which contains all six elements is *The Lady of the Fountain*, translated into English from the Welsh version of the story told by Chrétien de Troyes in *Yvain*; but as this story was analysed in *The Real Camelot* other examples will be used to extend the argument here.

The great number of 'challenge' incidents in the romances involve a substantial number of defenders. There are rather fewer challengers, including all the well known heroes such as Gawain, Lancelot and Perceval. The site of the battle is most often a forest clearing with a tree, a spring and a pavilion in

---

[1]  *The Real Camelot*, Darrah, p. 26.
[2]  Some authors quite legitimately describe as 'challenger' the participant named here as 'defender'. The defender does issue a challenge to all comers, but here I use the term challenger for the attacker.

which the ever present damsel and her lover, the defender, reside; but a spring is not the only central feature, the conflict may take place at a bridge, ford, causeway, island or hill instead. The challenge, if made, is generally a beaten cymbal or a blast on a horn, the broken branch motif only occurring in one particular romance. 'Guardianship', that is the onus on a successful challenger to take over the defence, is indicated a dozen times or more. At stake is the person of the damsel and lordship over her widespread dominions. She is a very important individual indeed.

Before making a more detailed analysis of the 'challenge' theme, it is advisable to see why the different accounts of it show so much variation. It can be assumed that if this cult practice were once widespread, there would be numerous sites in which the underlying dogma would be expressed in slightly different ways. To take a classical example, the worship of Diana would not be identical at the various different sites dedicated to her, such as the temple at Ephesus and the lake called Diana's Mirror which was beside the woodland clearing at Nemi. So in different places there would have been variations in the original style of worship, enhanced later by the accidents of transmission and conversion to a literary format.

To return to the fundamental basis of the 'challenge' in all its forms, the dogma seems to have been that prosperity was favourably affected by human sexual activity in general and by that of kings in particular. Life was precarious in prehistoric times. Apart from accidents and ill-health, food supply would have been variable with occasional shortages due to pests and diseases of crops, to exhaustion of the soil and even to small changes in the climate. Control of nature must have seemed extremely desirable, and, however misguidedly, prehistoric people attempted to improve their lot by setting an example to creation at large by their own procreative actions. That this way of looking at life really existed is vouchsafed for by its survival in folk-customs which clearly show that the general licence at spring-time had the intention of releasing natural fertility. Frazer quotes a sixteenth century description as follows:[3]

"Against May, Whitsonday, or other time, all the young men and maides, all olde men and wives, run gadding over night to the woods, groves, hills, and mountains where they spend the night in plesant pastimes; and in the morning they return, bringing with them birch and branches of trees, to deck their assemblies withal. And no mervaile, for there is a great lord present among them, as superintendent and Lord over their pastimes and their sports, namely, Satan, prince of hel. But the chiefest jewel they bring from thence is their May-pole, which they bring home with great veneration, as thus. They have twenty or fortie yoke of oxen, every oxe having a sweet nose-gay of flours placed on the tip of his hornes, and these oxen drawe home this

---

[3] *The Anatomie of Abuses*, P. Stubbes, 1583, p. 94, under the heading: 'The maner of Maie games in Ailgna', by which the author means Anglia, i.e. England.

Maye-pole (this stinkyng ydol, rather), which is covered all over with floures and hearbs, bound round about with strings, from the top to the bottome, and sometimes painted with variable colours, with two or three hundred men, women and children following it with great devotion. And thus being reared up, with handkercheefs and flags hovering on the top, they straw the ground rounde about, bind greenboughes about it, set up some summer haules, bowers, and arbours hard by it. And then they fall to daunce about it, like as the heathen people did at the dedication of the Idols, whereof this is a perfect pattern, or rather the thing itself. I have heard it credible (and that viva voce) by men of great gravitie and reputation, that of forty, threescore, or a hundred maides going out into the wood overnight, there have scarcely the third part of them returned home again undefiled."

The author has no doubt about the pagan nature of this spring commemoration of natural plenty nor that the human activities recorded were intrinsic to it.

This sort of behaviour was, indeed, widespread, and not confined to Europe. Marco Polo, for example, found the same supposition of a link between sexual activity and prosperity during his travels in the East.[4]

In the district of Kamul by the Gobi desert the inhabitants have an unusual custom for entertaining visitors. 'When strangers arrive, and desire to have lodging and accommodation it affords householders the highest gratification. They give positive orders to their wives, daughters, sisters and other female relations, to indulge their guests in every wish, whilst they themselves leave their homes, and retire into the city, and the stranger lives in the house with the females as if they were his own wives, and they send whatever necessities may be wanted; but for which, it is to be understood they expect payment: nor do they return to their houses so long as the strangers remain in them. This abandonment of the females of the family to accidental guests, who assume the same privileges and meet with the same indulgences as if they were their own wives, is regarded by these people as doing them honour and adding to their reputation; considering the hospitable reception of strangers, who stand in need of relaxation, as an action agreeable to their deities, calculated to draw down the blessing of increase upon their families, to augment their substance, and to procure them safety from all dangers, as well as a successful issue to all their undertakings. The women are in truth very handsome, very sensual, and fully disposed to conform in this respect to the injunctions of their husbands. It happened at the time when Mangu Khan held his court in this province, that the above scandalous custom coming to his knowledge, he issued an edict strictly commanding the people of Kamul to relinquish a practice so disgraceful to them, and forbidding individuals to furnish lodgings to strangers, who should be obliged to accommodate themselves at a house of public resort or

---

[4]  *The Travels of Marco Polo*, Everyman, 1908, pp. 107/8.

*caravanserai.* In grief and sadness the inhabitants obeyed for about three years the command of their master; but finding at length that the earth ceased to yield its accustomed fruits, and that unfortunate events occurred in their families, they resolved to dispatch a deputation to the grand khan, in their names, to beseech him that he should be pleased to suffer them to resume a custom that had been solemnly handed down to them by their fathers, from their ancestors in the remotest times; and especially as since they had failed in the exercise of these offices of hospitality and gratification to strangers, the interest of their families had gone progressively to ruin. The grand khan, having listened to this application, replied: "Since you appear so anxious to persist in your shame and ignominy, let it be granted as you desire. Go, live according to your base customs and manners, and let your wives continue to receive the beggarly wages of prostitution." With this answer the deputies returned home, to the great delight of all people, who, to the present day [the late thirteenth century] observed their ancient practice.'

The origin of this custom clearly lay in religion, since it is stated that it was agreeable to their deities. And its intention was to persuade the earth to 'yield its accustomed fruits', in exactly the same way as the western May Day custom was intended to encourage the spirit of vegetative growth.

What Marco Polo observed was still continuing in the nineteenth century. Elphinstone in his description of Kabul[5] notes that 'in other parts of the country, there prevails a custom called Kooroo Bistaunt, by which the husband lends his wife to the embraces of his guests. At all times, if a husband finds a pair of slippers at his wife's door, he immediately withdraws.' The inhabitants of Caiader applied for and received an exemption from the Moslem prohibition of adultery 'on account of their old usage of lending their wives to their guests.'

So far we have been looking at the supposed effect on fertility and prosperity of sexual activity in the population at large. A special case, and one which concerns us here in this enquiry into the presence in Britain of similar customs to that of Nemi, was the fecundity of rulers. Even today, it is said, some African princes must give proof of their virility before they can be chosen as kings. This theme has been almost forgotten in the British Isles, but it can still be detected in the ancient lore of Wales, in which the people of Dyfed are said to have summoned their ruler, Pwyll, to meet them on the Preseli Mountains to voice their demand for him to have offspring if he wished to continue to be their king.[6] Kings in early times bore little resemblance to the secular monarchs of the historical period but were essentially religious figures: priest-kings or sacred kings. The principle that their virility was essential was applied extremely drastically to them. Kings were chosen specifically for virility and they were disposed of when it was lost. There seem to have been two ways of doing this. Either there was the system used at Nemi

5   *An account of the kingdom of Cabaul etc.*, Hon M. Elphinstone, p. 483.
6   *Mabinogion*, Penguin, p. 59.

where the king was continually on guard against potential rivals, or else kingship was limited to a fixed period after initial selection by success in battle. Our concern at present is with the first system.

To evaluate the pagan residue in the surviving material it is necessary to examine the channels by which it has reached us. In the French romances, those recollections of the Nemi style 'challenge' which have survived have done so as elements of a story which has been created, though not wholly imagined, by a narrator. The standard method by which the romances were built up, to be examined in more detail shortly, was to string several traditional incidents together as the exploits of a single hero. If the individual episodes were separate 'challenge' incidents, continuity was impossible unless the key factor, retention of the guardianship of the site, was suppressed. So that is what happened. For a variety of invented reasons the champion was let off the hook and allowed to travel on toward another violent encounter at bridge or ford or forest clearing. Only at the end of the romance could he be allowed to marry and settle down to rule the new domain which marriage had conferred upon him. Because of this built-in tendency to suppress it, 'guardianship', when it is found in the examples which follow, must be considered particularly valuable evidence for the practice in Britain at one time of a Nemi-type challenge system.

As a footnote to this comment on the construction of a romance, aggregation can be observed to have been taken a step further. Just as episodes were gathered into sequences, the sequences themselves were collected together by linking their heroes with the Round Table and the Arthurian court. Thus individuals, incidents and episodes scattered widely in real life in time and space have been gathered together into what has been skilfully tailored to look a homogeneous whole. The lives and loves of Tristan and Yseult is an example of a story which originally had no connection with the Arthurian court. However, though the narrator may have shuffled the pack, sufficient traces remain of the original pattern on the cards for us to recognise the suits and even some of the royal pictures.

### The Challenge as a Component of a Romance

A romance which displayed the primitive pattern seems to have underlain the *Lanzelet* of the Swiss Ulrich von Zatzikhoven.[7] To select only the challenge-type events from the adventures strung together in the course of this early German language version of Lancelot's story, the hero first spent a night at the castle of one Galagandriez, who was a forester, a possessive father and a stout fighter. During the night Galagandriez' daughter came to Lancelot wearing a chaplet of flowers and preceded by two maidens clad in green. They slept

---

7   Tr. K. G. T. Webster.

together. Next day Lancelot fought and killed the father. Through the girl, he inherited her father's people, land and possessions. In spite of this success, he went on to the Castle of Limors (probably from the original French la mort – death), owned by a certain Linier. Here at Linier's festival Lancelot killed a giant, three lions and finally Linier himself. Lancelot was now kept prisoner but was cared for by Linier's sister Ade, who became his lover.

After his release, still roving, Lancelot next came to Belforet, the Beautiful Forest, which never failed to bear leaves and fruit. Near a clearing was the small monastery of the Sorrowful Fief with a graveyard where the ruler Yweret buried his victims. In the clearing stood an evergreen linden tree with a cool spring at its base. From the tree hung a cymbal. Any knight who wished to marry Yweret's daughter Yblis had to beat the cymbal as a challenge to fight Yweret to the death in the glade. Lancelot struck the cymbal, defeated Yweret and cut off his head. As a reward he obtained, as usual, the young woman's person and inheritance and he also received from his water-fay foster-parent and protectress (here called the Queen of Maidenland but more familiar as Malory's Damsel of the Lake) the gift of a fine pavilion and she revealed that his name, which he had not previously known, was Lancelot.

Lancelot had yet another affair, this time at the Castle of Pluris (presumably from the original French pleurs – tears), where in a meadow adorned by a splendid tent the Queen of Pluris offered her person, her land and her honours to any knight who could defeat one hundred knights in a day. Of course, Lancelot was the only knight able to do this. He married the queen, and she kept him there for about a year.

After other adventures Lancelot settled down with Yblis to rule the lands which had been her father's. Lancelot's other liaisons are not mentioned again, and there is no reference whatever to an affair with Guenever in this romance.

The Belforet episode is a good example of the 'challenge' theme. Five of the six elements are portrayed, as follows:

(1) Sacred site: the glade, monastery and graveyard.
(2) Feature: the tree and spring.
(3) The defender: Yweret.
(4) The challenge: beating the cymbal.
(5) Guardianship: missing.
(6) The reward: the girl, lands and kingship.

Some concession has been made to preserving the mobility of the hero. The missing element, guardianship, which would have immobilised him completely, has been omitted. A series of affairs or even marriages is not so damaging to the continuity of the story as retention at the glade would have been, but retention has not been entirely eliminated in the adventures with Ade and with the Queen of Pluris, in both of which the hero was detained for some time.

Besides the Yweret episode, the others are pale shadows of the 'challenge', scarcely embodying more of the standard elements than the 'reward'. But it is only to be expected that oral repetition would result in most of the recollections which survive being eroded, battered and also, as in the case of the 100 knights at Pluris, embellished. So there is nothing here contradictory to the suggestion that the original of these other three incidents was the same cult practice as that in force at Belforet. As well as the 'challenge' incidents there are a good many other ancient motifs in the *Lanzelet* to reinforce the suggestion that paganism underlies the medieval story. Among them are the water-fay, and her son, Mabuz, who has been reliably identified with the British god Mabon. The anonymity of the hero, a common enough motif in the Arthurian legends, is reminiscent of a well-known taboo; and the forest without seasons, a memory of the style of Otherworld in the Celtic tradition, untouched by the rigours of winter.

As time passed, later generations of narrators modified the challenge, for instance by making the defender villainous or oppressive towards the heroine so that her immediate acceptance of her new lord was emotionally acceptable to a more sophisticated audience. They also multiplied the danger, as at Pluris, to magnify the prowess of the hero, and they enhanced the visual effect with new combinations of colour but they were remarkably conservative in retaining the significant features, as will be seen in the analysis of the elements of the challenge system which now follows.

## The Components of the Challenge Theme

### The Site

#### (a) The Glade

The presence of many tales in the Arthurian legends which repeat the theme of Diana's sacred enclosure at Nemi cannot be explained by a transfer of the cult to Britain during Imperial Roman times. By then the style of Nemi was already archaic and took little or no place in the religious spectrum of the day. It is therefore necessary to look much further back in time for the origin of the 'challenge', to a period when it seems to have been common to both Rome and Britain and probably to a good many other places as well. Whatever forms the practice of the cult then took, it will have diverged to provide those of Nemi and those of the British legends. We cannot therefore consider the classical system to be a prototype of those of the north but rather as to some extent a parallel development. It would obviously be wise to give greater weight to the Roman eye-witness accounts than to an oral tradition covering a gap of more than a thousand years, but if there are differences in the northern examples this does not necessarily mean that the transmission has been faulty. Nemi is itself a single example. There is only one Nemi. It may not have been a representative member of its class. So if the northern traditions provide variations on the theme of Nemi there can be no logical objection to inferring, from these variations, more detail of the 'challenge' system as it was once practised here in Britain than can be obtained from the classical accounts of Nemi.

When the sites at which challenges took place in the Arthurian legends are examined there is a very high degree of correspondence to Nemi in the popularity of a woodland glade or grove or forest clearing as the ritual site. The romances often use the word 'la lande' for the site of a joust.[8] This word in modern French means 'moorland', which may in some translations have obscured the earlier meaning of 'glade' or 'grassy woodland clearing'. There can be no doubt that Gerbert, for instance, did not mean a moor when he described the lande in which single combat took place as at the bottom of a valley (el fons d'un val);[9] and, to take another medieval view, the Welsh translator of Chrétien's 'Orguelleus de la Lande' calls him 'Syberw Llanerch', in which Syberw is equated with Orguelleus and Llanerch means clearing,[10] not barren moorland. The Proud Knight becomes Orilus de Lalander in German and in Malory, Sir Miles of the Launde – 'the Noble Soldier of the Glade'. The place of conflict is sometimes called a meadow (prairie or pré), but since it is usually surrounded by woodland, the sense is the same. The glade, like the other sites at which challenges take place, is no more than an arena. The focus of the action is more specific – a tree, a spring, or a tomb within the glade – and is discussed below under the heading 'significant feature'.

Although it is not used at all in the romances, the word 'nemus',[11] meaning a sacred grove or woodland clearing, has remained attached to British cult sites, both in Latin inscriptions and in modern place names, which latter presumably indicate the one-time presence of such a site. Ten 'Nemet'-names are listed in the gazetteer. Two of them are associated with spectacular springs: Nemetona was the name of the nymph of the hot spring at Bath, and Buxton was called Aquae Arnemetiae after the nymph of the sacred grove where the waters of the spa gushed from the ground. Another of them, Medionemeton, which is known to have been on or near the Antonine Wall, is thought to have been the 'henge' at Carnpapple, near Edinburgh. It would be interesting to know if similar structures survive at the other Nemus places. In the legends the field ordained for the battle for a girl is usually a natural arena but when it has been deliberately made it is sometimes described as enclosed by ditches and cords.

### (b) Other than the Glade

Another type of Challenge site, the island, is popular in the romances. For instance Arthur defeated Frolle, the king (in some versions) of France, in single combat on an island near Paris. In principle an island quite closely resembles a

8  The word 'lande' seems to have originated in the Gaulish 'Landa' with the meaning of enclosure, which gave rise to the modern Welsh 'llan' (see Ekwall, under lann and laund) – enclosure, yard, and hence church from the sacred enclosure in which the church was built. In another direction 'lande' has developed into the modern English 'lawn' via 'launde', the form used by Malory in the fifteenth century.
9  *Gerbert de Montreuil*, ed. Williams, lines 13699/700.
10  *Peredur*, Goetinck, e.g. p. 9 and note to p. 261.
11  But see pp. 182–3 below.

glade in the sense that it is a space enclosed by a natural boundary. In one of his many adventures,[12] Lancelot killed a giant who used to demand tribute every year at King Pelles' court. He then set up house on the giant's island with 'Elaine', Pelles' daughter, and her son the young Galahad. With them were forty dames and damsels but no squires or pages. There was a marvellous fine, tall, pine tree in the middle of the island. On it Lancelot hung his black shield which had Guenever's device emblazoned on it. He also had black armour for himself and a black caparison for his horse. When he had defeated any knight who challenged him by dashing down his shield from the tree, the damsels who had seen the joust bowed to the shield and began a dance round the tree singing, 'Truly this is the shield of the best knight in the world'. As long as Lancelot stayed on the island, the round dance, the 'carole', took place four times a day, winter and summer. From the great joy the maidens made so assiduously, the island became known as the 'Isle of Joy'. Damsels making joy at the prospect of a fatal encounter are also present at the battle between Balin and Balan. This is again on an island; however, a female audience is a standard feature of the encounter between knights in single combat and is not restricted to any particular type of site.

Most of the other sites used for single combat can be gathered together under the heading, 'rights of passage'. They are bridges, causeways, fords and cross-roads.[13] This category in total is about as frequent as the glade so it is likely to have had considerable original importance in spite of not corresponding to the system at Nemi. There are a number of links between this group and the sites already mentioned. One is a connection with water, the 'causeway' being frequently bordered by marsh or water. Another is that the glade is often still present, surrounding the cross-road or as a meadow beside the ford. And there are similarities relating to other aspects of the 'challenge' which have yet to be described.

Of these 'passage' sites, perhaps the most evocative of paganism is the Perilous, or Amorous, Ford. The defender of this ford was Urbain, son of the Queen of the Blackthorn. He lived with his lover in a pavilion in one of the most beautiful meadows in the world beside the ford. They enjoyed the delights of a palatial castle with servants and courtiers, but this was invisible except to themselves. Perceval provoked a fight by allowing his horse to drink at the ford. He defeated Urbain, who told him his story. One tempestuous night he had spied a damsel riding on a mule at great speed. He followed and tried to overtake her, but the night was black and only by flashes of lightning was he able to keep her in sight. Eventually she led him to one of the most beautiful castles in the world. There she welcomed him and consented to become his mistress, providing he would set up a tent at the ford and joust with all knights who attempted the crossing. He was now within eight days of

---

[12] *Le Roman en prose de Tristan . . .*, ed. Löseth, pp. 211f.
[13] A Romano-British inscription in Scotland reads 'to the Celestial Goddess of the Woodland and the Cross-roads', L. J. F. Keppie, *Proc. Soc. Antiq. of Scotland*, 1983, p. 113.

completing a year. If he had been able to retain the ford for a year, he would have been considered the best knight in the world. Now he had been defeated, the victor, Perceval, would become the guardian and if he succeeded in keeping the ford for a year would gain the greatest prize in the world. Perceval declined, thereby provoking a tumult and a thunderstorm. The Damsel of the Ford, enraged by this insulting refusal, set a large flock of black birds on him which tried to peck out his eyes. One he killed with his sword. As it fell dying to the ground it changed into a beautiful young woman. The birds were the damsel and her maidens. They carried off their dead comrade to the island of Avalon, where all would be well with her.[14]

This account of events at the perilous ford is scattered with pagan themes. The 'Queen of the Blackthorn' (the white flowers of which are conspicuous in early spring) is probably a significant title in this context; the midnight chase on horseback is a motif which in the *Mabinogion* can be recognized as pertaining to a goddess;[15] there is a reference to 'lordship' being restricted to a year; and the Otherworld island goddess with her sisters who can change their shapes into black birds is a thoroughly pagan concept.[16] Under all this, their pagan character emphasised by these pagan associations, we can see: the sacred site; the watery feature; the defender; the challenge: the reward, love (emphasised by the alternative title, 'the Amorous Ford') and lordship; and, by implication, since it is expected, the continuation of the custom. Here are all six elements of the challenge theme.

In another story of single combat at a ford marked by a thorn tree the affair took place against a red knight on Midsummer Eve, an important date in the pagan calendar.[17]

The only other places at which this particular kind of single combat occurs are hills,[18] tombs or vaults and in one case a hill-top fire. All three examples are at sites which we can reasonably believe to have captured the pagan imagination as being significant for cult purposes and the elements of the 'challenge' are present at them in much the same way as at the glade and island. One of the tomb sites is comparatively well known as it features in the English Arthurian story *Sir Gawain and the Green Knight*. The Green Knight long inhabited the Green Chapel, which was a tumulus.[19] The place was perilous to approach for he loved fighting and killed all passers-by of whatever rank without mercy.

Perceval had a battle with a knight who guarded a tomb, the Black Knight of the Arcel de la Sepouture en la Lande (the Vault of the Grave in the Glade);[20] the same motif is repeated in Peredur's battle with the Black Man who came

---

[14] Didot *Perceval*, ed. Roach, pp. 198f.
[15] *Mabinogion*, Penguin, pp. 52–4.
[16] *Studies in the Fairy Mythology of Arthurian Romance*, L. A. Paton, p. 34 n. 2.
[17] *Lai de l'Espine*, ed. Zenker, ZRP XVII 1893, lines 188–90.
[18] E.g. Sornehan, *Vulgate*, V, pp. 5 and 9.
[19] See p. 165 below.
[20] See West *Verse Index* under Arcel for references. The Black Knight of the Tomb is linked by

out from under a stone,[21] and in his battle against the Black Worm which lived in the barrow named the Sorrowful Mound.[22] In each case the defender is black.

Markale points out that the word 'tertre', meaning a mound or hillock, is often used to mean a tumulus. 'Tertre' is also often used in the romances to describe an eminence defended by a 'challenge' knight. Perhaps more challenge sites than at first meet the eye were indeed tumuli, sites which combine both hill and tomb.

When Arthur passed the barrier[23] on leaving the glade he was safe from pursuit. Usually this feature of the sacred enclosure is mentioned on entry rather than departure. Crossing a boundary is referred to in several descriptions of the run up to 'challenge' events. Sometimes the barrier is not a material one. The battle ground of Erec and Mabonagrein, like the Queen of Danemarche's enchanted garden, is surrounded by an impenetrable wall of air or hedge of mist, which has in it an entrance and in the case of the enchanted garden, often an exit as well, which may lead to a deserted castle. At other times there is a physical barrier, as there was for Arthur at the entrance to the Perilous Glade. A common barrier is a ring of stakes such as that faced by Bors at the Tertre Desvé.[24] To cross the barrier was equivalent to a challenge. The palisade of sharpened stakes served a double function. Besides being a boundary it provided a suitable place to display the heads of previous victims at the Isle d'Or;[25] at Brandigan, the battle-ground of Erec and Mabonagrein;[26] at Maduc's challenge site in the forest of Sarpenic;[27] at the place where travelling knights fought for possession of a pucele in *Mule sans Frein*;[28] again in *Le Chevalier as deux Espees*, where the battle ground was encircled by a ditch as well as sharp stakes with heads on them;[29] and in the forest of Malvern, where Yder defeated two giants.[30] For what it is worth, the last is the only instance in which the story indicates the location of a cult site surrounded by stakes.

Worship in forest clearings is well attested for Celts, Teutons and Slavs, and also for the non-Indo-European Finno-Ugrians. The latter's sacred groves, which like their counterparts to the west had sacred trees as their central features, were always enclosed by a fence.[31]

---

the pursuit of a white stag with Maduc, the Black knight who defended a site with heads on stakes.
[21] *Mabinogion*, Penguin, pp. 255/6. The episode of Peredur and the Black Man from under the Slab follows after the killing of a magic stag.
[22] *Mabinogion*, Penguin, pp. 241–4.
[23] See p. 8.
[24] *Vulgate*, V, p. 240.
[25] *Bel Inconnu*, R de Beaujeu, ed. Williams, lines 1955f.
[26] *Erec et Enide*, ed. Hilka, lines 5741ff.
[27] *Vulgate*, VII, pp. 73/4 and 143; Maduc's defended site is also described in *Vengeance Raguidel*, lines 621f and 715f.
[28] *Two old French Romances*, Johnson and Owen, lines 433–7 and 774–83.
[29] Ed. Foerster, lines 4575f, 4584f, 4666f and 4730f.
[30] *The Romance of Yder*, ed. and tr. A. Adams, p. 221.
[31] *The Golden Bough*, Frazer, abridged, p. 111.

**The Significant Feature**

The tree which was central to the rite at Nemi is also the focus of many 'challenge' episodes. In only one traditional tale, to be discussed in detail later, has the broken bough motif come through. But in spite of the absence of this important feature the central position of the tree in the rite is clearly indicated, for it is always on this special tree that the cymbal, shield or horn is hung, by means of which the challenge is made. Usually there is only one tree, but sometimes two.

The tree is often described as particularly large, spreading and luxurious. From its branches often hang the trophies of a victorious defender – shields, helmets, or even corpses.

It will already have become apparent that the tree is not the only feature in the British glade. Equal in importance is the spring, usually called a 'fountain'. Generally tree and fountain go together. The fountain beside the tree in *The Lady of the Fountain* and the spring beside the linden tree where Lancelot fought Yweret for his daughter have already been mentioned. Other examples are the Fountain of the Two Sycamores, which Belyas defended with his brother Briadan; and the fountain defended by Terrican of the Deceiving Forest (see page 95). The act of defending a fountain is described in *Perceforest* as 'according to the ancient custom'.[32] When either tree or spring is on its own this may only be an accidental omission of one or the other and not significant, but it is interesting that the Lady of the Fountain in the Welsh story of that name takes her title from the spring and not from the tree which was beside it. She had great possessions, as had most of her kind, and a territorial title. We may therefore suspect that the surviving record of the rite at the Italian Nemi has underplayed the importance of the nymph and the spring. In the romances the spring and nymph are often central features. Here it is made clear that the local equivalent to the king of the woodland clearing owes his position to the nymph whose dominions he temporarily shares.

The scene of combat at a spring is characterized by extreme simplicity. There was merely a stone slab (usually called a perron in the romances) by the spring for the rain-making spell. Naturally the inhabitants of an isolated site would have used a simple shelter so a 'pavilion' is generally associated with the more obviously symbolic aspects of the challenge. However, the pavilion is so pervasive a motif, occurring even when there is a town or castle nearby,[33] that it may be supposed to be an essential feature[34] of the 'challenge' theme, especially so since the castle may be empty or even imaginary, only visible to those who live in the tent.

There are other reasons for supposing pavilions to have once had greater importance. In the description of the Isle of Joy, and also in the challenge site

---

[32] *Perceforest*, pt. IV, ed. Roussineau, p. 847.
[33] E.g. Isle d'Or or the incident involving Guerrehes and the Petit Chevalier.
[34] See Challenge Sites in Gazetteer, part b, list (a).

set up by Perceval's sister, it is made clear that the combination of pavilion, spear and tree with shield hung on it was to be taken as a signal that passing knights were invited to joust. The importance of tents in the romances as a whole has probably not been generally realized; there was even a Queen who bore the title 'of the Tents'. Tents ranged from a small tent of buckram[35] to a magnificent pavilion brought to Cornwall from Ireland as part of Yseult's dowry on her marriage to King Mark.[36] This pavilion was later used for the annual celebration of Tristan's defeat of Morholt who was mortally wounded in the combat on an island for the tribute of Cornwall and for the person of the queen's daughter of Ireland. Another notable pavilion was given by the Queen of Maidenland to her protégé Lancelot as a reward for the killing of her enemy Iweret.[37] Occasionally the tent in a challenge situation is described, as when the Proud Knight of the Glade set up a fine pavilion of samite with a leather cover in a meadow by a ford, in which, as Goetinck has pointed out, the Proud Damsel (in the Welsh version) sat in royal splendour, wearing a golden head-dress. In a few instances the pavilion is replaced in another version of a story by a 'Welsh hut' – a bower of fresh leafy branches – as in the meadow by the Perilous Ford.[38] In one instance the main hall at a spring festival was constructed in this way; the knights rose early to the sound of 'Sarrassin' horns, they jousted during the day, then there was a banquet in a very rich bower of branches in the middle of the meadow. Later there was caroling with great joy on all sides. That night the squires who were about to be knighted kept vigil in the temple to the Sovereign god in whose name the feast had been ordained.[39] The link between bowers and cult activity survived the introduction of Christianity. Missionaries in Britain in the Dark Ages were instructed not to object to certain minor expressions of paganism including the building of bowers round churches, and the practice of building bowers at a festival still continued in the sixteenth century, when the maypole already described had 'summer haules, bowers and arbours' set up beside it. Whether the arbours gave lovers privacy, or whether their leafy construction reflected the vegetative aspect of the celebration can only be guessed.

## The Defender

The hero of a romance is always the challenger. The defender never gets much kudos, he is always at the receiving end and is generally inactive, waiting to be challenged in his pavilion in a glade. So he turns out to be an uninteresting personage.

The most obvious visual feature of the defender is his colour, which is

---

35  *Parzival*, tr. Hatto, p. 397.
36  *Roman de Tristan etc.*, ed. Löseth, p. 123.
37  *Lanzelet*, tr. Webster and Loomis, p. 90.
38  *Le Bel Inconnu*, ed. Williams, line 327.
39  *Perceforest*, pt. IV, ed. Roussineau, p. 24 line 669.

usually either red or black, divided roughly equally between the two colours but with red predominating. Examples of red knights are Meleagant, Oriols, Raolais, Belynans, and the first knight killed by Perceval; of black, Agravadain, Brunor, Maduc, Maugis, Terrican and the unnamed guardian of a tomb. Different versions of an episode may use either of these colours for the same character, as in the case of Esclados the Red who is replaced in the Welsh version of the same story by the unnamed black knight whose wife was the Countess of the Fountain. Other knights who turn up at one time as red and another as black include Belyas, Bors, Mabon and Lancelot. The almost complete absence of white knights is unexpected, because a similar combat in the *Mabinogion*, in which the defender, whose name Hafgan is said to mean Summer-White, has been interpreted as an annual conflict between winter and summer. White is not an unpopular colour in the romances but it is generally used for the robes of priests, for women's wear or for the garments of new knights when they were being initiated.[40] The only hint from the romances as to the meaning of the colours is that red is stated to have been reminiscent of the colour of the fire which descended from the heavens on to the disciples at Pentecost. On the other hand, such few calendar links of the 'challenge' as have survived are with Midsummer Day.[41] The challenger does not seem to have a uniform colour, but when he has won and taken over the office of defender, he takes on the original colour of the defender as well as his possessions.[42]

Though defenders are not important characters individually in the Arthurian story, they are an important class, and, more than any other class of character, they are known by a single description: 'Proud' – in French, 'Orguelleus'. The name of one knight, Orguelleus de la Lande – the Proud Knight of the Glade – can be taken as the generic name for all defenders. In later French versions the name Orguelleus has been eroded to Oriols, and eventually to Raols and Raolais.[43] In spite of their slightly different names the identity of these characters is confirmed by their actions and attributes, for instance all are red knights.

---

[40] Narrators sometimes use colour to distinguish opponents who otherwise have similar characteristics. For instance, Malory's Beaumains fights in succession black, green, red, and blue knights, but the underlying conformity to the challenge theme is revealed by the titles of two of them – of the Black *Launde* and of the Red *Launde* (Malory's Launde is equivalent to Glade) – and by a challenge made by blowing a horn hung on a sycamore tree. In one text Lancelot deviates from the rule by being a white knight; and in a number of instances knights change their colours to deceive the onlookers.
[41] The Thunderstorm Fountain in *Yvain* and the Thorntree Fountain in *Lai de l'Espine*, see pp. 29–30 for references.
[42] E.g. *The Countess of the Fountain*, Mabinogion, Penguin, pp. 200–207.
[43] Raolais the Red Knight of Estremores is on one occasion called Belynans. I interpret this to be a variation on the name of the god Belenus (see Who's Who?). For the proud defender of a 'challenge' site to represent Belenus is in accord with other observations: Belyas, another version of Belenus, defended a fountain, and another personage from the same name group, Belinans, defended a river crossing, the Pont Norgalois. Belenus was a god of the sun (Hutton, *Pagan Religions*, pp. 151/2): both the Thunderstorm fountain and the Perilous Ford are linked with Midsummer Day.

Names tend to get altered in transmission, so we can expect the name of this often spoken of knight to come through in a variety of different forms. That is the price of, indeed the proof of, fame. He was very aptly called after his principle attribute, 'the Proud'. He can clearly be seen as the Proud Knight of the Clearing in *Peredur*, living with his lover, the Proud Damsel, in a pavilion. When a proud knight defends a glade it often contains a spring and a tree; proud knights may also be found defending an island, a ford or a passage. In one series of battles (in *Parzival*) the proud knight Orilus de Lalander is several times challenged by Gawain; the defender's *amie* sits under a sycamore tree or an elm, wearing a circlet of gold round her head; she has cost many men their lives. In this series the damsel's sister acts as a go-between or 'minder', and when Gawain defeats the proud knight, Orguelleus, the proud damsel, Orguelleuse, takes him to her bed after he has broken off a garland from the defended tree. At this point Gawain could be expected to become a defender himself. This is not explicitly stated but can be inferred since he was then forbidden to leave the castle except to fight. On another occasion, in spite of the tendency for major heroes to keep their freedom of movement, Gawain does get stranded for six years as a defender whom, because of his great prowess, no-one can conquer. The narrator has to get him off the hook by sleight of hand (p. 57 below).

Needless to say, this is a composite picture. No single 'challenge' knight in reality defended more than one site. But Orguelleus well represents the whole range of defenders, and his lover, Orguelleuse, provides us with the only instances in the romances of the broken branch motif (otherwise only recorded of Nemi) and also with a clearer view of the personality of the nymph of the glade as being proud, demanding, dangerous and requiring the death of her lovers.

The defender may be assumed to have fought for his life, but strength may not have been the sole requirement for success. In the episode in the *Mabinogion* in which Pwyll fought a year end combat, the result was foreordained. Pwyll was instructed to strike one blow only, which his adversary would not survive, and so it came about. And in the conflict between Erec and Mabonagrein in the ring of stakes the defeated Mabonagrein complains that he has been 'enchanted' by Erec. There was evidently more to the 'challenge' than brute force.

## The Challenge

The battle for kingship of the Woodland Clearing at Nemi could only take place after a bough had been broken off a particular tree. There are relics of this feature in the British tradition of the battle in the Glade, though in only one romance is the motif identical. In the local version, the challenge is generally made by blowing a horn, the horn being, typically, hung from the significant tree. Or it can be a cymbal or shield which hangs from the tree and has to be struck to make a formal challenge. As in other instances where there is a divergence from the rite at Nemi, the alternative in the shape of an audible challenge makes good sense. The end product of repetition may vary from the presumed original but can still preserve the meaning. Thus as Balin approaches the scene of the challenge he is first warned that he has crossed the bounds, then 'he heard an horn blow as it had been for the death of a beast. That blast, said Balin, is blown for me, for I am the prize and yet I am not dead'.[44] The challenger is often warned that 'crossing the bounds' is equivalent to a challenge and makes a battle inevitable. The horn, though in this instance not blown by Balin himself, signalled that the challenge had been made. Galahad is given a similar warning when he approaches the Castle of Maidens.[45]

Gawain, too, found crossing the bounds a significant step; entry was all that was necessary to make a challenge when he came[46] to a beautiful grassy clearing, with a pavilion in the middle, all surrounded by a palisade. At the entrance there was a damsel of great beauty sitting under the shade of an oak-tree. Gawain greeted the damsel when he came near and she welcomed him. 'Whose is the pavilion', he asked, 'and why are the barriers here?' 'A knight has established that he will fight any knight-errant who enters within the bounds. He is in the pavilion now'. 'Damsel', said Gawain, 'go to him and tell him a knight wishes to joust with him'. 'There is no need', replied the maiden, 'just enter within the barrier'.[47]

The one occasion on which the broken branch motif comes through is particularly interesting from the point of view of the development of the tradition. It is mentioned first in the *Perceval* of Chrétien de Troyes, who was the original populariser of Arthurian romances. In the episode in question there are two themes muddled together. Gawain is sent across the Perilous Ford by Orguelleuse, the Proud Damsel, to obtain a garland from the trees and flowers on the opposite side of the river. It looks as if the original narrator, some precursor of Chrétien, has put the perilous crossing motif before the broken branch to make it a testing adventure, not realising the true significance of obtaining a garland from a defended tree as an act of the greatest daring in itself. In *Parzival*, a later version of the same story by the German writer Wolfram von Eschenbach, there is the same confusion of the same two motifs, but the reason for gathering a garland from a specific tree with an 'owner' is clearly stated to be to provoke a challenge. The author of this work, written soon after 1200, has evidently translated from similar source material to that used by Chrétien. We can tell that by the repetition of the mixed motifs referred to above. But Wolfram has made what now, since the publication of *The Golden Bough*, is a

---

[44] E.g. *Morte Darthur*, Malory, bk II, ch. XVII.

[45] *Vulgate*, VI, pp. 34f.

[46] *Vulgate*, VII, p. 295.

[47] Another knight who found himself in a similar situation was Hector, told by a dwarf: 'Sir Knight, you go too far'; and he was also warned by a damsel sitting under an elm before fighting Marigart, who defended an open space, surrounded by stakes, in a garden of trees. *Vulgate*, IV, pp. 349/50.

convincing interpretation of the source material; the correspondence to the Nemi type challenge by breaking a branch leaves little room for doubt about its genuineness, while Chrétien's version is feeble in the extreme, sending an armed man on a perilous expedition for no better reason than to gather a bunch of flowers. Here is a clear example of a factor which has been commented on often enough; the 'second generation', that is, post-Chrétien, romances tend to transmit more mythological and folk-lore material than Chrétien himself.

Wolfram's story is as follows.[48] Orguelleuse told Gawain: 'You must get me a garland from the twig of a certain tree. If you will give it me I will praise your exploit, and then you may ask for my love.' They rode over the fields towards an escarpment till they saw the tree of the Garland. 'Sir', she said, 'that tree is tended by the man who robbed me of my happiness [he had killed her husband and wished to take his place]. If you will fetch me down a twig of it no knight would have won such high renown for love's sake as a lady's servitor.' Taking the twig did not involve Gawain in an immediate joust but he and the owner of the tree agreed to fight in two weeks time. Meanwhile, Gawain and Orguelleuse were bedded after a feast at the Castle of Maidens. This was only one of several contests initiated by Orguelleuse. Gawain merely took his place in a series of lovers. Great heroes are protected by the narrators of such tales from receiving their due, so, unfortunately we will never learn what actually happened to him. But Orguelleuse was an extremely sinister character. Not only had she cost many of her lovers their lives, but Anfortas, Wolfram's equivalent of the Maimed King, had suffered castration in her service. So we may be reasonably sure that Gawain also suffered some such drastic fate. This is perhaps hinted at by his presence in the fateful cart after the adventure of the testing bed in the Castle of Maidens, appropriately enough, the very place where he enjoyed Orguelleuse's bed.

The broken branch motif occurs twice in the same romance – Perceval also broke a branch from the tree in an attempt to provoke a fight with the same individual as Gawain. Later in Wolfram's story, Parzival says: 'I shall be happy to wait for the man called Rois Gramoflanz [Giromelant in French versions of this story]. Early this morning I broke a twig from his tree for a garland so that he should come and attack me . . .'[49]

## The Continuation of the Custom

It could be argued that contests of strength, some even with fatal results, have always taken place at fairs and similar gatherings, and that some of the sites defended – fords, bridges and causeways – might naturally be defended to preserve rights of access or to obtain a toll. The most certain indication that a

---

48 *Parzival*, tr. Hatto, Penguin, pp. 302f.
49 *Parzival*, tr. Hatto, Penguin, p. 350.

particular encounter is not run-of-the-mill violence is the *continuation* of the custom of guardianship. This, particularly when the wording implies an unending sequence of guardians, is a powerful argument in favour of this behaviour being derived from the same original as the rule at Nemi. This is especially so because, as we have seen, the way in which the romances were constructed, by stringing episodes together as the adventures of a single hero, tended to suppress incidents which immobilized the hero. Only where a way round this obstacle could be found would a description of 'guardianship' get through into the story.

Now follow some examples of the continuation of the custom. We have seen that a horn sounded when Balin crossed the bounds as he approached a certain castle which was bounded on one side by the sea and on the other by a fast flowing river. He found that he was obliged to joust with the knight of a tower on an island. The island, the tower, and the country all around belonged to a lady. In her youth a knight swore he would stay in the tower and keep her company night and day. To avoid loss of skill at arms he swore also to fight any passing errant knight to the death for possession of the lady and the isle. The challenger, if victorious, was obliged to take his place. We are told that no one who crossed to the island would ever leave it alive, since even if he was initially successful and he became a defender, his ultimate defeat was inevitable. The original holder had made the people of the town swear to maintain the custom after his death.[50] In the event, Balin found himself opposed to an unknown red knight who later proved to be his brother. They were equally matched and both died from the effects of the encounter. The defender Balan's dying words were: 'Here it happed me to slay a knight that kept this island, and since then might I never depart, and no more should ye, brother, an ye had slain me as ye have, and escaped yourself with the life'.[51] The custom has certainly brought the flow of the narrative to a standstill in this instance.

The 'Tertre Desvé' – the Deceiving Hill – was held for twenty years by Clochidés, the strongest, cruellest and most able fighter in the world.[52] When he was newly knighted he fell in love with the daughter of King Esclamor of the Red City. Her father refused him, but she agreed to marry him if he would defend her against all comers. He therefore built a castle on the hill where he took his bride with the great treasure she had obtained from her father. Clochidés reduced the paths leading to the top of the hill to a single one and erected a sign warning potential visitors of their peril. There was also a strong palisade of stakes with a gate, through which a challenger was allowed to pass only after he had sworn that he would, if victorious, take over the defence all his life until he too should be defeated by a stronger. Strangers could expect to lose their lives if their challenge was unsuccessful. Bors, having taken this oath and defeated the defender, became the guardian. Later Lancelot followed the

---

[50] Huth *Merlin*, ed. Paris and Ulrich, vol. II, p. 54.
[51] *Morte Darthur*, Malory, bk II, ch. 18.
[52] *Vulgate*, V, pp. 235ff.

same pathway up the hill, on foot. At the top there was one of the most beautiful 'sycamores' he had ever seen. Nearby, attached to an oak tree was a horse with black coverings, and there were lances leaning against the trunk. From a branch hung an ivory horn bound with gold and silver, which a dwarf from a pavilion said must be blown to fetch the defender. Lancelot did so and fought Bors until they recognised each other. After that the guardianship seems to have been abandoned. Both heroes could continue their adventures.

In the romance called *Le Bel Inconnu*, the hero was accompanying the damsel Elene on his way to rescue her mistress, the Lady of Sinadoun. On the way they came to a castle surrounded by an arm of the sea. It was the Isle d'Or, the Island of Gold. It could be reached by a bridge which led to a causeway. At the end of the causeway was a pavilion in front of a palisade of sharp stakes, each with a dead man's head on it. The defender of the causeway was the lover of the damsel of the castle. She would marry him if he was able to defend the causeway for seven years. The defender was called Malgiers the Grey, or in another version, the black giant Maugis who believed in the pagan god Teruagant. The damsel of the castle, Dame d'Amour – white as a flower, and whose beauty was likened to the light of the moon – bade the victorious Bel Inconnu be lord of herself, her city and her castle. He stayed there a year before his guide, Elene, recalled him to a sense of duty and they continued on towards Sinadoun. Meanwhile, he was not expected to guard the causeway, indeed, he was specifically excused from doing so. His lover's phrase; 'I declare you quit of the usage of guarding the causeway' underlines the existence of the custom and at the same time neatly allows him to continue his journey.[53]

Even the greatest heroes could get entangled in the position of defender. One day King Arthur, travelling in the Severn valley, came to the causeway into Sorelois known as the 'Chaucie Norgalois'. He saw it to be very high, very large and very long. It was trenched at the sides and had a good stone bridge over the water which flowed below. It was surrounded by coppice which had been planted round about. As soon as the king mounted the end of the causeway, the knight who guarded it armed himself and came up to the bridge to meet him. When Arthur arrived the defender challenged him as follows:

'Sir knight, where do you wish to go?
'I wish to cross into Sorelois', said the king.
'You cannot pass unless you are of Galehot's country'.
'I am not. I am a knight from another country'.
'Then you must agree to fight me and ten men-at-arms if you wish to pass ... and if it should happen that you conquer me and the ten you must agree to guard the chaucie until a new guardian is sent by the lord of this country'.

The idea of guardianship is watered down here by the words 'until a new

53 *Le Bel Inconnu*, ed. Williams, lines 2265ff.

guardian is sent', but in the event Arthur recognised the defender as King Ydier of Cornwall and the promise was forgotten.[54]

The same motive of recognition is used to break the sequence of defenders in another incident. After Hector ran off with the wife of a certain Argon, the latter had a tower built with a bridge which he guarded for the rest of his life. After his death his four sons maintained the custom that a knight was set to guard the bridge until he was defeated; his victor was then obliged to succeed him as defender until defeated in his turn. Chance brought King Hoel to this place and he defeated the defender, so becoming defender himself. In due course his own son, Kahedin, came up against him. Fortunately they recognized each other and stopped the fight. The custom, once again, seems to have been forgotten in the interest of preserving the life of an important personage.[55]

A rather more subtle variation in the rules was introduced at the Castle of the Ten Knights. Here a challenger was obliged to fight in succession ten knights who resided in ten tents in front of the castle. If so far successful he then fought the lord of the castle who, if defeated was, contrary to the usual custom, not immediately killed but was allowed to depart. This deviation from the standard procedure produced what is probably the longest sequence of named defenders in the romances. First Hector, who killed his predecessor, then Erec, then Gawain (who waited six years before any challenger could defeat the ten), and finally Lamorat of Wales. The latter came there by chance right at the beginning of May. After defeating the ten he unhorsed Gawain and would have ridden away, but the people of the castle seized his rein and led him to the castle willy-nilly. Never was greater joy made over a knight's arrival. The people of the place cried out with one voice: 'Welcome, sir, welcome', and others; 'Blessed be God who has given such a knight to be our lord and master'. Lamorat was amazed that they honoured him so much. When he came into the principal palace and his armour had been removed, an old man came before him and gave him the keys of the castle. The manifestations of joy continued as before. The old man explained that by defeating the knight who guarded the castle, he had won both the castle and the people and was now their liege lord. On the other part they made great joy for the sake of the most beautiful damsel in the world, their lady, who Lamorat would have for wife, and because God had ordained so knightly a person to be her lover. Lamorat replied that he did not want a wife nor for anything in the world would he leave off chivalry. He was told that he would be forced to comply and was put in prison. Evidently the narrator could not imagine how he could have entered into an agreement to conform to the rule voluntarily. However, finally he consented to see the girl. She pleased him, and they were married amongst the greatest possible rejoicings. So Lamorat by marrying the lady was able to leave prison to became lord of the castle and the country.[56]

---

[54] *Vulgate*, VII, pp. 226/7.
[55] *Roman de Tristan etc.*, ed. Löseth, p. 81.
[56] *Roman de Tristan etc.*, ed. Löseth, pp. 208/9 and 212; *Folie Lancelot*, ed. Bogdanow, pp. 72–5.

This most important element of the challenge theme, the continuation of the custom of guardianship, is well represented in the romances, considering the odds in favour of its suppression. In so far as the survival of memories of the continuation of the custom provides evidence for the one time religious practices of the past, the examples given are backed up in the usual way by others in which the principal feature is less clearly defined.

The triumph of Christianity over 'evil customs' is a principal feature of the romances. There are plenty of obviously wicked activities which get suppressed by one or other of the principal champions of Christianity, notably Perceval and Galahad. The Age of Salisbury cathedral was not likely to fail to notice the spiritual triumphs of its literary heroes. So the romances provide a set of circumstances in which the powers of good are on the winning side. The heroes carry the banner of Christianity – to all appearances. Indeed, no one would deny that the wicked customs were wicked, nor that the heroes triumphed over them. It is only when one examines what the romances provide as replacements for the evil customs that a suspicion may arise that these events, though they do seem to be inspired by a clash between two religions, have nothing to do with Christianity.

There are two clear examples in *Perlesvaus*. Potvin's index refers to Perceval's adventure at the Castle of the Black Hermit as the conversion of the inhabitants of the castle to Christianity. But what actually happened? Perceval was accompanied by the Damsel of the Cart, who has previously been noticed here when she came to a St John's Day festival at Arthur's court with a cart loaded with severed heads. During her travels with Perceval she had had the heads forcibly taken from her by the Black Hermit's knights, who overcame Perceval's resistance. When, in the 'conversion to Christianity' of his castle, the Black Hermit was killed she got her most important heads back again. Not a result which would have pleased a devout Christian who understood the pagan importance of severed heads.[57]

The contest between Perceval and evil customs is described as a contest between the Old Law and the New. The Damsel of the Cart says that, if Perceval does not hasten to the land which was King Fisherman's (i.e. the land of the Grail religion), the New Law that God has established will be brought low, for the King of Castle Mortal has announced throughout the country that all who wished to maintain the Old Law and abandon the New would have protection from him.[58] The meaning of the word law in this context is 'religion', as when the Old Law is said to have been represented by a woman riding on a serpent.[59] No one would argue that this was not a potent representation of a religion, but look what has replaced it: the cult of severed heads and the Grail cult which Perceval professed during his reign at Corbenic,[60] –

---

[57] See chapter entitled Severed Heads and Sacred Waters.
[58] *Perlesvaus*, tr. Bryant, p. 152.
[59] *Vulgate*, VI, p. 74.
[60] Potvin VI, lines 45330–4.

the place where Alfasein had been wounded in the thighs with a spear by a fiery men.[61] In spite of an uncritical assumption that the Grail cult has Christian significance, a closer look at its maimed kings; its vessel of blood refilled from the bleeding spear; and its parody of the eucharist when real blood was drunk from a crystal cup in *Diu Crône*;[62] shows that it was not Christianity.

## The Reward

The standard reward for a victorious challenger is, as we have seen, the Lady's person, her dominions and a territorial title. It is 'a basic feature of the theme' that the conflict at the ford leads to possession of the lady;[63] whoever comes looking for the maiden must fight and will have his head impaled on a stake if he loses;[64] and so on. This motif, that so puzzled Cervantes, is so often repeated as to need no further examples. But the Lady herself is not the only female character in many of the incidents. Take for example an adventure Gawain had one night when travelling in unknown country. There had been a violent storm and it was very dark. The moon had unaccountably failed to rise according to its usual course. However, from a hill he saw a distant fire on the top of a round mountain, to which he was irresistibly attracted (he was not to know it was in fact a trap set for him). When he arrived, he found a fire of charcoal in the middle of a beautiful salon. Nearby, in spite of the lateness of the hour, knights and ladies were sitting eating. A damsel explained the local rules to Gawain as follows: 'Sir, it is the custom for all knights errant who wish to enjoy hospitality here that they should agree to joust with a knight of my lady's who is within and to agree to fight over this fire in the middle of this hall. And do you know how the errant knight is rewarded if he beats my lady's knight? He will eat this evening with my lady and sleep with her and have his pleasure as with his own lover.' . . . in due course, Gawain having won and the meal being over, this damsel, called the Damsel of the Harp, who was the lady's sister, led him to the lady's bed – however, at this point there was an interruption and a lengthy interlude followed before he finally got into it.[65]

In the Damsel of the Harp we have an example of one of the staple characters associated with the challenge theme. At St Augustine's chapel her counterpart is the managing young woman under the oak tree at the entrance to the glade, who orchestrates the proceedings and explains the meanings of actions and of symbolism. She is particularly useful to the narrator when he is faced by what to medieval ears seemed a complete turn about by the Lady in

[61] *Vulgate*, I, p. 289.
[62] *Diu Crone* . . ., Jillings, p. 123.
[63] *Diu Crone* . . ., Jillings, p. 39.
[64] *La Mule sans Frein*, ed. Johnson and Owen, lines 774ff.
[65] *Vulgate*, VII, p. 172f.

accepting as her new husband the killer of the old. So it is Luned, who has been acting as the hero's 'minder', who has to persuade the Countess of the Fountain that to marry her husband's slayer is the correct course. The same motif is apparent in the story of the Queen of the Tents, who occupied a glade surrounded by a great long white sheet, like a wall. Inside were many tents and a great number of joyful dames and damsels of great beauty. Perceval came there after having killed a certain Cahot the Red in a joust, whereby he was given the submission of a Castle called the Key of Wales. This knight, Cahot, was deeply mourned by the Queen of the Tents. The Damsel of the Cart, who happened to be present, said to her:

'My Lady, behold the good knight for whose coming the pavilions were set up ...'
'Oh,' she said, 'he has killed the finest knight of all my family, who always defended me against my enemies.'
'My Lady,' replied the maiden, 'this knight could protect and defend you, for he is the finest knight in the world and the fairest.'
The queen took him by the hand and bade him be seated beside her.
'Sire,' she said, 'however the adventure may have fallen out, my heart bids me rejoice at your coming. . .'
The queen looked him straight in the face, and her heart lit up with such love that she almost threw herself upon him.
'Sire,' she said, 'if you will grant me your love, then I will forgive you for killing Cahot the Red.'[66]

The narrator in all episodes of this type takes a male chauvinist point of view. To him, the successful challenger obtained the girl as a prize. To him, the girl's quick change from her original lover to the new had to be explained. He was wrong on both counts. The man was the prize of the girl (ultimately of the goddess), and he was her victim, bought with a temporary display of wealth and power; and her change of heart was entirely heartless. The new 'lover', though enjoying sexual union, indeed there for that purpose only, would be discarded and destroyed without a pang, when his time ran out, as his predecessors had been and successors would be in the future.

Unfortunately for the Queen of the Tents, Perceval was required (in the story) to continue his adventures. Perhaps in some real life original she did enjoy his presence and protection, at least until she found a replacement.

In this incident the challenge theme, if that may be supposed to have been at the heart of it, is somewhat garbled. The interesting feature is the importance of the part played by the personage described by Luttrell as 'the emissary', who in the Chateau de Pesme Aventure *warns* the hero not to spend a night in the castle, *informs* him of the custom of the city and *advises* him to turn back.[67]

---

66 *Perlesvaus*, tr. Bryant, p. 100.
67 *The Creation of the first Arthurian Romance*, p. 199.

A similar role is played by both Luned in *The Lady of the Fountain* and the Damsel of the Cart in the episode above, particularly in persuading the resident lady to accept her new lord as a replacement for the one he has just killed. A managing role is also played in *Le Bel Inconnu* by the messenger, Elene; in the story of Gareth by the messenger Linet;[68] and again in rather different circumstances by Brangain, the accomplice of Tristan and Yseult. In spite of great apparent differences between these characters, the presence among them of the Damsel of the Cart reveals common features in this group of personages. At the mid-August festival at Carawent, the damsel in the cart is none other than the Damsel of the Lake. In this form she is known among other names as Elaine (according to Sommer); and as the Damsel Cacheresse (the 'Huntress') she was a local equivalent of Diana. So of our organizing damsels, Elene is linked to the Damsel of the Cart/Lake by her name; Luned is linked by the meaning of her name, the moon (an attribute of Diana); and Brangain (whose name is not to be distinguished from that of Branwen, sister of the god Bran), also represents the moon (see below p. 168). Behind the available real woman for whom the hero fought was a goddess egging him on, and at whom his devotion and self-sacrifice were aimed. Though, paradoxically, she has apparently been demoted to little more than a handmaid on occasion, some of her characteristics and names have persisted in the 'matter of Britain', allowing us to observe what an important part she plays under various aliases.

So far there are five apparently distinct personages tentatively bracketed together as alternative designations for what will soon be seen to have been a major goddess.

(1)  The Damsel of the Cart.
(2)  The Damsel of Diana's Lake, who also rode in the cart and who was called Elaine, among other names.
(3)  Elene/Linet, a managing damsel, has, as Elene, the same name as the above.
(4)  Luned, another managing damsel, has the same name as Linet. Her name meaning 'moon' links her with Diana.
(5)  Brangain also represents the moon, which links her via Diana with the Damsel of the Lake and Luned.

There are plenty more of the same kind. For instance, there are the many damsels travelling to Arthur's court, often apparently as the agents of royal mistresses in need of champions in what turns out to be a challenge type combat for the lady and her lands. On one particular occasion, at Arthur's marriage to Guenever, it was the Damsel of the Lake herself in her role as the Damsel Cacheresse who rode into the court following a white stag. Where a supernatural being is seen to play the role, it becomes apparent that the status of the rest of the messenger damsels has been undervalued. They are really slightly obscured images of the more powerful figures listed above, as their

[68] *Morte Darthur*, Malory, bk VII.

purpose in the story – to organize the combat and cheer on the attacking hero – demonstrates.

These requests for help were always 'adventures' which preceded an Arthurian festival and evidently betokened some ritual involving the supposed presence of the goddess, possibly in a dramatized representation.

Others who play a somewhat similar part are listed below on p. 87. They include Orguelleuse who organized the affairs of Gawain. The presence of Orguelleuse in the group emphasizes the demanding nature of these damsels. This is a feature recurring several times among them. They often deserve the title 'Maledisant' – Evil-tongued – earned by one of them for her haughty behaviour, an entirely appropriate characteristic for a divinity.

Writers interested in the origins of the Arthurian legends have pointed out that the countess or queen who by marriage confers county or country on her husband has an analogy in the mythology of Ireland. A divinity called the Sovereignty of Ireland had exactly that capacity of bestowing the kingship of her country on her consort. She sometimes appeared transformed into an excessively ugly form or else animal shape, which made a sexual advance towards her an adventure in itself. This latter magical feature occurs in *Le Bel Inconnu*, in which the ultimate objective of the hero, release of the lady of Sinadoun, is gained by kissing a serpent which, of course, turns into the lady herself, whose marriage confers on him the kingdom. This change of shape is the exception. More often the bestower is notably attractive and much sought after. Indeed, the best known player in this role is Guenever. That is the reason for all those abductions she suffered, a point to be taken up in the next chapter.

In this analysis of the six elements of the 'challenge' theme only a small number of the clearest examples have been quoted. They are backed up by a large number which themselves cannot be used as evidence of the local practice of the rites of Nemi because they do not contain enough of the elements. Such often repeated motifs as 'a knight set up a pavilion by a fountain in a glade and challenged all passing knights to joust' or 'Yvain was offered the king's daughter and his country after defeating him' do not carry conviction on their own but as representatives of scores of eroded versions of the Challenge theme they can be categorized as having their origin in the widespread practice of Nemi-type activities in prehistoric Britain.

# TOURNAMENTS
# AND THE SPRING MARRIAGE

The last chapter has provided illustrations of the selection of a priest-king by single combat after a challenge. The challenge, following Frazer's description of the rite at Nemi, has generally been assumed to have taken place at any time, but there are indications, in the much more varied tradition reflected in the romances, that the same objective, ensuring a virile monarch, could be attained in another way, by restricting the length of his rule. Thus we have seen the guardian of a ford having to survive for a year and in another version it is seven years; and at a passage or an island there are limits of seven years and of sixty days.[1] Periodicity is not restricted to the romances. In Welsh legend there is single combat at the year's end between two kings for their respective dominions in which Pwyll, King of the Otherworld, defeats a neighbouring king called Hafgan and receives the subjection of his people. The combat took place on a specific day well known to all the people, but what day it was is not revealed. Another event which sounds as if it may have been annual was the combat at the Thunderstorm Fountain where Arthur kept vigil on Midsummer Eve and after which the countess released Yvain until the next Midsummer Day. In much the same way there were more 'adventures' – that is, manifestations of paganism – at the Ford of the Thorntree on Midsummer Eve than in all the rest of the year put together. These periodic events are probably reflections of some past religious system. Certainly annual kingship is a well-known feature of paganism and seven years is mentioned often enough to suggest the original importance of this period, too.

Annual kings were not only selected as winners in single combat but seem also to have been chosen from among the victors of group conflicts. These were often annual events taking place in spring. They have been identified by narrators with medieval tournaments and are always so described, but they retain traces of their origin as a system for selecting temporary ritual kings who attained that position as the consort of the 'queen' or 'princess' of the

---

1  E.g.: The Perilous Ford in Didot *Perceval*, ed. Roach, 1 year; the Amorous Ford in 2nd Cont, 7 years, in Potvin, lines 24314–42.

country, who was the real power in the land. When the circumstances are examined, this interpretation is obvious enough. For example: the Queen of Waleis (Wales) put herself and her kingdom up as the prize at a tournament.[2] This motif inevitably degenerated in the literature of a male-chauvinist society into the woman being regarded as a mere chattel, as in the account of Perga-mon's twelve nieces being offered to the victors of tournaments at twelve successive full moons,[3] but if the tradition is examined closely it will be seen that traces remain of the memory that tournaments were originally organized by women for the benefit of women. Like the Queen of Wales, the Damsel of the Glades (des Landes) declared a tournament at which she herself would wed the winner,[4] and the Dame of the White Castle held a tournament at which her daughter's hand and great wealth were the prize.[5] In the case of a tournament at Pomeglai (a place on the boundary between two kingdoms), the patrons were the lady of Nohaut and the lady of Pomeglai. Queen Guenever was present, and the objective was marriage. The damsels attending tournaments, who came more to marry than for any other reason,[6] were expected to choose as their lords those who did well at the tournament.[7] All damsels and maidens of high parentage were taken to every tournament within two or three days journey, according to a custom originated by Uther Pendragon. The women watched the fighting from temporary stands. They encouraged their lovers by giving them as tokens pretty items of their clothing to wear – sleeves, hats, mantles, chemises and habits. In return the successful warriors brought back whatever tokens they had captured from the knights they had defeated. These were triumphantly displayed on the railings of the shelters from which the women were watching the fighting. According to an account in *Perceforest*, a romance which contains many references to prehistoric acts and buildings, this procedure was carried out with such abandon that they stripped to their underwear. They went away bareheaded, with their hair down, bare-armed, without sleeves, wimples, mantles and chemises.[8]

In the system described in the romances the women, far from being chattels, are the originators and beneficiaries, in that it provides them with spirited and vigorous mates, at whatever cost to the losers. Though it cannot be expected that every recollection in tradition will preserve these features as clearly as the examples above, the tournament at the castle of la Marche (the Boundary) displays many of them. It was held at the anniversary of the coronation of its king, Brangoire, and was intended to provide his unnamed daughter with a husband who would enjoy all her honour and riches, and to provide husbands for twelve other damsels. The winner and the other twelve bridegrooms were

2  *Parzival*, tr. Hatto, p. 41.
3  *Le roman de Perceforest* . . ., Lods, p. 28.
4  *Roman en prose de Tristan* . . ., ed. Löseth, p. 21.
5  Didot *Perceval*, ed. Roach, pp. 222/3.
6  *Guiron le Courtois*, ed. Lathuillère, p. 211 para. 30.
7  *Yvain*, tr. Comfort, p. 342.
8  *Le roman de Perceforest* . . ., Lods, p. 232.

selected by the women, and the winner chose the twelve brides. It was Sir Bors who after much fighting was chosen as the bravest and most handsome. He was put on a golden throne in a pavilion and given a vermilion robe by the princess and there was much feasting and dancing of caroles. Bors and the princess slept together that night and a son was conceived who, as Helain the White, was destined to do great deeds in the quest of the Grail. Bors himself was required by the narrator for further adventures so had to decline marriage. He tried to decline the princess altogether, since his continued virginity was required in his role as Grail-seeker, but evidently physical union was too significant a feature of the story to be ditched, so his scruples were overcome by a magic ring.[9] Perhaps the real-life original of this hero, not being required to move on like Bors, settled down to enjoy a year of love and royalty before his inevitable replacement.

There are several interesting features here:

(1) the tournament takes place at a boundary;
(2) it seems to be an annual event, taking place on the anniversary of Brangoire's coronation;
(3) since Brangoire can be argued to have been a deity[10] (the god Bran) it is a religious occasion;
(4) women choose the victor;
(5) his reward is the princess;
(6) the golden throne and the date, being the anniversary of the coronation, suggest that kingship is involved;
(7) and bed and conception are reminders of the ancient role of royalty in encouraging the fruitfulness of nature by sexual activities.

Although we are not told at what time of year this annual event took place, there is a substantial lead in the coincidence of the tournament and the anniversary of a coronation. Both tournaments and coronations take place most often at Pentecost, which as the principal spring festival, generally falling in May or early June, would also be the appropriate season for the spring marriage. The point is made most directly in *Perceforest* where on one occasion, at a May 1st festival – a time in that romance for the selection of kings – there is general love and conception,[11] and on another it is said that the numerous unions exalt and honour the feast.[12]

Accounts of kingship limited to set periods, or won by success in tournaments which took place on fixed dates, have survived more often in the stories of less important characters. But the same rules were applied to the great ones of the land, though only the merest hint may now survive. Lancelot, for

---

*Vulgate*, IV, pp. 264ff.
[10] The portrayal of Brân Fendigaid in the second branch of the Mabinogi forcibly suggests that Brân is a euhemerized deity, *Trioedd Ynys Prydein*, Bromwich, p. 284.
[11] *Perceforest*, IV, ed. Roussineau, vol. II, p. 1129.
[12] *Perceforest*, IV, ed. Roussineau, vol. I, p. 49.

instance, was the winner of a three day tournament. To honour him, the king gave up his own bedroom for the night.[13] Taken at its face value, this is an odd reward. But we are also told that at the time Guenever was being unfaithful with Lancelot and had provided him with arms for the occasion. Has an editor, unable to comprehend the original story, described the outcome of the cult conflict as adultery, therefore to be concealed, and as a result left the hero with an empty bed – a hollow substitute for the spoils of victory?

It is usually difficult to pinpoint a specific locality where a rite was performed but there may be an exception in the events at the castle of the March (see Gazetteer), which has been identified by Loomis as where the ruins of Castle Dinas Bran now stand, near Oswestry in the Welsh Marches. It is also possible to find a solution to the problem in more general terms. Brangoire's tournament took place at the castle of the Boundary. Other tournaments took place at the same kind of site, such as the one at Pomeglai, on the border of Logres and Gorre; that at Leverzerp, on the border of Logres and Sorelois; that at Taneborc, on the border of Logres and Norgales; and another between Arthur and the King of Outre les Marches de Galonne which took place on the border between their two kingdoms. The protagonists are generally the kings of the countries. (For reasons already explained, queens are not often recorded as originators.) The kings assemble small armies for the conflict. The matter is dealt with on what seems to the narrators to have been a national scale, though the 'countries' involved are more likely to have been tribes or clans. We see another aspect of tournaments here. As well as being for the choice of royal bridegrooms, they were miniature wars, taking place at the boundaries between the two kingdoms concerned. These formal battles are to be distinguished from real wars which are dealt with later in this book.

Some trace of this sort of behaviour may have persisted into modern times in an activity called 'faction-fighting' referred to as follows in the *Guide to the Dingle Peninsula*:[14] 'The fairs here were notorious for [it], a custom particularly associated with the early nineteenth century but which harked back to a form of symbolic tribal skirmishing associated in many cases with hilltop assemblies. Many such assemblies, and the later fairs, took place at meeting places of natural boundaries and brought together people from different sides of mountains or of major rivers, and people of different tribes and kinship groups. A story is told of two families of the locality who were particularly renowned for fighting it out at Ballinclare fair. A daughter and son of the opposing sides were courting and wanted to marry, and for the sake of the young couple the heads of the feuding families agreed to give up faction fighting. At a meeting in one of their houses they each hung up the long sticks they reserved for fighting and shook hands. Come the day of the next fair the two of them were sitting in the same house, each privately longing to be out fighting. Suddenly they heard a great clatter and looked up to see that their two sticks were

13 *Vulgate*, V, p. 194.
14 Steve McDonagh, 1985.

beating hell out of each other on their own. Further thought was unnecessary; they took down the sticks and headed off to the fair!'

The tournament as a ritual conflict to select a virile mate for a goddess may seem here to have degenerated into fighting for fighting's sake. Nevertheless, the Irish story depends on a romance between individuals of the opposing sides. In the complex web of interactions at the boundary tournament, fighting was only one aspect. Exogamous marriages, avoiding inbreeding, are likely to have been another benefit of the system.

The remarkable longevity of Irish popular tradition, unaffected by the rule of Roman legions and apparently less severely frowned on by Christian missionaries than in the rest of Britain, furnishes many examples of continuity from the pagan past. Great gatherings at particular sites have been going on for a score of centuries or more. Horse-fairs held on each August 1st until recently at Tara, Teltown, Wexford and the Curragh show a direct and unbroken link with the boisterous horse-races and games of the Iron Age there. And the link can be much longer still. At Tara a Neolithic passage-grave, later also used by Food-Vessel people, provided the original open-air sanctuary. A. Burl suggests that we can find traces of the practice of healing, betrothal and fecundity rites, at sites such as those mentioned above, in legends that have endured since those distant times, though diluted and misunderstood.[15] Such rites were performed on the great annual festivals such as May 1st, August 1st and the eve of All Hallows, November 1st.

Burl goes on to say that the rite of coronation took place in Ireland at such assemblies. It involved selection of the prospective monarch in a dream by a druid who was sleeping on the skin of a white buck, the candidate touching the coronation stone, Lia Fail, which was supposed to shriek; and a ritual marriage took place with the goddess of Sovereignty, without which no king could reign. There is no reference to hand to hand combat in this account, though R. A. S. Macalister remarks that, in the Bronze Age, 'As in the sacred grove of the Golden Bough at Aricia the king of Tara reigned, as a rule, by virtue of having slain his predecessor.' Macalister is referring to Nemi – Aricia, nowadays Ariccia, was the nearest town to the lake.

The scene at a national gathering on a day of festival, as described in Irish tradition, can be imagined as being very similar to that of a coronation in a French romance which was held in the temple of Venus on the day of her festival.[16] There it was the custom for the people to assemble on the evening before the feast for an out-door occasion. Pavilions and tents were erected for the royal party and for the barons. The rest made do with leafy bowers. People brought goods for sale and in a few days the place was as well provisioned as the best city in the kingdom. The barons, bourgeoisie and merchants were allotted sites according to their estates.[17] In another account of a temple of

[15] *Rites of the Gods*, pp. 197, 230 etc.
[16] *Perceforest*, pt. I, ed. Taylor, pp. 150/1, lines 3038/9 and 3063–5.
[17] *Perceforest*, pt. I, ed. Taylor, lines 3072ff.

Venus the event took place on a boundary, that between Cornwall and Loenois, it was celebrated during the first week of May, and the kings of both countries took part in the ceremonies.[18]

The hero Bors did not stay to enjoy the privileges which would have followed marriage to Brangoire's daughter. Only in primitive stories like *Lanzelet* and *Peredur* could the hero be tied down in 'marriage' to the representative of the Sovereignty that he has fought for and won. In much the same way, the real significance of the personages representing sovereignty is often obscured by the absence of a resident hero. At the end of the chapter on the 'Challenge' it was noted that it has been suggested that Guenever, 'to whom all Britain and Ireland do belong'[19] might well have played the role of sovereignty, that is, to have been a goddess.[20] How is it to be decided if that was the case? Perhaps first we should look at the residue left in traditional tales by generally accepted goddesses to see what criteria will justify the use of the appellation 'divine'. In Welsh tradition there are Don and Modron, the first a close parallel of the Irish Danann in name and in the names of the subsidiary members of her pantheon. The second, literally the Mother, widely accepted to have been a goddess who was mother of a young god. In the 'matter of Britain' there is Morgan le Fay, often called a goddess and an enchantress; and there is Diana of the Woods, again described as goddess and resembling the classical Diana in her love for the chase. Less obvious female deities are:

(1) the Lady or Damsel of the Lake (Diana's Lake), who parallels Diana in being a huntress, is an enchantress and, in a German Arthurian story, *Diu Crône*, is specifically called a goddess;

(2) the Grail-bearer who is also called a goddess in the same work; and

(3) Enid of the romance *Erec et Enide*, who is now thought to have represented the territory of the Veneti of Vannes. [21]

It will be seen that there are three factors involved; being called a 'goddess'; having a name resembling a known goddess; and behaving like known goddesses.

Who else in the romances springs to mind as qualifying for the description goddess after we have exhausted the first two testing factors and come to behaviour? There are the many women who do actually provide their hero husbands with kingdoms, so revealing themselves as representing Sovereignty. These include, for instance, the Queen of Waleis and others of the same kind mentioned above, and Lancelot's several princess/prizes. In all these instances, as in the case of the Damsel of the Lake, Enid and Elaine, the narrators of the romances fail to make a distinction between the human

---

18 *Roman en prose de Tristan* . . ., ed. Löseth, p. 11.
19 *Sir Gawain at the Grail Castle*, tr. Weston, p. 7.
20 *Peredur* . . ., Goetinck, pp. 213–250; *King Arthur and the Grail*, Cavendish, p. 54; *Le roi Arthur et la société Celtique*, Markale, pp. 293/4.
21 Bromwich in *études Celtique*, IX, fasc. 2, p. 465.

representative and the divinity who guided her course of action, but thanks to the Irish parallel what was going on is clear enough.

These spirits of sovereignty have a common feature. Their function requires them to be restricted to the locality they have made their own, like the nymphs of the springs at Bath and Buxton. They are in direct contrast to the highly mobile challengers of joust and tournament. The goddesses stay put, scattered around the countryside, waiting for a wandering hero to fall into their well-advertised trap of temporary kingship. Their generally static nature has not encouraged narrators to build up romances round them. They do not fit into the 'string of episodes' formula which has carried the male heroes onward. The case is different with, Guenever, however. She is the one heroine who has 'collected' a string of incidents in which she is successively abducted and fought for. Perhaps the best known example is the occasion when Mordred was left in Logres as regent while Arthur was away in Gaul. He forcibly married Guenever and seized the throne. Here in the open is the element of kingship which is implied in most of the other examples. Discussing this phenomenon, Webster[22] deals with a dozen or so abductions of Guenever. She has evidently been as successful in 'collecting' abduction episodes as Lancelot has challenge ones. We have seen that a narrator sometimes collects together a series of episodes of the same type, and portrays them as the adventures of a single hero or heroine. When this happens it could be argued that like attracts like. Just as a single individual called Lancelot could not have been the hero of all the tales told of him, but we can guess him to have been a figure who personified the type, which allowed narrators to use him to usurp the positions of others of the same kind, so with Guenever. The stories told of her reveal her type – the personification of sovereignty. That is the reason for supposing she represented a divinity. Her name which is said to mean 'White Phantom' tends to confirm the view that she had a supernatural origin; but two incidents, her marriage at the spring festival and her unresisted abduction by Melwas when she was maying in the woods, suggest a human involvement. Although she is never described in the romances as a goddess there is a hint of divinity in an ancient Welsh triad which refers to three Guenevers. Triplication is a common feature of Celtic deities. The triads are a literary formula in which three of a kind are grouped together, so the formula itself might have given rise to the triplication, but it is just possible that an original triplication might explain an odd feature of the romances, that both Guenever and Yseult are duplicated. There are the indistinguishable true and false Guenevers, and Tristan was in love with Yseult the Fair and married to Yseult of the White Hands. Is this duplication, nonsensical as far as the story is concerned, an erosion of an original triplication?

One cannot help wondering which of the many battles for Guenever was the one which first brought her to the notice of the originators of the romances.

---

[22] *Guinevere: A study of her abductions,* passim.

It would not be unlikely for this critical incident, perhaps even the sole recorded incident in which she participated herself, to have been the one which gave rise to her marriage with Arthur. Guenever had many lovers in the stories, both before and after marriage, but her lover until Arthur took her was Gasozein and the scene of the combat between the two of them for possession of her was Cardoel. A link with Cardoel fits another feature of her marriage to Arthur, that her dowry was the Round Table which was originally made at Cardoel. Cardoel seems to have been a haunt of deities (see Gaz. Cardoel). Half a dozen are linked with it, so it must have been an important pagan cult site. A battle for her at Cardoel is clearly another association between Guenever and paganism. However, unlike all the other manifestations of sovereignty, she did not stay put, but travelled, with the Round Table and its company of knights errant, from Wales to Camelot in Logres.

The ways in which a virile partner was chosen for a goddess have been explored in this chapter and the previous one. In them the question posed by Cervantes has been answered. Her needs would not be satisfied by the heir of a family which had exercised power for generations, but were to be met in the shortest term possible. What she wanted was an immediate display of fecundity, ideally during the first night which the hero shared with her human representative. The hero – hero, indeed, who took on this seemingly thankless task ending so soon in a shameful death – has left his own mark on the story for readers in posterity to ponder. The combination of sexual attraction and devotion (to a goddess, of course) has left the imprint of the figures of two great lovers on the 'matter of Britain' and hence on all subsequent literature.

# FIRE FROM HEAVEN

Arthur's opponent at St Augustine's Chapel wounded him with a flaming lance. Such fiery weapons are common enough in the romances but they are not normally used in personal combat. More often they strike from heaven without human intervention. There are three typical scenes: the victim is a ruler and is struck between the thighs by a fiery lance at the Grail castle; or an unauthorized person sits in the Perilous Seat at the Round Table and is consumed by fire; or a hero sleeps in the Testing Bed in the Grail castle and is assailed by a burning lance. Items one and three are directly linked with the Grail; and since we know that the act of sitting in the Perilous seat initiated the Grail Quest and the 'adventures' of Logres, so is item two. As F. Lot, a well-respected reviewer of Arthurian matters, comments: 'There is a mysterious rapport between the lance, and also the Grail, and the 'marvels' or 'adventures' of Logres'.[1] The fiery lance, often accompanied by thunder, fairly obviously symbolizes lightning; the wound between the thighs is assumed to be a euphemism for castration;[2] and the 'adventures', I have suggested, are pagan religious observances, probably dramatized. These three manifestations of fire from heaven are among the principal features of the Grail cult and account for much of the religious background of the romances.

## The Ruler Struck by a Lightning Weapon

Starting at the beginning of the most complete version of the 'matter of Britain', the first character to attract attention by the misfortune of being struck by symbolic lightning is the enigmatic Joseph of 'Arimathea'. The suggestion that he came here after the time of Christ is improbable. Without this fictitious date, I would argue that he can be recognised as a pagan figure, who brought a pagan religion – the Grail cult – to Britain.

As well as bringing the Grail to this country, Joseph was wounded between the thighs by an angel with a countenance as bright as lightning.[3] He took with

---

[1] Quoted in *The Romance of the Grail*, Bogdanow, p. 163.
[2] E.g. in *Parzival*, tr. Hatto, p. 244.
[3] *Vulgate*, I, p. 77; *Le saint Graal*, ed. Hucher, II, pp. 299/300.

him on missions to convert the natives both the Grail and the head of the spear which had wounded him. The relationship between these two talismans is fairly constant. It is demonstrated clearly in one story by the act of an angel who holds the lance over the holy vessel, so that the blood drips into it.[4] In another instance, to obtain healing blood a vessel was held under the spear-head when this had been replaced in the wound.[5]

A strange feature of the romances is that this bloodthirsty cult should not merely have been confused with Christianity but should have, in the words of one commentator, positively invited identification with it – owing to the self-sacrificing nature of the heroic figure at its centre.

Joseph's first attempts at conversion to this new cult seem to have taken place in Wales, and were accompanied by military action. After capturing a city near the Severn, he built a minster to 'Our Lady' (who may be presumed from what follows to have been some female divinity). Here, in what reads like a dedication ceremony, his ally Evalac (the king who had a temple to the sun and worshipped a goddess-dolly) was too closely exposed to the Grail. There was a lightning flash and the ark which held the spear-head and the Grail was seen to be shimmering with burning fire. Evalac fell to the ground and lay there like a piece of meat, blinded and paralysed. He was, the story has it, to be healed by Galahad after four centuries of 'maimed kingship'. Meanwhile, his nephew Celidoine was married the next day to a certain Sarracinte, they were crowned king and Queen of Norgales in the city of Galatone, and that night a male heir was conceived.[6]

In an alternative version Evalac was wounded by a sword full of flame and fire[7] but otherwise the sense of the account is the same, and is similar to that of the wounding of the many other 'maimed kings' who were unlucky enough to be guardians of the Grail.

A city in Wales called Galafort was a centre of missionary effort for the Grail cult. From there two successful expeditions set out, one to the city of Camelot in Logres, at that time the richest city of the Sarrassins in Great Britain and their principal religious centre,[8] and the other to Terre Foraine – the oddly named 'Foreign Country' – which will later be located in the south-east of Wales. The latter foray was led by Alain le Gros, who travelled with the Grail and a party of followers to find empty lands in which to settle. In due course they came to Terre Foraine where there were plenty of small people who new nothing except how to cultivate the land, and whose king, Kalafes, was a leper. The Grail people offered to cure him if he would give up the Sarrassin customs and throw down his idols. This he did, and, having been cured, decided to build a castle to hold the Grail and to offer his daughter in marriage to one of

4   *Vulgate*, VI, p. 189.
5   *Parzival*, tr. Hatto, p. 249; *Le saint Graal*, ed. Hucher, II, p. 310.
6   *Le saint Graal*, ed. Hucher, III, pp. 492–8.
7   *Perceval le Gallois . . .*, ed. Potvin, vol. VI, p. 247.
8   *Vulgate*, I, p. 244; *Le saint Graal*, ed. Hucher, III, p. 195.

Alain's brothers, Josué. The first Sunday after the castle had been completed the Grail was carried into the palace and the betrothal of Kalafes' daughter and Josué was announced. The marriage took place that same day, and the couple were also crowned king and Queen of Terre Foraine and received the homage of the people of the country. Kalafes spent that night in the place in which the Grail was kept and, like Evalac, came too close to it for his own good. A man all in flames let fly a lance at him which struck him between the thighs. The place, Corbenic, became known as the Adventurous Palace and many knights who attempted the adventure were found dead the next day. Only Gawain was able to survive, at the expense of much shame and injury. The night of the wedding and coronation, the night, that is, of the maiming of Kalafes, a male heir was engendered on Kalafes' daughter by the new king.[9]

Yet another ruler who suffered the wound between the thighs was Pellinor of Listenois, a country in the south of Wales (see Gaz. L). He was struck with the Lance Vengeresse, and the nature of the wound led his wife to be described thereafter as the Widow Lady of the Waste Forest. The description of Pellinor's wife as a 'widow' after this misfortune is as near as the French romances get to describing the wound between the thighs as castration. Only in a German version is the wound of Anfortas specifically so called. The weapon which wounded Pellinor, the Lance Vengeresse, is the same that wounded Pellehan (this is not surprising, since Pellehan is an analogue of Pellinor, see Who's Who), the effect of this latter event on the surrounding countryside being so devastating as to earn this act the name Dolorous Stroke.[10]

Finally, the story of Joseph's misfortune occurs in an alternative version, mysteriously transposed to Norway, in a romance entitled *Sone de Nausay*. In this account Joseph expelled the Saracens from Norway, slew their king, married his daughter and was crowned. For marrying a heathen princess he was punished by god with a wound in the 'reins' (literally kidneys) and below. He then became known as Fisher King and his country Lorgres (evidently Logres, not Norway after all!) was comprehensively blighted on account of the nature of his wound. Later he established a community on the Island of Galosche (which sounds like the French word Galesche, meaning Welsh) where after his death his body was preserved as a holy relic.

There are numerous links between the various characters mentioned above, and between the various scenes of their ritual injury. Most of these can be described later, but one factor of great significance springs directly from this comparison of the circumstances in which pagan kings came to be castrated. In the cases of both Evalac and Kalafes, mentioned above, the event took place at the moment of the succession to the throne of a new king. For Evalac, King of Sarras, his replacement was his nephew, his natural heir in matriarchal times, who married a certain Sarracinte. For Kalafes it was his daughter by whom the kingdom was passed on to her husband, another manifestation of a

9  *Le saint Graal,* ed. Hucher, III, pp. 287–92.
10  See next chapter for details.

less patriarchal age. At both marriages castration coincided with coronation, copulation and conception. The fertile royal union, looked on as something much more than merely a good omen, is contrasted here with its diametrical opposite, the king whose power of reproduction has been totally lost. The puzzle of how a ritual figure could exist whose characteristic attribute negated the principle of the fertile royal union is entirely explained by the timing. In both these instances, castration has taken place at the moment of the succession of a vigorous replacement. The original ruler's task had been to promote prosperity by fertile sexual union. To remove his now unwanted sexual function after he had been replaced has a harsh logic. In the event, Kalafes is said to have died after ten days but Evalac to have lived several centuries and to have eventually been cured by the application of blood from the Grail. Perhaps the latter's long survival is a memory of the continued existence of the system over a long period of time, involving many individual participants.

The new Queen of Sarras bore the same name, Sarracinte, as the old queen, Evalac's wife. To have continuity in the name of the queen whose marriage conveys kingship, and for her name to incorporate the name of her city, Sarras, suggests that she may have represented the sovereignty of her domains. The same can probably be said of the Saracen princess in Sone. Joseph, in that romance followed a familiar progress in first killing the king and marrying his daughter, and he paid the same price as Evalac.

The events which were distant precursors of the strange tales recounted above seem to have taken place at a period of religious change. The Grail protagonists were obviously evangelizing, and their temples were often founded in place of an earlier structure representing a deeper layer of paganism. Thus in a variant on Joseph's castration with a lance by a fiery angel, he was struck between the thighs by a Sarrassin with a sword at the castle of the Rock. He later called down thunder and lightning to destroy the Sarrassin idols – Mahomet, Jupiter, Teruagant and Cahu – and built a chapel to 'Our Lady' where they had been set up.[11]

This is a somewhat similar story to the accounts of the events at Galatone and Corbenic, where Evalac and Kalafes respectively were deprived of their reproductive functions at the inauguration of foundations dedicated to 'Our Lady'. Since the date is unlikely to be in the first century AD, the ambience is likely to be pagan so there can be no question of Christ's mother being involved in this primitive ritual. The repetition of the four motifs; the wound between the thighs; the lightning stroke (represented by the fiery prime mover or the flaming lance); the construction of a religious structure; and the dedication to a female – seems to imply that a goddess was the central focus of this cult – in the case of Sarras, her name seems to have been Sarracinte.[12] How-

---

[11] *Vulgate*, I, pp. 253f; *Le saint Graal*, ed. Hucher, III, pp. 705ff.
[12] The second Sarracinte was originally called Florée, perhaps an indication of the style of her cult.

ever, if she was referred to by some title such as 'the Sweet Lady of Paradise', it is easy to see how a temple dedicated to her could have turned up as dedicated to Our Lady.

## The Perilous Seat

The second way in which Fire from Heaven was manifested was at the Perilous Seat at the Round Table or at that table's precursor and prototype, the Grail Table. The latter was situated on the Giant's Hill, two days journey from Camelot. One Friday Bron and Joseph of Arimathea's son Josephé were sitting at this table with a space between them sufficient for a man to sit in. A certain Moys requested permission to sit there. When he did so he was seized by fiery hands and began to burn like a dry bush.[13]

Much the same happened to a knight called Brumant the Proud. He went to Camelot at Pentecost to demonstrate his valour by sitting in the Perilous Seat, where he was struck by lightning and burnt to ashes in a short time.[14]

The only individuals who were able to sit in the seat with apparent safety were Perceval and Galahad, really the same personage, for the latter seems to have replaced Perceval later in the development of the romances. When Perceval attended Arthur's court at Pentecost the king was fêted by the crowd and had fresh spring herbs – iris and mint – spread before him. He then gave out robes and insignia to the knights and squires. There was jousting at which Perceval, spurred on by Elainne, Gawain's sister, excelled. His success seems to have qualified him as a candidate for the Siege Perilous. He sat in it. The stone split underneath him, shrieked in anguish and there was thunder. He escaped death only because he was descended from a line of holy kings.[15] The shrieking is paralleled in Irish legend by the Lia Fail, the coronation stone at Tara, which indicated in this way a rightful occupant of the throne. Perceval may therefore be supposed to have been elected to the kingship at this point, but it is considerably later in the story that he is to be found established at Corbenic as the Fisher King.[16]

Galahad, like Perceval, sat in the Siege Perilous at Pentecost. He indicated his kingship by drawing the sword from the stone (like Arthur himself), he was dressed in red, because this colour was evocative of fire, and he became in due course king of the holy city of Sarras,[17] where Evalac had earlier held court in a sun-temple. Galahad's story has been heavily edited to make his 'achievement' of the Grail seem like a sublime act of faith. No doubt it was, but not of the Christian faith, for Galahad can clearly be discerned to have been an

---

[13] *Le saint Graal*, ed. Hucher, III, pp. 200/1; Didot *Perceval*, ed. Roach, p. 149.
[14] *Vulgate*, V, pp. 319/20.
[15] Didot *Perceval*, ed. Roach, p. 149.
[16] Didot *Perceval*, ed. Roach, p. 242 line 1902.
[17] E.g. *Morte Darthur*, Malory, bk XVII, ch. 22. 'So they made Galahad king by all the assent of the holy city . . .'.

annual king;[18] he met his end in the presence of the Grail and the terrible lance after exactly a year's rule. When Galahad's spirit left his body spread-eagled on the ground in front of the altar, at the very moment when he 'achieved' the Grail, the watchers saw a great miracle. A disembodied hand came from the sky and took up the Grail and the lance and presented them to a crowned and sceptred being in the heavens, surrounded by angels. This being's flesh and face were scarlet as though he were on fire and Galahad's companions Perceval and Bors had to look away. They were then stunned by a blast of hot wind and lay shattered on the ground.[19]

The editing of this account of the death of a sacrificial victim has failed to conceal the 'fire from heaven' which was seen to have accompanied his end. Though when he first sat in the Perilous Seat he escaped a ritual death, it caught up with him at last, as it did all the others who essayed this 'adventure'.

As soon as Galahad was dead the inhabitants of Sarras wished to elect Perceval as their next king. He wisely declined the offer and became a hermit instead, but he still died in a year and three days.[20] Perhaps there are traces here of the original story which was told of Perceval before Galahad appeared on the Arthurian scene.

## The Adventurous Bed

Three of the principal Arthurian knights – Gawain, Lancelot and Bors – endured the adventure of the 'testing bed' in the Grail castle. The account of Gawain's visit to Corbenic, the most complete of the three, runs as follows:

After failing, despite using all his considerable strength, to pull a woman out of a tub of scalding water, just outside the gate of the castle of Corbenic, Gawain entered and was welcomed. The king, Pelles, being maimed and so unable to walk, was carried into the hall in a litter. Then a white dove flew into the palace with a golden incense burner in its beak, filling the place with sweet odours. All kneeled and prayed. Next a beautiful damsel came from the same room as the dove, carrying above her head the most beautiful chalice ever seen by man. All kneeled as she passed, and when she returned to the room she had come from, the tables had been filled with delicious food. (The bleeding lance, which usually accompanies the Grail, is missing in this version.) All had their fill except Gawain, who failed to eat because he was incapacitated by the great beauty of the girl who carried the Grail. After the meal the rest left but Gawain found the gate firmly shut. A dwarf assailed him with a stick and forecast that he would not leave without being shamed. Gawain then went to the top end of the hall, where he saw one of the richest beds imaginable. Being ready for

---

18 *The Real Camelot*, Darrah, p. 45.
19 *Vulgate*, VI, p. 195n.
20 According to one account, in *Vulgate*, VI, p. 198n.

sleep he was about to lie down on it when a damsel called out: 'If you sleep on it unarmed you will die, for this is the Adventurous Bed.' She showed him armour and he put it on as best he could and sat on the bed. He then heard the most hideous voice he had ever heard, like the voice of the devil. Then a lance came at him with its head all in flames and struck him so fiercely that it penetrated shield and hauberk and pierced his shoulder. Gawain being seriously wounded stayed semi-conscious on the bed having visions of serpents, leopards, battles, thunder and lightning, and of being healed by the Grail. Next, many people came in who seized him by the arms and the feet and the shoulders, carried him out of the hall and tied him to a cart in the middle of the court, where he stayed till dawn. When the sun rose and he recovered consciousness, Gawain found himself in the cart with a beggarly nag between the shafts. Mad with pain and grief he was conducted through the town by a hag with a scourge. Behind followed the hue and cry of minstrels who pelted him with filth, dung and old shoes. When he had been taken out of the town and across a bridge he was released by the old woman, and thought himself the vilest knight in the world.[21]

Bors had a somewhat similar adventure, in which the Grail procession which preceded the hero's ordeal included the lance dripping blood. During a night vigil on the 'bed of Marvels' he was struck by a lance with a fiery point and wounded in the shoulder. There was thunder and lightning and events similar to those in Gawain's adventure, but Bors escaped the cart and seems to have been unharmed at the end of his ordeal.[22] However, he was on another occasion to be found in the cart, followed by a jeering crowd and pelted with ordure.[23] (see p. 79 below for more detail)

Lancelot is twice recorded as being the victim of similar adventures. In one account he came too close to the Grail on its silver table in the Grail castle and felt a fiery wind strike him, which left him unconscious for two weeks.[24] In the other, he was in a castle near the border of Wales and Logres where he was shown the beautiful bed. He slept in it, in spite of having been warned by a damsel that he would be shamed or killed. At midnight the house shook. There was a great noise, as if God thundered. A whirlwind swept through the house, and Lancelot saw a brightness so great he thought the house was on fire. From this brightness came, with great force, a lance burning like hot coals, which merely grazed him but set fire to the bed. After putting out the fire, he calmly went to sleep again[25] and was allright in the morning. Lancelot did endure the shame of the cart and the jeering and pelting, indeed, the title of the story of Lancelot and Guenever is *The Knight of the Cart* but in Chrétien's account the episode of the cart came just before the testing bed.

---

21 *Vulgate*, IV, pp. 343–347.
22 *Vulgate*, V, p. 298.
23 *Vulgate*, IV, pp. 215/6.
24 *Vulgate*, VI, pp. 179–181.
25 *Vulgate*, IV, p. 166.

There are features common to all three testing bed 'adventures' and also to the castration of Kalafes at Corbenic. They are: the place, a pagan cult site, usually the Grail Castle; what Loomis calls 'the attack by the storm god',[26] which is typified by the flaming lance and by thunder and lightning; and the reception of a wound. Although the latter is not castration in the case of Gawain, Lancelot and Bors, and fertility and prosperity are not mentioned, tradition does seem here to have preserved several facets of the dogma that has previously been described.

## The Cart

The three heroes, Gawain, Lancelot and Bors, who encountered the lightning bolt in the perilous bed are the only personages in the first generation of the romances who found themselves in trouble in the demeaning cart, jeered at and pelted with ordure. Indeed, they are almost the only individuals to ride in wheeled vehicles in the whole of the romances. In the romances the normal means of travel for living people not on horseback was a litter. Apart from the few personages mentioned in this section, the only occupants of wheeled vehicles were dead: the corpse of a knight accompanied by a damsel who wore her clothes inside out as a sign of mourning, and the corpse of Raguidel, whose bier was on a cart in a magically propelled boat. Not only the rarity but also the special significance of a cart in the romances has not generally been realised. Its importance was sufficient to give Chrétien's story about the love of Lancelot and Guenever the title *The Knight of the Cart* and in it Lancelot is called the 'knight of the Cart'. Yet the cart does not play a correspondingly important role in the action. True, Lancelot took a ride in a cart on the trail of the captured Guenever when she had been abducted by Meleagant, and he travelled in it to the place where he endured the perils of the Adventurous Bed. However, it is not the ride itself which was noteworthy but the status of the cart, which is said to have been so demeaning as to shame a knightly rider for the rest of his life. At that time a cart was such a frightful object that it was impossible to sit in one without loosing all self-respect and honour. In those days even large towns had only one cart,[27] and when they wished to take a man's life, he was made to mount it and led through the town so that he could be seen by all.[28]

A closer look at the background to cart incidents will show that the carts of the Arthurian court were exclusively occupied by ritual figures. Those who were male and received shameful treatment in the cart are also distinguished by being the only three knights who endured the adventure of the bed. In one instance the bed itself was on wheels; and so not to be distinguished from the

[26] *Celtic Myth and Arthurian Romance*, Loomis, p. 172.
[27] *Le Chevalier de la Charette*, tr. Comfort, p. 274.
[28] *Le Roman en prose de Lancelot . . .*, ed. Hutchings, p. 16.

cart, which seems in this case to have been the place where the hero lay when he was hit by symbolic lightning.

It has been mentioned above that Bors' ride in the cart is entirely dissociated from his adventure in the bed, but it took place on a significant date and was followed by an interesting sequel. The episode occurred when King Arthur was at Carawent in Wales (generally assumed, from the resemblance of the name only, to have been Caerwent in Monmouthshire between the mouths of the Wye and the Usk). Mid-August came round and he was obliged to hold a court and wear the crown, as was the custom at major feasts. On the day of the festival, after mass, he saw a cart approach driven by a fat dwarf with, in the shafts, a horse docked of ears and tail. In the cart was a knight with his hands tied behind his back and with his feet tied to the shafts of the cart. He was wearing a dirty and torn chemise. His white armour was near him and his white horse followed behind, tied by the reins to the cart. Seeing the king the knight exclaimed 'O God, who will deliver me?' at which point all the knights came out of the palace. The king then asked the dwarf what the knight had done to incur such punishment. 'The same as the others', he was told, and the knight could only be released if another took his place. The dwarf then drove through the town below, where the victim was jeered at and pelted with filth and old shoes. Having seen an adventure the king could, as the custom then was, sit down to his dinner.[29]

Later the dwarf returned with a woman in the cart. It was the Damsel of the Lake. The queen also mounted the cart, followed by the king and other knights. It was thus cleansed of its evil reputation.[30]

A cart appeared at King Arthur's court on another occasion, containing 150 heads and in the charge of a damsel, an episode to be discussed in more detail below.[31]

Finally, a cart is mentioned in the 'matter of Britain' on the occasion when Lancelot and a company of knights met a very fine four-wheeled cart covered in rich red samite in which Brangoire's daughter was travelling. She made as much of her child, Bor's son Helain the White, as if he had been the son of God.[32]

The pagan status of the women in the carts is as follows: the Damsel of the Lake is a local parallel of the goddess Diana; Brangoire's unnamed daughter is a daughter of the god Bran; the Damsel of the Cart, who is also the Grail bearer, is daughter of the god Beli under the name Pelles. Thus it will be seen that when carts were not occupied shamefully by battered heroes, they were occupied honourably by 'women' of divine rank. There are other links between the participants in the adventure of the cart. Brangoire's daughter bore

---

[29] *Vulgate*, IV, pp. 215f.

[30] *Vulgate*, IV, pp. 217/8.

[31] See pp. 83f below.

[32] A princess riding in a cart would have been a common occurrence in the Middle Ages. It is only in the special circumstances of the romances, where carts are so rare, that this incident has to be recorded to complete the list.

a son, who was to be a Grail-hero, to Bors, a carted knight. Pelles' daughter bore a son, who was to be a Grail hero, to Lancelot, a carted knight. The pair of carted knights here, Lancelot and Bors, were both brought up by the Damsel of the Lake in her underwater home, Diana's lake.

There is too much symmetry about this group of motifs for them to have been gathered together by chance. Not only did the carted foster-sons of the Damsel of the Lake engender Grail heroes on the daughters of gods, they both had to be persuaded into their beds by enchantments. Yet there is no suggestion that either story has been derived from the other. It can only be supposed that both are independent recollections of the cult associated with our local Diana, an impression which is reinforced by the date. Mid-August corresponds very well with Diana's yearly festival which was on the thirteenth of that month before it was replaced by the Christian festival of the Assumption of the Virgin on the fifteenth.

Looking round outside the local scene, a classical association between Diana and a cart drawn by deer is described by Pausanius.[33] On the annual feast of the huntress goddess Artemis Laphria (Artemis was Diana's Greek counterpart) her virgin priestess rode round Patras in a chariot drawn by yoked deer in a procession of the greatest grandeur. Again in a classical report, the chilling aura of the Arthurian cart is reflected in the description of the chariot in which Nerthus, Mother Earth, was drawn by cows in a triumphal procession through northern Germany. This vehicle inspired 'a mysterious terror and an ignorance full of piety as to what that may be which men only behold to die'.[34]

Archaeology carries our knowledge of the cult of a goddess in a cart even further back in time, perhaps before the classical era. A four wheeled cult vehicle in bronze from Strettweg in Austria, dating from the seventh/sixth centuries BC, has a central female figure carrying a bowl over her head (like the British goddess of the Cart, who in her capacity as Grail bearer carried the Grail over her head in the Grail procession). She is surrounded by horsemen and foot-soldiers to a smaller scale than herself and is obviously a goddess.[35] Nearer home, an undatable carved stone in Meigle churchyard in Scotland was said in 1560 to be of a goddess in a cart drawn by two horses, though so much detail can no longer be discerned. The practice of displaying a cult figure in a cart is also attested from the Iron Age by the remains from Dejbjerg in West Jutland of a most elegant wagon with a throne for a single person.[36] Though there are no remains of carts at Caerwent, we know rather more about the comparable cult practice in this country than can be deduced from the wood and metal dug from the Danish bog. The cart was four-wheeled, as in Jutland, and it had a brilliantly coloured canopy of rich fabric; its occupant was a priestess of the religion of either Bran or Beli; her baby son was part of

33 Bk VII, Ch. 18.
34 Tacitus, *Germania*, Loeb ed. . . . , p. 321.
35 *Gods of the Celts*, Miranda Green, p. 34.
36 *The Bog People*, P. V. Glob, p. 121.

the act, they were worshipped as a pair; he had been engendered by the victor of an annual tournament and would himself grow up to be a sacred king.

There are now enough clues to piece together a probable original for the group of tales about heroes in carts. Uniformity is not to be expected, but there is a surprising conformity between the adventures of the three heroes, except as far as the sequence is concerned. For Gawain, the cart followed the adventure in the bed; for Lancelot, it immediately preceded the bed; and for Bors, it is completely separated from it. The sequence seems to make most sense in Gawain's adventure, where the demeaning ride follows the lightning stroke. It would be quite in line with the general run of the romances for Lancelot's and Bor's adventures to be altered versions of a similar original to Gawain's. Narrators who did not understand the story they were repeating (including Chrétien)[37] sometimes rearranged the motifs in the hope that the story would then make sense to their audience.

Evidently wheeled transport was important early in its history as an adjunct to religious ceremonial. For the 800 years between 1250 BC and 450 BC carts seem not to have been made for heavy duty nor to have been subjected to wear from constant use. During this period they 'occupied a vital cultural role'.[38] The sinister impression created by the cart of our story (particularly in Chrétien's *Le Chevalier de la charrette*) can only be explained if it has been remembered from a period when the cart was a ritual vehicle and capable of exciting feelings of the utmost awe in any beholder.

In the three adventures of carted knights there is conformity to the principles of 'fire from heaven' which have already been discussed. We can probably discount the survival of the hero unharmed. The flaming lance was clearly intended to wound, presumably, by analogy with Kalafes and Pellinor, to castrate. The event occurred on the replacement of a sacred king whose task had been to demonstrate his vigour by engendering a child. The tenure of office of the father might have been for a period of a year or some longer specific period, but a few episodes suggest that in one expression of paganism he was disposed of as soon as the priestess had been served, so his reign was restricted to one night. Bronze Age Scandinavian rock carvings show axe-men with long handled axes at the sacred marriage[39] and, in Malory, Sir Gareth was dragged from his bed, from the very arms of his lover, aptly called 'the lady of the Perilous Castle', and wounded in the thigh with a gisarme – a pole axe.[40] This episode is but one of many violent incidents in Gareth's career and not by any means the last. There is no means of telling if the interpretation proposed is correct, but a glance at the relationships of the principal characters suggests that cult activity is likely, for their relations are all divinities. Gareth's father

---

[37] 'Chrétien rips his sources apart into fragments . . . to inspire his own quite different putting together.' *The Creation of the First Arthurian Romance*, Luttrell, p. 250.
[38] Use of wagon in later prehistory, C. Pare, *Antiquity*, vol. 63, no. 238, 1989, p. 81.
[39] *The Chariot of the Sun* . . ., Gelling and Davidson, revised 1982, p. 28.
[40] *Morte Darthur*, Malory, bk VII, ch. 22.

was King Lot, suggested by Loomis to have been the equivalent in the romances of the Welsh god Lleu, and his brother was the epitome of all Celtic cult heroes, Gawain. Gareth's lover had a brother who was the lord of the Isle of Avalon, and a sister who was called Linet (equivalent to Luned, the moon), otherwise called the Savage Damsel – the Cruel Goddess of the next chapter.

# SEVERED HEADS AND SACRED WATERS

The damsel who was sitting under the oak tree played a significant part in King Arthur's adventure at St Augustine's chapel, notably by asking him to cut off his opponent's head and bring it to her. She later travelled with this macabre trophy to a hermitage,[1] where Gawain found her waiting for the hermit, with the head tied to the saddle-bow of her mule. She was sitting under a tall spreading tree which was beside a spring in front of the chapel. The purpose of her visit was to find from the hermit the whereabouts of a knight who would enable her, by means of the head, to recover a castle which had been stolen from her. Though nominally Christian, what faith the hermit professed is in doubt. He is described as serving the Fisher King who was the guardian of the Grail, rather than the Christian god. On account of his association with the Grail the hermit preserved a youthful appearance, seeming only forty, when he had been a squire and a knight for two score years, followed by over thirty years as a hermit. The same motif of unexpected youthfulness associated with the Grail occurs again[2] in the account of the ancient knights at the Grail Castle, each of one hundred years of age or more but who seemed not over forty. Perpetual youth is a typical piece of pagan wishful thinking, and as a characteristic of the hermit is a pointer to the pagan origin of this episode. The damsel carrying the head prayed before the altar of 'Our Lady' at the hermitage, but she did not discover where the knight who would help her, Perlesvaus (that is, Perceval), was to be found. She was told instead to take the head to the castle of the Black Hermit and there to find the Damsel of the Cart.

That is the last we hear of the unnamed damsel with the single severed head, unless she is the similar damsel carrying the head of Perceval's cousin, who appears later in the story. However, the Damsel of the Cart, whom she was sent to meet, collected heads on a larger scale, and she plays a more significant role in this version of the story of Perceval than is generally realized. She first comes to notice when she arrived at King Arthur's court on a Midsummer Day with two companions, bringing a cart drawn by three white harts. She was beautifully dressed but bald, and she carried her right arm in a

1 *Perlesvaus*, tr. Bryant, pp. 41–3.
2 *Perlesvaus*, tr. Bryant, p. 79.

sling and let it rest on a gold embroidered cushion. She was carrying the severed heads of a king and queen sealed with silver and she had another one hundred and fifty heads in her cart. Her baldness reflected the magical barrenness of the land and it would be cured at the same time as the land was retrieved from its wasted state by the actions of a hero. Meanwhile, her head was covered by a hat of the most sumptuous richness.[3] The reason for the sling and cushion was that she was the woman who carried the Grail in the Grail procession, and she wore her arm in a sling because she had held that most holy object and could not afterwards put her hand to baser uses.[4]

Later the Damsel of the Cart travelled with Gawain on his search for the land of the King Fisherman. They came one day upon a hideous black castle, where 152 black knights carried off the 152 heads on their spear-points. Next, the three damsels of the Cart went to see Perceval, at the home of his mother, the Widow Lady who lived in the second Camelot in the farthest parts of Wales, to warn her of danger from the King of Castle Mortal. Later one of the damsels of the Cart came to warn Perceval, Arthur and Gawain that Perceval's mother was in danger of attack from Aristor, a knight who abducted damsels, married them and killed them after a year. In yet another adventure she took part in with Perceval, the Damsel of the Cart came again to the castle of the Black Hermit. This time the hermit was defeated, and the stolen heads of the king and queen were returned to the damsel. Finally, the Damsel of the Cart took Perceval's mother and sister to Perceval's own most holy castle, which since it held the Grail may be presumed to have been the Grail Castle. The Widow Lady brought with her the body from the chapel near the castle at Camelot in Wales, which seems from a comparison with other similar sepulchres to have been that of Perceval's father.

Although the story of Perceval is presented as if it were the triumph of Christian principles over the forces of evil, there is a good deal in it which may have been recollected from pre-Christian times, particularly the extraordinary importance of severed heads. In this one romance, as well as the damsel at the entrance to the glade and the three damsels of the Cart, there are also Perceval's sister, who has a head thrown into a river; there is the younger maiden of the Tent, who is given Brudan's head to take to Arthur's court; and there is the damsel carrying Perceval's cousin's head in an ivory casket,[5] for whom Perceval restores her castle.[6] The prominence of severed heads in *Perlesvaus* is closely matched by the importance of the young women with which they are so closely linked. These women play significant parts, inciting the heroes to action, guiding, advising, warning and explaining. They are indeed supernatural

3  *Perlesvaus*, tr. Bryant, pp. 33f.
4  *Perlesvaus*, tr. Bryant, p. 54.
5  *Perlesvaus*, tr. Bryant, pp. 229/30 and 234.
6  In *Peredur*, the hero (who corresponds to Perlesvaus in this Welsh version of the story of Perceval) sees his cousin's head carried on a platter by two damsels in a Grail-type procession. *Mabinogion*, Penguin, pp. 226 and 256. Are these two references to Perceval's cousin's severed head descended from a common original?

beings, the Damsel of the Cart, as her other self, the Grail-Bearer, being described as a goddess.[7]

Severed heads have been a feature of religion since the earliest times. The Neolithic causewayed camp at Hambledon Hill had skulls in the surrounding ditch, obviously deliberately set at regular intervals; and skulls were being deposited in the river Thames in the Bronze Age. Severed heads, both as representations and actual human skulls, are often present at sacred sites, particularly watery ones. There are many examples from Britain and Gaul from the centuries immediately before and during the Roman period. Even well after the Romans left, in the sixth century AD, St David was in conflict with a certain Boia, a local pagan chief near the place which is now St David's. Boia's wife[8] one day 'invited her step-daughter, Dunawd, to go with her to the wood of Glyn Hodnant to gather nuts. Presently she sat down and asked the girl to lay her head in her lap so she could dress her hair. When the girl did so, the stepmother cut her throat, and a clear fountain arose in the place where her blood flowed to the ground, which abundantly cured many diseases of mankind, which place the common people call the Martyrium of Dunawd to this day'.[9]

Much the same explanation is given of the holiness of the well at Holywell in Flintshire – that it sprang up one Midsummer Day[10] where a severed head fell to the ground, a saint's on this occasion. Looking at this type of legend in practical terms there is a suggestion that a head was thrown into the spring at its dedication to a deity. There was a real skull in, for instance, the well of the native divinity Coventina in Roman times at Carrawbrough on the Wall, and until quite recent times the water of a Welsh healing well had to be drunk from a human skull for the cure to be considered efficacious.[11]

Against this particular religious background, and given that the legends are a repository of pagan memories, it is easy enough to recognise that some other episodes in the romances reflect the practice of the head cult in distant times. Among them are several in which, as at St Augustine's glade, it is a woman who asks for the head to be cut off. For instance, Lancelot, travelling through the forest, was challenged by a knight whom he fought in a glade. When Lancelot had defeated the other knight, a damsel rode into the glade on a palfrey and begged for the knight's head. Lancelot killed him and gave it to her. She took it, tied it by the hair to her stirrup and rode to an ancient, dried-up well at the end of the glade, into which she impetuously cast the head.[12] There is a trace of the 'reward' theme from the 'challenge' in her

---

7  As gotinne in *Diu Crone*, L. Jillings, p. 188.
8  Boia's wife was responsible for attempting to seduce St David's monks, see Gaz Aroie.
9  *The Holy Wells of Wales*, Jones, p. 41.
10  *Tours in Wales*, Tennant, p. 47.
11  *Pembrokeshire Antiquities*, Rhys, *et al.*, 1897, p. 75.
12  *Vulgate*, IV, pp. 197/8.

behaviour, for she would have married the defeated knight if he had been the victor. In return for the head, this young woman played the part of guardian angel to Lancelot later in the story when he was imprisoned by Morgan le Fay.

Though we are not told her name, this damsel was Meleagant's sister, that is, she was the daughter of Baudemagus, the god Bran in one of his many disguises (see Who's Who). Webster[13] considered her to have been one of those organizing damsels who have already been mentioned.

At the wedding of Arthur and Guenever there was a characteristically obscure Arthurian adventure, in which a white hart rushed into the hall pursued first by thirty couple of black hounds and then by a small white dog, described as a brachet, which bit the hart. The huntress was the Damsel Cacheresse, a title of the Damsel of the Lake, and when her white brachet was seized by a knight she requested the king to have it returned to her. At that moment a knight rode in and snatched away the damsel herself, and the white hart fled away. Merlin explained that these were significant events and could not safely be disregarded. Therefore, Gawain was sent to get back the white hart, Tor to obtain the brachet and Pellinor to bring again the lady and the knight, or else the knight must be slain. Each of these quests resulted in a severed head. Gawain returned with a lady's head tied round his neck by the hair; Pellinor came back with his own daughter Eleine's head that he had found by a spring; and Tor, having defeated Abelin the Proud, the knight who had taken the brachet, cut off his head at the request of an unnamed damsel.[14]

There are other examples of women being involved in beheadings. After Balin (a manifestation of the god Beli) had obtained a special sword at Arthur's court the Damsel of the Lake came in and asked Arthur for Balin's head or that of the girl who had brought the sword, or both (her plea was unsuccessful, Balin cut off her own head and took it away to Northumberland);[15] the nine witches of Gloucester were responsible for cutting off the head of Peredur's (i.e. Perceval's) cousin;[16] and finally, Guenever requested Lancelot to cut off Meleagant's head when this knight who had abducted her had been defeated.

Celtic women were no strangers to violence. According to a Roman authority, Strabo, priestesses cut the throats of large numbers of prisoners and saved the blood in large tubs, presumably for ritual purposes. There is no trace of this particular activity in the romances, but an analysis of the women in the romances who ask for heads to be severed shows that they have several attributes in common. They belong to that group of women whose role in the story is far from passive, which has already been mentioned. Like the damsel under the tree in Arthur's adventure in the glade, they originate, guide, instruct and explain. To take another instance, Perceval (in *Perlesvaus*) has often

---

13 *Guinevere. A study of her Abductions*, Webster, pp. 45/6.
14 Huth *Merlin*, ed. Paris and Ulrich, II, p. 112.
15 Huth *Merlin*, ed. Paris and Ulrich, pp. 213ff.
16 *Mabinogion*, Penguin, pp. 226 and 256.

to be told by the Damsel of the Cart the significance of the events he takes part in, and she shepherds important people, exhorts, and carries news, playing a most important part in the story. The characteristics of the damsels on the list on p. 61 may now be amplified, since one of its members, the Damsel of the Cart, has now been identified with the Grail bearer; and Brangoire's daughter is another passenger in a cart.

## The Characteristics of an Organizing Damsel

(1) She guides, instructs, explains and provides magical aid to the hero when he is in difficulties. This applies to most of the Arthurian damsels so far mentioned.

(2) Her name was a variant of Elaine: this was the name of the Damsel of the Lake (according to Sommer), of Elene/Linet, and of Pelles' daughter (if she was called Elaine) and if so the Damsel of the Cart.

(3) She has a link with watery cult sites: the Damsel of the Lake, Meleagant's sister (though in her case the well was dry), and Lunete, founder of the Thunderstorm Fountain.

(4) She has a link with Diana or Diana's attribute, the moon: the Damsel of the Lake,[17] Brangain, Luned, and Elene/Linet.

(5) She has a close link with severed heads: Diana herself,[18] the Damsel of the Lake,[19] the Damsel of the Cart, the Damsel at the entrance to the Glade, and Meleagant's sister.

(6) She is one of the only Arthurian heroines mentioned as riding in a cart: the Damsel of the Lake, the Damsel of the Cart, and Brangoire's daughter.

(7) She is linked as sister, daughter or lover to the Welsh god Bran, whose severed head was an important talisman: Brangain, who was his sister; Brangoire's daughter; Meleagant's sister, whose father was Bran, as Baudemagus; and Lunete whose lover was a cousin of Bran, as Branduz.

(8) The fact of being an emissary distinguishes some of the organizing damsels from the 'Prize', the woman who, in several classic instances, sent the emissary to get a champion and who was actually fought for and won by the champion. Lunete does not marry Yvain nor Elene the Bel Inconnu. The organizing damsel may seem to be the inferior of the prize, but she is often the prime mover, setting up the system; so the

---

[17] The Damsel of the Lake under her other name of Cacheresse parallels Diana the Huntress; as lover of the Lord of the Animals, she parallels Diana with Faunus; and she inhabits the lake in which Diana's body was thrown.

[18] The Diana of the romances had her head cut off and she was thrown into the lake named after her.

[19] The Damsel of the Lake asked for Balin's head or that of the damsel who provided him with his sword. However, he cut off her own head and took it away with him.

view that she is a mere handmaid may be a mistake on the part of narrators. A distinction between emissary and prize is not always made. At the Perilous Ford and the Tomb in the Glade they are the same person.

The behaviour of the organizing damsels, analysed as above, may seem to be a fairly haphazard collection of characteristics attributed to some or other of seven or eight distinct, or sometimes overlapping, personages. To look at it so fails to take advantage of our knowledge of the nature of the evidence and the nature of pagan divinities. Observation has already shown that oral repetition is likely to leave an incomplete reproduction of the original 'verbal icon'. In spite of this, there are strong links between the various women on the list. As well as those links which have been enumerated here, there is the previously mentioned relationship between Pelles' daughter, Brangoire's daughter and the Damsel of the Lake. The first two both bore sons, who were to be Grail heroes, to protégés of the latter. The Damsel of the Lake and Lunete were cousins. And there is a general association with deities, with Beli (Pelles) as well as his 'brother' Bran, though the link with the latter is the most clearly marked. Perhaps this is not surprising, since he is principally remembered in Welsh legend for his talismanic severed head, and this group of organizing damsels is also closely linked with severed heads. There are in addition several references to enchantment in the affairs of the damsels, which is often in this tradition an indication of divinity. Thus Pelles' daughter and Brangoire's daughter both need the help of magic to get their reluctant partners into their beds, and Brangain provided it for Tristan and Yseult (in the form of a love potion) with the same result.

The association with deities and enchantments suggests the possibility that the composite personage being examined has many of the characteristics of a goddess herself, perhaps linked with Bran and Beli in some sort of pantheon. Just as these two gods are described sometimes as brothers and sometimes with other relationships, so this damsel is daughter of one or the other, or lover of Bran's son or cousin. Such ambiguities of kinship are not unknown in a pantheon. Perhaps she should not be thought of as a composite except in the sense that we can recreate the original by superimposing the multiple images that have survived. We seem to be observing in this group several descriptions of a single goddess in each version of which some of her characteristics are present and some absent. It must be remembered that the local deities of our ancestors were not departmentalized like those of Greece and Rome, but were all-purpose deities, covering all aspects of life and death. A Celtic tribal god or goddess could be invoked at one time for help in time of war, at another in famine or in illness. So it is found that a particular Celtic god may be equated with several different Roman gods in inscriptions on altars during the period of Roman rule.[20] The same principle applied to goddesses. They were not

---

[20] E.g. Ross.

limited to the feminine aspects of life, so there is no inconsistency if they include within their spheres of influence war and hunting as well as sponsoring kingship in general and the kingship of the sacred glade in particular.

It is interesting to note the lack of a specific name for many of the manifestations of this multi-faceted goddess. The personal names of deities were too potent to be uttered, so by-names had to be used. From this follow the descriptive titles by which the members of this group are almost invariably known. The titles 'of the Lake', 'the huntress', 'of the Cart', 'Pelles' daughter', 'Meleagant's sister', 'Brangoire's daughter', 'queen of the Land of Maidens' – are entirely in line with the proposition that a divinity is involved. Even when a name is provided it may be merely descriptive, thus Helen/Elaine may mean shining, entirely appropriate in association with the moon.

To have a single goddess appearing under no less than seven different aliases may seem *embarras de richesse*, but a large number of appearances of the same personage as apparently distinct characters is an exact parallel of the outcome in tradition of the well-established deity Bran and also, as will be seen, of his brother Beli (see Who's Who).

The goddess whose form gleams fitfully through the mists was a divine huntress whose interests lay in the natural increase of the earth in the form of wild vegetation and herds. She was linked with the moon, and several of her names indicate 'brightness' or 'white'. Her consort was Faunus, Lord of the Animals, one of the most primitive of woodland deities, who in this local version would sometimes appear as a stag. She, like Diana at Nemi, was patroness of the sacred glade and provided sovereignty to the incumbent of the position of king of the Glade; but unlike the chaste Diana she was the mother of a god in her personification as queen of Maidenland. This mother and son pair correspond to the divine mother and divine son of Welsh tradition, Modron and Mabon. She was closely linked with water, or in one case perhaps a ritual pit, into which the severed heads she demanded as sacrifices were sometimes thrown. She initiated the system of guarding springs, she provided a human companion for the sacred king, and she also provided a retinue of singing and dancing priestesses, whose joy at the prospect of death by single combat is a feature of the romances. Any sons of the royal union were destined to play roles similar to those of their fathers. When her lover had served his purpose and been replaced his mutilated body was exposed in the cart to the jeers of the crowd. Later her own image would be carried in procession in the same cart.

It may come as a surprise to hear that Guenever, as well as playing the part of the Sovereignty, has several of the characteristics of the protean goddess just described. She was a daughter of Bran (see Who's Who); she was asked by the Damsel of the Lake to ride in the cart; she asked Lancelot to cut off Meleagant's head when the two men had fought for her at a fountain in a glade; and the element 'Guen' in her name means 'white', a colour often associated with cult figures other than challenge knights. There is perhaps some risk in drawing conclusions from the activities of an important figure with a great deal of 'collecting' power, but in so far as these characteristics really belong to Guenever, they tend to confirm the view already expressed that she was a goddess (pp. 68f).

The victim of beheading was of either sex. Most were male, inevitably so, as in the tradition which has survived men are represented as playing more active roles. But as the examples given above show, a significant proportion was female. This includes the Damsel of the Lake, and a similar fate befell her alter ego, Diana, whose head was cut off beside the lake to which she gave her name by being thrown into it.[21]

Did a goddess have a head to lose? There is more than one way of answering this question. The wells at St David's, and Holywell apparently took their names from the head-losing founders. If this was a general rule the skull in Coventina's well would have been regarded as Coventina's own, however non-material she may have been as a water-nymphs. Deities in all mythologies are often spoken of as if they had human characteristics. Their births, marriages and infidelities are a commonplace. But in the romances the emphasis is on real human participants. Thus the head which Pellinor (Beli, again) brought to court was that of the lover of a defeated challenge knight, the Knight of the Glade (Sir Miles of the Launde), who died by the spring he defended; the woman decapitated by Gawain was the lover of the knight he defeated in the fight for the brachet; and the amie of the Proud Soldier was unable to survive the defeat of her man. It could be that the real-life consorts of defeated heroes lost their lives, a mode of death reflected in other episodes (p. 122).

## Rivers, Lakes, Fords and Fountains

In the early days of Christianity many major cult sites may have been taken over by the Church but as it was the nature of paganism to be thinly spread over innumerable local natural features, by far the greater number of them were not built on. Worship at such pagan sites as survived was severely prohibited between the fifth and seventh centuries by church councils at Arles, Rouen, Tours and Toledo which denounced those who offered vows to trees, wells or stones; and there was a requirement for every priest to forbid the worship of fountains. In this country, in the sixth century, the cleric Gildas denounced the old beliefs in mountains, fountains, hills . . . to which the blind people paid divine honour in former times. But some centuries later the church was taking a different view. By AD 1100 or so, bishops were using their authority to sanctify wells. The change of heart seems to have been because

---

21 *The Romance of the Grail*, F. Bogdanov, p. 181; Huth *Merlin*, ed. Paris and Ulrich, II, p. 148.
22 *The Holy Wells of Wales*, F. Jones, pp. 21f.

the people retained their ancient attachment to the wells on account of their supposed magical powers, often in spite of rededication to a Christian saint.[22] The history of the Church thus shows twelfth century examples of the recollection of pagan beliefs, demonstrating that such beliefs had survived into the very period in which the Arthurian source material was collected, and it shows that they had survived with such forcefulness that they were able to deflect the church from outright opposition to a guarded tolerance quite unlike the earlier attitude. It is thus well within the bounds of possibility that the twelfth century oral traditions used by Chrétien and his successors were also carrying recollections of deities, heroes and heroines. These pagan figures were later almost forgotten in a disintegrating Welsh oral tradition which apart from the verses of French poets did not get preserved in written form except for a small and possibly unrepresentative sample.

Watery sites and their associated divinities were very important in Celtic religion. These included springs, rivers, lakes and even boggy ground. Knowledge of these cult sites depends on Roman inscriptions and other written records, on the discoveries of archaeologists, on Christian prohibitions and other responses, and on recorded folklore. Thus it is known that, apart from Coventina's well already mentioned, the following were cult sites sacred to the deities named after them in brackets: the source of the river Seine (Sequana); the hot spring at Bath (Sulis); and the rivers Wharfe (Verbeia) and Ribble (Belisama).[23] And sumptuous deposits in, for example, an inconspicuous small lake called Llyn Cerrig Bach in Anglesey, and of swords in the river Thames, aptly described as 'ritual Excaliburs',[24] show the same sort of veneration. The siting of St David's cathedral in a boggy place on an isolated headland tells a similar story, and countless folk-tales attributing healing and other magical powers to lakes and wells do the same.

The romances have little new to say about the mythology of rivers, except that Perceval threw a cauldron containing human blood into one (p. 130), and not much about lakes. The best known example of the latter type of site is the lake of Diana, so often mentioned in these pages. It took its name from the deposition of her body in the lake. The same link between death and the naming of a watery sacred site is recollected in the case of the Severn, which took its Welsh name from a young woman called Habren who was thrown into the river (with her mother, Estrildis) so that the river should be called by the damsel's name 'whereby it cometh to pass that even unto this day the river in the British tongue is called Habren, which by corruption in other speech is called Severn'.[25]

Only two other lakes deserve mention. There is the lake inhabited by fées

---

[23] *Pagan Religions* . . ., Hutton, p. 154. Mac Cana, *Celtic Mythology* p. 48, adds the rivers Marne (Matrona), Saône (Souconna), and the many rivers whose names derive from the stem 'dev-' meaning simply 'divine'; also the sources had their divinities Aventia (Avenches), Vesunna (Périgeux) and Divona (Cahors, Bordeaux).
[24] *Current Archaeology*, 67, June 1979, p. 251.
[25] *Historia Regum Britanniae*, tr. Evans, bk II, ch. 5.

(that is, supernatural beings) from which, in an alternative version to the sword from the stone, Arthur obtained the sword Excalibur[26] and into which it was eventually returned; and the pool called Estanc Alain, from which Alain le Gros drew out a fish for a ceremonial meal.[27]

Looking at these episodes in more detail, Excalibur, the main feature of the lake of the Fées, is probably best seen as a symbolic weapon representing lightning, in line with the various weapons which represent the lightning bolt in the hands of Jupiter and his congeners – Arthur's enemies were confounded by the bright light shining from this sword.[28] But that is no bar to an actual sword being used in this ritual act. Take away the artistic embellishments from the pages of Malory and his precursors who describe the death of Arthur and the casting of Excalibur into the waters and we may have an account of a specific event which followed the great national cataclysm of the collapse of the Arthurian system after the battle on Salisbury Plain, just as the deposition of the weapons and other prestige articles into the pool in Anglesey may well have been sparked off by the fall of that island, the last bastion of druidism, to the Roman forces.

If this episode from romance really is a record from the past it carries with it the name of the god associated with the sword, Beli[29] and the information that, since the sword was *returned* to the goddess called the Damsel of the Lake, it had been dedicated to her in the first place. That is, it was possibly a ritual weapon from the beginning, not intended for practical use.

The Alain mentioned above as linked with a lake, Alain le Gros, was the first and greatest of the many Alains in the romances. He was a nephew of Joseph and the first guardian of the Grail in this country after his father Bron (Bran).[30] The ceremonial catching of the fish was evidently an event of great importance, because it gave him the title Rich Fisher (or Fisher King), a title which was carried by the line of guardians of the Grail which followed him, continuing through many generations. Alain was (in some accounts) the father of Perceval, and he died at Corbenic on the same day as Kalafes at the time when Josué married Kalafes daughter and became Grail keeper and Fisher King. Alain's name and other characteristics reveal him (see Who's Who) to be a form of Belenus, like Balin and Pellinor who have already been mentioned as linked with watery sites, and also Belyas who appears in this chapter on account of his connection with a fountain.

Fords and other river crossings are common enough sites for 'challenges'. A superficial examination of these incidents might suggest that commercial traffic was concentrated here and sometimes tolls had to be extracted by force. But

---

26 Huth *Merlin*, ed. Paris and Ulrich, I, pp. 196/7.
27 *Vulgate*, I, pp. 250–2.
28 *Morte Darthur*, Malory, bk I, ch. 9.
29 *The Real Camelot*, Darrah, p. 118.
30 The proposition that Bron in the romances owes his origin to the Welsh Bran has been put forward by Newstead, Loomis etc. See West, *Prose Index*.

in the romances, the details show something different was involved. The Thorntree Ford (p. 30), for instance, was associated with Midsummer Day and other aspects of paganism, including the continuation of the custom. The description 'entries' for some of these river crossings which are at boundaries, and their defence by the ruler of the country they lead into, gives a clue as to their significance. The Pont or Chaucie (i.e. causeway) Norgalois, leading into Sorelois, is a case in point. It was the scene of a challenge leading to the continuation of the custom (p. 56). Its guardian was Belinans, a name also used by the King of Sorgales, suggesting that the king defended his country in person at a particular place on its boundary. Confirmation of this view comes from an incident in the *Mabinogion* in which Pwyll and Hafgan fought their year-end battle, by which the kingship of Hafgan's country was decided, at a ford thought by Loomis to have been on the boundary of their two kingdoms.

In contrast to the relatively small number of references to rivers (except for river crossings) and lakes, the romances are full of accounts of events at 'fountains' as springs are always called in the French texts. In particular, springs are the staple of the 'challenge' theme. They were generally defended on behalf of a female supernatural being of some sort, a nymph or fée. Quite apart from the 'challenge', springs were widely linked with this sort of local divine personage in popular thought. 'The people who lived in the forest said they had seen very beautiful women at the fountain of the Fées under a sycamore tree and as they were uncertain of their origin they called them fées'.[31] In spite of their beauty, these fées were no pretty fairies with gossamer wings. Like Celtic goddesses in general a fountain fée combined all aspects of divinity and, as we have seen, was just as often to be found demanding the death of her devotees as she was to be invigorating her territory by sexual activity with them (in the form of a human proxy, of course).

Chrétien de Troyes' story of Yvain, with versions deriving from it or influenced by it, is the most complete surviving description of a spring cult. The owner, Laudine, the Lady of the Fountain (the Countess in the Welsh version), conferred territorial rights on her consort, the defender for the time being. He wore black for the task, and could be challenged by throwing a cup of water from the spring on to a stone slab beside it. This was a rain-making charm and produced a storm, heralded by thunder and lightning. Midsummer Day was particularly associated with this system. The analysis in The Challenge enables several pagan themes to be discerned in this short account. Also, the lady of the Fountain's name is Laudine, which seems likely to be derived from the French l'undine, meaning a water-spirit – an exact description of her role.[32]

The origin of the challenge at the fountain is described in two ways. In one it is attributed to Merlin, who is said to have made a chapel over a small perron and to have provided a basin, and to have made a spell so that no knight errant could throw water from the basin without it producing thunder and

---

31 *Vulgate*, IV, p. 305.
32 See Lothian in Gazetteer.

lightning.[33] In the other, Merlin himself says that it was Lunete who made it. In the account of an incident which took place on the way to the fountain there is a whimsical description of a deity which may very well be authentic. It does not seem to have sprung from the polished pen of a court poet. A traveller taking the route to the fountain met Merlin, strangely transformed into a herdsman. He was in a great clearing in the forest, on a bank by a ditch close to an old mossy oak. He was dressed in great shaggy skins, neither black nor white but seemingly wolf skins. He was lord of all the animals of the forest and he summoned stags, deer and bucks and all manner of other wild beasts to pasture there. They were entirely under his command, and when he cried out in a rage they dare not eat without his permission. As it was raining a little he used one of his enormous ears as an umbrella and wrapped himself up in the other, waiting for the traveller. When he came, Merlin told the traveller that the beasts drank at a nearby fountain which was guarded by a friend. No one dared throw water on to a perron from a basin which was attached to the 'sycamore' beside the fountain. The guardian was a brave and hardy knight whose amie was Lunete, who had arranged for the fountain to be guarded for ever, in the same way as it was guarded at that time. The fountain could be visited between three and nine o'clock in the morning.[34]

In other versions of this incident in the romances the figure represented by Merlin is a black giant and his ugliness and capriciousness are mentioned. The place is more obviously a cult site, for the ditch and the bank with its ancient oak are replaced by a mound in a clearing; and the figure is more obviously a divinity, for the animals bow down before him. And in a Welsh version the corresponding figure has one eye in the middle of his forehead and only one leg.[35] He shares these odd features with his Irish equivalent, the Bachlach.[36] It seems likely that the recollection of a deity lies behind these personages.[37][38]

Merlin went on to say that when he was first acquainted with Niniane she had a cousin of great beauty, who was wise, skilful and religious. She was friendly with a brave knight who was a cousin of Branduz of the Isles (lord of Dolorous Gard and the brother of Mabon). Branduz's cousin desired love from the beautiful Lunete. She made it a condition that he should set up the fountain in Broceliande, with a chapel above and a small perron and a basin, and

---

[33] Godefroy, under foudre.

[34] *Vulgate*, VII, pp. 124–6.

[35] *Mabinogion*, Penguin, p. 196.

[36] I. L. *Foster in Arthurian Literature in the Middle Ages*, ed. Loomis, p. 197.

[37] The characteristic of being one-legged and one eyed is shared by the god Lugh, *Celtic Mythology*, Mac Cana, p. 58; Odin also was one-eyed, *Scandinavian Mythology*, Davidson, p. 31.

[38] It is interesting to see that although the Welsh *Owein* is generally regarded as closely resembling Chrétien's *Yvain* (e.g. *Mabinogion*, Penguin, tr. Ganz, p. 192) it contains in this episode an authentic piece of mythology which is missing in the French version. Perhaps the Welsh redactor had access to a common original version which provided the one-eyed, one-legged giant who had been tidied up by Chrétien for his more sophisticated audience. A similar explanation would account for the hart's head given to Enid as a prize, a barbaric object replaced by Chrétien with a kiss.

made a spell so that if any knight errant cast water from the basin on the perron there would be thunder and lightning. She then inaugurated the jousting custom.[39]

The mythological background of watery cult sites has now widened to include the following divinities: Lunete, whose name suggests she represented the moon; the Lord of the Animals, equivalent of the classical Faunus, whose part is played by Merlin; the Damsel of the Lake, who arranged to meet Merlin at a fountain on Midsummer Eve; Branduz who is a form of Bran; and Mabon who is the Welsh god of that name. Lunete may have been religious after her fashion, but her religion was certainly not Christianity.

Other fountains have links with paganism: at that of Terrican of the Deceptive Forest the trees were pines, three of them. The spring gushed from an arch, through a silver tube, on to a marble slab and thence into a lead vessel as big as a barrel.[40] Terrican, a black knight, had defeated sixty knights before being killed by Lancelot in single combat at the spring, like Belyas, another black knight who defended a spring. The pagan significance of Terrican's fountain, apart from its being a clear-cut example of the 'challenge' theme, is underlined by the spring being decorated with leaves and pine branches,[41] linking it with vegetative abundance. Terrican is not a well-known character in the 'matter of Britain'. As well as the combat with Lancelot, his castle was a meeting place for knights on St Magdalen's day, July 22nd, and his brother was Karados of the Dolorous Tower, but otherwise nothing is known of him unless, by a slight and not improbable variation of the name, he is really the 'Sarrassin' god Teruagant whose name sounds much the same. We would be on rather surer footing in assigning divinity to Belyas, whose name is so close to Beli, and who with his brother Briadan has been suggested by Loomis[42] to have been yet another of the Beli/Bran pairs (see Who's Who).

Trees and springs are associated with many other challenge episodes. The instances given here have been chosen because they once again link springs and the challenge theme with the names of gods.

By no means all meetings at springs involve fighting. Sometimes the hero comes by chance upon his fairy lover bathing in a fountain,[43] an invitation he, unlike St David's monks (see Gaz. Aroie), is unable to resist. And there is an interesting group of incidents in which the residents are often women on their own, perhaps with a dwarf as a servant but usually with no knight present. For instance, three knights travelling in the adventurous forest of Aroie were

---

[39] *Vulgate*, VII, pp. 125–6.
[40] *Vulgate*, V, pp. 89/90, and p. 205.
[41] The earliest reference to well-dressing is said to be in 1350, when the well at Tissington in Derbyshire was decorated in thanksgiving for the protection its clear waters had given the inhabitants of the place against the plague (*Well-Dressing*, Womack). That this was no new idea but a recollection from a pagan past is strongly suggested by this earlier reference in a thoroughly pagan setting.
[42] West, *Prose Index*.
[43] *Elucidation*, ed. Thompson, pp. 43/4.

guided to the Adventurous Fountain where 'adventures' (which according to the view expressed here imply ritual activity of some sort) were sure to occur. In a deep rocky valley there was a great fountain set off by noble trees. Under the trees sat three damsels whose ages were fifteen, thirty and seventy, the latter of whom always wore her white hair loose under a golden circlet. The damsels offered to lead the knights to the adventures for which they were searching, and all were to return to the spring in exactly a year's time at mid-day.[44] In what follows, the significant features seem to be the Perron of the Stag, which was a notable landmark connected to the marvels of the Grail, and the Rock of the Maidens, where Merlin had set twelve prophesying damsels who were, as Gawain and le Morholt found, in spite of the name of the place, not at all dedicated to maidenhood.[45]

A somewhat similar scene to that at the Adventurous Fountain met another travelling knight, Guerrehes, who came to a fine meadow in the forest in the middle of which was the most beautiful fountain in the world, which gushed out at the foot of a 'sycamore'. Under the tree sat three damsels, of over sixty years of age, about forty, and of under twenty. They had spread a cloth on the grass and were eating venison pasties. There were no men there except a dwarf who served them from a silver cup. They arose to greet the strange knight and invited him to eat, which he did after washing.[46] The same alfresco theme is repeated with other errant knights. In one instance the knight came upon a fountain in a meadow where two damsels and a dwarf were eating venison pasties under two elms; they invited him to eat and the dwarf gave him water to wash before he did so.[47] In another, on a hot day, as if it were the festival of St John, the traveller came upon a beautiful meadow. Under the shade of two sycamores two damsels and a knight had spread a white cloth upon the green grass. They invited him to join them. He washed his hands and sat down.[48] In yet another instance the two damsels with their squire were sitting under two elms eating venison. A fight occurred shortly after with the black giant Mauduit.[49]

The first episode in which there are three 'damsels' can reasonably be argued to represent a visit to the cult site of a triple goddess.[50] Triplication of a divinity is 'absolutely fundamental to Celtic mythology.'[51] Representations in stone of triple goddesses occur in Britain. For instance, the native divinity Coventina of the spring at Carrawbrough appears as a triple being in one carved representation. There is some doubt about the sort of separation of

44 *The adventures of Gawain etc*, ZRP 47 1913, ed. Sommer, pp. 12–14; Huth *Merlin*, ed. Paris and Ulrich, II, pp. 245/7.
45 *The adventures of Gawain etc*, ZRP 47 1913, ed. Sommer, pp. 61f. The eldest of the damsels was the Damsel of the Lake.
46 *Vulgate*, V, p. 15.
47 *Vulgate*, V, p. 305.
48 *Vulgate*, V, p. 71.
49 *Vulgate*, V, p. 133.
50 *The Real Camelot*, Darrah, p. 127.
51 *Pagan Celtic Britain*, Ross, p. 241/2.

divine duties which may have occurred in triplication. At the spring in the forest of Aroie and in the alternative version given above the division seems to have been into three phases of female sexuality, each figure presumably with her appropriate sphere of influence in promoting the well-being of her devotees.

As might be expected, narrators have strung these episodes on the adventurous life-stories of well-known heroes. There would be little to gain by naming those involved because of the possibility that the names of the original actors have been replaced. But there is one case in which watery cult sites are so consistently linked with one name, or rather, family, that the link may be significant. It so happened that a certain King Lancelot (Sir Lancelot's grandfather) had his head cut off when he was visiting a hermit in the Perilous Forest. Since the event took place on Easter Day and the severed head fell into a spring,[52] we can reasonably guess that this was a ritual act. This impression is strengthened by the story that the well then began to boil and it was prophesied that it would continue to do so until Sir Galahad (Sir Lancelot's son) came to quench it. There are other links between this family and sacred waters. An earlier Galahad, King of Wales and son of Joseph of Arimathea had been christened at a spring;[53] and Sir Lancelot himself was christened at 'the fountain stone'. He was actually named Galahad then and only learnt the name Lancelot after he had proved himself to the Queen of Maidenland by killing an aggressive neighbour of her son Mabuz.[54]

What all this adds up to is a long list of watery associations for the Lancelots and the various Galahads, in addition to Lancelot's upbringing by the Damsel of the Lake, which gave him his name, 'of the Lake'. Lancelot occupies a strange position in the romances since he is a major hero yet has no Welsh original. He appears to have usurped Gawain's position of premier hero during the development of the legends, much as Galahad has usurped Perceval's. For this reason, Lancelot has often been stated to have been entirely a creation of poetic imagination. If this were so, it is improbable that such a consistent set of pagan associations would have been provided for him by narrators largely unaware of the pagan nature of the material they were using. The name Lancelot may be a twelfth century French invention, but the pagan characteristics of the underlying character hang together. He was brought up in an enchanted palace under a lake by a fay; he became king of Dodone by defeating a water-fay's father at a well (p. 43); he cut off a knight's head to be thrown into a well; he was lowered into a well after a defeat;[55] and, though he may not have had his own severed head thrown into a well, his grandfather certainly did.

---

[52] *Le Saint Graal*, ed. Hucher, pp. 303/4.
[53] *Le Saint Graal*, ed. Hucher, p. 500.
[54] *Lanzelet*, tr. Webster and Loomis, p. 93.
[55] *Vulgate*, V, p. 155.

Although there is a strong streak of cruelty in the nymphs of Arthurian springs they were also remembered with affection on occasion. The goddesses gave as well as taking away, and their replacement by another cult seems to have been regretted, as the following account demonstrates.

Before the land of Logres became dead and deserted there used to come out from the wells at all times of day a most beautiful damsel who carried a cup of gold in her hand and provided larded meats, pasties and bread for the refreshment of travellers. She was accompanied by another damsel with a towel. Together they took delight in serving travellers with the foods of their choice.

Unfortunately a certain King Amangons failed in his duty of protecting the damsels and forced one against her will and took her cup. His action was copied by his vassals, who as a result drove the damsels away, so that they no longer provided refreshment for visitors to the wells.

The effect of this sacrilege was to bring devastation on the land. The wells disappeared, the trees bore no leaves, the meadows and flowers dried up and the waters diminished. Never again could be found the court of the Rich Fisher, which had made the land resplendent with precious metals, costly furs and fabrics, and other luxuries.[56]

---

[56] *The Elucidation*, ed. Thompson, vv. 29–98.

# HEALING BLOOD
# AND THE DOLOROUS STROKE

When the organizing damsel at St Augustine's chapel told Arthur that the blood of the knight who had wounded him would heal his wound, she voiced a widely held opinion, no doubt justified more by the desire for revenge than by any previous success in the use of this treatment. The same motif is apparent in the recipe for healing a maimed king in *Perceforest*, that he should be anointed with ointment made from the marrow of the tusk of the boar which had wounded him in the thigh (shades of Adonis);[1] and it appears again in the stories recounted below of the adventures of Balin. But there is, from the point of view of paganism, another significant aspect of this theme in the romances, namely, that the blood should be that of a sacrificial victim. The prime example is that of the healing of another maimed king, also, wounded 'between the thighs', by blood from the Holy Grail, but before dealing with sacrificial victims, let us examine some of the many attempts to heal by the application of blood.

As usual, not all accounts of healing blood conform to a standard pattern. In the case of the wounded Agravain, a son of Lot, King of Orkney, the cure was a helmetful of blood from Gawain (his brother),[2] or Lancelot,[3] in both instances obtained by a damsel. Gawain was fighting several knights for possession of a damsel – 'Gain me,' she cried – but the odds of ten to one proved too great, so she took him prisoner and ransomed him for the blood The theme of healing blood has been used merely to provide an adventure story.

A more interesting episode is the supposed healing of Joseph of Arimathea's son, Josephé, who was the first 'bishop' of the Grail cult in Britain. He had been struck in the thigh by a lance cast by an angel with a face as red as burning lightning.[4] The head broke away from the shaft and remained embedded in the wound, which could not be staunched. This happened during the conversion to the Grail religion of the inhabitants of Orcaus, a city belonging

1 *Perceforest*, pt. II, ed. Roussineau, pp. 1178 n. 707/505 and 1175/6 n. 670/589
2 *Vulgate*, III, pp. 314/5.
3 *Vulgate*, III, p. 405.
4 *Vulgate*, I, p. 77.

to King Evalac of Sarras. When the head of the lance was eventually taken out
it was regarded as a talisman and was kept with the Grail. Later, after Evalac
and the Sarrassins had been 'converted', an angel in white took the headless
lance from the ark which held the Grail and reinserted it into Josephé's
wound. When the spearhead was withdrawn and put in a box it spurted gouts
of blood until the container was filled. The angel used this blood to cure
Josephé's wound and also the blindness of a certain Nascien, which had been
a divine punishment for too close an approach to the Grail.[5] Evalac (of the sun
temple and the goddess-dolly, renamed Mordrains on conversion to the Grail
cult), suffered the same misfortune of being wounded between the thighs,[6] so
earning the title of 'Maimed King', in the same fashion as the evangelizer who
converted him. Such seems to have been the way of the Grail religion.
Evalac/Mordrains remained in this unenviable state until 'cured' much later
by Galahad by the application of blood from the Grail.[7]

Another instance of supposed healing by blood, closely linked with pagan
themes and characters, occurred when Balin (who is argued in Who's Who?
below to have shared his name with the god Belenus and the Welsh ancestor
deity Beli) was travelling with a damsel. They came to a well-sited castle
called Castle Felon in a valley. There the damsel was asked to undergo the
custom of the castle, which was that all damsels passing must bleed a dish of
blood in order to heal the lady of the castle, who was suffering from leprosy.
She could only be cured by the blood of a virgin who was the daughter of a
king and queen. The damsel agreed in spite of the risk of death. Unlike the
occupants of a cemetery reserved for the victims of this treatment, she survived, but the lady was not healed and the custom continued.[8] It was the
blood of Perceval's self-sacrificing sister which is said eventually to have
cured this lady, but at the expense of her own life. Her body was put in a boat
which floated without human guidance to the holy city of Sarras.[9] There she
was buried in the Spiritual Palace,[10] where Galahad later achieved the Grail
and was himself buried.[11]

During Balin's travels a knight who had been put in his safe-keeping had
been treacherously slain by one Garlan, a knight who could be invisible at will.
The damsel with whom Balin was travelling when they came to Castle Felon
had been the lover of the dead knight and she had been appointed to lead
Balin on a quest which would lead to the revenge of her former lover. When
they had travelled to such a distance from Camelot that the language had
changed so much they could scarcely understand what the people said, they
met a hospitable lord whose son had received an incurable wound from this

---

5  *Le Saint Graal*, ed. Hucher, II, pp. 307f.
6  *Le Saint Graal*, ed. Hucher, III, p. 492–4; p. 00 above.
7  *Vulgate*, VI, p. 185.
8  *Le Roman de Balain*, ed. Legge, pp. 65f.
9  *Vulgate*, VI, pp. 168–73.
10  *Vulgate*, VI, p. 194.
11  *Vulgate*, VI, pp. 187/8.

same invisible Garlan and could only be cured by Garlan's blood. The lord knew where Garlan was to be found and took Balin and the damsel to the court of Garlan's brother, Pellehan, King of Listenois, who was holding a great festival on a Sunday at the castle of the Perilous Palace.[12] There was a condition of entry that every knight should bring his wife or lover, so Balin and the damsel went in, leaving the lord outside. During the meal, Garlan insulted Balin, who killed him with a blow of his sword. 'Host, now you can have Garlan's blood to heal your son', he shouted. Then the damsel gave him the shaft of the spear used to kill her lover, which she had been carrying about with her, and he thrust it through Garlan's corpse from side to side.

In the uproar that followed, Balin's weapon was knocked from his hand, and he ran through the palace searching for another, pursued by King Pellehan. Eventually he came to an exceptionally fine room without parallel for beauty anywhere in the world. In it was a silver table on three pillars. In the middle of the table was a vessel of silver and gold. Over this a lance *hovered upright*, without any support. A voice called out that it would be sin to touch the lance, but he paid no heed, seized the lance and struck Pellehan *through both thighs*. Balin then withdrew the lance and replaced it over the vessel, where it stayed upright as before. The result of this blow – the Dolorous Stroke – was that the palace collapsed and the kingdom became barren and was afterwards known as the Waste Land or Terre Foraine, and would remain in that condition until the maimed king was healed.[13]

In this episode the vessel over which the lance was suspended was the Grail, but, as is often the case, the whole story has not quite been told. The objective of that particular configuration, with the lance over the Grail, was that the blood from the lance should drip into the vessel. This is made quite clear in several other instances, such as the initiation ceremony for the Grail quest, at Pelles' castle, when an angel held the bleeding lance over the holy vessel so that the blood dripped into it. The blood from the lance was put to ritual use as follows. It was this blood, which dripped into the Grail from the lance (said by Christianizing narrators to have been the lance with which Christ had been pierced on the cross!)[14] which Galahad later used to anoint the Maimed King's wounds, so, it is said, healing him.[15]

That the Dolorous Stroke took place on a Sunday has no relevance to Christianity. The events described in the last few pages, in which the victim is struck by a burning lance or by a lance propelled by a supernatural being with a face of fire, are often accompanied by thunder. Although it is not so in the case of the Dolorous Stroke, this event is evidently one of a category of visitations resulting in castration and barrenness in which the stroke represented

---

[12] *Le Roman de Balain*, ed. Legge, pp. 67ff.
[13] *Le Roman de Balain*, ed. Legge, pp. 70ff and *The Romance of the Grail*, Bogdanow, pp. 242ff. Where in italics in Bogdanow only.
[14] *The Romance of the Grail*, Bogdanow, pp. 253–5.
[15] *Vulgate*, VI, pp. 189/91.

lightning. A supernatural origin for lightning is a common enough aspect of mythology. Zeus and Thor, and some less familiar gods, all wielded the levin. There is a possibility that Balin did so too, if he can be equated with Beli. The reason for believing Beli to have been a lightning god is that Arthur's sword Excalibur, which routed his enemies by the brilliance of the light it cast, was called in Welsh 'Caledvwlch', a name that has been explained as meaning the sword of Beli.[16] As well as the link with lightning some of the personages and events that have been mentioned are associated in other ways with heavenly phenomena: Evalac with the sun temple at Sarras; and the Celtic god Belenus, whose name resembles Balin, was associated by the continental Celts with the sun. Looking further afield, Gawain's strength increased with the power of the sun; Mabon is consistently equated in epigraphy with Apollo;[17] and Lunete, whose name clearly means moon, originated the thunderstorm fountain. There was no marked departmentalization in Celtic mythology, unlike the Mediterranean pantheons where lightning and the sun were the distinguishing symbols of different deities.

It seems that the result of the Dolorous Stroke was twofold in pagan eyes. Castration of the sacred king would create the magical barrenness of his land (unless, of course, he had been providentially replaced at the right moment) and it would provide talismanic blood for magical purposes. The Grail was the vessel in which the blood of the victim was collected, a fact which twelfth century attempts to assimilate the Grail stories to Christian dogma have failed to conceal. The Grail was supposed to have other magical properties, still to be examined, but consideration of what went into it and what came out of it leads to the inescapable conclusion that its main function was as a receptacle for the blood of a human victim.

Sometimes the blood is said to have been applied to the wound in the expectation of a cure, but more often the contents of the cup of blood is referred to as a 'host', that is, the consecrated food of the Eucharist, and sometimes specifically as being drunk. This aspect of paganism is referred to in more detail on p. 134 below.

There are two other events described as the Dolorous Stroke. In one the victim was Lambor, King of Terre Foraine, slain by Varlan, King of Wales, who himself also died for the sin of handling the sacred sword with which the blow was struck. This event took place in a boat, and the weapon was a sword, not a spear, but the result was the same – from it arose such a great destruction in the two countries that they never after repaid labourers for their toil; there was no corn or other crops, trees would not bear fruit nor rivers fish; from this the land of the two countries, Wales and Terre Foraine, was called the Waste

---

[16] *Early Irish History and Mythology*, O'Rahilly, pp. 67–9; *The Real Camelot*, pp. 116/8.
[17] It has been stated that there is no trace in the Irish or Welsh literatures of any deity associated with the sun. As far as Mabon is concerned, the deity has been remembered but the link with the sun has been forgotten except for classical epigraphy.

Land.[18] In the other it was King Pellinor who came by chance upon a boat when travelling towards Ireland. In it he found a sword which he drew from its scabbard and he was immediately smitten through the thighs by a spear which struck him without human agency.[19] The change of scene to a ship, of the weapon to a sword, and the death of Varlan, as opposed to wounding, do not entirely invalidate comparison with the stroke struck by Balin. The principle that the wholeness of a sacred king was necessary for the prosperity of his realm has been expressed for the same kingdom as in the other version, there called Terre Foraine in Wales, and for Lambor, the father of Balin's victim Pellehan, but expressed in an entirely different fashion. It is a likely outcome of oral tradition that a vigorous original should survive by more than one route, giving rise to what seem different stories but which nevertheless encapsulate the same basic motifs in modified forms.

The Dolorous Stroke was a critical event in the Arthurian story. It heralded the Adventures of Logres – a new sort of paganism which began at the moment the fatal blow was struck – and it marked the end of a previous system – it coincided with the death of Merlin at the hands of the Damsel of the Lake and at the same time the torches which Merlin had contrived to burn to mark Midsummer Day were miraculously extinguished.[20] In this episode there is a faint but clear trace of a change which actually took place in prehistory. The emphasis on the position of the sun on the horizon, which characterized the system which produced New Grange and the bluestone circle at Stonehenge, was at some stage replaced by something new – Merlin's defeat by the Damsel of the Lake parallels a change to more emphasis on watery cult sites which actually took place during the Bronze Age.

The descriptions of these strange events tell of several personages with similar names. There is Pellehan (alternatively Parlan or Pelleans), King of Listenois; there is Pellinor, who was also King of Listenois; there was a second Pellinor[21] who yet again was King of Listenois. Pellehan and Pellinor were entitled Maimed King, and the Maimed King is sometimes called Pelles, who was Pellehan's son, Lambor's grandson, and brother of one of the Pellinors and cousin of the other. One of these Pellinors resided at the Grail Castle, like Pelles, and Pellehan was healed there by Galahad. The extraordinary way in which the misfortunes of the wound between the thighs and its concomitant, the devastated land are concentrated in this one family begs for an explanation. The analysis is continued in the Gazetteer under Listenois.

In two of the events maiming takes place in a ship. Since in certain scenes depicted in Scandinavian rock-engravings ships seem to be the scene of cult activities, there is a possibility of a correspondence between archaeology and a story from romance. And so there is in the account of the last voyage of

---

[18] *Vulgate*, VI, p. 145ff.
[19] *Vulgate*, VI, p. 150.
[20] Huth *Merlin*, pp. 262/5.
[21] See *Prose Index*, West.

Perceval's sister to the place of her burial – the Spiritual Palace in the holy city of Sarras. Just like the better known 'Lady of Shalott' (based by Tennyson partly on the story of the Damsel of Escalot in a French Arthurian romance), she made her last voyage before interment by boat. Is this a recollection of the burials in boat shaped coffins which took place in the Bronze Age? Can the same question be asked of Arthur's departure in a boat to an Otherworld island, accompanied by three goddesses? We shall never know but there is an intriguing possibility of the survival of what was (as far as the Celtic west is concerned) the memory of yet another Bronze Age custom.

PART TWO

FURTHER ASPECTS OF PAGANISM
IN THE ROMANCES

# THE BIRTHS, LIVES AND DEATHS OF
# HEROES AND HEROINES

The adventure at St Augustine's chapel has introduced many of the main strands of British paganism, but it by no means tells the whole story. To do that it is necessary to follow the whole course of the lives of 'heroic' human participants and to make a more detailed study of the various deities involved. That is the concern of this section of the book.

## Ancestry

The system of challenge knights and tournaments which was used to select heroes seems to have assured that the selection was based on merit alone and not birth, where 'merit' may be taken as fighting skill. However, heroes frequently claim descent from deities. Perhaps entry into the competitions of arms was restricted to priestly clans who regarded themselves as having a special relationship with divinities; or the package received by a winner might have included the acquisition, late in life, of divine ancestry. For whatever reason, the personages who are described as the parents of heroes and heroines generally seem to have been gods and goddesses, a feature of the tradition which it will be interesting to explore. There is a difference here from the Welsh royal houses of the Middle Ages who also claimed descent from deities. For these petty kings it is an ultimate ancestor, many generations back, who is Beli or Anna (mother of the Virgin Mary) or Aballac. For the hero of romance it is generally the immediate parent.

To examine this relationship involves defining the types of legendary beings concerned. Who, for instance, qualifies as a hero or heroine? They are easy enough to recognize but difficult to define. The majority of the personages who might generally be considered as being in this category, as will be seen, can be linked with a deity in one way or another.

To arrive at such a conclusion involves another dividing line. As well as deciding which personages are 'heroic', we have to decide which figures in the romances are of divine origin. A number of these have already been mentioned. Their status has been decided in three ways: either by a specific description as a deity; behaviour recognized as appropriate to a deity; or on the appearance of their names as deities in the Celtic or classical traditions.

One of the most prominent gods in the romances is Bran. A glance at the *Index of Proper Names* shows a surprising number of names which begin with 'Bran-'. There are also some names which have -bran as their last syllable and some in which the name has been twisted into forms such as Uriens and Ryons. These extraordinary variations have been followed through in Helaine Newstead's *Bran the Blessed in Arthurian Romance*. Her research was made entirely into Bran as a literary character in the romances and places no emphasis on paganism. But that aspect of Bran's original character can be discerned both in Welsh legend and in the romances. The various forms of Bran[1] are almost all described as 'kings' – for instance, the following: Brangoire, whose unnamed daughter was a heroine; Ban, whose sons Lancelot and Hector were heroes, and so on. A substantial proportion of the list of heroes and heroines can be categorized as related to Bran. Amongst the better known there are, in addition to those mentioned above: Lionel, Bors, Lore of Branlant, Meleagant, and Meleagant's unnamed sister.

The next group of heroes who seem to be descended from a god is the family of Lot, who is identified by Loomis as equivalent to the Irish god Lug and to other 'kings' of romance, such as Luce, who seem to have represented light. It is probably not an accident that Lot was buried in a chapel dedicated to St John. Lot's family of heroes and a heroine includes Gawain, Guerrehes, Gaheriet, Mordred, one of the Elaines, Agravain, and in a second generation Gawain's son Guinglain, hero of the Bel Inconnu group of stories.

Another substantial group is formed by the descendants of Beli. Beli is one of those names which have in the course of repetition diverged until it is represented by a number of apparently distinct individuals.[2] The process is admirably illustrated by the list of Maimed Kings in West's *Index of Proper Names in French Arthurian Prose Romances* under the heading Roi Mahaignié (the Maimed King). These are: Pellehan, Pelleans, Pelles, Evalac, Pellinor, Parlan and Alain de l'Ile en Listenois. These kings, mostly closely related and with overlapping characteristics, are tied together by being 'maimed', that is they were mutilated sacred kings, and several of them are credited with being father of Perceval. As with the spread of names beginning Bran-, the Pel-names indicate the name of the common original. For reasons to be gone into later, this is likely to have been Beli/Belenus, whose initial 'B' has been altered at a language boundary to 'P', a phenomenon which is common enough on the Welsh border. In Alain the initial consonant has been lost altogether; again, this is not without parallels.[3] The list of maimed kings above can thus be

---

1    See Who's Who below for more details.
2    See Who's Who below for more details.
3    *The Grail, from Celtic Myth to Christian Symbol*, ed. Loomis, p. 234. Bruce and other scholars have pointed out that 'proper names in manuscript transmission sometimes lose their initial letter.' E.g. Morgan becomes Argante in Layamon.

regarded as consisting entirely of variants of a single pagan original. There are a dozen or so descendants of Pelles/Pellinor/Alain including Perceval and his sister Dandrane; 'Elaine' (Pelles' daughter) and her son Galahad; Lamorat; Florée and her son Guinglain (also a descendant of Lot); Agloval; and Tor.

A few other heroes who fall outside these three family groups are linked in one way or another with easily recognizable deities. Examples are: Mabonagrein with Mabon; Girflet the son of Do, Don or Doon (by his name) with Gilfaethwy, one of the children of the goddess Don; Yder son of Nut with Nuada; and Karados brother of Terrican with Teruagant. Two of these, Mabonagrein and Girflet, though performing the human function of defender or challenger of a cult site, themselves bear the names of gods. They are accompanied in this respect by Belyas le Noir, also the guardian of a fountain, whose original is probably Beli (i.e. Belinus or Belenus).

These heroes and heroines whose parents or grandparents are deities can at once be seen to provide most of the interest of the Arthurian court. This was recognized by Malory in *Morte Darthur*, where the importance of the kin of King Ban, the kin of King Pellinor, and the kin of King Lot is clearly stated and the quarrels between the three families are given considerable prominence since they lead ultimately to the final catastrophe.

It will be observed that in the case of Lot and the Pellinor/Pelles group, the gods are again like Bran described as kings. The remark that ancient gods tend to turn up as kings in the legendary history of Britain, originally made more in the context of Geoffrey of Monmouth's *Historia* than of the romances, has once again been demonstrated to be true. Indeed, the relationship between royalty and deity in the romances is quite definite. Bran was 'king' of Gorre and of Benoic, and, disguised as Bandemagus and also as Urien, again of Gorre; and as Eurain of Brandigan. Lot was King of Orcanie and, like Luce, Pelias and Apollo, of Loenois. The Pelles/Pellinor group were mostly kings of Listenois and/or Terre Foraine.

Looking at the ancestry of heroes and heroines from another angle brings out two other interesting features of the legends. They are the importance, in the ancestry of heroes, of the royal house of 'Ireland' (the name is put in inverted commas here because the Ireland of the romances seems to be a religious influence in Britain, not the present country of that name); and the extraordinary importance of Arthur's sisters and step-sisters, the daughters of Ygerne.

As far as the first is concerned, King Lancelot, Lancelot's grandfather, married a princess of Ireland; Guenever was sister of a King of Ireland; and Yseult was a princess of Ireland. Nothing is known about King Lancelot's wife, but the parallel stories of the other two, Yseult and Guenever, seem to be based on a particular principle, the devotion of a hero for a goddess.

The large number of heroes and heroines descended from Ygerne include one daughter, Morgan le Fay (herself described as a goddess), and the following children of other daughters: Mordred, Gawain and his brothers; Yvain; Galeschin; and King Aguiscant. Even more remarkable is the consistency with which the husbands of Ygerne's daughters are the rebel kings in the uprising against Arthur when he had just acceded to the throne. They are: Lot, Urien, Neutre and Aguiscant. With equal consistency the sons of these erstwhile rebels (except for Mordred) are his most loyal supporters after their fathers have been united in the grand alliance at the great gathering on Salisbury Plain.

The position of Ygerne in the 'matter of Britain' can be elucidated by a closer look a her name. This is generally spelt Ygerne or Yguerne. In thirteenth century French 'g' and 'v' (or 'gu' and 'w') were interchangeable, according to Hucher.[4] Following this mutation, Ygerne is also called Yverne, though in one instance only (West Verse). The name Yverne happens to be an early title of Ireland, Iverne, more familiar in its alternative form Iverna or Ivernia. Whether the link between Ygerne and Ireland is to be taken seriously or not, it is still a fact that almost all the great heroes at the Arthurian court are descended from, or otherwise linked with, Ireland or Ygerne. In an Arthurian context, Ireland is not to be thought of as pertaining to the present country of that name but as representing in Britain a religious principle which persisted in both countries and later gave to Ireland proper the name used of that country today.

## Conception

In the romances conception is not always an incidental by-product of sexual activity but is sometimes the outcome of a planned demonstration of the forces of reproductiveness and fertility, intended to encourage nature to release its bounty. This is made specially clear in a particular case mentioned below, where the outcome of the union was the birth of Galahad, but it also follows from the numerous matings which take place after the spring marriages of royal personages.

Two days before Lancelot encountered Galahad's mother he was the victor of a tournament at the castle of the Harp.[5] Having established his supremacy, he slipped away into the forest to preserve his anonymity. He was then conducted to Corbenic by a female guide. There, after several obscure adventures, including being threatened with the shameful cart,[6] he was welcomed by Pelles, King of Terre Foraine who was also called Fisher King, and who, like others with the same title, guarded the Grail at Corbenic. Lancelot was badly

---

4    Hucher, in respect of a pagan king called either Avrés or Agrestés, says in *Le Saint Graal*, III, p. 694 note: 'le g et le v permutent au XIII^e siècle, témoin le nom Guillelmus ou Willelmus.' Hucher might have added Gualguanus or Walwanus and Gualbroc or Walbroc (Geoffrey of Monmouth); Guincestre or Winchester, Guindresores or Windsor, Gautier or Walter (all in West, *Prose Index*, the latter under Map); Guenever or Wenhaver; Gododdin or Votadini; Garvic or Warwick, Guincent or Wissant and Gultessire or Wiltshire; and Waheriet or Gaheriet, (all in West, *Verse Index*). The same rule applies to common nouns, e.g. guimple or wimple.
5    *Vulgate*, V, p. 97.
6    *Vulgate*, V, p. 105.

needed because it was prophesied that he or one of his kin would deliver the country from the strange adventures from which it suffered and that he would reinvigorate the wasted and deserted land and recover the lost crops. The king knew that this could be achieved if Lancelot were to be bedded with his daughter (called Amite in the *Vulgate* but generally known, from Malory, as Elaine). However, Lancelot's well publicized attachment to Guenever meant that his union with the daughter could only be obtained by deception and a plan was made to obtain the co-operation of 'the knight God had sent them'.[7] First there was a ceremonial procession, to be described later in more detail, in which the Grail was carried by the king's beautiful daughter. After the meal which followed, the daughter's old nurse, Brisane, lured Lancelot to her mistress's bed by pretending Guenever was there, and Galahad was engendered. In this way the best and most loyal knight and the most beautiful and high-born damsel were brought together; it was done for no other purpose than to restore la Terre Foraine to its former fertility and prosperity which had been lost through the Dolorous Stroke.[8] Though Pelles was not the recipient of the Dolorous Stroke in the examples already given, he was a Maimed, that is, castrated, king, with a wasted kingdom, so the description is appropriate. The local people, supposing their welfare would benefit, were delighted by the news of Elaine's pregnancy.[9] As often happens in the romances, an important event is repeated in a different version. A similar story of Lancelot being tricked into Elaine's bed is told of another occasion at a Pentecost court at Camelot.[10]

There is another detailed description of the conception of a hero, which has considerable resemblances to the above. Bors' success at the tournament held annually to commemorate King Brangoire's coronation (the date is not stated, but by far the most popular date for coronations was the late spring festival of Pentecost) has already been mentioned on pp. 27 and 34.

Events in which fertility is much to the fore are described several times in the late romance *Perceforest*. Here the action takes place before Christ and the gatherings are at temples or standing stones on May 1st instead of Pentecost. The central feature is usually a royal marriage. There is a tournament after which the winner is rewarded with the queen's daughter and her lands; for the remaining knights, Love, offering an immediate reward, that very evening, indeed, gave strength and courage to force of arms. After the fighting there was a feast either on the grass or in a leafy bower. The young people attending wore chaplets of flowers. Damsels and amorous knights joined in round dances, followed by numerous unions which honoured and exalted the festival of the god in whose temple those proceedings took place. The feast ended

7  *Vulgate*, V, p. 109.
8  *Vulgate*, V, p. 110.
9  *Vulgate*, V, p. 112.
10 *Vulgate*, V, 379.

early so that the newly weds could go to bed. Many children were conceived, among whom some would grow up to be doughty knights in their turn.[11]

There are clearly similarities between these three sets of circumstances in which heroes were conceived. The scene is the residence of a god – Beli or Bran – or else a cult site (the tournament in *Perceforest* took place beside a standing stone or at a temple). All the accounts refer to tournaments, feasting and caroles, followed by bed with a princess or else by a royal marriage, followed again by conception. The *Perceforest* episodes are tied to May 1st, confirming what was only a guess in the other two that the main spring festival was involved. The royal marriage on May 1st backed up by numerous other couplings and conceptions conveys the same implication as the more direct reference to general fertility and prosperity in Lancelot's adventure. Kingship is less obvious at the festival at the castle of the Boundary, but it can be discerned in the background for this is an event commemorating coronation, and Bors sits in a golden chair which sounds like a throne. And though the hero Lancelot shows no sign of royalty at Corbenic himself, his son Galahad was in due course to become an annual king at Sarras and Galahad's Welsh equivalent, Perceval, became Fisher King at Corbenic. Is there a suggestion from the annual events above that the ceremony may have been an annual one at which the god's 'daughter' regularly exchanged her royal lover for a new one? We may have confirmation of this from the mention in two of the accounts of the presence of Lancelot and Bors in the demeaning cart, which seems to have acquired its sinister reputation from its use in disposing of a deposed sacred king.

**Upbringing**

After birth came a naming ceremony, at the fountain stone in the case of the person known as Sir Lancelot, who was in fact named Galahad after an ancestor so called. It is common enough in the French romances for characters to acquire a different name later in life. Other examples are:

| | | |
|---|---|---|
| Florée | became | Sarracinte |
| Evalac | | Mordrain |
| Kalafes | | Alfasein. |

and several personages whose names were originally unknown acquired names in adult life.

Heroes may sometimes have faced an unexpected hazard early in life. There are hints of exposure. This was indeed the fate of one of the greatest heroes, Gawain. In later life he came by chance upon a ruined ancient chapel, deserted except for one aged priest and his clerk. The priest told Gawain that his

---

[11] *Perceforest*, ed. Roussineau, Part IV, pp. 49, 69, 969 and 1129.

mother had wished to expose him soon after birth, but he was provided for by the owner of the place, a certain lord Gawain from whom Gawain inherited both name and estates. Afterward his mother (who was Arthur's sister or half-sister) married Lot, King of Orkney. These events were recorded in richly coloured paintings in the chapel.[12] That the circumstances of Gawain's birth should have been recorded in a chapel seems to be an indication, unnoticed by any censor, of the religious importance, in a pagan sense, of the personage whose life-history was so preserved.

Another son of that same mother is said to have been born on May 1st and exposed at sea.[13] This was Mordred, who was foreseen by Merlin to pose a threat to Arthur, who accordingly had all the children of noble birth born that Mayday cast adrift at sea. Mordred was one of the few survivors, and the expected calamity came to pass. This account sounds too much like its biblical counterpart to be taken at face value, but there is a basis outside the bible for future heroes being so exposed in, for example, the story of the Welsh Taliesin, who was floated on a river but was providentially found in a fish-weir one May Eve.[14]

If he survived the immediate threat of death, the hero-child is supposed to have grown with exceptional speed. The high prince Galehot was a marvellous child who at three months had developed as much as a normal child in a year.[15] This fiction is entirely in keeping with Celtic traditional tales of supernatural beings.

In appearance the hero in the romances is always described as 'beau', having the meanings of both fine and fair. Thus the prototype of all Arthurian heroes[16] is called Libeaus Desconus or le Bel Inconnu, that is, 'the Fair Unknown'; Gareth is called in Malory 'Beaumains' – Fair Hands; the young Perceval is 'Beau Fils' – Fair Son; and Tristan's wife and lover are called Yseult of the White Hands and Yseult the Blonde, respectively. This epithet 'beau' is paralleled elsewhere in Celtic tradition. The Irish hero Finn has a name which actually means fair, and the comparable word in Welsh, guen, also means white, as in Guenever – White Phantom. It will be seen that many of the names of heroes and heroines are no more than nick-names. Their real names were carefully concealed. For instance Lancelot had to wait until after he had embarked on his career as a knight errant and defeated an enemy of the son of his protectress before she revealed to him that his name was Lancelot; and Perceval still did not know his name when he had reached maturity, but guessed it correctly when asked what he was called![17]

The taboo on mentioning names is extremely deep seated. Even today there are many people who are offended to be addressed by strangers by their

---

12 *Perlesvaus*, tr. Bryant, p. 197.
13 Malory, bk I, ch. 27
14 *Celtic Myth and Arthurian Romance*, Loomis, p. 340.
15 E.g. *Perceforest*, Roussineau, p. 471.
16 *The Creation of the first Arthurian Romance; a Quest*, Luttrell, 1974.
17 *The Grail, from Celtic Myth to Christian Symbol*, Loomis, p. 37.

Christian names, prized possessions only to be shared with intimates. How much more the same principle applies to deities is clearly stated in the romances when Perceval was being taught by a hermit and was told that the name of Our Lord must not be spoken for fear of death.[18]

One of the peculiarities of Celtic legend is the part taken by women in the upbringing, arms training and arming of heroes. This is reflected in the romances in a number of ways. Lancelot, with his cousins Bors and Lionel – both also important heroes in their own right – was brought up by the Damsel of the Lake to the moment when she presented him when eighteen years old at Camelot to be dubbed a knight on St John's Day.[19] Galahad was also brought up by women, by the nuns of an abbey near Camelot. A youth of matchless physique, he was presented, also at the age of eighteen, by three nuns to Lancelot, Bors and Lionel for knighting, which took place after a night vigil in St Stephen's Minster.[20] This happened immediately before his appearance clad in red at Arthur's Pentecost court, where he drew the sword from the stone and took his seat in the Siege Perilous.

We may assume something similar in the upbringing of Perceval, whose mother kept him isolated, away from the company of men; and his Welsh equivalent Peredur, in a fashion more like that of his Irish counterparts, certainly received his warlike education at the hands of female supernatural beings. The story contains several mythological elements. It is as follows: 'And at daybreak Peredur could hear a shrieking, and quickly Peredur arose in his shirt and trousers, and his sword about his neck, and out he came. And when he came, there was a witch overtaking the watchman and he shrieking. Peredur fell upon the witch and struck her on the head with his sword until her helm and headpiece spread like a salver on her head. Thy mercy, fair Peredur son of Efraug, and the mercy of God!' 'How knowest thou, Hag, that I am Peredur?' 'It was fated and foreseen that I should suffer affliction from thee, and that thou shouldst take horse and arms from me. And thou shalt be with me awhile, being taught to ride thy horse and handle thy weapons' . . . Peredur then 'set off with the witch [who was one of the nine witches of Gloucester] to the witches court. And he was there three weeks on end. And then Peredur took his choice of horse and arms and set out on his way'.[21]

Comparing this with the upbringing of Galahad, it can be seen that the terrifying female divinities of the Celts have been tamed and transformed in the romances into an abbey of nuns. This is another example of the pagan elements of a Celtic original being reconstituted in later versions as a medieval counterpart – witches turn up as nuns, temples as abbeys or castles, gods and goddesses as kings and queens, human sacred kings as challenge knights, their female counterparts as damsels, and so on.

[18] *Le roman de Perceval*, ed. W. Roach, lines 6484–91.
[19] *Vulgate*, III, pp. 118ff.
[20] *Vulgate*, V, pp. 408 and VI, pp. 4f.
[21] *Mabinogion*, Everyman, p. 199.

## Knighthood

A youth aspiring to knighthood would have been tested among his peers in the arts of war before being chosen as a knight. Once he had had his sword belted on by a king or senior knight he was licensed to fight others of the same order, and was expected to travel in search of 'adventures'. 'It was the custom in Great Britain and all the islands of the sea for young knights to ride armed throughout the kingdom seeking adventure and to prove their force and power and to enhance their skill at arms'.[22] The 'adventures' have been identified here as being pagan religious observances of some kind, often challenges for kingship of the glade. Knights were bound by a code of behaviour, which is revealed in snippets here and there in the romances. Some rules were trivial and not always kept, like not staying more than one night in a place,[23] or not travelling in parties of more than two. Others, which seem to have been more fundamental, govern the knights' relationships with women. Leaving out for the time being the special requirement for chastity which restricted those who undertook the Quest of the Holy Grail, knights seem to have enjoyed the favours of women freely enough; Lancelot's intention to be faithful to Guenever was something of an exception. And the female counterparts of the knights, damsels, far from being resigned to their fate as prizes, actually incited the knights to fight so that they could choose the bravest.

The rules were that:

(1) a knight must take up the cause of any woman who comes to court asking for help;[24]
(2) a knight must help any woman whether she has a good cause or not;[25]
(3) a knight may not harm any damsel on her own, unprotected by another knight;[26]
(4) a damsel can choose freely between knights;[27]
(5) when a damsel is accompanying a knight, she must follow the victor if her knight is defeated, whether she wants to or not, and he can have his will of her.[28]

The last item reads like an element of the 'challenge' which has escaped the confines of the glade and taken to the open road, no doubt assisted by careless narrators.

The behaviour of the heroes and heroines associated with the Grail was entirely different. Chastity, for both sexes, was an essential. Thus, 'those knights who are resolved on serving the Grail must forgo women's love'.[29]

---

22 *Perceforest*, ed. Roussineau, pt IV. p. 410.
23 *Perceforest*, ed. Taylor, pt I, p. 242.
24 *Vulgate*, II, p. 320.
25 *Vulgate*, V, p. 461.
26 *Yvain*, tr. Comfort, p. 287.
27 *Guiron le Courtois*, Lathuillère, p. 413.
28 *Guiron le Courtois*, Lathuillère, p. 413; *Le Chevalier de la Charrette*, tr. Comfort, p. 287.
29 *Parzival*, tr. Hatto, p. 251.

The successful Grail seekers, Galahad[30] and Perceval were both virgins, the former being enjoined to take this course by a hermit who came often to visit him in the abbey where he grew up. And it was Lancelot's failure in this respect which prevented him from being a successful grail-contender.

As far as the women were concerned, the Grail bearer in the Grail procession had to be of perfect chastity.[31] Pelles' daughter was obliged to give up her post as bearer after she slept with Lancelot.[32] The woman most closely connected with the Grail quest was Perceval's sister. She accompanied Galahad on his journey towards the holy city where he was crowned and died. She too was a virgin, and in that capacity was qualified to give blood to heal the leper lady. And, in another incident, when the Dolorous Stroke had been struck and the striker lay dead in a ritual boat, a virgin girl was sent to retrieve the body since there was no man in all the country brave enough to enter the boat.[33] Young girls clearly played important parts in the pagan dramas recollected in the romances, and so they did in a Welsh memory of prehistoric times. The life of Math, who must have been a sacred king, was hedged by a taboo which required him to keep his feet in the folds of a virgin's lap.[34] His foot could not touch the ground except in time of war. His 'foot-holder', Goewin, had to resign the office when she lost her virginity to Gilfaethwy son of Don – the Welsh equivalent of the Arthurian knight, Girflet.

The particular section of the romances which provides most of the examples of chastity above shows every sign of having been heavily edited by a monkish hand, which might have resulted in the emphasis on chastity for the Grail-seekers. However, the last example shows the importance of virginity in a completely pagan context. The central figure of the Grail cult is the castrated Grail king, in a rather surprising antithesis to the main theme that sexual vigour in a king was beneficial and necessary. This emphasis on sex and potency suggests that there may have been other restrictions on the sexual activity of participants in the original pagan religious drama.

## Combat

The principal occupation of knights was fighting. Their battles fall into four categories: single combat; tournaments; wars on a national scale; and one massive expedition abroad in which Rome is said to have been conquered.

It has been shown by a number of instances that typical examples of the first two categories have the characteristics of ritual engagements. Analysis of many episodes has revealed a number of factors which point to a common framework which, though often degraded and substantially added to, can still

---

[30] *Vulgate*, V, p. 385.
[31] *Parzival*, tr. Hatto, p. 125.
[32] *Vulgate*, V, p. 141, lines 35/9.
[33] *Le Saint Graal*, Hucher, p. 295.
[34] *Mabinogion*, Penguin, p. 98.

be recognized. For 'challenges' and 'tournaments' it is thus possible to propose the explanation that an original group of tales which embodied recollections of pagan practices has been preserved, though considerably extended by invented material.

The origin of the wars is not so easy to decide, but since the enemy can sometimes be recognized as a deity – Ryons, King of Ireland (among other places), for example, can be argued to be Bran under one of his many aliases – a possible explanation is that they were wars of religion. The most formidable challenge to Arthur's position was the war with the rebel kings, which ended at the great confederacy on Salisbury Plain, when both parties ceased fighting each other and turned on the Sarrassins instead.

The fourth item is again difficult to explain. It would be naive to take it at face value. At no time did a British-led army from this country inflict damage on the Roman Empire to the extent indicated by this story, and no emperor can be found called Lucius Hiberius, the name of the defeated emperor in the romances. A possible explanation is that some local event has been magnified to enhance Arthur's reputation. It has been pointed out that the course of the expedition to Rome is closely paralleled by that of the action against the rebel British kings already mentioned.[35]

## Opponents

In Welsh legend, King Arthur's adversaries were giants, hags and monsters ; he and his men undertook journeys to the Otherworld to rescue prisoners and to carry off treasures; he was 'rude, savage, heroic and protective.'[36] This primitive Arthurian court is well represented in the French romances, less well so in Malory. Though it is still present in the selection made by the latter author, he has tended to leave out the inexplicable. Here is an example of the sort of episode he omitted.

King Arthur, wakened by thunder and lightning, rose up alone and saw a boat drawn to the shore by a swan. In the boat was a dead knight on a rich couch with a broken spear protruding from his breast. A letter asked that the corpse should be displayed in Arthur's hall for a year and a day. Any knight who drew the spear out would be under an obligation to avenge the knight's death by killing his unknown murderer with the same weapon.

Meanwhile, far away, Gawain's brother Guerrehes came upon an empty marble castle in the course of his travels. He looked out of a window into a garden and saw that two pavilions of great richness were pitched in it. From one a dwarf carried a silver cup into the other, where it was used by a beauti-

---

[35] 'The account of the campaign against Lucius corresponds point for point to the account in the *Suite de Merlin* (Huth *Merlin*) of Arthur's war against King Loth.' Parry and Caldwell in *Arthurian Literature in the Middle Ages*, quoting Tatlock, Legendary History, *Speculum*, VI, 1931, pp. 206–220.

[36] *Mabinogion*, Everyman, p. xxv.

ful damsel to feed a large wounded knight lying in the tent on a vermilion bed with white silk sheets. He was dressed in a purple cloak edged with ermine. Guerrehes descended from the window and went into the tent. The wounded knight became very angry. Almost at once a very small knight came up and challenged Guerrehes to single combat. The dwarf knight won, although Guerrehes was a great champion, in the same class as his elder brother Gawain, and the tiny victor compelled him to promise to return at the years end to fight again or else to become at once a slave of the wounded knight and work as a weaver with many other captives. Guerrehes chose the former, then went back through the window where he was taunted by a great crowd of maidens and on leaving the castle he was pelted with refuse in the market place.

Later on at Arthur's court Guerrehes drew out the spearhead from the corpse, almost by accident, had it fixed on a shaft, and took it on the anniversary of his defeat to the castle with the two tents. This time he was the victor over the dwarf knight, and he also fought and killed with the fatal spearhead the large knight who had previously been wounded, and who [it becomes clear at this stage in the story] was the object of retaliation. A damsel then took Guerrehes to the castle of the knight he had avenged, where he was received with great joy. The next morning, Arthur found the swan boat with Guerrehes asleep in it at his court at Carlion. The damsel took the year-old body of the dead knight away in the boat, after explaining that he was called Brangemuer and had been the child of a mortal and the fairy Brangepart. He had been obliged to die before he could be taken permanently to his mother's kingdom. The date was Hallowe'en.[37]

There are plenty of mythological motifs here, but in the context of 'opponents' our attention is drawn to the dwarf knight. Dwarfs are usually described as of perfect physique, sometimes kings, persons of honour, aggressive towards knights,[38] and evidently playing some significant part in the story, though what it is not always clear. The subject has been extensively researched by V. J. Harward in *The Dwarfs of Arthurian Romance and Celtic Tradition*. He points out a link between dwarf kings and the god Beli, and regards dwarfs as resulting from the same pagan thinking as created the 'little people' well known in the folk-lore of the West.

The general picture provided by this detailed look into the affairs of the Arthurian court tends to show dwarfs as persons of influence and importance. They are generally present on formal occasions which may be suspected of having a ritual origin. For instance it is a dwarf who recognizes the anonymous hero at Arthur's court and announces his ancestry and his mission; a dwarf is often present on the occasion of a 'challenge', sometimes acting as master of ceremonies, blowing the horn, or striking the challenger to provoke a conflict; a dwarf is often an attendant at the alfresco meal at which the hero

---

37 *First Continuation*, Roach, lines 14519 to end. Line 15204 for Hallowe'en.
38 *Vulgate*, V, pp. 240 and 442 and III, p. 281.

eats with goddesses; and, finally, the attendants of the messenger damsels who travel great distances to court to ask for champions for their mistresses are invariably dwarfs, who sometimes play significant parts in the pagan tableau which marks the beginning of an Arthurian court festival.

More obvious opponents of Arthurian knights were giants. These may often have been brought into play by narrators anxious to emphasize the prowess of major heroes, but it is still possible to discern a pagan conception of a deity underlying some of them. Since giants are said to have been, with Sarrassins, the original inhabitants of the land before the people of Brutus or the Grail missionaries came, it might be said, as it has been of the dwarfs, that giant was a term used for some set of the original inhabitants or their deities, though of course the people themselves were neither abnormally large or small. A medieval explanation of the origin of giants was that they were the descendants of a woman settler called Albine (presumably a hypothetical name-giving founder of Albion). The thirty daughters of a king were expelled from Greece and after a long journey adrift at sea came to Britain, which was then uninhabited except for devils. These seduced the sisters, who bore the race of giants which populated the country in the days before Brutus is said to have arrived.[39]

The connection of the giants of the romances with paganism is as follows: the several versions of the god Bran are usually described as larger than life-size,[40] much as the derivatives of Beli are smaller; and both the giant herdsman of 'The Lady of the Fountain' and the one-legged giant of Tristan's underground lover's den are clearly versions of a Celtic mythological figure.

Another large category of knightly opponent is the dragon, otherwise described as a serpent or a worm. Once again there is no reason to suppose that any such creature ever existed, whether winged and fire-breathing or not. But primitive people may have worried that they existed and therefore required their heroes to defeat them. Peredur had three battles against such creatures. In one a black serpent inhabited a tumulus, otherwise called 'the sorrowful mound'. Serpents sometimes play a part in dreams, for instance in Gawain's adventure before he was placed in the shameful cart; and also Arthur's dream-time serpent which he had painted in a church (p. 179). So even dragons may once have seemed vivid enough to paint, and have been much more real than a mere literary device on the part of narrators, intended to provide a happy ending for the knight and for the inevitable rescued damsel.[41]

---

[39] *Des granz geanz*, ed. G. Brereton.

[40] For instance, the large knight in the story of Guerrehes is an example used by Newstead of an unnamed figure representing Bran.

[41] There may have been some connection between serpents and paganism, since the figure of a woman riding on a crowned serpent is said to have represented the religious code of the Sarrassins, which perhaps corresponds with the appearance of such a figure in pagan iconography.

## The Knight Errant

The knight errant, riding through strange countries in search of marvellous adventures, is the stock figure of Arthurian romance.[42] The word 'errant' applied to this class of knight derives from the French verb 'esrer' and means to travel rather than to wander or go astray. This way of life is characteristic of the romances and fundamental to them, but little thought has been given to it. It seems to have been accepted as just another peculiarity of an unreal world in which the unexpected may occur at any turn of the woodland path or in the next forest clearing. Here, we have seen that these 'adventures' were often ritual combats conforming to the system described as the 'challenge'. If the sequel to these battles is followed up, a standard pattern emerges. The defeated knight is sent to surrender to the king or, quite often, to the queen[43] at a festival court, usually Pentecost, and as often as not finds himself later on elected, for no very obvious reason, to be a knight of the Round Table or an officer of Arthur's household.[44] What began as a ritual event is continued at a pagan festival and ends, a little unexpectedly, in election to a ceremonial position. Evidently the 'challenge' system was a method of recruitment for the Round Table.

As has happened before in this analysis, a German language version of a French romance provides useful information not otherwise available. Speaking of the Grail companions, we are told in *Parzival*: 'If a land should lose its lord and the people see the hand of God in it and ask for a new lord from the Grail company, their prayer is granted . . . God sends men out in secret but bestows maidens openly . . . in order to have progeny, in the hope that these children will return to serve the Grail and swell the ranks of its company. Those knights who are resolved on serving the Grail must forgo woman's love. Only the king may have a spouse in wedlock, and those others who God has sent to be lords in lordless lands'.[45]

Is the description of these knights with their far-flung domains an alternative version of the knights errant who by success in challenges provided lords in distant lands and at the same time acquired spouses (or at least legitimate lovers)? The god of the Grail system has, as already pointed out, nothing to do with Christianity. The German text makes this quite clear by calling the knights 'templeisen', that is 'temple-knights' or alternatively 'knights of the Grail Castle'.[46]

---

[42] E.g. *Vulgate*, V, p. 142.

[43] E.g. *Vulgate*, III, p. 320, III, p. 400, and V, p. 307.

[44] E.g. *Manessier*, Potvin, lines 41163–41312; and in *Morte Darthur*, bk VII, the various different coloured knights defeated by Gareth are made knights of the Round Table (in chapter 35).

[45] *Parzival*, tr. Hatto, p. 251.

[46] Grimm's German Dictionary

## The Round Table

The Round Table was made by Merlin for Uther at Cardoel in Wales and dedicated at Pentecost. Its construction reflected that of the Grail Table of Joseph of Arimathea. The Table was, indeed, closely linked with the Grail for it contained the Perilous Seat, in which only the individuals destined to achieve the Grail escaped immediate death. Medieval narrators have inevitably described the table in terms of what was familiar to them, but they have not excluded some information which points to archaic origins. For instance, looking at the Table from the viewpoint of the individuals who made up its companions, we are told that while the Table was at Cardoel no one was allowed to sit at high feasts unless he was wounded in the face, and on one occasion, after a Christmas court, a wounded knight was allowed to die in his seat at the Table over the next two or three days. Later the Table came into the possession of Leodegrance. It then passed to Arthur as Guenever's dowry, and its rededication at Camelot coincided with Arthur's marriage. In its new situation in Logres, only *successful* 'challenge' knights were allowed to join the Table at high feasts.[47] Whether in the old way or the new, we see the complement of the Table being provided from ritual figures, either mutilated ones or challenge knights. It will be argued here that among the company of 'kings' and 'knights' and their female counterparts there were several deities, but in these descriptions of triumph and suffering there is a hint that real people were involved in some centralizing pagan system. What evidently began as a pagan organization has been transformed by medieval narrators into something which corresponded with contemporary ideas of the relationship between king and the nobility.

Apart from its roundness, details of the structure of the Round Table are provided in only one comment: 'Even as the spaces at a hayrack are marked off by wooden bars, so are there pillars at the Round Table which separate the seats from one another.'[48] The Table seems to have been characterized by a ring of pillars. It also had an astronomical function (astronomy in the romances means astrology, but nevertheless implies observation of the movements of the heavenly bodies), for 'in its name it mirrors the roundness of the earth, the concentric spheres of the planets and of the elements in the firmament . . .'[49]

## The Beauty Contest

So far we have been looking at 'adventures' in which male heroic figures compete, usually by strength and skill at arms. Heroines were apparently chosen for their looks, and judged by their female peers. For instance, at a tournament which followed a beheading incident and the dubbing of new

---

[47] *Vulgate*, V, pp. 129/31.
[48] *The Quest of the Holy Grail*, tr. Matarasso, p. 170.
[49] *The Quest of the Holy Grail*, tr. Matarasso, p. 99.

knights, the queen, ladies and maidens assembled to elect the most beautiful maiden, who for her beauty would sit in the best seat in the grandstand and would reward the winner of the tournament with a kiss.[50] Is this a bowdlerized version of a more primitive situation described in an earlier romance concerning Tristan? In it, a certain giant Dialeces who lived in or near the Lontaines Isles, furious at the success of Joseph of Arimathea's missionary efforts, killed his own twelve sons and had a castle built on the Isle of Giants, on the soil soaked with the blood of his victims. Here he lived with the most beautiful woman he could find, and had all passing strangers imprisoned until such time as either he or his lady were defeated, he in bravery, she in beauty. This custom lasted from the time of Joseph to that of Arthur, when it was terminated by Tristan. At the time of the latter's arrival at the castle the seigneur was an Irish knight called Brunor who had defeated the previous incumbent and married his widow. Tristan claimed precedence for himself and Yseult. A jury gave the prize to Yseult. At the same time Tristan defeated Brunor in single combat. Both the losers were beheaded. Tristan now became lord of the castle after two days of fête, and found that like other winning challenge knights he was forbidden to leave the island except to fight another knight.

Whether the losing lady's fate was really decided in this way cannot be determined, but the incident is full of pagan detail. As well as two challenge episodes in which the defence of the site is taken over by a successful challenger, the lady in question was the Fair Giantess, whose son Galehot was later buried in what sounds like a secondary burial in a Neolithic grave (p. 180).

Tristan and Yseult played a somewhat similar role in an encounter with Mennonas and his lady, Grysinde. The latter was fated to be beheaded if she should be excelled in beauty. The enchanter Mabon sent a magic boat to fetch Tristan and Yseult to challenge Mennonas and Grysinde. Mabon also provided them with a squire and a dwarf for their convenience while travelling. Tristan and Yseult each had the better of the encounter and sent the heads of the losers to Mabon.[51]

One wonders if these stories of Tristan and Yseult are relics of a past system, or are they merely a twelfth-century insertion to please a royal patroness? However, since in both accounts there are a number of other pagan motifs, it is reasonable to consider the possibility that they stem from pagan originals. Perhaps, since Yseult, princess of Ireland, seems to have been a territorial goddess, the overthrow of an earlier regime and the replacement of its principal figure is at the root of this story.

---

[50] *Perceforest*, vol. II, CXXV, recto col. 2.
[51] *Le roman en prose de Tristan*, Löseth, pp. 250/2.

## Imprisonment

Systematic imprisonment of large numbers of knights is quite frequent in the romances. Notable instances in addition to the one recounted in the last section are the Dolorous Gard, the Dolorous Tower, the Dolorous Chartre, the Valley of No Return, the Valley of Bondage (Servage), Turning Island, the Magic Orchard of the Queen of Danemarche, the Tertre Desvé, Terrican's fountain, and the Fountain of the two Sycamores. This may seem a long list of varying types of site, but there are several common features amongst them. In almost every case the captor is immediately recognizable as a deity. Those who fall into this category are: Branduz, Morgan le Fay, Nabon (a form of Mabon), Belyas (Beli) and probably Terrican. And in every instance except Val sans Retour the captor is defeated in single combat by a well-known hero – Lancelot, Gawain, Tristan or Bors – and the captives released. The sites, though varied, are identified in some cases as cult sites by the challenge theme, and in others are hedged about with enchantments which implies the same thing. Whatever the original significance of these stories may have been, there is remarkable unanimity in their structure: a hero defeats a deity at a cult site and releases his captives alive. There may be a record here of the taking of prisoners as part of the challenge system, or it may be that the challenge theme has been used as a vehicle for a pagan myth of retrieval of dead souls from purgatory.

## Madness

An unexpected humiliation undergone by great heroes, including Lancelot, Tristan[52] and Owein,[53] is madness. The same derangement also affected Merlin. Madness took the form of wandering in the woods as a wild man, eating fruits and roots and other products of the natural environment. The 'wild man of the woods' seems to have been a sacred figure of some kind and in one version of Merlin's conception his father was such a being. According to this view, Merlin acquired from his father a hairy skin and his supernatural abilities. Behind this improbable story there lies the memory of Merlin as Lord of the Animals (or Faunus), a dim recollection of an ancient deity.

Lancelot is so strongly linked with madness that he is on record as having three separate bouts. In one his mental balance was disturbed by Guenever's displeasure at the easy way he kept on being deceived by Elaine's old nurse into sleeping with Elaine. He retained his strength and ferocity but not his memory, and his appearance became so unkempt that he was unrecognizable. Eventually after enduring solitary hardship in the woods he came by chance to Corbenic, where he was healed by exposure to the Grail.

The meaning of this episode is far from obvious, but the circumstances are

---

[52] *Le roman en prose de Tristan*, Löseth, p. 83.
[53] *Studies in the Arthurian Legend*, Rhys, p. 100.

exclusively pagan, so it may be a reflection of the ancient link between madness and sanctity, a link widely exploited by shamans who used their ramblings while in a state of trance to impress their credulous victims.

## Tests

The major underlying themes of the romances are contests for positions of honour. The rewards may seem inadequate to us when what a young man risked his life to obtain was a temporary kingship retained by constant fighting, or annual kingship followed by certain death, or the embraces of a goddess followed by castration and the cart. The Celtic thirst for honour at all costs was not for the faint-hearted. It is perhaps best exemplified in the romances by a remark in *Perceforest* on the aftermath of a tournament. 'Some of the dead and mutilated had not been armed (that is, wearing armour) like the rest, hoping thereby for greater honour.'[54] And in *The Vulgate Version of the Arthurian Romances*, on the occasion when Galahad drew the sword from the stone, some of the contestants in the jousting which followed chose not to wear armour or carry a shield, for the extra honour they obtained if they survived. It is indeed a fact of history that Celtic warriors went into battle naked against the Romans. So it should be accepted that even the certainty of death would not deter heroes from pressing forward in attempts to gain sacred kingship. Merely for Lancelot to 'sleep in the king's bed' after winning a tournament[55] seems an inadequate reward for the ultimate in risk of life and limb – unless, perhaps, Guenever was in it, the story does not say. No doubt the hero's true reward was the regard of his fellows and the supposed fertility and prosperity of his realm.

The aspiring hero was tested in various ways in his ascent to sacred kingship. We have seen the 'challenge' and the tournament as methods of selection. In the latter, at the castle of the Boundary, there was a hint, in its occurrence on the anniversary of the king's coronation, that the battle for the princess was an annual event; the fight between Pwyll and Hafgan for the kingship of the Otherworld seemed to take place yearly, for it took place at the end of a year, and Hafgan had fought his rival on a previous occasion; and the Thorntree Ford[56] and the Thunderstorm Fountain[57] were both linked with Midsummer Eve, itself of course an annual event. There may be traces here of annual kingship, which is a well documented system. Many examples are given by Frazer. It is most clearly expressed in the romances in two adventures which happened to Lancelot.[58] In *Perlesvaus*:

---

[54] *Perceforest*, ed. Roussineau, pt IV, p. 1131.
[55] *Vulgate*, V, p. 194.
[56] See p. 30 note 62.
[57] Chrétien's, *Yvain*, ed. Roques, lines 668/9.
[58] Another example of 'collection' – even Lancelot could not be expected to die both by burning and beheading.

The story tells that Lancelot made his way through strange forests in search of adventure, and rode on until he came upon an open country outside a huge city which seemed to be of great importance. As he rode across the fields he looked towards the city and saw a great company ride out, with a mighty noise of bagpipes and flutes and viols and other instruments. They were coming along the road along which Lancelot was travelling, and when the foremost neared him they halted and redoubled their joy, crying:

'Welcome, Sire!'

'My lords,' said Lancelot, 'who are you preparing to meet with all this rejoicing?'

'Sire,' they said, 'our masters will tell you that: they are coming up behind.'

And up came the provosts and the lords of the city to meet Lancelot.

'Sire,' they said, 'this whole city is overcome with jubilation out of love for you, and all these instruments are sounding their joy at your coming.'

'Why should they sound for me?' said Lancelot.

'We will tell you,' they said. 'This city has begun to burn in one quarter ever since the death of our king, and the fire will never be put out until we have had a king to be lord of our city and its fief for a year's term. At the end of that year he must cast himself into the fire, and thus it will be extinguished. Until then it cannot be quenched, nor will it die. And so we have come to meet you to bestow our kingdom upon you, for we have heard that you are a great knight.'

'My lords,' said Lancelot, ' I have no need of such a kingdom, and may God save me from the honour!'

'Sire,' they said, 'you cannot be saved from it since you have come to our land; and it would be a great pity for such a beautiful city as the one you see there to fall to ruins to avoid the death of one man. And its fief is great indeed – it would be a high honour for you. And at the end of the year's term you will be crowned in the fire to save this city and its great people and win high praise indeed!'

Lancelot was filled with awe at what they said, but they crowded round him and carried him into the city. Ladies and maidens climbed up to great stone windows to cry their joy, saying to one another:

'Behold, they bring the new king! In a year's time the fire will be quenched!'

'But God!' cried some. 'What a great shame that so fair a knight should die in that way.'

'Silence!' said others. 'It is a great joy that so fine a city as ours should be saved by his death, for all the kingdom will pray for his soul evermore.'

Rejoicing, they led him into the palace and said that they would crown him. Lancelot found the palace strewn with reeds and hung with rich silken drapes, and all the lords of the city were standing to do him homage; but he stoutly refused, saying that he would never be their king or their lord in this way. Just then a dwarf entered the city with one of the most beautiful maidens in the kingdom, and he asked what had caused so much rejoicing and commotion.

He was told how they wished to make a knight their king and how he would not agree, and he was told about the fire, too; whereupon the dwarf and the maiden dismounted before the palace, and climbed the steps, and the dwarf cried out to all the lords and the most powerful men in the city:

'My lords, since this knight does not wish to be king, I will accept your crown most willingly, and govern this city at your pleasure and do all that you require.'

'In faith,' they said, 'since the knight has refused this honour and you wish to accept it, we grant it to you most gladly. Now he may take up his journey once more, for we declare him free.'

With that they set the crown on the dwarf's head, and Lancelot, filled with joy, took his leave and commended them to God. Then he climbed on his horse, and as he rode through the city in all his armour, the ladies and the maidens spoke of how he was not willing to be king and die so soon.

He was glad indeed to leave the city behind, and he passed once more into a great forest and rode until the sun went down. . . .[59]

This tale of a realm whose safety is ensured by a king killed annually is obviously a recollection of annual kingship. It may have been written down for the first time in the Middle Ages, but by then it must have been preserved in oral form for thirty generations or more, from the time when such a practice actually took place. The account is so clear that no comment is necessary except, perhaps, as regards the position in the calendar of the election of the new king. At different times and places the beginning of the year has varied widely. It began with March in Rome before Julius Caesar; it began with the spring equinox (or a couple of days later) in medieval England; the first month was June, in four years out of five, in the continental Celtic Coligny calendar; the year began with September in Byzantium; and it began on the eve of November 1st for the British Celts. In spite of the spate of coronations at the spring festival in the romances – coronations implying the replacement of a previous ruler – Hallowe'en is quite a likely date for the death of a king by burning, in a Celtic context. A certain Irish king called Muirchertach met his death in a burning house at this season, perhaps significant because his grandfather also perished by burning.[60] [61]

It is remarkable that, as well as the episode of the burning city just described, Lancelot should have 'collected' yet another clear instance of annual kingship. The second now follows, in which there is a succession of crowned youths who die at annual intervals, this time by beheading. The story is as follows:

59 *Perlesvaus*, tr. Bryant, pp. 106/7.
60 *Celtic Heritage*, Rees and Rees, p. 340.
61 In Britain the effigy which is burnt annually is not that of a king, but it would not be unreasonable to suppose that an original fire ceremony has been displaced from the eve of November 1st to the 5th.

Then Lancelot left the hermitage and rode until he passed out of the forest and found before him a waste land, a land stretching far and wide where there dwelt neither beasts nor birds, for the earth was so dry and poor that there was no pasture to be found. Lancelot gazed out far before him, and a city appeared in view; he rode on towards it at a swift pace, and saw that the city was so huge that it seemed to fill an entire country. But he could see its walls crumbling round about, and the gates leaning with age. He rode inside to find the city quite empty of inhabitants, its great palaces derelict and waste, its markets and exchanges empty, its vast graveyards full of tombs, its churches ruined. Through the great streets he rode until he found a huge palace which seemed to be in better condition and less ruined than the others. He drew rein before it, to hear knights and ladies lamenting bitterly and saying to a knight:

'Oh God! What a shame and sorrow it is that you must go and die thus, and your death cannot be delayed. Well may we hate him who condemned you!'

And the knights and the ladies swooned as he left. Lancelot heard all this but he could see no-one. But just then the knight came down from the hall; dressed he was in a red coat with a rich belt of silk and gold around him, and a beautiful brooch was pinned at his neck clustered with precious stones, and a golden hat he wore on his head, and in his hands he clutched a huge axe. He was fair indeed and only young. Lancelot saw him coming, and it brought him joy to behold the knight with his fine appearance. And the youth said to him;

'Dismount, sire.'

'Gladly, fair sire,' said Lancelot, and he climbed down and tethered his horse to a silver ring which was set in a great stone at the steps of the palace, and he took his shield from his neck and laid down his lance.

'What would you, sire?' he said to the knight,

'Sire,' came the reply, 'you must cut off my head with this axe, for I am condemned to death with this weapon; if not, I shall cut off yours.'

'By my life!' cried Lancelot. 'What are you saying?'

'What you hear, sire,' said the knight. 'This you must do since you have come to the city.'

'Sire,' said Lancelot, 'he would be a fool indeed who could not see how to get the better in this game, but it would be to my discredit to kill you without due cause.'

'Truly,' said the knight, 'you cannot leave otherwise.'

'Fair sire, ' said Lancelot, 'you look so fine and noble: how can you go so calmly to your death? You must surely know that I would sooner kill you than have you kill me, since that is the choice.'

'I am well aware of that,' said the knight, 'but you must swear to me before I die that you will return to the city in a year's time and offer your head freely, without contest, just as I offer mine.'

'By my life! 'cried Lancelot. 'Nothing you could say would persuade me from deferring death rather than dying here and now. But I wonder that you are so well prepared to receive death.'

'Sire,' said the knight, 'he who is to go before the Saviour of the world must cleanse himself of all the wickedness and all the sins that he has ever committed, and I am now truly repented of mine, and I want to die so.'

And with that he handed him the axe. Lancelot took it and saw how keen and sharp it was.

'Sire,' said the knight, 'stretch out your hand towards that church that you can see.'

'Willingly,' said Lancelot.

'Will you now swear to me on the relics in the church,' said the knight that you will return here a year from this day, at the hour at which you kill me, or before, and offer your head freely, without defence, as I shall in a moment offer mine?'

'I swear it,' said Lancelot.

And with that the knight knelt down and stretched out his neck as straight as he could. Lancelot clutched the axe in both hands and then said:

'Sir knight, for God's sake, have mercy on yourself.'

'Willingly, Sire. Let me cut off your head. Only thus can I find mercy.'

'That mercy I will not grant you,' said Lancelot, and he raised the axe and smote off the knight's head with such a terrible blow that he sent it flying seven feet from the body. The knight crashed to the ground when his head was cut off, and as Lancelot threw down the axe he thought that he would do ill to linger there, and he returned to his horse, took up his arms and mounted. When he looked back. . . . he heard a great mourning and crying of knights and ladies far off in the city; they were bewailing the good knight, and saying that he would be avenged, God willing, at the agreed time or sooner. Lancelot rode out of the city, hearing every word that the knights and ladies said.[62]

A year later Lancelot, true to his word, returned about noon to the 'Waste City', which he found as deserted as the first time.

In this city to which Lancelot had come there were many derelict churches, and magnificent palaces that had crumbled to ruins, and many great, deserted halls. But he had scarcely entered the city when he heard great wailing and lamentation of ladies and maidens, though he did not know where it was coming from. They were all saying together:

'Oh God! How we have been betrayed by the one who killed the knight, for he does not return! The day has now arrived when he should come to keep his promise. We should never believe the word of knights, for this one has failed to return. The others before him have failed us, and now he will do the same for fear of death, for he beheaded the finest and fairest knight in this kingdom, and he should now be beheaded likewise, but he is trying to avoid his fate if he can.'

---

[62] *Perlesvaus*, tr. Bryant, pp. 90/1.

So said the maidens; Lancelot heard them all too well, but wondered where they could be, for he could see no one anywhere. He came up to the palace where he had killed the knight and dismounted, and tethered his horse to a ring fixed in a marble stone. He had hardly done so when down from the palace came a knight, tall and fair and strong, and assured; dressed he was in a splendid tunic of silk, and in his hand he held the axe with which Lancelot had beheaded the other knight. . . .

Preparations were made for Lancelot to be beheaded in his turn, but at the last moment he was saved through the intercession of a maiden. He was told that 'this ruined city . . . would never have been inhabited . . . if a true knight like you had not come. At least twenty came here just as you did, and each one killed a brother of ours, or an uncle or a cousin, by cutting off their heads, just as you beheaded the knight; and every one swore to return on the day declared. All of them broke their promise, for none dared return; and if you had failed to return on the day like the others had done, we should have lost this city for ever, and the castles which belong to it.'

The knight and the maidens led Lancelot to the palace and had him disarmed, and in the forest near the city the greatest rejoicing in the world could be heard.

'Sire,' said the maidens, 'now you can hear the townspeople and those who dwell in the city rejoicing from your coming, for now they know the news.'

Lancelot leaned at the windows of the hall and watched the city fill with the fairest people in the world, and the great halls were brimming, and clerks and priests were coming in great processions, worshipping and praising god that they could return to their churches, and offering their blessings to the knight who had enabled them to return.'[63]

This story is very similar to that of Sir Gawain and the Green Knight. In each the hero beheads a stranger and is obliged to present himself for the same treatment in a year's time. In neither case is the punishment exacted. There is a link with paganism in one case with the waste city being returned to prosperity, and in the other in the site of the return blow being a barrow defended by a challenge knight. More or less the same story is also told in Irish legend, the hero being Cuchulain. This theme is sometimes called 'the beheading game', but there are several factors in the account of the waste city to indicate that it was not a game at all but the real thing. First of all, this is yet another pagan episode gathered into Lancelot's life story. When this happens there is a condition imposed by narrators that the hero should escape death or immobility, so the hero's escape may very well not have been part of the original story. We are left with the inference that the rich dress of the youth and the golden hat indicate kingship; that a successful conclusion to the adventure is expected to bring back prosperity to the city; that it is an annual event, taking place at

[63] *Perlesvaus*, tr. Bryant, pp. 182–4.

the year end; and, from the great ceremonial, it is a ritual event in which the whole populace is involved.

It may reasonably be supposed that the same rule – that in a romance composed of a string of incidents the hero must survive – will also have influenced the narrators of the stories of Gawain and Cuchulain. The survival of these heroes is probably a fiction. The underlying original is likely to have involved a long sequence of sacrificial victims in annual beheadings.

We have seen burning and beheading as the means of ritual killing. There is another method which was used by Perceval to dispose of a lord who attacked the Maimed King's widow, who lived in the West Wales Camelot. He had eleven knights decapitated and collected their blood in a cauldron, in which he had his enemy's head immersed until he drowned. Perceval's method of disposing of the vessel afterward may strike a chord with archaeologists. 'The vat with all the blood was thrown in the river'.[64] Is this a recollection from late prehistoric times when ritual vessels, among other prestige objects, were deposited in watery places?

### The Grail Hero and the Grail Procession

Of Chrétien's four romances only one, *Le Conte du Graal*, often referred to as *Perceval*, is about the Grail. This was Chrétien's last Arthurian romance and he left it unfinished. Over the next few decades successors came forward to fill the gap, and produced four versions of the missing ending, totalling five or six times as many lines of verse as were in Chrétien's own unfinished work. Others wrote two prologues and there were alternative versions, not all in French. There have been, of course, many scholarly works written on the relationship between these romances, but here I shall look on them from the point of view of recollections of paganism. The question is, to what extent did these authors, and later authors and translators, have access to the Celtic tradition on which Chrétien himself drew, and so may be able to add to our knowledge of Celtic tradition? If all these successors to Chrétien merely copied him and added embellishments from their own imaginations, there would be no point in considering them here.

An instance from another romance will make the point. Chrétien's *Yvain* was translated into Welsh and appears as a section of the *Mabinogion* in modern versions of that group of stories. For the most part, the Welsh version is directly comparable to the French. However, there are some differences. For instance, when the adventurer approaches the Thunderstorm Fountain, he first encounters the giant lord of the animals, who has complete control over all the wild creatures of the forest. In the Welsh version of this story, but not in the French, he is said to be a black giant sitting on a mound in a clearing and

---

[64] *Perlesvaus*, Nitze and Jenkins, pp. 234/5; trans. Bryant, pp. 151/2.

he has only one leg and has one eye in the middle of his forehead.[65] These are the characteristics of gods in Irish and Scandinavian tradition. It is not hard to believe that the Welsh translator may have added back to the story detail suppressed by Chrétien as unsuitable for his more sophisticated audience. The episode can be recognized as a sketch of a god only in the Welsh version.

Turning now to *Perceval*, one of the prologues is entitled the *Elucidation* and contains a report on the ravishing of well-maidens and the loss of the prosperity provided by the court of the Fisher King. A. W. Thompson comments that, although the connection between the prologue and Chrétien's romance is not obvious, 'someone at an early date in the development of the legend thought it did have a connection. Probably that fact is one more proof that the Grail was not of Christian origin.'[66] Evidently Thompson thought that the writer of the Elucidation had access to Celtic material not used by Chrétien.

The other 'prologue', called 'Bliocadran', is more of an alternative account to Chrétien's of Perceval's youth. It is, in fact, closer to the versions provided in other romances than it is to Chrétien's *Perceval*. To quote Thompson again: 'that fact is often taken as testimony for a pre-Chrétien form of the story.'

The *Continuations* contain incidents similar to those in Chrétien, but there are often substantial differences in the treatment of well-known episodes, for instance, when Gawain visits the Grail Castle it is at the end of a long spit of land and although the Grail is present, with the bleeding spear, there is no procession in which they are paraded. The *Continuation* of Manessier records the end of Perceval's story. He is crowned as successor to his uncle the Fisher King and becomes a Fisher King himself. Perceval's successor in the development of the post-Chrétien romances, Galahad, at the end of his life was crowned at Sarras, where he reigned for a year before his death in 'achieving' the Grail. Not much attention has been given to this aspect of the Grail hero's life, but since they are both remembered as becoming king, in rather different ways, there is a substantial chance that this is an archaic feature.

If Chrétien was recycling a Celtic traditional tale also known in Wales, it is not unexpected that a Welsh author should be in a position to re-introduce material which sounds as if it came from the underlying tradition. What is more surprising is that the same thing has happened in two instances in a German version of Chrétien's story, Wolfram von Eschenbach's *Parzival*. It has generally been conjectured that, in the French romances, the wound between the thighs of a ruler, which causes magical barrenness, is a euphemism for castration. Only in *Parzival* is this stated openly. And this is also the only Arthurian story in which a 'challenge' episode includes the broken branch motif recorded in the classical descriptions of the rite at Nemi.[67] Wolfram has his hero gather a garland or break a twig from the special tree to provoke a

---

[65] *Mabinogion*, Penguin, p. 196.
[66] In *Arthurian Legend in the Middle Ages*, ed. Loomis, p. 209.
[67] It is perhaps not surprising that the other original qualification for a challenger, that he should be a runaway slave, plays no part in the romances.

challenge in two episodes, one involving Gawain, the other, Perceval. Chrétien, in his version of the same episode, has the Proud Damsel send Gawain across the Perilous Ford merely to gather a bunch of flowers.

The consideration of the relationships of the various versions of the texts mentioning the Grail legend is necessary because of the effect on our approach to the romances as a whole of two aspects of the 'matter of Britain'. One is that, as he was the originator of the genre, Chrétien's sanitized version, in which one drop of blood drops from the lance, tends to take precedence over later versions in which the Grail is a receptacle for blood. The other is that in some versions the Grail story has been adapted to provide what Matarasso calls, in the case of the *Queste del Saint Graal*, 'a guide to the spiritual life aimed at the court'.[68] But even in this heavily edited work 'it is quite clear that ancient legendary material has been reinterpreted to make it relevant to a society whose beliefs . . . were far removed from those of the ancient Celts.'

If Chrétien tends to suppress the less courtly aspects of his original, and if the educational system of the Middle Ages meant that the literate were trained by the church, where are we to turn for versions of Perceval's quest which preserve the flavour of such archaic material in the Celtic traditions of Wales and Ireland? The answer seems to lie in two works which least follow the general run of Chrétien and his immediate successors, *Perlesvaus* and *Peredur*. The authenticity of the first of these, from the point of view of paganism, is vouched for by the presence of the two episodes involving Lancelot recounted above, which can only be accounted for as recollections of annual kingship. This work is characterized by other archaic motifs: bloodthirsty damsels, severed heads and, indeed, all the aspects of paganism which stem from Arthur's adventure in the glade and which provide the basis for the first part of this book. *Peredur* is a Welsh version of one of Chrétien's themes which is far from being a translation, though many incidents are recognizable. To illustrate the difference, *Peredur* introduces the most bloodthirsty example of a Grail-type procession in which the centrepiece is two girls 'bearing a large platter with a man's head covered with blood on it.'[69] The differences between *Peredur* and the other versions of the Perceval story are of the greatest importance in understanding its relationship to mythology.[70]

A third important source of information about the Grail is the work of Robert de Boron, who tells of Joseph of Arimathea and the introduction into this country of the Grail and its associated symbolism: the lance directed by a fiery angel, the wound between the thighs, and healing blood.

The many texts referring to the Grail provide a large number of different version of its relationship to the lance and the associated ritual. The lance may have a single drop of blood on it; or it may drip blood into a container which is not the Grail; or it may drip blood into the Grail. The Grail and the lance may

68 *The Quest of the Holy Grail*, tr. P. M. Matarasso, p. 9.
69 *Mabinogion*, tr. Ganz, Penguin, p. 226.
70 Presented in detail by G. Goetinck in *Peredur* . . .

be merely be present; they may be carried in a procession; the presence of the Grail may magically provide food, or healing, or destruction by the fiery lance. How is this strange affair to be explained?

An examination of the Grail and its associated symbolism leaves little doubt that the background of this cup-shaped container contains pagan elements. Even a heavily Christianized version, such as the *Queste del Saint Graal*, contains many markers of paganism, such as Galahad's year of kingship. But from all the variations, how are we to decide what is original, and thus may be significant, and what is imaginary? The degree of variation is in itself a clue. There is none of the sense of derivation or pastiche which pervades, say, *Fergus* or *Perceforest*. The wide variation, the wildness, the lack of compatibility, are what one might expect from a garbled tradition rather than from the recycling of other authors' motifs. And identifiable aspects of paganism are not hard to find.

The Grail is to be found in the Grail Castle, Corbenic, the home of the line of Grail keepers, who are invariably maimed or languishing, often with the wound 'between the thighs' indicating the nature of his disability. The scene is set in a wasted, barren land. The Grail hero, in his most primitive form, kills the pagan king and marries his daughter, the Sovereignty. He thus becomes king himself, but suffers emasculation by a fiery lance. The resulting magical barrenness can be cured by the succession of a vigorous successor. In later variations, in which the contender is Gawain, Lancelot or Bors, the fiery lance strikes from heaven and the method of disposal of the sacrificial victim is recalled by the shameful cart, however the continuation of the story requires the survival of the hero. But in those other variations in which the successful hero is either Galahad or Perceval, a major aspect of paganism which has survived is Grail kingship at Corbenic or the 'holy' city of Sarras. The fatal nature of the adventure, as far as Galahad is concened, has been remembered even in the *Queste*, and the death of the sacred king is accompanied by fire from heaven in a less edited version of this event.

An interesting part is played by the pagan princess. She is the mainspring of the system. As the Proud Damsel she caused Anfortas to be emasculated. She appears as the Empress who offered the cup to Peredur, and for whom he fought against all comers. And she appears in an attenuated form as all the damsels of ford and fountain who were fought over by challengers and defenders.

Amongst all the other unreal supernatural events, the Grail procession has a particular air of pagan provenance. The main features are: the Maimed King (for instance, Pelles) is present, carried into the hall in a litter; the proceedings are initiated by a dove which carries a censer in its bill, filling the place with the delightful odours of incense; a sumptuous vessel is carried in by a virgin, (Pelles' daughter was a Grail bearer); she is followed by another maiden (who may be Pelles' niece, the mother of Perceval) who carries a silver platter; after this candles, tapers or torches are carried past; then comes a youth with a lance which drips blood, accompanied by general wailing; and as the Grail is carried past the tables where the spectators are sitting, the company is miraculously satisfied with the food of each individual's choice.[71] That night the hero is subjected to the adventure of the fiery lance in the testing bed[72] and finishes up in the demeaning cart[73] or else in due course he becomes a Fisher King himself, replacing the one he has 'cured'.[74]

Whether such an event or dramatised representation ever took place is impossible to say, but there are interesting features. Behind the food-producing capability of the Grail there seems to lie a eucharistic function. It is a cup of blood from which a 'host' – a symbolic consecrated meal – is provided for the worshippers. The Maimed King (in this instance, Evalac/Mordrains) is said to have been sustained solely on the host from the Grail.[75] This host is several times said to have the form of a child or a man,[76] and the blood which the Grail contains drips into it from the spear which has been used to castrate the victim. These hints of what Frazer calls the 'eaten god' have survived in spite of the Christian veneer superimposed on the tradition by later authors. In this story of the Grail we are taken back into the past when such rites were actually performed – several versions of the Grail story refer to consecrated blood being drunk from it or from some other costly vessel[77] – mercifully now superseded by the symbolism of the Eucharist. Ironically, the means used by Christianity to defuse a terrifying ancient cult seems to have resulted in the recollection of the actual practice of that cult being given a Christian gloss.

There is an attractive explanation for the form of the Grail procession in which it is said that the golden Grail represents the sun, the silver platter the moon, and the candles the stars.[78] Since sun, moon and planets were at one time the objects of worship of the very sect which also worshipped the Grail – Evalac was ruler of Sarras where there were temples to the sun, moon and planets – this interpretation has a great deal to commend it. It is supported as far as the platter or carving dish is concerned by a comment in the Continuation of Gerbert de Montreuil which describes the dish as 'plus clair que lune'.[79]

However, the link between the Grail and the sun is only a minor one in the expression of this cult. The association between the Grail, or an associated container, and blood is very strong. Apart from the many instances of blood dripping into it from the lance, in one episode grails are said to have contained 100 boars heads. The word sangliers for boars is thought to be a mistake for

---

71 *Vulgate*, VI, p. 13.
72 See pp. 76f.
73 See pp. 78f.
74 Potvin, bk VI, lines 45157/8. The healing of the Fisher King follows Partinal's death by Perceval's hand. Perceval later succeeds to the kingship at the Grail Castle and takes the title Fisher King.
75 *Le Saint Graal*, Hucher, III, p. 503.
76 *Vulgate*, VI, pp. 180 and 189.
77 Göppinger Arbeiten zur Germanstik, p. 123, Jillings, L. In both grail scenes in *Diu Crone* the old man partakes of sacred blood.
78 *King Arthur and the Grail*, Cavendish, pp. 137/8.
79 M. Williams, ed., line 10412.

the similar word sanglantes, meaning bloody. This was at the castle of Brandelis;[80] bloody heads on grails would be quite appropriate at a site dedicated to Bran, the god of the severed head.

As well as these examples, Peredur was presented with the bloody head of his cousin on a large platter which seems to have taken the place of the Grail in a procession similar to the Grail procession – the head had, significantly, been cut off by the witches of Gloucester, a fate redolent of paganism.

There is perhaps something to be learnt from the divergent underlying traditions of the Welsh Peredur and the French Galahad. Perhaps the Celtic tradition still extant in the twelfth century had been altered and added to in entirely different ways. The Welsh tradition suffered a century or two more of damage and loss in a disintegrating oral tradition. The French was stabilized in writing much earlier, but suffered at the hands of uncomprehending narrators. The end result, as far as the romances are concerned, is that the stratum of tradition is heavily overlaid by invention, but the tradition is there, easily recognisable when pointed out, and it is closely related to the Welsh in style and content. But there are basic differences to be discerned between the two, apart from the substitution of Galahad for Perceval. For instance, in the romances the Arthurian power-base is more consistently seen to be in Logres than in Wales or Cornwall. This may provide a clue to the differences between the two Grail heroes. One legend could stem from the performance of the system in Wales, the other from its performance in Logres, a possibility which will be seen to be enhanced by a later discussion on the times and places at which these events occurred.

## Burial

The cult practices described in the romances resulted in many deaths. The most prestigious victims were buried with great ceremony. They were after all the prime religious figures of the day, the contemporary bishops and archbishops. So they had their last resting place in the equivalents of Westminster Abbey. They were buried at Camelot in St Stephen's or St John's, or in the Spiritual Palace at the holy city of Sarras, or in the Grail Castle,[81] or in the cases of Uther and Ambrosius, on Salisbury Plain and at Stonehenge, respectively. For those who met their fate at outlying cult sites, local cemeteries were available with chapels for the proper religious ceremonies. This was the situation at Belforet for Iweret's victims, and there was a cemetery with twenty four tombs of princesses who had bled to death where Perceval's sister gave her life to heal the leper lady.

Sometimes the emphasis is on where the victim fell. Thus Galahad was buried where he fell in front of the altar at Sarras; and Lanceor, prince of

---

80 *Sir Gawain and the Lady of Lys*, tr. Weston, pp. 29f.
81 *Perlesvaus*, tr. Bryant, p. 263.

Ireland, and his lover were buried where they fell,[82] he killed by Balin, at Merlin's Perron near Camelot.[83]

Knights were buried fully armed and with their swords beside them.[84] This is noted particularly of the King Galahad who gave the name Wales to Hoselice and of his namesake the high prince Galehot.[85] King Galahad's tomb consisted of a stone slab supported by four pillars.[86] Since the stories of these two Galahads are so similar as to suppose them to be derived from the same original, this may be taken as a more detailed description of Galehot's grave, suspected to have been a dolmen.[87]

After death ceremonial figures retained their importance. The talismanic body of King Galahad of Wales was taken away from its tomb, the largest in a cemetery of thirty four tombs, by a great body of 'converts' after the grave had been opened by Lancelot on the day after Ascension Day.[88] The body of King Galahad's brother, Josephé, was taken away to the abbey of Glay in Escoce to avert a famine;[89] and the 'holy' body of Joseph of Arimathea, father to both the above, also exerted a talismanic function, founding a castle in the island of Galosche in the romance *Sone de Nausay*.[90]

The use of human remains for ritual purposes is entirely in accordance with archaeological findings from the Neolithic era, so tends to support the proposition that the description of King Galahad's tomb as a stone slab supported on pillars, and of Galehot's as a reused pagan stone tomb, are recollections from Neolithic times.

---

82 Huth *Merlin*, I, p. 230.
83 *Morte Darthur*, bk II, ch. 5.
84 *Vulgate*, VI, pp. 27/30; *Prose Lancelot*, ed. Hutchings, p. 45.
85 *Vulgate*, IV, p. 279.
86 *Prose Lancelot*, ed. Hutchings, p. 45A.
87 See p. 180.
88 *Vulgate*, IV, p. 176.
89 *Vulgate*, I, p. 285.
90 *Sone de Nausay*, ed. Goldschmidt, lines 4557/8.

# THE NATURE OF PAGANISM IN BRITAIN

## The Demotion of Deities

The Celtic gods Bran and Belenus/Beli turn up in Geoffrey's *Historia* as Brennius and Belinus, kings of Britain. The degeneration of gods into superior mortals is an accidental effect of tradition and is a phenomenon demonstrated again by the same pair when Brennos and Bolgios, supposedly human, are said to have led their armies into Macedonia in the third century BC. Anne Ross's explanation is: 'The Celtic tribes in general claimed their descent from a divine ancestor and it is only to be expected that the eponymous deity would be one whose reputation would incite his followers to heroism.'[1] The result is that gods are sometimes seen as historical characters. Another influence tending in the same direction is the presence of deities in genealogies as the ancestors of royal lines. Avallach is a case in point. Three major Welsh dynasties traced their descent from Aballac, who is described as the son of Amalach, the son of Beli and Anna. Amalach and Aballac are probably doublets of Avallach, and if I am right in supposing Avallach to be a form of Beli, the same deity has appeared three times in succession. If this is so, it is easy to see why. The court genealogist has not necessarily been venal or stupid. Tradition may have presented him with the same genealogical table in three versions, after the name of the deity in question had diverged into distinct forms. He therefore combined the three. The Anna of royal ancestry is discussed on p. 139 below.

As well as believing deities to have been their ancestors, Celtic kings incorporated the names of deities in their own. Cunobelinus is an example. It is evident that the gods seemed much closer to human beings in Celtic times, and, in the case of kings, sometimes indistinguishable. This may explain why personages who exhibit the behaviour of or associations with supernatural beings also appear as historical characters. Arthur may be an example, but there are several others who are less conspicuous and so more easy to analyse. Ambrosius, for instance, is authenticated by Gildas, but was there an Ambrosius associated with Stonehenge, who formed the basis for Geoffrey's

[1] *Pagan Celtic Britain*, p. 221.

characters with that title? If not, how did the place-name Amesbury, Ambro's burg, arise?

There was also a historical Peredur, and two other historical characters who consistently show mythological behaviour in the romances and in Welsh tradition are Urien Rheged and his son Owein. Urien has been interpreted here as a god who is married to a goddess, Morgan le Fay. His son in the romances is the hero Owein/Yvain who wins the Lady of the Fountain from the guardian of the spring and guards it in his turn; and in the Welsh *Dream of Rhonabwy*, he is assisted by a band of ravens which is more than a match for Arthur's knights.[2] The mythological background to this story is explained by the episode in which the ravens which come to the aid of the defender of the Perilous Ford are the transformed sisters of the damsel who was the spirit of the ford; they were immortal and they lived in Avalon. Morgan, looking after her son Owein/Yvain, behaves like an Irish goddess who does the same. Clearly, being human does not prevent one's name being a vehicle for the transmission of information about mythology. Perhaps the fact that important people chose to incorporate myth into their own 'histories' has been a critical factor in the preservation of the myth, in much the same way as a Christian gloss may have been responsible for the survival of a memory of the events at Corbenic.

## Deities in the 'Matter of Britain'

The names of about four hundred Celtic gods and goddesses are recorded in inscriptions, mostly continental, dating from the centuries around the time of Christ. Three quarters of them occur once only,[3] which suggests that, although there may have been a few general deities corresponding to widespread wonders such as sun and moon, thunder and lightning, sexuality, birth and death, by far the greatest number were the names of the deities of individual tribes or else the names of the supernatural beings associated with the natural features which were common objects of worship in every locality – particular trees, glades, springs and so on. Presumably only a very small proportion of the deities had their names inscribed on altars and most altars will have perished, so the real number of these minor deities must have been many times the three hundred mentioned above. Most of the inscriptions preserving the names of deities have been found in Gaul, where on the fringe of the literate Mediterranean world written commemorations were more usual, but there is no reason to suppose that the same pattern would not also have prevailed in Britain.

The oral tradition is by no means so lavish in the number of names of deities it has preserved. Taking the narrowest possible definition of 'deity', it has been said that the only gods and goddesses which feature in the Welsh *Mabinogion*

---

2   *Mabinogion*, Penguin, p. 189.
3   *The Gods of the Celts*, M. Green, p. 32.

are Lleu, Don, Mabon and Modron.[4] A wider, but still conservative, sweep would add to these Bran, Beli and Rhiannon, the first because of his great size, his talismanic severed head, and his mysterious wound;[5] the second because of his position among the ultimate ancestors in the genealogies of Welsh royal houses; and the third as a horse-goddess from her name Rigantona (Great Queen), from her supernatural ability as a horsewoman and her punishment of having to carry strangers to court on her back.[6]

Court bards seem to have used descent from the gods as a normal means of flattery, so a position high in the list of ancestors of early medieval Welsh kings provides names which might be those of deities but for which there is usually no way of confirming this status because there are no detailed descriptions. For instance, when the personage in question is Avallach, two other similar names spring to mind, Avallo, the name-giving patron of the Isle of Avalon and 'father' of the priestesses there, and Evalac the sun god with the goddess-dolly, but there seems to be no means of finding if these three, or any two of them, are the same person. And when the ultimate ancestor is Anna, mother of the Virgin Mary, we may again suspect, but cannot prove, an original of a name similar to Anna and with high pagan status; perhaps the goddess called Anu (an alternative name for the Irish Danann, leader of the Tuatha De Danann), who gave her name to the mountains called the Paps of Anu in county Kerry, or perhaps the forbidding hag remembered as Annis in British folklore.

Non-Welsh sources are less reticent about describing their characters as deities. Morgan le Fay and Diana, as already mentioned, are specifically so described, and so are a couple of little known native gods, Teruagant and Cahu. As well as these, several deities appear under recognizable names such as the classical deities Venus, Faunus, Sebile, and the Celtic Bran, Beli, Mabon, Nut (Nodens, Nuada), Lear (Llyr), Do and his son Girflet (Don and her son Gilfaethwy), Branwen, Enid (the Sovereignty of the Veneti), Florée (Flower maiden) and Helen.

## Bran and Beli

Of those deities in this list who get more than a cursory mention, the one who appears most frequently and about whom most is known, both from Welsh and French sources, is Bran, followed by his 'brother' Beli. These two may as well be taken together as they are often linked and because, though they are entirely different personages, the traces they have left in the tradition are very similar. The large number of personal names beginning Bran- in the romances has often been remarked on, and the same can be said of those beginning Bel-.

---

4  *The International Popular Tale in Wales*, K. H. Jackson, p. 128.
5  Bromwich, in *Trioedd Ynys Prydein*, p. 284, refers to 'grounds for supposing Bran to be a euhemerized deity'.
6  *Mabinogion*, Penguin, p. 61.

In each case the name seems to have been compounded with prefixes or suffixes and to have been modified and eroded but still left in a recognizable form. A score or so personages have names that can be linked with Bran and rather more with Beli. Even allowing some scope for error in compiling the lists, which are detailed in Who's Who below, these groups of names which are phonologically connected and also have linked mythological characteristics provide a powerful argument in favour of regarding the original bearers of the names as having been wide ranging deities. Both groups include goddesses, of which the one linked with Beli – the 'British Helen', represented by all the Elaines in the romances – though previously almost unrecognized as a deity, now reveals a very substantial profile (see the British Helen below).

Briefly, there are resemblances between Bran and Beli as well as clear cut differences. The title Fisher King occurs in both groups and with it guardianship of the Grail. Both are connected with islands and with the challenge theme. Both are kin to each other, usually as brothers, and to other deities. On the other hand, Bran is often a giant, while Beli is a knightly dwarf. Bran has more links with Ireland (as a religion, not the present day country) and with severed heads; Beli with lightning and with fountains. A Roman traveller reported that Cronus slept in a cave on an uninhabited island off the west coast of Britain. It is possible to see this figure, enshrouded in darkness, as Bran, while Beli is linked with the skyward pointing rocky pinnacle of Mt St Michel by its earlier name, Tombelaine, and also with lightning and with brightness. More details of these two gods and also Morgan le Fay and Diana of the Woods can be found in *The Real Camelot*, pp. 72–80.

## Mabon and Modron

Mabon is perhaps the most obvious deity, among those on the Welsh short list, who can also be recognized as a god in French romances[7] (and who as it happens is also vouched for in inscriptions). He is described as an enchanter,[8] a sign of a supernatural being; he is brother of the god Bran (as Branduz); he is the black defender of a cult site enclosed by a barrier of air as Mabonagrein; he has a ford named after him at which he fights Gawain for the fay Marsique[9] he is a black oppressor as Nabon le Noir, holding many knights prisoner in the Val de Servage;[10] he is son of the water-fay Queen of Maidenland in the German *Lanzelet*, herself the equivalent of the Damsel of the Lake (again, arguably a divinity); and he is a parallel to the great hero Yvain (Welsh Owein) in which form his mother is, in one tradition, Morgan le Fay.[11] These

---

7   And see Gazetteer, Lochmabenstane.
8   West, *Prose Index*.
9   Huth *Merlin*, II, p. 222. Called here Naborn the Enchanter, who is accepted by West as a synonym of Mabon.
10  *Roman de Tristan*, Löseth, para. 61.
11  *Prose index*, West, under Yvain[2].

references to the divine parentage of Mabon match the Welsh version, in which Mabon and Modron are an inseparable mother-and-son pair, she the divine mother and he the divine son. In terms of classical mythology, Mabon is always equated to Apollo, who plays the same 'son' role relative to his mother Latona as does Mabon to his mother, Modron. Latona, according to Hecateus,[12] was born in an island larger than Sicily off the north coast of Gaul, presumably Britain. In general terms, the French romances tell us, the 'Mother of God' was more honoured in one place than elsewhere in Christendom, but since the place in this quotation is Chastel Orguelleus, a jousting place where the god Bran did well,[13] it may be supposed that some pagan precursor of Mary was intended when they speak[14] of 'the mass of the glorious mother of god'. In one way or another, both Mabon and Modron are well represented in the 'matter of Britain'.

## Don

The presence in the Irish and Welsh traditions of roughly equivalent pantheons headed respectively by the goddesses Danann and Don might lead to an expectation that an active goddess of much the same name would appear in the romances. This would be asking too much, for neither of these two played any part themselves in the *action* of the underlying Celtic traditional tales which record their existence. It was their 'people' or their 'children' who were participants. In terms of importance in the story in the romances, the inactive (male) Do, Don or Doon of Cardoel, and his active and adventurous children Girflet and Lorete have roughly the same relationship as their Welsh counterparts, the inactive goddess Don and her adventurous children, including Girflet's counterpart, Gilfaethwy.

The traditional histories of the British Isles show several odd traits. One, the name-giving founder, has already been mentioned. Another is the ascription of the origin of invasions to some specific country, generally Spain or Greece or Troy. Danann was a descendant of Nemed, who is said to have come from the Greeks of Scythia. Now Scythia happens to be watered by the two great rivers whose names Rees and Rees consider to have been derived from the same root as Danann and Don – the Dnieper and the Dniester (and one cannot help suspecting that the same applies to the Donetz and the Don).[15] Is there a connection here? It would be asking too much to suppose that there was a prehistoric invasion from the steppes which has been remembered in tradition, but the recollection of the same name Don as a river name in the Ukraine as well as in Britain has marked two surges in the wide spread of an ancient people, as if by the distinctive sediment from some ancient sea.

---

12 For more detail see Gazetteer under Salisbury Plain.
13 *First Continuation*, ed. Roach, lines 11725–11736.
14 *Vulgate*, VI, p. 102.
15 *Celtic Heritage*, Rees and Rees, p. 53.

## Lleu

The equivalent of Lleu in the romances is by no means obvious, but it has been pointed out that the Arthurian King Lot of Orkney corresponds in some ways. Following this identification through, it can be seen that Lleu was probably the original of several important but rather shadowy characters – Luce, king of Britain; Lot, who was leader of the rebel kings and the father of the heroes Gawain and his brothers; and perhaps even Lucius, the 'emperor of Rome' (called Luce in the romances) who, like Lot, was defeated by Arthur.

## Flora and Faunus

The principle of growth and reproduction seems to have been all-important in the romances – a guiding force which has shaped the systems of kingship in several ways. If we search for a deity who might represent this principle it is likely to have been a goddess and was probably a personage called Florée or some similar name. It was no doubt in her honour that participants in the spring rituals wore chaplets of flowers[16] and wore green or else dressed in leaves. She does not occupy much space in West's *Index of Proper Names*, but when we examine the details they are quite interesting. Under the alternative name of Sarracinte she is argued here to have been the name-giving goddess of sovereignty at the holy city of Sarras, and she was married to a certain Celidoine, the principal astronomer in Joseph of Arimathea's entourage. It was she who conceived on the night of her husband's coronation following the maiming of the Maimed King, Evalac of Sarras. This event is said to have taken place at the city of Norgales but the characters are also connected with Sarras, which was of course astronomically significant, as its city contained temples to the sun and planets, so a suitable setting for Celidoine. Perhaps the same ritual was performed at both places.

In another incarnation Florée was the mother of Guinglain by Gawain. Guinglain under the anonymous title 'le Bel Inconnu' is the literary prototype of all the knights errant, and, if the speculation that he is a British equivalent to Cuchulain is correct, a figure whose true eminence has declined on this side of the Celtic Sea over the millennia.

The doings of the Florées are only an introduction to this complex deity. Her name, like others, has been eroded by the loss of the first letter,[17] so still more information about her is available from the personages called Lore or Lorete in the romances. What might appear to be two different Lores (West's Lore[1] and Lore[4]) are almost certainly the same. One was called 'of Cardoel' and was said to be daughter of the master-butler of Logres by one of Arthur's sisters; and the other was daughter of Do of Cardoel, Uther Pendragon's master-forester.

---

16 *Perceforest*, Roussineau, part IV, p. 394.
17 This is an accident that often happens. Loomis suggests it for Florée in *Arthurian Tradition and Chrétien de Troyes*, p. 161.

This Lore was a sister of Girflet, equivalent to Gilfaethwy who was one of the children of Don. Thus Lore's brother was a divinity, which tends to confirm her own status as a supernatural being.

Lore's parentage can be represented either as:

She was the daughter of the master-butler of Logres and one of Arthur's sisters, and she was entitled 'of Cardoel'

or:

She was the daughter of the master-forester of Uther Pendragon, King of Logres, and her father was called Do of Cardoel.

These two statements could be variants on a single original in which Lore's parents were Do of Cardoel and one of Arthur's sisters. Of Arthur's sisters, one can speculate who was involved in this marriage with Do. It could have been Anna, who, since she has been equated with Danu and hence with Don, would be an entirely appropriate consort for Do.

Lore may have a parallel in the Damsel of the Lake in that both are 'descendants' of goddesses. Perhaps this means they were the goddess in her human phase, able to participate in 'adventures' and ceremonials. These two have another resemblance. They are both the daughters of foresters. And, in so far as the Damsel of the Lake resembles Diana 'of the Woods' and Lore is an equivalent of Florée, both may be thought of as spirits of vegetative growth.

Lore's position in the scheme of things may be clarified by a look at the links between Diana and other classical deities. It has already been pointed out that there is a strong convergence between the two couples Diana and Faunus on the one hand and the Damsel of the Lake and Merlin on the other. The relationship between them and other divine personages who are known to be linked with or parallels of Diana is now set out in tabular form. The personages in each column are merely different names for the same underlying deity.

### In the classical tradition

| Goddesses | | Gods |
|---|---|---|
| Juno | consort of | Zeus |
| Jana | consort of | Janus |
| Diana | consort of | Dianus |

### In the 'matter of Britain'

| Diana | lover of | Faunus |
|---|---|---|
| Damsel of | lover of | Merlin |
| the Lake | daughter of | Dianus |

Diana and the Damsel of the Lake were both huntresses, their lovers were both 'Lord of the Animals', and the women both killed their lovers by incarcerating them alive in a stone tomb.

Diana and the Damsel of the Lake were both kin to Dyonas, a hunter in the woods and lord of a great forest. He seems to fit in the right hand column of male divinities above and links the huntresses of the romances to the classical goddesses by the identity of his name with Dianus, hence with Janus[18] and ultimately with Zeus, who was linked with oak trees and with lightning. Diana's roots can be traced via Artemis to a fertility goddess and her name 'of the woods' links her with vegetation. It may be guessed that Florée is another evocation of the same principle and she may be placed tentatively in the column graced by Diana. Faunus seems to have played the same kind of role as far as the animal creation was concerned as Diana for the vegetable. The table above may therefore be completed, as far as British deities are concerned, as follows:

| Florée, | Faunus |
|---|---|
| an alternative | |
| to Diana as | |
| vegetation goddess | |

Flora has now been partnered by Faunus. Evidently we are seeing in the local tradition a more primitive version of the patriarch of the gods, and his variously named consort, than in the Olympian hierarchy, but a version which is not so different that the members of it could not have evolved from the same originals.

Merlin in the right hand column has a link with the thunder and lightning of Zeus, for he was closely concerned with the setting up of the thunderstorm fountain, setting it up himself according to one version,[19] and he inserted the lightning sword of Beli into the floating stone (p. 172 below).

The British end of this spectrum of goddesses can be displayed by setting out in tabular form, as now follows, the relationships of the several personages called

Florée and Lore and also those lovers of Gawain who though not so named correspond to her in behaviour:

Florée, the Sovereignty of Sarras, was crowned, married, and conceived the night the previous king **Evalac** was maimed.

Florée, the daughter of Alain of **Escavalon**, bore a child to **Gawain** and later married **Melian** de Lis.

Unnamed sister of Guinganbresil of **Escavalon** bore a son to **Gawain** and later married **Melian** cousin of Lore de Branlant.[20]

Lorie of Roche Florie, a fairy, was lover of **Gawain**.

---

[18] The supposed bust of the king of the Woodland Glade found at Nemi was two-faced, linking him with the two-faced stone heads of the western tradition. His leafy head-dress might be taken to represent Sylvanus/Faunus.

[19] Godefroy, under foudre.

[20] *Prose Index*, West, under Melyant[2].

Blancemal, a fairy bore a child to **Gawain**.

Guilorete, the Pucele de Lis, bore a child to **Gawain**. Her brothers were **Melian** and Bran de Lis.[21]

Lore or Lorete was daughter of Do of **Cardoel** and sister of Girflet.

Lore of **Cardoel** was lady in waiting to **Guenever**.

Lore de Branlant was lady in waiting to **Guenever** and loved **Gawain**, whom she wished to kill so that she could be buried with him.

Lore, Queen of Caradigan, deposited a horse hobble in the Waste Chapel and retrieved a scrap of cloth from the altar.

Lorete the blonde was a lady in waiting at Arthur's court.

The principal theme seems to be love for Gawain and the bearing of a son to him. The circumstances of the affair are made clear by the identification of Lorie as a fairy, that is, in terms of the British tradition, a supernatural being. To confirm the view that there is a recollection of some feature of pre-Christian religion here, there are in the background several other prime indications of paganism: the goddess of sovereignty; Sarras, the pagan capital city; Guingan-bresil who was brother of Giromelant, the guardian of the Tree of the Garland; Gawain, the taker of the garland from the defended tree; the god Bran in Lore's title 'Branlant' and as Guilorete's brother; and Lore's close kinship with Do and Girflet, representatives in romance of the divine Children of Don. It looks as if the original was an extremely archaic story of the union of a hero and a vegetation spirit. The existence of other Lores and Loretes unconnected with Gawain does not mean they are irrelevant. Battered versions of the story may still reveal original links with Sarras, Avalon and Cardoel.

## The British Helen

There are a great many characters in the Arthurian tradition called Elaine, if they are women, or Alain, if they are men. The spelling varies a good deal. Sometimes they have an initial 'H'. To add or remove an 'H' at the beginning of a word used to be a feature of the English language which depended on local usage up to recent times, so its presence or absence has no value in distinguishing one form from the other, and can be disregarded. There is also a certain amount of variation in the initial vowel, which is sometimes 'A' and sometimes 'E'. These variations occur in different versions of the same story, for instance Alain le Gros may be spelt Alein, Elain, Ellain or Helain. It is therefore not possible to distinguish one Alain or Elaine from another merely on account of the spelling of the name.

Out of about a score of such individuals about half are of each sex. To deal

[21] 'Lis' here probably signifies 'isle', since Bran de Lis looks like a doublet of Brandiles, i.e. Bran of the Isle.

briefly first with the men, they include amongst their number several person-ages of considerable pagan importance. There is Alain le Gros, who was the first Rich Fisher and Grail guardian, and was father of Perceval; Alain, King of Terre Foraine, another Rich Fisher and brother of Pelles, of Pellinor and of the Widow of the Waste Forest; Alain, King of Escavalon; Helain the White, son of Bors and Brangoire's daughter, born to be a Grail hero; and an Elian, prince of Ireland, who took Lancelot's place at the Round Table after the latter had been expelled for taking Guenever off to Joieuse Garde. The presence here of a high proportion of individuals linked to the Grail can scarcely be an accident.

When we come to the women, their pagan importance is equally clear. The full list of all the Elaines is as follows:

**'Elaine'** the Damsel of the Lake, who fostered Lancelot. In *Diu Crône* Lancelot's foster-mother is called a goddess.

**'Elaine'**[22] the Grail bearer, Pelles' daughter, mother of Galahad by Lancelot. The Grail-bearer in *Diu Crône*, under a different personal name, is called a goddess. The Grail-bearer appears in *Perlesvaus* as the Damsel of the Cart. She married the King of Maroune (a country neighbouring Wales) who followed Perceval as Grail King when the latter abdicated.[23]

**'Eleine'**, Pellinor's daughter, who killed herself when her lover the Knight of the Glade was killed at a spring. Pellinor found her severed head by the spring and took it to Arthur's court.[24]

**Leone**, who killed herself when her lover, the king's son of Ireland, Lanceor, was slain by Balin at Merlin's perron.

**'Elaine'** the Fair Maid of Astolat, who died of love for Lancelot.[25]

**Elainne** sister of Gawain, whose love inspired Perceval in the tournament which took place immediately before he acceded to the Perilous Seat.

**Elene** the organizing damsel in *Le Bel Inconnu*.

**Helaine** the wife of King Ban and mother of Lancelot.

**Helaine**, after whom pagan of Mont St Michel was called Tombelaine (according to one interpretation of that name).

**Helen** the empress of Rome in *The Dream of Maxen*.

**Helen**, supposed British wife of the Emperor Constantine.

**Heliene** without Equal, the incomparably beautiful wife of Persides the Red.

(The unnamed empress of Constantinople, with whom Peredur reigned for four-teen years.)

---

22  Helizabel or Amite in *Prose Index*, West.
23  *Verse Index*, West.
24  *Morte Darthur*, bk III, ch. 15.
25  Another instance where the name is provided by Malory, bk XVIII, ch. 9.

Some of these names are shown in inverted commas because Malory is the only source for them. This applies to the most famous Elaine of all, Galahad's mother, though on occasion H. O. Sommer, the extremely knowledgeable editor of the *Vulgate Version of the Arthurian Romances*, supports him.

The Elaines are without exception important and interesting. Only one, 'Elaine' the Grail bearer, is directly concerned with the Grail, but several of them are closely linked with Grail heroes in one way or another. We are fortunate in having a substantial number of characters to analyse, for several themes can be seen to be repeated more than once in the list above. For instance, three of the loves proved fatal to the woman, that of Lancelot for the Fair Maid of Astolat, that of Lanceor for Leone and that of the Knight of the Glade (Sir Miles of the Launds) for Pellinor's daughter 'by the lady of the Rule'. It can be argued that Lanceor and Lancelot are two apparently distinct images derived from a single original personage. Lancelot's father is said to have been Ban, but he is a god, so as far as human ancestry is concerned he must be an interpolation in Lancelot's family tree. The next step back is to King Lancelot, who married a princess of Ireland, so, apart from the close resemblance of name, both Lancelot and Lanceor have a link with Ireland. There is thus a basic similarity between the stories of Leone and the Fair Maid, though not reflected in the detail; and if we consider all three of these Elaines who died for love it will be seen that there is a common factor in that their men were all challenge knights.

A somewhat similar argument can be used to collapse together the affairs of the wife of Persides and of Perceval's lover, Elainne. There are strong indications that the original of Perceval was married as, indeed, his prototype Peredur was. Since one of Perceval's most prominent characteristics was that he was a red knight, it has been suggested that Persides the Red has been derived from Perceval. If so, Peredur's unnamed consort, the Empress of Constantinople, would have been called Elaine. Perhaps she was so called, like the other two 'empresses' in the table above.

It looks as though the original Elaine was a goddess of considerable importance who has surfaced as two or three separate 'empresses'; also as the cruel goddess who inspired heroes to deeds of selfless bravery; as the organizing damsel who put them through the hoop; as the head-hungry spirit of springs; and who appears, as could only happens with a deity, as their mother, their lover and the mother of their sons.

## The Sovereignty

The clearest exposition of the principle of sovereignty occurs in Irish legends in which the goddess Eriu represents the land of Ireland itself and bestows kingship on her consort. Although this principle is not so clearly stated elsewhere, the territorial nature of goddesses is sometimes hinted at in classical inscriptions. Where divine couples are recorded in the Celtic west, the female partner generally has a local name while the male, whatever his true name, may have been assimilated to a Roman god who has travelled with his legionary devotees. She is the goddess of the place, he an incomer. She is static, he is mobile. The 'matter of Britain' abounds in examples of the same kind of system, slightly differently expressed. It can be discerned in the conflicts of the challenge type and in tournaments. The touchstone for this type is that she is a prize, like Guenever.

Guenever is far from being the only territorial goddess who was fought over. Lancelot's devotion to her is paralleled by Tristan's to Yseult (princess of Ireland). Here the territorial motif may be present in Tristan's battle for the 'truage' (that is, tribute) of Cornwall for seven years, seven years being one of the standard periods for temporary kingship; and it is just possible that the cup of wine presented by the goddess to seal the contract in other examples of 'sovereignty' appears in this story as the love philtre given by Brangain to Tristan and Yseult. Brangain from her name and her character as organizing damsel seems likely to have originated in the goddess Branwen. The same Branwen, with her name slightly eroded to Ronwen (in later versions, Rowena) was the provider of the cup of sovereignty to Hengist on one of those other occasions when Geoffrey of Monmouth has got ancient myth tangled up with post-Roman history. Another abduction episode which might originally have been of the same kind is the fight for Ygerne leading to Arthur's conception. It is interesting to note that as well as Eriu, the goddess of the land of Ireland, the 'Ireland' of the romances has links with most of the other examples of 'sovereignty'. Guenever was brother of the King of Ireland (West Verse); Yseult was daughter of the Queen of Ireland; the name Iweret (Yblis's father) is very close to the medieval Welsh name for Ireland; Branwen (who as Brangain organized the affair of Tristan and Yseult) was Queen of Ireland;[26] and one version of the name Ygerne, Yverne, is, as already noted, one of the names of Ireland.

One characteristic of the Sovereignty is an alternation between beautiful and ugly, but this feature is not restricted to her for other deities such as the Irish Morrigan show the same trait. In the romances it is displayed by an odd personage – the Loathly Damsel, an extremely ugly young woman wearing a sumptuous hat and rich clothing embroidered with the Grail emblem, the dove. She sometimes turns up with a significant message. Loomis points out that she is not a separate individual but another phase of the beautiful Grail bearer. Here is a link with Celtic roots, and perhaps a slight indication that sovereignty may have been one of the aspects of the Grail bearer.

The most complete survey of the Sovereignty was made by Goetinck and comes from an analysis of the Welsh *Peredur*.[27] Here it is pointed out that Orguelleuse, prime example of the 'challenge' damsel and hence of Sovereignty, wore a heavy gold diadem, in effect, a crown, in her pavilion in a glade

---

26 In *Branwen, daughter of Llyr*.
27 *Peredur. . . .*, G. Goetinck, passim.

by a spring; that Enid, whom we have seen was the eponymous goddess of the Veneti of Vannes,[28] was set up to marry Gereint if he won the Sparrow hawk challenge, and so represents the Sovereignty; so does the Maiden of the Fortress, who offered herself to Peredur in return for his championing her; and so does the Empress, who offered a cup three times to Peredur before he lived with her and ruled her kingdom.

## The Sun and the Moon

It would be remarkable if any primitive system of paganism omitted to worship the sun and moon, the most conspicuous of what the ancients called the planetes – the wanderers, the objects which move in the sky against the background of fixed stars and which occupy that narrow band in the heavens called the zodiac by the Arabs. The daily life of civilized people is still regulated by those one-time gods who share their names with the sun, the moon and the planets:

| SUN | MOON | MARS | MERCURY | JUPITER | VENUS | SATURN |
|-----|------|------|---------|---------|-------|--------|
| Romance | | | | | | |
| | LUNDI | MARDI | MERCREDI | JEUDI | VENDREDI | |
| Germanic | | | | | | |
| SUNDAY | MONDAY | TUESDAY | WEDNESDAY | THURSDAY | FRIDAY | SATURDAY |
| | | TIW | WODEN | THOR | FRIG | |

The sun comes through most clearly into the romances as a named deity in the person of Mabon, since the latter is equated with Apollo. It is also obviously an object of worship in temples stated to be dedicated to the sun, such as that of Evalac at Sarras, and in temples (though called churches) dedicated to St John. There is a third way in which the sun shows its influence, in the behaviour of knights. Gawain, in particular, felt his strength double through the morning but in the afternoon it declined.[29] This characteristic is not quite restricted to Gawain. The Red Knight of the Red Glade also displayed it (his strength increased sevenfold at noon),[30] so Loomis's identification[31] of this knight as Mabonagrein rings true since the element Mabon- in that name signifies the sun.

The moon is represented as a named individual by Luned/Lunete, the *dea ex machina* who provides magical support for Owein/Ywain, the winning challenge knight in The Lady of the Fountain. She is a cousin of the Damsel of

---

[28] And perhaps also of the other tribes which bear the same name. This might include the Venedotians of Gwynnedd. Markale, *Le Druidism*, p. 181 etc.
[29] E.g. Huth *Merlin*, II, p. 239.
[30] *Morte Darthur*, bk VII, ch. 17.
[31] *Celtic Myth and Arthurian Romance*, p. 72.

the Lake, from whom she learns magic, by which means she sets up the thunderstorm fountain and works the spell which produces lightning when water is thrown onto a perron.[32] She sets up the cousin of Branduz des Illes (brother of Mabon) as the first defender of the fountain. The clarity with which Gawain and Lunete portray sun and moon calls forth the following comment from the medieval narrator of *Yvain*. 'He who was lord of the knights and who was renowned above them all, ought surely to be called the sun. I refer, of course to my lord Gawain, for chivalry is enhanced by him just as when the morning sun sheds its light abroad and lights all places where it shines. And I call her the moon, who I cannot do otherwise because of her sense of courtesy. However, I call her so not only because of her good repute, but because her name is, in fact, Lunete'.[33] To the narrator this likening to the sun and moon is a literary device. But to us just another of the many marks of paganism which are clearly visible in both their characters.

Sun and moon are also given human shape in the romance of Tristan. This time it is Yseult, the Queen of Ireland's daughter who is the sun (see p. 168). In the story of Tristan, Brangain plays a rather similar role as a magical protectress to that other representative of the moon, Lunete – both having been demoted, by the vagaries of repetition, from their original high state as goddesses to that of mere helpers, once their divine status had been forgotten. Nevertheless, clues to the importance of the sun in Tristan's story still survive. As mentioned in the Calendar of Arthurian Romance under Midsummer Day, this date is linked with his challenge to Morholt and is also the date on which he and Yseult drank the love potion.

## Animals

Writing in *King Arthur and Celtic Society*, Markale notes traces of totemism in Celtic epic cycles, displayed by names of animals used as personal names and by transformations into animal form. Thus he points out that the Irish Finn, whose real name was Demne, equivalent to the French 'le daim', a deer, married a girl whom a druid had transformed into a doe and had by her a son called Oisin, meaning a fawn. Examples of such traces of totemism, and other forms of animal and bird symbolism, can also be seen in the French romances. For instance, a certain Ourseau (in *Perceforest*) has both the name and the hairy pelt of a bear; Merlin's body was covered in hair and he transforms himself into a stag; Tor is transformed (again in *Perceforest*) into a bull; the Lady of Sinadoun is transformed into a serpent by enchanters; the dove and swan are symbols of the Grail; and so on. Most of these are incidental to the story, and their pagan significance would have escaped notice if totemism had not been known of from other sources. Not so the fish caught by Alain le Gros which

32 *Vulgate*, VII, p. 126.
33 *Yvain*, tr. Comfort, p. 211.

being magically multiplied to satisfy his hungry companions earned him and his successors the title of Rich Fisher or Fisher King. Here, in spite of the impossibility of magical multiplication, the impression is given of an actual ceremony in which the ruler formally catches a fish in a particular lake to symbolize prosperity from fishing and to encourage its continuation.

Equally vivid though entirely divorced from reality is the crow or raven symbolism attached to Morgan le Fay and her parallels in Irish literature. In one episode ravens fighting on the side of Owein (suggested by some to be the son of Morgan) defeat Arthur's knights; in another, the damsel for whom a knight guards a ford turns herself and her maidens into large black birds when her knight is defeated and the victor will not take his place as guardian. They attack the reluctant victor, who strikes one with his sword. Dying, she turns into a beautiful young woman and her corpse is carried away by her avian companions to Avalon, where all will be well with her.[34] Avalon was the home of nine priestesses led by Morgan, thus reminiscent, in this context of transformation into birds, of the island of Sein, reported in Roman times to be inhabited by nine priestesses reputedly able to fly through the air (Gaz. Avalon). It sounds as if Morgan's ravens were considered a threat to those humans who offended her. Perhaps it was not entirely an empty one, as these powerful and aggressive black scavengers were noted for disposing of corpses after battles.

In surviving Celtic traditions the prevalence of stories about horses suggests that they were some of the most important animal symbols. In the *Mabinogion*, Rhiannon rode a horse which could not be overtaken, at whatever speed it was ridden. For this and other reasons she is widely recognized as a horse goddess. In his *Topography of Ireland*, Giraldus Cambrensis (1146–1220) describes a coronation ceremony at Tyrconnel in Ulster at which the Sovereignty took the form of a mare. Copulation with her entitled the new king to his crown, and she was afterwards formally eaten by the members of his tribe. We might expect this emphasis on horses to be reflected in the romances but, unless perhaps as the mounts of heroes, they scarcely appear in a cult context, except that King Mark's name seems to mean horse, and the presiding goddess at the ford mentioned above acquired her lover after a chase on horseback reminiscent of the way Rhiannon got her lover in the *Mabinogion*.

Stags, on the other hand, are obviously important in the romances. This is particularly so in the episode of the capture of the white stag, or the stag with the white foot, a story which is repeated several times. Success in this hunt seems to be linked with marriage to the princess representing sovereignty and hence with kingship. Perhaps it is not an accident that such a chase after a white hart took place on the occasion of King Arthur's wedding, leading to episodes of great pagan significance.

Another potent symbol was the serpent. It was depicted in St Stephen's after Arthur's dream, it was engraved on the reliquary holding the four elements in the temple of the Sovereign God in *Perceforest*, and it was

[34] See pp. 46–7.

transformed by a kiss into the beautiful lady of Sinadoun. The crowned serpent ridden by a woman is used as a symbol to represent the old 'law', that is, the old religion of the pre-Arthurian inhabitants of these islands, the Sarrassins. In one instance the crowned serpent is likened to Guenever,[35] neatly emphasising her status as a divinity and her position in that great coalition of deities, the Arthurian pantheon, as the representative of an older, indigenous, religion.

---

35 *Vulgate*, IV, p. 28, lines 13 and 15.

# CEREMONIAL AND RITUAL

## The Arthurian Court

Apart from the Grail Castle where the Grail procession took place, the Arthurian ceremonial centre was, of course, the court in whatever place it might have been held. Courts were held on days of festival and were attended by the great and powerful men and women of the surrounding district or, at times, the whole country. There was some form of religious observance, for instance at a Pentecost court mass was sung at the Round Table, not in any church. The king's path was strewn with iris and mint as he distributed robes and insignia to the knights and squires. Typically there was a great feast followed by a tournament, then music and dancing. If it was the spring festival there may have been numerous marriages between the garlanded knights and damsels, and the proceedings ended early so that the newly weds could get to bed.[1] This scene might have been set in almost any age and is not at first glance notable for any pagan content until that exclusively Arthurian feature – an adventure before a feast – is encountered. The king has frequently to be reminded, when about to eat, that it is a custom that he should wait for an adventure to occur before the meal can begin. At once something strange happens which, though its meaning is often obscure, seems to be of great significance. Some examples follow:

At a court held on the day of mid-August Arthur made a vow never to sit at dinner on a feast day until some adventure was reported to him. His knights in turn vowed to help any damsel coming to Arthur's court in need of assistance.[2]

At a great court at Christmas at Carlion, while the king was waiting for his meal, a beautiful damsel rode in on a mule, accompanied by a dwarf. She brought a message from her mistress Lore de Branlant asking for assistance. At once she was abducted by a knight who was brother of Karacados of the

---

[1] *Perceforest*, ed. Roussineau, pt IV, lines 2061–2067.
[2] *Vulgate*, II, pp. 319f.

Dolorous Tower, so the abductor possibly represented the god Teruagant, Karacados' only recorded brother.[3]

At a court at Glastonbury (or in the French version, Carlion) the visiting damsel was Elen (Elene or Helie), who was accompanied by the dwarf Teodelain. She requested help for her mistress the lady of Sinadoun. The newly knighted Fair Unknown, son of Florée and Gawain, was given the task, much to Elen's openly acknowledged disgust.[4]

At this Glastonbury court we meet again the organizing damsel, now called Mesdisant or Maledisant – evil-tongued – after the outspoken Elen. She is a stock figure, always railing at her inexperienced and often anonymous charge. A young woman of the same kind came to court with a shield taken from a knight called 'the Amorous', who had been killed at a fountain leaving an adventure unfinished. She requested a champion to continue the adventure, which eventually led her to Castle Orguellous.[5]

At a Christmas eve feast of Arthur's at Quimpercorentin, a beautiful damsel entered, before the meal had begun, carrying the severed head of her brother. She requested a champion to avenge him. The king sent Yder son of Nut.

At Camelot where the king was holding his pentecost court, he was reminded by his steward Kay that he was obliged to see some adventure before he could eat at a high feast. At once a squire announced that a great perron was floating on the river. It had Balin's sword fixed in it, the withdrawal of which inaugurated Galahad's period of supremacy as Grail hero, the 'adventures of Logres', and the Grail Quest.[6]

The wedding of Arthur and Guenever at Camelot coincided with many interesting events: the arrival of the Round Table as Guenever's dowry; the re-establishment of the table and the election of new knights to bring it up to full strength; and Guenever's coronation and Gawain's knighting. An odd adventure preceded the wedding feast in which a white hart dashed into the court, pursued by the Huntress Damsel and her pack of hounds while all the companions were sitting at the Round Table. This episode resulted, it will be remembered, in three heads being severed, and in the Damsel of the Lake being brought to court, where the queen agreed to prefer her above all other women.[7]

However strange and obscure these activities may be they have a single thread running through them, whether we look at the personages or the actions, and that thread is paganism. In the background there are deities, some clearly delineated: Nodens (who appears as Nut, the father of Yder), Mabon and Bran (the enchanters at Sinadoun), and Beli (whose sword was fixed in the floated stone). As well as these there are those less obvious supernatural personages described in these pages, whose characters merge into those of the

3  *Vulgate*, VII, p. 74.
4  *Sir Libeaus Desconus*.
5  Prose *Tristan*, Löseth, ch. 66f.
6  *Vulgate*, VI, p. 6.
7  Huth *Merlin*, p. 136.

human beings who represent them on earth: Florée/Lore, Elen, Guenever, the Damsel of the Lake, and Gawain. And we have typically pagan actions and attributes: the challenge where the challenger must swear to guard the passage for seven years if victorious;[8] the amorous knight's reward for winning is the love of the resident damsel, herself called (at the Isle d'Or) 'd'Amour'; the castle of the Proud Knight, the archetype of the defending knight in the challenge system; the severed head; the floating stone; the significant withdrawn sword and the Grail hero.

If the 'adventures' that take place before great Arthurian feasts are so heavily imbued with paganism, what conclusions can be drawn? It seems unlikely that on such important occasions the assembled notables would sit back and wait for some chance occurrence. If they are not wholly imaginary, the adventures are likely to have been part of the programme, and the element of surprise, which is often present, to have been introduced by narrators. One may doubt if a real stag was introduced into a pagan arena. If not, the observance which preceded the feast may have been a dramatic representation or a liturgical recital. We are dealing here with myths, with verbal icons. A brief statement, like the Damsel of the Lake came to court and was preferred over all other women, may encapsulate a religious change of the greatest magnitude, which may have taken place over years or decades of conflict. It is an intriguing thought that such a move may really have taken place, and that amongst the descriptions of pagan pageants there may be a recollection in this instance of the religious switch towards deities whose ritual involved water which did actually take place in the prehistoric period to which the legends are here attributed.

Now it has been mooted that the part of the Arthurian ceremonial which preceded the feast may have been ritual, it will be worth looking again at the other elements of 'court' life and to see if they can equally well be classified as pagan rituals. The so called mass was not in a church; the spread flowers, though of course not exclusive to any period, fit the pagan spring festival very neatly; alternatively, when it is a winter festival which is being described, dancing and farandoles round a leafless tree hung with silk cloth[9] sounds equally pagan; distribution of goods by both the king and queen[10] often takes place at these courts and is a typical feature of the level of economic organization likely to have prevailed in a heroic society; ritual meals are common enough in the romances; conferring knighthood can be explained as initiation, always preceded by the significant night vigil in what *Perceforest* makes clear was a temple; and the business of multiple marriages has a distinctly pagan flavour. It is thus possible to characterize the whole scene of 'adventures before festival meals' as pagan, and parts of it would be very difficult to explain in any other way.

---

[8]  *Li biaus descouneüs*, ed. Williams, p. 59.
[9]  *Guiron le Courtois*, ed. Lathuillère, p. 404.
[10] E.g. *Vulgate*, VII, p. 133.

**Away from the Court**

*The Toilet*

The pagan adversary of St David, Boia's wife, invited Dunawd to place her head in her lap so she could dress her hair before cutting her throat. Other incidents in which hairdressing took place indicate that this activity had some hidden significance. One such is Culhwch's[11] visit to court on New Year's Day to ask Arthur to cut his hair as a prelude to obtaining his support in the winning of Olwen. This is not an aspect of Celtic practice which has penetrated into the romances, unless it is in a challenge episode in which the damsel in the tent is having her hair dressed,[12] but another facet of the toilet, washing, is quite prominent, even though it does not reproduce exactly the pattern which appears in the Celtic tradition. There a goddess washes at a ford before being taken by a god. In the 'matter of Britain' it is springs not fords in which the damsels choose to wash.[13] We may guess they did so in a provocative way, as they did for St David's monks, on that occasion openly inviting their timid adversaries to join in (Gazetteer, under Aroie). When Guingamor, lord of the Isle of Avalon and lover of Morgan le Fay, did join in he stayed three hundred years with the damsel he saw washing in a spring below an olive tree, though it only seemed to him like three days.

Men are less often recorded as bathing. An isolated instance is Tristan taking a bath at the court of Ireland, attended by Yseult and the Queen of Ireland and other dames. There is no internal evidence from the behaviour of those present that this episode has any cult significance, but since Yseult was worshipped in the form of an idol we may suppose at least one of the female participants to have supernatural characteristics, so the episode may once have had some pagan meaning, now hidden.

**Ceremonial Meals**

Washing is also prominent as a prelude to the ceremonial meals already mentioned[14] as having taken place beside springs under, in one case, the aegis of the triple goddess. Washing before meals is, of course, to be taken for granted as taking place in any human society for reasons of hygiene and good manners. But the numerous repetitions in the romances of this commonplace motif suggest a concealed significance. Narrators do not usually bother with the obvious, like tying one's shoelaces. So there may be significance in the washing which takes place before the Grail procession and also precedes meals on many occasions. There is a common thread running through these passages in that the food eaten is almost always wild game: venison patties under two

---

11 *Mabinogion*, Penguin, p. 140.
12 *Vulgate*, III, p. 281.
13 E.g. *Guingamor, Lanval, Tyolet and Bisclavet*, tr. Weston, p. 18.
14 See pp. 96f.

elms by a fountain; venison patties again at the fountain under a sycamore with the three damsels of twenty, forty and over sixty; harts, hinds and wild swine at the widow lady's Camelot before a tournament; barbel, salmon, perch and pike for Perceval on one occasion, and on another, at the Castle of Maidens, birds, pike and salmon; and for Gawain at the same place, plovers, pheasants, partridges and venison. Another ceremonial meal in a decidedly pagan context was the eating of the unnamed fish caught by Alain or Bron, the Fisher Kings. This, like those listed above, was eaten out of doors. Other links between these episodes are to be found in the pagan surroundings – the springs under trees; the Grail Table; the second Camelot, home of the Fisher King, Pellinor; and in the pagan personages: the triple goddess; Perceval, who later became a Fisher King; and the sun hero, Gawain.

In other contexts, washing takes place prior to the dubbing of knights;[15] and also before the meal which precedes the Grail procession. The latter of these is a pagan ceremony, so it may be added to the other pagan associations of this simple act, the number of which suggests that we may reasonably guess that washing performed before eating a meal was an element of a pagan ritual. Often the ritual seems to have involved the celebration of the bounty of wild nature, in slightly different ways in different places. The scene is set by the presence of the Fisher King, who appears several times in the various accounts of the ritual, and whose title and the ceremony which gave him his name exactly fit him to preside over a ritual meal.

The Damsel of the Lake and the goddess Diana, in spite of their link with hunting, seem to be almost completely absent from this particular group of incidents. Whether this is due to the vagaries of the oral tradition or some difference in the original style of worship is unlikely now to be discovered.

## Song and Dance

Singing and dancing have been a normal element of festivities in all ages, and so they are in the romances. They also feature in the 'matter of Britain' in descriptions of events in which there are expressions of joy, of greeting and of sorrow. The invariable description of joyful dances is 'caroles'. The word carol is more or less restricted in English nowadays to hymns celebrating the Nativity but in the original French of the romances probably meant a round dance with singing, with an implication of joy and festivity. Caroles are a constant feature of Arthurian festivals, for instance they were part of the fifteen day Christmas celebrations at Camelot which were the occasion of Gawain's encounter with the Green Knight.

It is only when we come to singing or dancing at what is clearly a religious festival that it can be seen that these activities may have been of a ritual nature. For instance, (in *Perceforest*) there are caroles at the dedication of the Temple of

---

[15] Chrétien's *Conte du Graal*, tr. Linker, p. 185.

the Sovereign God, an occasion marked by a royal marriage, the appearance of the Perilous Seat and the mysterious arrival of a perron sent by the Queen Fée;[16] and there were also caroles at the great feasts in honour of the Sovereign God in the month of May, when maidens and squires caroled and sang joyfully round a sweet-bay tree.[17] Another May-time festival (in *Guiron le Courtois*) celebrated the death of two giants who had once taken a tribute of youths, maidens and attractive women each May 1st; this festival had a complementary winter version in which dances took place in front of the leafless tree mentioned above. At Corbenic, while Gawain was enduring the adventure of the testing bed, there was a lament sung by twelve maidens and there was a chant sung by many voices expressing glory and praise; or in another version of the testing bed episode, Bors listened to a lament sung by a harpist with snakes wound round his neck.[18] And at the Isle of Marvels, when Balin approached before his fatal encounter with his brother, he was met by a hundred damsels who clustered round him, caroling, dancing and singing before and behind and making the greatest joy in the world; this welcome was because, by jousting with the lord of the island, the strange knight would give the greatest possible pleasure to all the dames and damsels of the castle.[19]

In the instances above song and dance seem to be merely a part of the ritual at a pagan religious event. In others, the carole in particular stands out as a principal feature. At the Isle of Joy[20] Lancelot's retinue of damsels danced at a challenge site round a very fine pine tree in the middle of the island on which his shield was hung, but it was not the shield he used for combat. The shield on the tree had on it a picture of the queen and a knight kneeling before her, and seems to have been an icon, some sort of heraldic representation, rather than a means of defence. After a joust the damsels would bow to the shield and then carole round the tree, singing: 'Truly this is the shield of the best knight in the world!' They used to carole at least four times a day, summer and winter, and the island took its name from the great joy they so assiduously displayed.[21] A somewhat similar performance is described as having taken place near Escalon. There Galehot came upon a grove of trees beside a well-sited stronghold. Near it were girls and women and plenty of knights. They were all caroling round a particularly fine pine tree which had Lancelot's shield fixed to it. The dancers bowed to the shield as if to the body of a saint. An old man told Galehot that they reverenced the shield because it belonged to the best knight in the world, who had delivered their castle, Escalon, from darkness by his prowess.[22] Reverence was also shown for Lancelot's shield in

16 *Perceforest*, ed. Roussineau, pt IV, pp. 387ff and pp. 398/9.
17 *Perceforest*, ed. Roussineau, pt IV, pp. civ and 10.
18 *Vulgate*, V, p. 300.
19 *Le Roman de Balain*, ed. M. Legge, p. 100.
20 See pp. 45–6.
21 Folie Lancelot, Bogdanow, *Beihefte zur ZRP*: 109, heft 1969, pp. 67ff: *Vulgate*, V, pp. 403ff.
22 *Vulgate*, IV, p. 144.

more formal surroundings; it was treated like a holy relic when it was hung in the minster of St Stephen at Camelot.[23]

In another episode involving a carole, the central feature was not a tree but wooden effigies of a crowned queen and an imprisoned knight. Tristan found one hundred and fifty dames and damsels enjoying a carole round these representations.[24]

It is interesting to see Tristan once again associated with effigies. He is also to be seen taking delight in the images in the groves and embracing the image of Yseult in the underground chamber.[25] The images of the queen and the captive knight in this latest carole correspond to the pictures of the queen and the kneeling knight on Lancelot's shield which too was the centre of a carole. It would be reasonable to suppose that the figures represented are Tristan and Yseult in one case and Guenever and Lancelot in the other. In both these love affairs, the hero expresses his complete subservience to his lady – in this context of images she was the representation of a goddess.

The link between Tristan and images continued after his death. His defeat of Morholt was then celebrated annually, when his image was crowned and his sword and shield treated like the relics of a saint.[26]

Returning to caroles, there is still to be described the one about which most information has been provided. Lancelot came upon it in a forest clearing where there were thirty pavilions. In the middle there were four great pine trees which surrounded an ivory chair covered in scarlet samite and with a heavy crown of gold on the seat. Around this caroled many knights and damsels. They were singing and striking their feet together. On the way towards the carole Lancelot had been warned that whoever took that route would never return. It was the carole which was the fatal attraction. Any passing knight was irresistibly drawn into the circle, even Lancelot, who took a damsel and gave himself up to the joyful performance, singing in Escoutois (Scottish) a song of Queen Guenever: 'Truly we have the most beautiful queen of all! Truly love is wonderful!'[27] The carole seems to have been performed continuously by relays of dancers and Lancelot was abandoned by his squire to a life of continuous singing and dancing. However, that evening a damsel told Lancelot that he must sit in the chair and wear the crown. This had the effect of breaking the spell and the dancers recovered their freedoms and their long-lost memories.

Afterwards, an old man said that the system had been founded just before Arthur's marriage. On their way to attend the wedding, King Ban (Bran) and his brother Guinebaut, who had learnt some of Merlin's magic, came across

---

[23] *Vulgate*, VI, pp. 313/4.
[24] Prose *Tristan*, Löseth, p. 295A.
[25] See p. 168 below.
[26] Prose *Tristan*, Löseth, p. 415.
[27] *Vulgate*, V, pp. 123/4.

the site in the Forest Sans Retour. There was a king's daughter sitting in the chair and six other women dancing. Ban surveyed the scene for some time and thinking it better that there should be an equal number of men in the dance, ordered six of his knights to join in. The damsel in the chair was delighted and wished the carole could go on and on. Guinebaut offered to make it do so for ever in an even more spectacular form in return for her lifelong love. He made an enchantment whereby any passing true-lover would be constrained to join in eagerly, but those joyless spirits to whom this happy accident had never occurred would be excluded. The dancers were to live on the site and to perform their carole every day without fail until after vespers. They would forget everything except to be festive. But there was a proviso for its ending. As it had been created for the most beautiful girl in the world, it would come to an end when the best and most handsome knight in the world should sit in the throne and wear the golden crown,[28] which had been provided by King Ban in one version, by King Bors in another.[29]

It is not to be doubted that singing and dancing are often an integral part of religion. As far as the former is concerned, perhaps universally so. But dance seems to have played a negligible part in Christianity, so when dancing is found as part of a religious ceremony the event is clearly pagan, particularly since the personages involved are often recognizable as pagan deities or their human counterparts. One would expect that the results of dancing most likely to be utilized in the furtherance of a pagan religion would be either the production of a state of trance, to be followed by supposedly prophetic utterances, or else its erotic effect. The former seems to be completely absent in the 'matter of Britain', while the latter is well represented, particularly in descriptions of the spring festival. From what we have so far found, the course of such a festival might have run something like this:

| Programme | Ritual |
|---|---|
| The adventure | A dramatic representation of a mythological episode. |
| The meal | A celebration of the bounty of the natural world under the auspices of the Fisher King. |
| The tournament | Selection by personal combat of a new king of proven potency. |
| Caroles and bed | A celebration of the stimulating effect of human sexual union on the productivity of the natural world. |

As well as providing a general view of the significance of dancing in pagan terms, the romances seem to have thrown up several examples of dancing round a tree which sound entirely factual. One may suppose that, in some of the recollections of paganism which have survived in the romances, an impossible idea has taken root, such as the transformation of a priestess into a bird, which has impressed itself so profoundly on susceptible minds as to

28 *Vulgate*, V, pp. 148ff.
29 *Vulgate*, II, pp. 244/5.

have acquired the appearance of reality, however little it may conform to the laws of nature. Here, in contrast, there is a simple procedure which is described clearly several times, allowing its constituent features to be picked out. These are: an association with a hero; a representation of a goddess with a subordinate male, to which reverence is shown; this is a centre round which dancers perform a joyful carole indefinitely. The odd way in which the ending of this ritual is described has similarities to other accounts of pagan practices in which there is a beginning in the times of Bran, before the Arthurian period proper, and an ending brought about by Lancelot or his son Galahad.

Such a system could have a parallel in historical times in the endowment of chantries in which a community of monks was engaged to pray daily in perpetuity (it was hoped) for the souls of their benefactor and other persons nominated by him. Though the objective was very different, we are perhaps being told, in this group of tales, of a prehistoric equivalent in which the help of a deity was sought by joyful pagan dances instead of the drone of prayers.

The possibility that such a system once existed is enhanced by survivals in folklore of several of the elements of the 'carole' in association with the may-pole and by the discovery of trampled earth in prehistoric monuments, suggesting that dancing may have been a part of the ritual activities of those engaged in its construction.

Dancing as a ritual act may have left a more distinctive trace in the ground than mere footprints. The path followed by the train of dancers may have been formally marked on the ground in some combination of arcs and spirals resulting in the sort of pattern found in the most primitive mazes, in which there is only one route through with no dead ends. Though no surviving maze in North West Europe has been shown to be prehistoric, the distribution of similar patterns of mazes from Etruria in Italy to Britain in the west and Finland in the north suggests a general spread throughout Europe from the earliest times, rather than introduction by some more recent, identifiable, folk-movement or invasion. And even the dance step may have been preserved in tradition. At Stolp in Pomerania, at a shoemakers festival up to the beginning of this century, the dance took place on the Tuesday after Pentecost, when a May King had been elected. The course of the dance was guided by a spiral maze and the dancers used the 'lapwing' step (the lapwing jumps about a metre, stands on one foot and slightly raises the other). This dance has been imaginatively identified with the crane dance performed by Theseus and his companions on the sacred island of Delos and also with a dance performed by the Ostiaks of Siberia, wearing the skins of cranes, in the eighteenth century. Though there is no conclusive evidence, a credible picture emerges of a prehistoric association between ritual dances and some kind of traditional pattern, marked on the ground, a pattern which may have survived in the form of the early, uncomplicated, mazes or labyrinths which chart a course rather than providing a puzzle.[30]

[30] *Mazes and Labyrinths*, W. H. Matthews, 1922.

It has been noted that the folk-names of stone circles often incorporate the word dance. A favourite explanation for a ring of standing stones is that they are a group of dancers turned into stone for dancing on a Sunday. Stonehenge itself was known to Geoffrey of Monmouth as 'the Giant's Dance'. The Latin word he used for 'dance' was 'chorea', a word related to the 'carole' of the romances. If caroles did take place at summer-solstice oriented Stonehenge, the most likely day of the week on which they would have taken place is, of course, a *Sun*day.

Dancing in the romances is almost invariably described as an expression of joy. The importance of this emotion is demonstrated by the title given to the account of a particular episode, the 'Joy of the Court', in *Erec*. Erec won a typical 'challenge' and, although the denouement, which might have been expected from the analysis here of the 'challenge', does not take place, the joy of the population is reminiscent of that which occurs when a new ruler has been selected by the challenge procedure, as appears in so many descriptions of this event. It is likely to have been the joy made by the whole population for the provision of a new vigorous lord which gave its name to this episode.

Perhaps the coincidence here of 'joy' with the wall of mist and the severed heads on stakes indicates that joy in the romances had a more sinister side. We have already seen expressions of joy when a new sacrificial victim arrives at a cult site.[31] Here the Joy of the Court takes place at Brandigan under the auspices of King Eurain. Both the place and the king carry the name of Bran, whose head was buried to protect the realm of Britain. After Erec had won, he had the heads buried, but the story does not say if the 'mist' persisted.

There is a hint of change in a snippet of ancient Welsh tradition in which as a sequel to the burying of Bran's head as a protection for Britain, Arthur much later dug it up, on the grounds that under his rule protection should be by no one's strength but his own.[32] The inference is clearly that at a certain stage the magical protection provided by the head ceased to be believed in. After that, proper defences would have to be erected round defended sites. This episode fits the general rule in the romances that customs originally pertaining to the age of Bran were superseded in the time of Arthur; and it also suits the proposition, to be made later, that Bran was Neolithic, like the skulls at Hambledon Hill, which were afterwards superseded by real ramparts.

---

31 See pp. 46, 57 and 125 above.
32 *Trioedd Ynys Prydein*, Bromwich, p. 89.

PART THREE

THE PHYSICAL BACKGROUND
TO THE ROMANCES

# CONSTRUCTIONS

The objective of this chapter is to see to what extent the physical background to life in pagan times is reflected in the romances. On the face of it, the landscape described in these stories is much as might be expected of the time in which they were written. There is the vast mysterious forest with its hermitages at convenient intervals in which travelling knights could find shelter and sustenance; there are roads, causeways, bridges, fords and all the normal features of the British terrain; there are castles, abbeys and, in the few towns, churches; and there are encampments of tents, single pavilions and even shelters of leaves and branches. Unlike the tell-tale behaviour of some of the supposedly human participants in the stories, there are no obvious indications that any of these familiar features of the countryside are anything other than what they seem. Yet there are a few references to pagan places, and a few buildings and places have described as having links with pagan personages or practices such as the worship of images or idols. A well-known example is the 'green chapel' in *Sir Gawain and the Green Knight*, which since it consisted of a grassy mound in a launde, that is, a glade[1] and had a hole at the end and either side and was 'hollow within – nothing more than an old cave or a crevice in an old crag', may reasonably be supposed to have begun life as a tumulus.[2] Its situation was beside a stream bubbling below a waterfall, and it was in the north-west of England, but there is not enough detail for its position to be identified.

One of the most obvious places to have pagan connotations is Camelot, which is described as having been, in the earliest times, the richest city that the Sarrasins had in Great Britain. Its authority was so great that the pagan king was crowned there and paganism flourished there more than anywhere else in the kingdom.[3] The accounts of the spread through Britain of the cult of the maimed king and the lance bleeding into the Grail, interpreted as Christianity,

---

[1] *Sir Gawain and the Green Knight*, Tolkien and Gordon, lines 2171ff.
[2] It has been rendered as 'barrow' in the translation of J. A. Burrow, p. 122.
[3] *Vulgate*, I, p. 244. 'La plus rice cité que li Sarrasin eussent en la grant bartaigne & estoit de si grant auctorite que li roi paien i estoit corone & i estoit la mahoumerie plus grant & plus haut quen nule autre cyte qui el roialme fust.'

describe several places, such as Sarras and Camelot, as having temples and mention the names of some deities. In Terre Foraine, for instance, the king, Kalafes, on conversion burnt his idols before building Corbenic, the Grail Castle;[4] and in the forest of Broceliande Argon and his people worshipped idols representing Mahomet, Teruagant, Jupiter and Apolin or Cahu.[5] Mahomet, who lived much later than even the historical Arthur, is unlikely, if he had known about it, to have been flattered by this juxtaposition with Celtic deities, whether under their local names or indicated by a Roman equivalent. One of these native deities appears again in an entirely different context. At the Isle d'Or the black giant Maugis, defender of what has already been identified as a cult site with its heads on stakes and continuation of the challenge custom, believed in the god Termagant[6] (that is, Teruagant). There are a number of other references to deities and to places with temples and idols. They will be discussed in more detail later in the book under the headings 'Geography' and 'Who's Who'; they are mentioned here only to show that the writers of the romances did in some instances link paganism with named places.

Some of the constructions which can be identified as pagan are actually called temples. Others are not so described but a link with paganism can be inferred from their use. Thus in one of the examples of underground chambers which follow a personage in such a chamber is described as a goddess and is worshipped as such in the form of an idol. A wide selection of descriptions of chambers has been put forward for consideration, of which it will be seen that most are variants on a single theme. Excluded are burial chambers, such as the one in which Merlin met his end, and storage chambers.

## Underground Chambers

The underground chambers to be considered below are all man-made. They are described as follows:

(1) Geoffrey of Monmouth tells a romantic fictional tale of the colonizing of Britain by a certain Brutus from Troy, who is supposed to have given his name to the country of Britain when he became its king. Brutus' eldest son Locrine likewise gave his name to his share of his father's kingdom, Loegria, the country called Logres in the romances, now England. Although married, Locrine kept a mistress named Estrildis in an underground chamber, where she was honourably served by the attendants of his household. Here he kept her in secret for seven years, and as often as he was minded to go to her he would feign that he made hidden sacrifices to his gods. Estrildis bore a

---

4   *Vulgate*, I, pp. 286ff.
5   *Vulgate*, I, pp. 252/4.
6   *Sir Libeaus Disconus*, tr. J. L. Weston, p. 51.

daughter to him, Habren, who it was that was thrown into the Severn to give it its Welsh name, in Geoffrey's day, of Habren.[7] Welsh versions of the *Historia* have Essylt for Estrildis, Essylt being the Welsh equivalent of the Yseult of the romances.

(2) There was a holy city called Sarras, where Galahad eventually achieved the Grail. Earlier in the story the inhabitants worshipped the sun, moon and planets. The temple to the sun was the finest of their temples, for they held the sun in greater honour than the other planets.[8] At the entrance to this temple was a very fine, tall and beautiful shelter, where the king, Evalac, sat surrounded by his subjects.[9] At night he copulated with a richly dressed wooden idol, which he kept in an underground chamber.[10]

(3) Tristan and Yseult, living a wandering life in the woods of Cornwall, came upon a giant's cave near three lime-trees in a clearing with a spring below them. They used it as their home until their hiding place was accidentally discovered by King Mark's huntsman. He saw them through a little window and returning to his master, reported that he had seen a man and a goddess in the lover's cave.[11]

(3a) A description of the Giant's cave in Gottfried von Strassburg's *Tristan* is as follows: the cavern had been hewn in the wild mountain in heathen times, before Corynaeus'[12] day, when giants ruled there. They used to hide inside it when, desiring to make love, they needed privacy.[13]

(3b) In an alternative version of the same cave, it is described as 'a secret place beside a certain water, and in the hillside, that heathen men let hew and adorn in olden time with mickle skill and fair craft, and this was all vaulted and the entrance digged deep in the ground, and there was a secret way in running along below ground. Over the house lay much earth and thereon stood the fairest tree upon the hillside.'[14]

(3c) The Giant's cave is described in yet another way by Thomas of Britain. There was 'a rock round and all vaulted within, hewn and graven with the most art' at Mont St Michel. It had been built by a giant from Africa who kept in it Elaine, daughter of Duke Howel of Brittany, whom he accidentally slew due to his great weight and size – he split her to the navel when making love.[15]

(4) At one period in the long story of Tristan and Yseult, the lovers were

---

7  *Historia*, ed. Wright, vol. I, Sect. 24.
8  The ancients described all the objects in the sky which move against the fixed pattern of the stars as 'planetes', that is, wanderers.
9  *St Graal*, ed. Hucher, II, pp. 130f.
10  *St Graal*, ed. Hucher, II, p. 318.
11  The *Tristan* of Gottfried von Strassbourg, tr. Hatto, p. 271.
12  Corynaeus was supposedly the name-giving founder of Cornwall.
13  *Tristan*, tr. Hatto, p. 261.
14  S. C. Harris, *Romania*, 98, p. 316, taken from the Norwegian *Tristanssaga*.
15  *Trystram and Ysolt*, Thomas of Britain, ed. Loomis, pp. 215f.

separated and Tristan spent some time in exile in Brittany with his friend Kahedin, who was in love with Yseult's companion, Bringvain (as her name is spelt by Thomas). The young men used to hunt in the forest and fight in tournaments in the marches, 'and when they would go for to sojourn, they would go unto the groves to behold the fair images. On those images they had delight as of the ladies they so loved. By day they had solace there to pay for the loneliness they endured at night'. According to Thomas, Tristan's love Yseult was the sun, and Kahedin's love Bringvain was the moon.[16] Gottfried von Strassburg, in a German version, makes exactly the same attribution. He calls Queen Yseult (the Queen of Ireland, Yseult's mother) the Glad Dawn; the resplendent maiden Yseult (Tristan's lover) the sun; and Brangain, the lovely Full Moon.[17]

In the course of his fighting, Tristan defeated a giant, who lost a leg in the battle, and took over his cave from him. He had the chamber richly embellished, and under the arch he had placed a richly clad and beautiful image of Yseult. Next to her on one side was a smaller image of Brangain proffering a covered cup, and on the other side an image of the one-legged giant, brandishing with both hands a club above his head, as if to defend the others. His shoulders were covered by a large, hairy goatskin cape which reached only to his navel, below which he was naked. There were also images of a lion and a dog, and in a less important position two humans who had behaved maliciously towards Tristan and Yseult. When Tristan 'came before the image of Yseult he kissed her' and 'took her in embrace and put his arms about her neck as she had been on live' and with many loving words rehearsed before the image the joys, dolours, pains and woes of love.[18]

(5) Geoffrey of Monmouth tells how Cordelia, being 'mistress of the helm of state in Britain' after her father Lear's death, buried him 'in a certain underground chamber which she had bidden to be made under the river at Leicester. This underground chamber was founded in honour of the two-faced god Bifrons [often equated with Janus], and there, when the yearly celebration of the day came round, did all the workmen of the city set hand unto such work as they were about to be busied upon throughout the year'.[19]

There are a number of common features in these accounts of underground chambers. The structures seem for the most part to be deliberately made, not natural caves; most are linked with deities or religion; and most of them are used for love-making. The odd one out is Geoffrey's account of Cordelia's chamber with its unrealistic situation under a river. Even so it is not without interest, with its connections with three divinities: Bifrons, whose two faces

---

[16] *Trystram and Ysolt*, Thomas of Britain, ed. Loomis, p. 263.
[17] *Tristan*, tr. Hatto, p. 187.
[18] *Trystram and Ysolt*, pp. 218/221.
[19] *Historia*, ed. Wright, vol. I, Sect. 31.

remind us of the many Celtic stone heads with two faces;[20] then Lear, who is the Celtic god Llyr differently spelled (and who obeys the rule that ancient deities tend to turn up in popular tradition as kings and queens); and finally Cordelia, who seems to have begun her career as a supernatural being, for she was fated to be fought for by two champions each May 1st until doomsday.

Geoffrey's other contribution (1) also seems a little out of line, but Welsh translators of his work have recognised Estrildis as their own Essylt, that is to say, the Yseult of the romances. However garbled his version may be, it looks as if Geoffrey has independently picked up a tradition of an underground chamber, love-making, and Yseult and that it was something to do with religion, so tending to conform to the French sources. Once Estrildis has been identified as Yseult, Yseult can be seen to be an occupant of the underground chambers in three of the examples, (1), (3) and (4). Apart from the one at Leicester, the only exception is Evalac's, and that is linked to the rest by the theme of love-making with an idol.

The religious background comes through in each instance – Locrine made sacrifices to his gods, Evalac had a wooden idol, a 'goddess' was reported to have been seen in the lover's cave, and it is to be seen most clearly in the description of the activities of Tristan and Kahedin in exile, for they visited the groves to behold the fair images. Worship in groves or glades is so well attested in prehistory that the latter is surely an exact description of pagan behaviour. What they were worshipping in the groves is indicated by the phrase 'they had delight from the images as of the ladies they so loved.'

Against a pagan backcloth we see Yseult called a goddess in (3) and likened to the sun, and Brangain to the moon, and both of them adored in the form of idols in the underground chamber. Are we to suppose that this is a true picture, and that Yseult was never flesh and blood but a goddess worshipped in the form of an idol? There are two reasons why this is likely to be so. The first is that her companion, Brangain (under several different spellings), has a name barely distinguishable from Branwen, presumably a goddess as she was the sister of the Welsh god, Bran; and the last element in her name, 'wen' or 'guen', means white, an appropriate colour for the moon, so, though the early Welsh tradition is indifferent to the moon (and the sun) her attribution as a moon goddess seems reasonable enough. The second, which seems to me overwhelming, is the inclusion in the tableau in the chamber of the one legged giant. This strange, half-clothed figure is so exact a replica of the one-legged giants of Irish and Welsh mythology that he carries the stamp of authenticity.[21] It is perhaps within the bounds of possibility that an imaginative narrator could have supposed the exiled young men to have solaced themselves with

[20] The usual identification of Bifrons with the Roman Janus draws attention away from the perfectly good native originals for this deity.
[21] I. L. Foster in *ALMA*, p. 197; the black giant in *Owein* who is Lord of the Animals; the Irish god Lugh had, on occasion one eye and one leg – although a god of skill and craftsmanship and so completely different from the crude figure brandishing a club, this tends to confirm one-leggedness as an attribute of a god.

models of their loved ones, but for him to have included in an invented tale what is so obviously a real pagan figure is highly improbable. So the tableau can reasonably be taken at its face value as a depiction of the contents of an underground chamber, and our view of the relationship of Tristan and Yseult should be adjusted accordingly.

There is a striking parallel in Irish legend to the affairs of Tristan and Yseult. The runaway couple Diarmait and Grainne likewise sought shelter in the wilderness and in artificial caves which are remembered as love-making places. No less than forty Neolithic chambered tombs are named after them as 'Beds of Diarmait and Grainne', at which, up to recent times, a woman is said to have been unable to refuse a man's request for love. Mac Cana considers 'this theme to have concerned the rivalry of a younger and older deity for the possession of a goddess, and that at some stage in its development [it] assumed the character of a conflict between love and honour, a conflict which we find in the stories of Deirdre and Grainne among others and one which was to receive its ultimate and classical statement in the romances of Lancelot and Guenever and of Tristan and Yseult.'[22] The view expressed by Mac Cana that the stories in this group originated in tales of pagan deities finds confirmation in the romances in the description of Yseult as a goddess and in Tristan's worship of her in the form of an idol.

To turn from Tristan to Lancelot, that other hero noted for a single-minded romantic attachment. At one time the latter was captured by Morgan le Fay and incarcerated in a large and luxurious cell. He employed his time painting pictures of the story of his life on the walls of his prison. When Lancelot rose in the morning he used to look in the chamber where the likenesses of his lady were painted. He would bow to and greet her image and would approach it and kiss it on the mouth and have more pleasure with it than with any other woman except his lady.[23] The affairs of Lancelot and Guenever are a close parallel of those of Tristan and Yseult. Both the men display the same extreme devotion for the wife of their 'king'. Both are even driven mad and finish up as wild men of the woods. Is the kissing of the image of his lady by Lancelot just another parallel between his story and Tristan's? Or should the question be: 'Was the image of Guenever, like that of Yseult, a representation of a divinity?'

Suspending disbelief, for the moment, about the possibility of so long a span of transmission, if we enquire into archaeological parallels to these underground chambers of romance there seem to be only two possibilities. They could correspond to Neolithic burial chambers of the kinds which are accessible from the outside by passages, or else to a much later type of structure known as souterrains or, in Cornwall, as fogous. These are stone-built, roofed galleries which are to be found in Ireland, in the highland zone of Britain, and in Brittany. Their purpose is uncertain. Storage has often been suggested, but the remains of stored products have not proved conspicuous in

22 *Celtic Mythology*, Mac Cana, p. 112.
23 *Vulgate*, V, p. 218.

the examples examined nor has pagan religious use been demonstrated, though, a souterrain in Orkney was found to have four human skulls arranged round a stone pillar,[24] and a chamber of a very different kind hewn in chalk in Kent had a niche in a wall which is likely to have contained a carved stone head which was found in the filling of the chamber and is considered to have been an idol.[25] Such structures seem to have been constructed during the late centuries BC or early AD.

A suggestion has already been made that one of the examples (3b) shows a remarkable resemblance to a particular souterrain, according to S. C. Harris, who has compared descriptions of the shelter used by Tristan and Yseult with the actual appearance of a 'fogou' at Carn Euny in Cornwall. The main points of correspondence are: a corbelled chamber which was covered with earth, a long main passage and a creep-hole entrance.[26]

On the other hand the description in (3b) could equally well apply to a burial chamber and there is a link between burial chambers and the story of Diarmait and Gráinne. Another hint is provided by Merlin's burial place. It was a chamber hewn in the rock which had previously been used by two lovers, and they were buried there.[27] Is it possible that some such chambers served both purposes? Whatever the answer to this question, there is a surprisingly detailed picture in the romances of idols or images in the form of well-known female personages who are suspected for other reasons to have been goddesses; and there is an unexpected description of love-making in an underground chamber in four very different texts, in two of them with idols.

## Standing Stones

Features of the Arthurian landscape which, because they were above ground, would have been more conspicuous than underground chambers, were the 'perrons'. 'Perron' means a block of stone, often a pillar, not necessarily worked, but visually important and, in the context of the Arthurian legends, usually significant in some social context. A perron may be merely a marker at a parting of the ways, often inscribed with a warning and perhaps nothing more than a narrator's device to convey that warning to any knight errant who happens to pass close to an 'adventurous' site. But a perron may also be the most important place in the kingdom, where the people gathered to witness the crowning of their queen and the combats that led to the selection of her consort.[28] The perron where these last two events took place, in the late romance *Perceforest*, was at Cardueil (that is, Cardoel). It is described as 'The Marvellous Perron' or the 'Adventurous Perron', and was where the destiny

---

[24] *Rites of the Gods*, A. Burl, p. 217.
[25] *Current Archaeology*, no. 101.
[26] *The Real Camelot*, Darrah, p. 145.
[27] Huth *Merlin*, p. 192.
[28] *Perceforest*, Part VI, ch. XXIIII folio 57f.; Lods, p. 33, para 78.

of Great Britain was to be accomplished. It was the creation of the Queen of the Otherworld and there was an oracular severed head nearby. The general love-making which took place there following the royal marriage in the month of May suggests that the marriage was a fertility promoting event. The stone from which Arthur drew the sword at Camelot, which feat led to him being proclaimed king, is another stone described as a perron, indeed, it is the very same stone as the Marvellous Perron just described, which had the sword which Arthur later drew inserted into it on May 1st at Cardoel during the selection procedure for the consort of the Queen of Britain.

The majority of the Arthurian perrons are associated with Merlin. One such is 'The Perron Merlin', just outside Cardoel in Wales, which he set up to mark the place where he had killed two enchanters.[29] Another 'Perron Merlin' was just outside Camelot. At this second Perron Merlin, Balin killed the prince of Ireland in single combat.[30] A third perron associated with Merlin is a pillar put up on Mount Dolorous, wherever that may have been. As well as these, the editor of the prose *Tristan*[31] indexes as 'Merlin's Perron' the floating stone which arrived at Camelot and gave Galahad the opportunity to draw the sword from the stone. This is the stone in which Merlin fixed 'Balin's Sword', which seems to have been the 'lightning weapon' of a local Zeus and to have been an equivalent of Excalibur.[32] In a fourth instance, in Brittany, the great magician came upon another perron by the Lake of Diana, where he made the underwater palace in which the Damsel of the Lake resided, and, finally, no one knows where, he was himself shut under a 'great stone' by his too apt pupil, the Damsel of the Lake.[33]

Yet another stone marks a place and time of great significance. When King Arthur, in pursuit of Mordred, approached the fateful day when the glorious era of the Round Table would end, he came with his forces to Salisbury Plain. He knew it was here that Merlin and other diviners had predicted that a great battle would take place. Once they had arrived on the plain he told his troops to camp, and made his decision to face Mordred. That evening after dinner he walked on the plain and came to a great tall, hard rock which, since there are no natural outcrops on the plain must have been a standing stone erected by man. It had letters on it from long ago, saying; 'On this plain will take place the mortal battle by which the kingdom of Logres will be orphaned' – which was taken as a prediction of Arthur's own coming death. The prediction and the inscription must be taken with a pinch of salt, so Merlin is not so directly linked with this perron as with the other stones, but he has another connection with this site, for it is the place chosen by him for the great gathering, an event

29 *Vulgate*, III, p. 275.
30 *Morte Darthur*, Malory, bk X, ch. 5.
31 Ed. Löseth, pp. 281/2.
32 *The Real Camelot*, Darrah, pp. 116/18.
33 Huth *Merlin*, II, pp. 195/7.

marking the beginning of Arthur's country-wide rule exactly as the last battle marked its end.

Just as there are possible originals in the real world for the underground chambers of the romances, so there are possible precursors for the Arthurian 'perrons'. Perrons have already been described as blocks or pillars of stone with a social significance, but there is more to it than that. The significance is, for the most part, magical and there are many links with supernatural person-ages.[34] As far as the real world is concerned, the standing stones which seem most closely to correspond to them were erected in the Bronze Age or earlier. They are not inscribed, except possibly with symbols in rare instances; letter-ing on stones does not appear until Roman times, many centuries after stand-ing stones ceased to be erected. Later still the tradition of inscribing stones was continued in the Celtic western region under Irish influence, now using ogham instead of Roman letters. No doubt this script was also used for magi-cal purposes;[35] the word runes for the early Teutonic alphabet retains the connotation of magic significance. But slips of wood seem to have been used for that purpose; surviving stones marked with ogham are usually grave-stones and the inscription are generally of the most basic kind – here lies X son of Y. Only one, from Cornwall, seems to have a direct Arthurian connection as it refers to Drustanus, that is Tristan, son of Cunomorus. However, it comes from an era when the families of kings incorporated the names of deities into their family trees, they used the gods names as their own names, and they incorporated their actions into their own stories as we can see from Cunobelinus, whose name incorporates that of the god Belenus, and other historical characters to whom tales of deities have become attached.[36] So the name Tristan on a stone may mean no more than the localization of the name of a supernatural personage whose story had by then been told for many centuries.

As far as 'the tall, hard rock' on Salisbury Plain is concerned, commentators on the romances have not failed to notice that there are standing stones on Salisbury Plain, Stonehenge in particular, which might be referred to by the description 'great, tall, hard, inscribed rock'; and although others have pointed out that this is not the only monument on the Plain the inference is still that the 'rock' was a standing stone, that is, a Bronze Age (or earlier) monument. And in this context of stones on Salisbury Plain, it should not be forgotten that the most famous of them all, Stonehenge, was also linked with Merlin, and so are all the perrons listed above. I shall discuss later the many links between Merlin and stones, particularly moved and floated stones (see Geography below),

[34] There are records of stone pillars having been objects of worship in the past. In *The Myce-naeans*, Lord W. Taylour remarks: 'The worship of a deity in the form of a column, pillar or baetyl also takes place in rustic shrines, sometimes associated with the tree cult.' A baetyl is a sacred meteoric stone.

[35] *The Pagan Religions of the Ancient British Isles*, R. Hutton, p. 294.

[36] E.g. Urien Rheged and Peredur son of Eliffer.

meanwhile the site which is common to both the Great Gathering and of the final battle provides another link between Merlin, stones and Salisbury Plain.

## Temples in the 'Matter of Britain'

The most obvious temple in an Arthurian context is Stonehenge, important in the stories of Uther and Merlin, both individuals who are close to Arthur: its appearance in the romances will be described in more detail later. Apart from that there are several mentions of temples actually so called in the romances, though none of them have been repeated by Malory. It is necessary to go to an earlier stratum in the development of the legends to find them. For instance, we have already come across the temple to the sun at Sarras, which was not the only religious foundation in that city, for it is described as the most splendid of several temples there. Sarras is said to have been 'eleven days from Jerusalem' but seems really to have been in Britain and only got transposed to the Middle East by a confusion between the name of its inhabitants and the Saracens of the Middle Ages.[37] There was also the most important temple in the country at Camelot, where the pagan kings were crowned; there was a temple of Venus on the border between Cornwall and Loenois;[38] and there were several temples which are said to have had their idols thrown down and to have been replaced by 'churches' on the arrival of the Grail cult.

The narrator who ascribed a local temple to the Roman goddess Venus was probably making an interpretation. He has concealed the local name of the original deity under that of a universally known one, presumably on account of some resemblance in the style of worship, though it is unlikely to have coincided exactly with that of the Roman Venus. Other narrators seem to have made the same sort of interpretations but with Christianity in mind, so the dedications of the replacement 'churches' of the Grail cult to 'Our Lady' are probably informative about the original deity only so long as they are not taken at face value.

In none of the descriptions of the temples so far mentioned is the structure described. The only romance to provide information about the appearance of temples is a late one, *Perceforest*. This is different from all the other 'Arthurian' romances, as it does not mention Arthur or any of his entourage. Yet everything else is immediately recognizable as typically Arthurian except for the unique historical setting, which begins three centuries *before* the Roman conquest of Britain. The earlier date of the scene of action in this romance gives an entirely different tone to the religious background. Christianity and churches are completely excluded. Their places are taken by pagan divinities and temples. The pagan detail, as this analysis will show, seems authentic enough. Did the author have access to an earlier stratum of the tradition, remembered

---

[37] Above, Calendar of Arthurian Romance, p. 35.
[38] *Roman de Tristan*, ed. Löseth, p. 11.

from the time before Arthurian motifs became Christianized and transposed by over-imaginative narrators into post-Roman times?

*Perceforest* begins with a general description of Britain similar to that in Geoffrey of Monmouth's history. In it the author makes an excursion into Ireland, where we learn that a certain Barcolan constructed a place of stones in the manner of a temple on an island off the coast, and that the dead were 'placed on noble stones' so that the living could be familiar with their parents and ancestors. Barcolan, otherwise known as Bartholoim or Partholon is a well-known figure in the traditional history of Ireland. He is said to have led an invasion in which the following were introduced to an Ireland in which hunting and fishing had previously been the principal means of sustenance: ploughing (to sow grain), the quern (to grind grain), and ale, (made from fermented grain). Although the correspondence is not perfect, Barcolan stands out as representing the 'first farmers', that is the people of the Neolithic period when tilling of the soil became general and grain became the main support of life. A place of stones in the manner of a temple seems appropriate to such a period, and placing the dead on stones so that they could be familiar to the living seems to be a reference to the exposure of corpses, again appropriate to the Neolithic Age.

An inference about age can also be made about a series of British temples mentioned in *Perceforest*. Where their construction is described they are sometimes said to be in a flat space surrounded by a ditch; to be round and of stone; and to have an eastern entrance. Neither stone circles, nor oriented temples,[39] nor substantial round temples, nor indeed in Britain, prior to the Roman occupation, substantial stone temples of any kind, as opposed to mere shrines, are typical of any period after the Bronze Age, so the oral tradition may be passing on some very ancient memories here, though not necessarily as long standing as in the case of Partholon's Neolithic temple.

## Four Temples Described in *Perceforest*

### *The Temple to the Unknown God*

A good deal of what we are told of this temple sounds reasonable to a modern ear. It was situated on a low hill, in a clearing surrounded by a thorny thicket. Round about was a forest of great oaks. The place was very seldom visited by man. In the middle of the flat clearing was a round temple open to the sky, which had a vestibule at the east, indicating the entrance. The temple was served by the hermit Dardanom, who had founded it. There was a turret at the east where the hermit sat on a turning wheel, keeping watch far into the night, his eyes on the sky. Inside the temple was a curtained altar. There were no windows. Half-way round the outside was the path to a very fine dwelling.

---

[39] *Guide to the Megaliths of Europe*, A. Service and J. Bradbery, p. 18.

The door of the dwelling led into a large round hall with a central pillar which supported the stone vault.

So much for the apparently factual, but in the romances the magical is never far away. So we find that sharp spears are suspended from the sky and the floor was a mirror, giving the appearance of a terrible abyss thickly strewn with spears, above and below which a worshipper must walk to reach the altar. And on the pillar of the associated building was a shield which only a pre-determined hero could remove from its hook.[40]

In the factual part of this description there are two of the features mentioned above – roundness and an eastern entrance – which indicate an early origin and which also distinguish the temple from the standard form of church known to the mediaeval narrator. Yet we have a reasonably accurate picture of a stone circle with an entrance at the east and a priesthood interested in astronomy, an impression which will be reinforced by the examination which follows of the pagan attributes of the other temples in this series.

### The Temple of the Sovereign God

This temple was round, made of stone and painted green inside, without any other colour and without image or portraiture.[41] The simplicity and quietness of its situation favoured meditation and devotion. There were enough windows for adequate lighting. The temple was made completely round and the most rich and noble it was possible to make. The intention was to surpass all others in the kingdom in grandeur, beauty and nobility, just as the Sovereign God surpassed all other gods. There was an altar at the east end which had on it a rich gold reliquary decorated with crystal and interlacing serpents which held – to please the God of Nature – earth, air, water and fire, the four elements. The temple was surrounded by a fine wall and provided with a strong door and a drawbridge. Much later in the story, a travelling knight came across this temple in ruins. In a deserted countryside, occupied only by wild beasts he saw through great trees a well-made *round temple of ancient construction, covered with flat stones*. Coming closer, he found the old temple was in a space surrounded by deep ditches full of brambles. He continued round until he found the ruins of the drawbridge. There was now only a narrow plank to cross the *ditch* into the *arena*. At one side were the ruins of ancient buildings with the roofs fallen in. The knight walked across the arena and in through the door of the temple. He found the place in its simplicity the most holy he had ever experienced. There was an altar towards the east where he mused for a while. Turning to the right he then saw a rich throne. The *sun*, which was then *setting, directed a single ray through the door of the temple* on to the throne, illuminating it brightly. He now saw it contained the desiccated corpse of a very old man, clad in a sheepskin. After praying to the God of Nature the knight fell asleep and dreamed he saw an Otherworld queen who

---

[40] *Le Roman de Perceforest*, Lods, p. 108: *Perceforest* ed. Taylor, p. 243; ed. Taylor, p. 412; ed. Roussineau, pt IV, pp. 536/8 and p. 564.

explained an earlier dream, when he had slept in the temple of the Goddess of Dreams, in which a beautiful girl gave him a drink from a cup of gold and promised his issue the kingdom.[42]

### The Noble Temple of Protection

This temple in 'Scotland' was founded in honour of Venus by the Goddess of the Otherworld (otherwise the Queen Fay or the Queen of Scotland – 'Scotland' in this instance not being the present country, but a manifestation of the Otherworld). It was in an open space surrounded by a thorny thicket, and it contained on a pillar the severed head of a golden-haired giant and the shield of his slayer. Entrance could only be gained after defeating a guardian knight in single combat. Some visiting knights were met by the Queen of the Otherworld with maidens and youths in attendance. She showed them the head and the shield, then they washed and sat at table, where they were served a meal with her and her consort, the Maimed King. After eating they slept till dawn, when they found themselves in a meadow surrounded by sweet-briar and roses, as though it were mid-May.[43]

### The Temple of the Goddess of Dreams

This was a round temple. A visiting knight ate in it with the damsel who was travelling with him. Then they went to their repose on couches which were put ready for the use of passing pilgrims. In his sleep he dreamed that a lady of very great honour explained a strange adventure he had once had. On waking it was light and they rode away.[44]

There were other temples: to the God of the Desires of Maidens, to whom maidens prayed for the husbands of their choice; to Flora; and to Mars, but their construction is not described.

How does this series of temples match the prehistoric reality? Apart from roundness, there are a number of correspondences here with known ceremonial constructions. The temple itself is in the middle of a clear space, the 'arena' being surrounded by a ditch. It is in one case open to the sky and in another (painted?) green inside. There is a way across the ditch at the entrance into the arena, which in one case contained a round temple covered with flat stones. The reliquary on the high altar of the temple to the Sovereign God contains 'the four elements, earth, air, fire and water'. The residue of such an offering would in the course of time closely match the mixture of earth and ashes known as occupation debris, which is sometimes found as a ritual deposit. There is an emphasis on astronomy and orientation. The hermit sits on his tower at the eastern entrance keeping watch far into the night, his eyes fixed

---

[41] *Perceforest*, pt IV, ed. Roussineau, p. 1147 note 74/2232.
[42] *Perceforest*, 1528, Pt V, ch. 37.
[43] *Perceforest*, II, ch. LXXXVII; ed. Roussineau, IV, p. 1147 note 72/2162; Part III, p. 302.
[44] *Perceforest*, Roussineau, pt IV, p. 1017 and p. 1095, and *Perceforest*, pt VI, XVII and XVIII.

on the stars. At sunset a beam of light shines through the doorway, as it seems to at Maes Howe in Orkney about the winter solstice, a classic feature of prehistoric construction distinct from but reminiscent of Stonehenge and New Grange where the orientation is to the rising sun at the midsummer and midwinter solstices, respectively.

Tradition may be giving us a clue here as to the attitude of the users of oriented temples. In this account, exactly as happens at New Grange, the nub of the matter is that a ray of light falls on and illuminates a particular feature. Should the view be revised that the disc of the sun rising over the heelstone was what mattered to the worshippers at Stonehenge? Quite likely the assembled viewers had their backs to the sun and were observing some pagan pageant suddenly illuminated by sunlight shining through a slot between two upright stones on one of the few days near the solstice when this could happen.

Everybody knows that the axis of Stonehenge points to the rising midsummer sun. It is less widely realized that, as a matter of celestial geometry, if the axis is prolonged in the opposite direction it meets the horizon at the most southerly setting point of the midwinter sun, the marker for the winter solstice. Some observers have thought the winter solstice to have been more significant to pagans than the summer. Midsummer is obviously a time to celebrate the sun at its most powerful. At midwinter the attitude of the priesthood is likely to have been entirely different – an attempt would have to be made to appease the gods to prevent the continued decline of the season into darkness, cold and hunger. An instance at the present time is provided by the Hopi Indians of the South-West United States, a people who regulate the sequence of their agricultural tasks by noting the position of the sun on the horizon. Both solstices are marked by ceremonies but more emphasis is placed on the winter solstice. This is the most important ceremony of the whole year, the intention being 'to "call back" the sun from its southerly movement.'[45]

On a less material plane than physical orientation, the features associated with the temples – the beautiful girl who proffers a cup and promises kingship, the severed heads, the Queen of the Otherworld and the Maimed King are all recognizable pagan themes. Less familiar is the idea of sleeping in a temple, or in another instance not so far mentioned on a perron by a cross at a fork in a road,[46] in order to have dreams or to dream the explanations of earlier dreams. This is reminiscent of the Aesculapian rite of 'incubation' of classical times, in which prayer and sleep resulted in dreams and a healing vision of the deity. As far as British archaeology is concerned, this principal seems to have been applied in practice, during the Roman occupation, at the temple of the Celtic god Nodens at Lydney near the Severn, where buildings which are nowadays taken to be dormitories were provided, presumably for this purpose. Nodens corresponds to the Irish god or sacred king, Nuada or alternatively

---

[45] *Astronomy and Society*, Ruggles and Whittle, 1981, p. 280.
[46] *Vulgate*, VI, p. 93.

to the more shadowy Arthurian personage Nut, whose son Yder was born at Cardoel.

There are a large number of dreams and dream explanations in the romances, suggesting that dreams were important in the underlying tradition. One common situation in which an individual spends a night in a house of religion is the night vigil of a new knight prior to being dubbed. As dubbing is a form of initiation it would make anthropologically good sense for it to be preceded by a dream session in, since this is obviously a pre-Christian rite, a temple. In *Perceforest* the setting was in the times before Caesar's invasion. The young squires about to be knighted at the May festival kept watch the previous night in the Temple of the Sovereign God (the round stone temple covered with flat stones referred to above), and they did much the same on such occasions at Camelot in more conventional romances. For instance, Gawain, who was knighted at the time of Arthur's marriage, kept a night vigil in St Stephen's.

In Arthurian times affairs of state were often decided by dreams. They influenced Arthur's choice of Camelot instead of Cardoel for his capital city. On the occasion when he fathered his son Mordred, his murderer to be, Arthur dreamed of a terrible serpent. He had a picture of this serpent painted in St Stephen's 'church'. This action calls to mind the idea that certain primitive spiral designs may represent illusions seen in (possibly drug-induced) trance states.

## A Palace described in *Perceforest*

### The Noble Palace

This palace is obviously an imagined precursor of Camelot in a romance set in pre-Roman times. In the middle of the palace, on the evening of the Festival of the Sovereign God, a round tower containing a round table arose miraculously in the centre of the palace. This round table, in some accounts of ivory, but more often of stone, had places at which knights were only able to sit where indicated by magically appearing shields, and it had a Perilous Seat of similar characteristics to the one at Camelot. The Noble Palace is said to have been close to the temple of the Sovereign God and also to the Marvellous Perron, which without warning arose nearby. Perceforest, the king of Britain, ordained great feasts in the month of May at the palace in honour of the Sovereign God.[47] It was the centre of the political and chivalric restoration of the country.[48] The Noble Palace was the site of a great battle in which the proto-Arthurian forces were defeated by the Romans, and its ruins were visited by the knights of the later age when chivalry would be reconstituted.

The author of *Perceforest* seems to present a view of the Arthurian legend

---

[47] *Perceforest*, ed. Roussineau, pt IV, preface, page civ.
[48] *Perceforest . . .*, Lods, p. 109.

without its Christian veneer, in which Camelot is intimately associated with a round pagan temple of ancient construction covered with flat stones, and also a standing stone of considerable importance.

## Graves

### (1) Urbaduc's Grave

There are a few graves which sound from their description or associations as if they may have been pagan. The most obvious is that of Urbaduc, said to have been a pagan king.[49] A certain prince Galehot, lord of the Faraway Islands and son of the Fair Giantess, played an important part in the Arthurian story, being Arthur's major military rival, but he was persuaded by Lancelot to join the king instead of opposing him. He died young, according to the story, and having been buried elsewhere he was reburied by Lancelot at the stronghold known as Joyous Gard. Here Lancelot ordered a fine tomb to be made but he was told by an old woman that the most beautiful tomb ever made was already there. The old people of the place would tell him where. It was in the main chapel near an altar. It had originally been made for a certain King Urbaduc,[50] whom pagans and Sarrassins worshipped and who had possessed the Joyous Gard before Joseph of Arimathea came to this country. He had been buried in the tomb, which subsequently had never been disturbed. Lancelot was pleased with 'this adventure'. He had the tomb dug out and found it not to be of gold or silver but to be entirely surrounded by precious stones so marvellously jointed one with another that it did not seem made by earthly man. The tomb was carried to the appointed spot and Galehot's body was placed in it with weapons, as the custom was at that time. Lancelot gave him three kisses, covered the body with a rich pall and replaced the slab. In due course Lancelot was buried in the same grave.

Allowing for the effects of the imagination of narrators, this could be a description of a re-opening of, say, a passage grave. Leaving aside the adjective 'precious' and the removal of the tomb we have: a very ancient pagan tomb twice re-used, once for an excarnated body; it was underground and of stone, marvellously jointed etc., a description reminiscent of the underground chamber 'that heathen men let hew and adorn in olden time with mickle skill and fair craft'.[51]

### (2) The grave of Faunus

This tomb is called after a deity, so a pagan link may be presumed. When Merlin was travelling in Brittany with the Damsel of the Lake he offered to

---

[49] *Vulgate*, IV, p. 295.
[50] Alternatively spelt Norbaduc or Narbaduc. The name is reminiscent of Geoffrey of Monmouth's Gorboduc, who was an ancestor of Brennius and Belinus in *Historia Regum Brittanie*.
[51] *Romania*, 98, p. 316, S. C. Harris.

show her the Lake of Diana. She was very pleased to see it for she felt a rapport for Diana, the goddess of the chase, because of her own love of hunting, on account of which she had the alternative name 'The Damsel Cacheresse'. They came upon a large, deep lake in a valley and went along the shore until they came to a perron beside which was a marble tomb, that of Faunus, at one time Diana's lover, whom she had killed. Merlin told the damsel what had happened. Long before the time of Jesus Christ, Diana had travelled and hunted all through the forests of France and Britain. She found at this place a wood by a lake which pleased her more than anywhere else, so she stayed and made a manor on the lake, where she returned each night after hunting throughout the day. Of the many who desired her she chose Faunus, the son of the king who held that land. He became her lover and they lived together on the lake. Two years later she met another knight, Felix, in the same way as she had met Faunus, while out hunting. Felix persuaded Diana to do away with Faunus. She set about it as follows. The stone tomb was normally full of water, which Demophon, a local enchanter, had bewitched so that it became a cure for wounds. One day Faunus was severely mauled by a wild beast while hunting. Diana suggested that he should try the water in the tomb for a cure, but she treacherously removed the healing water. She told him to lie in the empty tomb while she went to fetch healing herbs. Instead she had the heavy stone lid put back on and poured in molten lead, which killed him instantly. Felix, when she told him, seized her by the hair and cut off her head and cast her body into the waters of the lake. As her body was deposited there and she had been so fond of the place, it has been called the Lake of Diana ever since.[52]

The Damsel of the Lake, when she had heard the story of Diana, asked Merlin to build a manor for her too at the lake. He sent for craftsmen who built houses and a hall as rich as any in the world. These he made invisible except to those who lived in them. Later, the Damsel of the Lake fostered Lancelot in this place until he was eighteen years old, and it was from the Lake of Diana that he obtained the title by which he is always known, Lancelot du Lac.

### (3) Merlin's grave

Merlin's account of the death of Faunus is a remarkably close parallel to the manner of his own death.[53] He was himself to be incarcerated under a rock by the Damsel of the Lake who closely identifies herself with Diana through her name, the Huntress, and by her residence on Diana's lake. It is easy enough to see the Damsel of the Lake as a local equivalent of Diana, but how does Merlin fit in with Faunus? Faunus was an early Roman god described as an earth deity, concerned with the woods and the fields and with the protection and fertility of flocks and herds. He was scarcely to be distinguished from another Roman woodland deity, Silvanus or from the Greek god Pan. Surprisingly, the

52 Huth *Merlin*, II, pp. 145ff.
53 Huth *Merlin*, pp. 195/7.

fit between Merlin and Faunus is remarkably good. We have already seen how at the beginning of *The Lady of the Fountain* Merlin was transformed into the Lord of the Animals. It would be difficult to imagine a closer correspondence with Faunus than that. It seems likely that Faunus was a primitive deity common throughout Europe and though picked up by the Romans as the ancestor of the first Latin kings, never admitted to the upper ranks of the deities in the fully developed pantheon. Whether the same name persisted in Britain is a matter of conjecture. The native Celtic 'Lord of the Animals' would have been immediately recognizable as Faunus to anyone versed in classical lore, whether during the Roman occupation in the first few centuries of the first millennium AD or at the time the romances were being written down, a thousand years later.

The underground chamber in which Merlin was trapped by the Damsel of the Lake had earlier been lived in by two lovers, who were buried there.

Markale has suggested that the story of Merlin's demise is a description of 'dolmen burial'. The links shown here of Merlin with deities reinforce the proposition that the character we known originated as a supernatural personage. His links with the erection of the bluestone circle and other standing stones suggest that Merlin's original belonged to the age when 'dolmen burial' and reuse of a burial chamber would have been well known.

## (4) *The cemetery of Salisbury*

The account of this graveyard comes in two versions; probably the most widely known is that of Geoffrey of Monmouth, in which a reference to the stones of Stonehenge being brought from 'Ireland' i.e., the distant west, has been suggested by Prof. Piggott to be a remnant of an otherwise lost Bronze Age oral literature. In this version, the victims of a massacre were buried on Salisbury Plain in the cemetery close to the monastery of Ambrius.[54] Later in the story Aurelius Ambrosius, the king of Britain, having pacified the country, decided to set up a suitable monument in memory of the dead. Merlin recommended the Giant's Dance and went to Ireland with Aurelius Ambrosius's brother, Uther Pendragon, to obtain the stones. When the Irish had been defeated (their king was later killed near St David's[55] which is close to the source of the Stonehenge bluestones) the stones were brought back to the Mount of Ambrius (named after the founder of the monastery, Ambrius). Aurelius Ambrosius then sent for the whole population of the country to set up the stones, as they had originally been set up in 'Ireland', round the burial place. This took place at a Pentecost festival at which Aurelius Ambrosius set the crown on his own head.[56] An alternative version of this story adds an interesting glimpse of prehistory at this point, saying that the king's court was not decorated with ivory and tortoiseshell but was merely 'nemus et frondes'

54 *Historia*, ed. Wright, vol. I, sect. 104.
55 Meneuia urbs, *Historia*, vol. I, sect .132.
56 *Historia*, ed. Wright, vol. I, sect. 130.

that is woodland and leaves.[57] Surely in this context of an important pagan ritual centre, the meaning of nemus must carry with it something of the sense in which it was understood by Frazer; a clearing which was a sacred enclosure. This sentence in the *Gesta* is evidently another candidate for being added to the 'fragment of Bronze Age tradition'. When Aurelius Ambrosius died he was buried within the Giants' Dance;[58] Uther (Arthur's father) followed him as king, and when his time came he was buried, beside his brother, at Stonehenge;[59] next Arthur succeeded Uther; then Constantine succeeded Arthur, and Constantine too, according to Geoffrey, was buried at Stonehenge.

The other version is in the Huth *Merlin*.[60] In it Uther and Pendragon are two separate individuals. Pendragon was killed in a battle, after which Uther buried the dead in the 'Cemetery of Salisbury', raising Pendragon's tomb higher than the rest. Uther then assumed the surname 'Pendragon'. Merlin brought the stones much as in Geoffrey's version and set them up where they still are to this day at the Cemetery of Salisbury.

Taken at its face value this account of the Cemetery of Salisbury is a description of burials made before the erection of a stone circle at Stonehenge. In conjunction with Geoffrey's references to moving the stones and to a 'nemus' at the Stonehenge site, the Cemetery may be thought of as the concentration of barrows on the Plain, a further addition to the Bronze Age tradition.

## (5) *The Perilous Graveyard*

There was a place called Escalon[61] which became enshrouded in perpetual shadows because one Easter Thursday a knight lay with the daughter of the lord of Escalon, she willingly, in the church. This sounds like a thinly veiled description of ritual copulation and sets the scene in deepest paganism. The enchantment could only be removed by success in an odd adventure. A hero had to penetrate a completely dark minster in a cemetery and open a door, letting in light. Usually the hero who attempted this feat was driven back by the cold and the stench of decay. In contrast, reapers outside in the sunshine were gathering grain for the people of the shadowed castle. It was the corpses of the people of the castle which caused the smell. Eventually Lancelot

---

[57] *Gesta Regum Britannie*, ed. and tr. Wright, p. 162 lines 353/5. When the author of *Gesta* describes the king's court in this way he is making an entirely unexpected statement. Geoffrey of Monmouth is recognized to have been wildly imaginative and unreliable. He might have been expected to embellish the details of the hospitality of the king of Britain towards his most honoured guests on the occasion of his coronation. Instead of this the author apparently reduces the background of the expected lavish hospitality to merely woods and leaves – no palaces, houses, feasts or lavish display. To say 'nemus et frondes' at this juncture is meaningless unless it is accepted that the occasion was a religious one and that the principal religious centre was a sacred enclosure.

[58] *Historia*, ed. Wright, vol. I, sect. 134.

[59] *Historia*, ed. Wright, vol. I, sect. 142.

[60] Ed. Paris and Ulrich, vol. I, pp. 89/93.

[61] *Vulgate*, VII, p. 136; and see Gazetteer.

succeeded and released Escalon from its spell.[62] Another adventure of a similar kind was that of the Perilous Graveyard, where from such time as the land was first peopled with folk, and knights began to seek adventure in the forest, all dead knights were brought for burial. Perceval's sister, on her own, for only one person was able to enter at a time, braved this terrifying place, undeterred by the spirits of the buried knights, to obtain a piece of cloth from the shroud of a dead knight whose corpse was lying on the altar.[63] She needed this strange talisman as a charm against a knight who was feuding with her family.

It may at first glance seem far fetched to suggest as an explanation of these events that they are recollections of visits to prehistoric burial vaults, but the episodes should be looked at in the context of the legends as a whole. To test the bravery and endurance of his heroes, the narrator has exhausted all the trials of the natural world and beyond. The heroes are undeterred by perilous fords, defended causeways, ten opponents at once, even hags and dragons. The most difficult tests that he can envisage, of a kind that only the peerless knight Lancelot can accomplish, are of an entirely unexpected kind. He has to penetrate the cold and stench of rotting corpses which have kept out all the rest; he has to wrench a great slab of stone, 3ft by 4ft by 1ft thick, from a tomb to reveal the fully armed corpse within; only Galahad can surpass him, by extinguishing a flame which burns miraculously in a tomb in a cave under a minster, a feat which marks him out as the eventual achiever of the Grail. How extraordinary that the ultimate tests for the earthly paragon, Lancelot, the spiritual paragon, Galahad, and the latter's female counterpart, Perceval's sister, should all have been the entering of tombs – unless the narrator was recalling some ancestral memory of the time when the courage to brave the spirits of the dead and to do just this was a necessary qualification of the upper ranks of the priesthood.

### (6) King Lot's grave

Lot was killed in battle by Pellinor. Twelve other kings were killed at the same time and were buried at St Stephen's at Camelot, but Lot had a tomb to himself. It was very fine and a chapel to St John was erected in his honour. A link with Midsummer, which may be supposed from this dedication, is confirmed by the lighting on that occasion of perpetually burning candles or torches.[64] Fires were traditionally lit at midsummer up to recent times.

### (7) Tristan's tomb

This, in the church of Tintagel, was second only to Galehot's and was embellished by copper figures of Tristan and Yseult. At the annual celebration of the defeat of Morholt (which was close to the solstice) the church was lit by the rays of the rising sun. At the hour of prime the church filled and King Mark

---

[62] *Vulgate*, IV, p. 110.
[63] A similar story is told of Lore.
[64] Huth *Merlin*, I, pp. 262/4.

placed his own crown on Tristan's image and kissed it. Tristan's sword and shield were treated like the relics of a saint.[65]

### (8) *Graves which were the site of heroic encounters*

One of Peredur's adventures was to kill the Black Serpent of the Barrow, which lived in the Mournful Mound. The corresponding feature in the romances, Mount Dolorous, thus seems to have been a tumulus. Merlin's unnamed daughter was entitled 'of Mount Dolorous' and Merlin set up a magic perron on top of this tumulus. Peredur's adventure appears to have a duplicate in which the cave had a stone pillar at the mouth of and was guarded by a monster.[66]

A black knight defended the entrance of a tomb in a glade until defeated by Perceval. This knight appears also as Maduc, who had the heads on stakes at his challenge site.

Malaquin, a black knight guarded the tomb of Darnantes at night (in *Perceforest*).[67]

Lanceor and his lover Colombe (in Malory) were buried in a splendid tomb where he had been killed by Balin, near Merlin's perron.

The green Chapel in *Sir Gawain and the Green Knight* was a barrow in a launde.

The graves listed here are all in one way or another linked with pagan practices or personages. Some of them correspond to what has been described, not to be too specific, as dolmen burial. There are several more burials which may have been in barrows. King Galahad's grave was a slab on four pillars[68] and one of Bran's sepulchres listed on p. 270 sounds much the same. Graves were marked by towers of stone (cairns) placed over them in the time of the Grail religion.[69] However, of all these the only grave which can be exactly located is that of Arthur's son Amr at the source of the river Gamber between the towns of Hereford and Monmouth, and, less specifically, it is said that Gawain's grave was on the seashore of South-West Wales facing the gap between the islands of Skomer and Skokholm.

---

[65] Prose *Tristan*, pp. 390, 411 and 415.
[66] *Mabinogion*, Penguin, pp. 241–5.
[67] *Perceforest*, ed. Roussineau, pt IV, p. 1025.
[68] *Le Roman en prose de Lancelot du Lac*, ed. Hutchings, p. 45(A). The names Galehot and Galaad are easily confused, This could be an alternative description of the pagan grave reused for Galehot mentioned on p. 180 above.
[69] Hucher, *Le Saint Graal*, vol. III, p. 344.

# THE GEOGRAPHY OF ARTHURIAN ROMANCE

## The Location of Named Places

As mentioned in the introduction, the geography of the Arthurian Romances presents many well advertised problems. It would be difficult to exaggerate the extent to which piecemeal attempts to identify places in the romances have produced complete confusion, largely because authors have relied almost wholly on resemblances between place-names in the romances and modern place-names. Centuries of verbal repetition, including translation into one or more different languages, have obscured the detail and corrupted the spellings of names in the romances. As a case in point, here is an example of a personal name, incorporating a place name, which appears in different forms in several different versions of the same story:

| | | |
|---|---|---|
| Orvale | de | Guindoel |
| Orgale | de | Guidel |
| Orgalle | de | Gindiel |
| Angale | de | Raguindel |
| Angrile | de | Granidel |

Except that we know from their contexts that these all belong to the same individual, who would have guessed that the last two and the first three are merely versions of a common original, whatever that may have been? Yet this is a fairly typical example of the effect on names of the long process of repetition. When a large number of instances is examined, a feature often observed is the constancy of the sequence of consonants in a name compared to the variability of the vowels. In this case there are in succession:

$$- r - v(\text{or } g) - 1 -  \quad de \quad g - n - d - 1$$

The order of the consonants is broken only by occasional omissions and a reversal ('gr' for 'rg' or vice versa).[1] The change between v and g is common

---

[1] The reversal of consonants in proper names in the romances is not unusual, examples: Goronilla for Gonorilla, *Perceforest*, pt 1, ed. Taylor, Index; Disnadaron for Dinasdaron and

enough, as, for example, Pays de Galles in French stands for native Wales, Gawain for Walwyn and so on.[2] The relative stability of the framework of consonants has not prevented considerable distortion. Except with a few of the best-known names, this degree of distortion is general, so it will be seen that a crisp solution to the problem of identifying places cannot be found by comparing their names in the romances with present day place names.

Another difficulty is the dream-like nature of so many of the place-names. Take the 'Castels' in West's *Prose Index*. They are as follows: the Castle of Dames; of Maidens; of Gazewilte; (a place on the border of North Wales); of la Casse (a place in the kingdom of Listenois); of the Chariot; of the Harp; of the Rock; of the Horn (or of the Heart); of the Thorn; of the Narrow Way; of the Mill; of the Hill; of the Passage; of the Enchanters; of Four Stones and of Merlin. Few of these are place-names in the ordinary sense, implying a unique location. They sound more like places in *Pilgrim's Progress* than names taken from a gazetteer of the real Britain underlying the romances. Though this is only a small sample of the 137 castles (mostly called 'chastel') in the *Prose Index*, many of the remainder fall into the same pattern. It will be seen that, because of the difficulties of spelling and what appear to be generic rather than specific place-names, a great deal of close attention to the material will be required before it will be possible to provide fairly accurate locations for any of the places mentioned above.

Yet another possible source of confusion is error on the part of narrators. Occasionally one place-name is substituted for another in different manuscripts describing the same event, Carlion for Cardoel, for example, or vice versa. Also there are apparently impossible juxtapositions, such as Ireland and Cornwall, and also Ireland and Scotland, apparently having common boundaries, which cannot be explained (in recent times, geologically speaking) except by error unless the limits of the countries concerned are redefined.

With all these obstacles it is not surprising that different commentators on the Arthurian scene who have attempted to unravel the geography have very often come up with alternative solutions to the location of particular places. As I have said in the introduction, it is possible to argue that the whole of the action took place in Cornwall, or that the major part was in Wales or in Scotland or in Brittany. But these arguments have been made with the historical Arthur in mind. In the romances there is a different emphasis, for a leading role is played by the Arthurian court at Camelot, which is definitely in Logres. The course of this enquiry will be guided by what is said in the romances and will not necessarily follow the same lines as have previous attempts.

---

Deneversire for Devonshire, *Verse Index*, West; Agron for Argon, *Prose Index*, West; Balan for Laban, Langlois; Elavachin for Evalachin, Hucher, II, p. 208: and Malory's Cameliard for French Carmelide.

[2] V and G were interchangeable in the 13th cent, see footnote p. 110.

To take a couple of examples of the sort of difficulty which has arisen in the identification of places; was a place called Ceroise on the river Suize in France or was it Saussy or Val Suzon? Was the Taneborc of the romances where Oswestry now is, on the Welsh border, or was it Edinburgh? The answers to these questions are not important. Nothing much happened at either of these places. But the reasons put forward for these localizations are of interest if we are to find more accurate answers in other instances. The identifications of Ceroise depend entirely on the resemblance of the name to modern place-names. That several similar sounding places are available in a comparatively small compass – Ceroise was on a journey between two places which are about eighty miles apart – reinforces a recent comment to the effect that names are 'slippery evidence'. Name resemblance has also been used in the identification of Taneborc with Edinburgh. A switch between 't' and 'd' is a likely effect of oral transmission, so, given the usual variability in vowels under these circumstances, there is a very strong likeness between the two names, involving a sequence of five consonants.

EDIN BURGH
TANEBORC

However, a more wide-ranging assumption than mere name-resemblance has been made in this case. Taneborc is described as being at 'the entry of Norgales'. Norgales is, of course, literally North Wales but did North Wales mean the same then as it does now? In the romances it sometimes appears to have been north of Northumberland. Scholars have pointed out that before the Anglo-Saxon conquest the original inhabitants of the whole country, even well into Scotland, included people indistinguishable from the then inhabitants of Wales. So, it is argued, the name North Wales could equally have been used of Scotland, much as North Britain is today. Hence the idea that Taneborc is Edinburgh rather than Oswestry. Which solution, if either, is correct does not matter for the moment. At this stage I am only concerned to examine the methods which can be used to pinpoint ancient places on modern maps. So far we have seen topography, exemplified by 'at the entrance to North Wales', and name resemblance. Another method uses journey times. As Carman points out, if it took two days to travel from Southampton to Camelot and the same time from Dover to Camelot then Camelot must be on a line stretching roughly from Brighton to London. On this line he chooses Westminster as being on a large enough river for the Fair Maiden of Astolat (alternatively Escalon, or as Tennyson has it, Shalott) to have floated down; and because Westminster has, like Camelot, a minster dedicated to St Stephen. This line of reasoning, which identifies Westminster as Camelot, is based on the assumption of a constant rate of travel of nearly forty miles a day and it leads, in Carman's view, only to the location which the author of that particular version had in mind for Camelot; in other words, that we can expect a narrator to adjust minor details like journey times to suit his own perception of reality.

These examples show that three main methods have been used in attempts to unravel Arthurian geography: topography, that is the description of the features of a district; name resemblance; and journey times. The last two are clearly extremely vulnerable to the vicissitudes of repetition and the manipulation of narrators. Descriptions of the first type, like 'the entry to North Wales' or 'on the boundary of North Wales and Logres' or 'where the Severn meets the sea' stand a better chance of surviving intact, particularly when well-known names such as those of countries and major rivers are involved since they are less likely to be susceptible to change on a letter to letter basis. This being the case, if attempts to identify legendary places are restricted to recognizing *topographical* features, then a more consistent overall view should be obtained than is shown by the erratic and contradictory results so far published.

## Topographical References

'At the entry to North Wales' may be an accurately remembered description of the position of Taneborc but it is still capable of being interpreted in many ways. We are not told whether the entry is to be made from the north-east, from the east or from the south. Nor do we know what the boundaries of North Wales were at that time. So, are there any other places which are topographically more clearly defined, however much or little they contribute to the story as a whole? Indeed, one can ask if there are any places in the whole of the romances which can be identified with reasonable certainty from internal evidence. This question probes the limits of the possibility of identifying places in the romances, for since the other possible lines of enquiry have been ruled out as unproductive, it is really asking the most fundamental question of all, 'Is there any single place in the romances which can be positively identified with reasonable certainty by any method whatever?' Among the very few possibilities, I believe the most distinctive to be a place called Leverzerp which is said to have been between two arms of the tidal Severn but is never said to be an island.[3] From this description it can be concluded that the place referred to is in the comparatively short space between Gloucester and the estuary proper, and is probably the Arlingham peninsula. The main assumption involved here is that the 'Saverne' of the romances means the river we know as Severn today. There are two reasons why it is likely to have been so. The first is that river names have more staying power than those of any other feature of the landscape. The second, that if the Saverne (alternatively Sauverne, Sauuerne, Surne, Assurne, Aisurne, Ausurne or Sabryne)[4] is assumed to be the Severn (the present day Severn – there is only one river of that name in Britain now) a consistent general view of the Arthurian scene follows. The Saverne,

---

3   *Vulgate*, Index under Leverzerp and footnote.
4   An initial 'A' is sometimes added to names in the romances. See footnote on page 193 below.

for instance runs close to Norgales and it is always the boundary between Logres and the Welsh kingdoms neighbouring Norgales to the south.

To identify one place only might seem an inauspicious beginning, but Leverzerp (alternatively Leveserp, Leverzep, Louverep, Loverzeph or Lovrezep) is by chance a very useful starting point for the exploration of Arthurian geography. It is a word with a five-consonant structure and its spelling varies little, so it is always immediately recognizable; it is not an important place in the romances, so it has not attracted editorial interpretations nor modern identifications; in the real world there is nothing noticeable there – no strange rock-formations or ruins which might have attracted to themselves a floating legend, as seems to have happened at Caernarfon and Caerleon; and finally it is, as will be seen, linked with several other places on the Severn whose positions, determined in several different ways, fit together in a mutually satisfactory fashion.

The persistence of river names has been demonstrated by comparing Roman geographical works with present day names. It is said that of some fifty British rivers listed by Ptolemy in the first century A.D., about half have survived, nearly all to the present day.[5] These river names were not Roman inventions but the Latin equivalents of native names, so a considerable proportion of our river names are well over two thousand years old. Names which were familiar to the Celtic Britons (though not necessarily given by them and conceivably of great age even then) have survived conquests by peoples speaking three different languages, Latin, English and Norman. The Severn, which is of the first importance in this analysis, is among those rivers with pre-Roman names. The Latin version of this river name, Sabrina, was considered by Milton to be the name of the nymph representing the river. Sabrina is etymologically the same as Severn, since a change from native 'v' or 'w' to 'b'[6] on translation to a romance language is not uncommon. The Welsh name, Haffren, is also derived from the same root. Here 'h' has replaced 's' (or vice versa). This is a well-known phenomenon, dividing Indo-European languages into two groups; the one which uses 'h' instead of 's' includes both Welsh and Greek. A widely known instance is provided by the group of elements including chlorine which derives its name 'the halogens', meaning 'salt-formers', from the Greek root (h)al- rather than the corresponding Latin sal-. Other instances are hexagon, for a six-sided figure and heptagon, for one with seven.

The name Severn, though unique as a river name in Britain, is paralleled in

5   *Early Irish History and Mythology*, T. F. O'Rahilly, p. 40.
6   V sometimes changes to B on translation to romance languages: e.g. caballero for cavalier; Hibernia for native Ivernia; Gobannium for (Aber)-gavenny; Oboka for Avoca; sorbus for service tree; Eboracum for Eferwic/Everwic; Abrincates for Avranches; Taba for Tava (Rivet and Smith); and Besançon for Vesontio (the tutelary deity of the place). Some changes from V to B (or vice versa) are not so obviously at a language boundary, e.g. Varlan for Brulan (*Prose Index*, West), taule for table (Hucher, p. 199).

Ireland by the Sabrann, an old name for the river Lee,[7] showing – like the rivers called Don – how the names of rivers are markers, like erratics stranded by a glacier, for the spread at some distant era of some distinctive factor of human culture.

The usefulness of rivers as topographical indicators, because of the persistence of their names, suggests that the other rivers of the romances should be looked at before we go on to examine their environs. Apart from the Severn, the rivers mentioned as being in Britain are the Arecuse, the Celice, the Charosche, the Drance, the Hombre, the Marse, the Marsonde, the Poynzaclins, the Ocire, the Salerne, the Tembre, the Thamise and the Toivre. Of these only the Hombre and Ocire are important in the Arthurian romances. Unexpectedly, the Thamise/Thames plays no part in the story, which has a very strong bias towards places in the west and rarely mentions recognizable eastern locations. A few of the lesser rivers are topographically interesting. The Poynzaclins, mentioned in a German version of the story of Perceval, is said to meet the Sabins at a place called Rosch Sabins, where the Sabins meets the sea. The Sabins may be a garbled recollection of the Sabrina, which would suggest that the Poynzaclins was the Wye, but there is little to be gained by speculation at this point. The Drance also makes a single appearance, again as an unidentified tributary of the Severn. The Ocire (alternatively spelt Oscure and Ousque) is yet another tributary of the Severn. It can probably be identified as the Usk from the name variant Ousque. Usque merely means water in Gaelic. For instance, dictionaries give the derivation of 'whisky' as from '*usque*baugh', literally, the 'water of life'. It is not at all surprising that a number of rivers should bear this name meaning water. Among them are, as well as the Usk, the Exe, the various rivers called Axe and Esk, and on the continent the Isch and others (Ekwall). The castles of Maidens and of Dames faced each other across the Ousque, and the castle of Maidens was on the Severn.[8] This limits the Ousque to being a tributary of the Severn, and although another of the rivers whose names come from the same root, the Axe, also runs into the Severn estuary, at Weston-super-Mare, the Usk is to be preferred for the Ousque because the castle of Maidens and the castle of Dames have links (to be mentioned later) with other places which can be identified as having been in Wales.

An unexpected feature of the rivers of legendary Britain is that where their course is indicated, they are almost all tributaries of the Severn – even the Hombre is said to have fallen into the Severn![9] Here there is a problem which seems to have no solution. Was the Hombre of the romances (alternatively spelt Honbre, Humbre and Ombre) the mighty Humber estuary which joins the North Sea between Yorkshire and Lincolnshire, with which it has

7  *Oxford Dictionary of English Place Names*, Ekwall.
8  *Vulgate*, VI, p. 34.
9  *Prose Index*, West.

invariably been identified; or was it an unknown tributary of the Severn; or, since the name Humber is far from being unique, could both be true?

To take up this point, in Celtic speaking times the name Humber (or something like it) was once used for several rivers and remained common in the past in England as a name for streams.[10] There are at the present day several rivers and places which have names incorporating the same root as Humber, which spreads out into forms like Ombr- and Ambr-. These include the river Amber in Derbyshire and the river Gamber in Herefordshire.[11] The latter has a specific Arthurian connection. The tomb of Arthur's son Amr is said to have been beside the source of the river Gamber, (which bears his name Amr – the G being a Celtic grammatical appendage and the b being an elusive letter, often omitted). Gamber Head (that is, the source of the river Gamber) is a little south of the conspicuous barrow known as Wormlow Tump on the A466. Amr's tomb was still visible there in about AD 800 as a low mound, variously estimated as from two to five paces long. The sources of rivers were often cult sites in pagan times. To have a personage buried at the source of a river to which he gave his name is clearly significant, though unfortunately Amr has been completely forgotten except for one reference in Nennius.[12] Although said there to be Arthur's son, he plays no active part in either the Welsh or French versions of the Arthurian legend. The Gamber falls into the Wye near Symonds Yat and thus ultimately into the Severn at Beachley.

There is another place-name prominent in the Arthurian scene which contains this same root Ambr-, though it is not that of a river. It is Mons Ambrius, the site of Stonehenge in the *Historia* of Geoffrey of Monmouth. The name has persisted, for Ekwall explains nearby Amesbury as Ambr's burg.[13] Ambr- also appears in the personal name Ambrosius, for whom, according to Geoffrey of Monmouth, the stones were moved and who was buried there; and this name again appears in the epithet Ambrosius given to Merlin, who is said by Geoffrey to have moved the stones.

The ramifications of the name which crops up in rivers as Humber demonstrate its original importance but obviously do not lead to any unique identification. All that can be said is that a reference to the Hombre does not necessarily lead to the present day Humber, nor does Norhombellande (and its variants) necessarily mean the present Northumberland. Indeed, almost all the links of this river and kingdom are with the Severn and Norgales, so, however improbable it may seem, a situation in the Severn valley is that which is generally indicated by the romances.

---

10 *Oxford Dictionary of English Place Names*, Ekwall.
11 For a comment on Gamber see K. H. Jackson in *Arthurian Literature in the Middle Ages*, p. 1.
12 The name Amhar son of Arthur also appears, in a list only, in Geraint and Enid, *Mabinogion*, Penguin, p. 260.
13 There is another Ambresbury, an Iron Age hill-fort in Epping Forest.

## The Marches

One of the most striking features of Arthurian topography is the frequency with which a place is described as being on 'la marche' between two terri- tories, 'marche' here meaning boundary, as in the term 'the Welsh Marches' used for the border between England and Wales. Unfortunately, though the border with Wales is the most obvious example of the use of 'marche' (nowa- days march) for a border, the use in this context gives an entirely different slant to our understanding of the word from its use in the romances. The Welsh Marches were politically important in the Middle Ages, especially at the time the romances were being collected, as the dividing line between two warring kingdoms, while in the romances themselves the 'marche' seems to be a zone of interaction as well as a division. Fairs, religious observances and gatherings often take place on marches, and though the gatherings often in- volve conflict, it is formalized as a tournament rather than outright war.

There is a particularly clear group of references to the borders between the territories – mostly kingdoms – in the Severn area. A kingdom called Sorelois, for instance, is described as having being enclosed towards Logres by a single great, swift, deep river called the Assurne[14] (i.e. Severn). On the other part it was surrounded by the sea. It contained castles, strong and delightful cities, and woods, mountains and other rivers in plenty, of which the most part fell into the Assurne which itself fell into the sea. Whoever went from Logres to Sorelois had to cross the Assurne, no easy task.[15] Sorelois is also said to have a border with Norgales (i.e. North Wales), which was itself contiguous with Logres. Between them these references place Sorelois in the south east of Wales, and contiguous with Norgales which is therefore in the north of Wales as might be expected. Almost all other topographical bearings confirm this conclusion, as will later be seen.

There are a number of other references to 'marches' which confirm the division of Wales into Norgales and Sorelois with the Severn separating them from Logres, and also extend this simple scheme to include other territories. First, the border between Norgales and Logres is mentioned several times. Norgales is often linked with the river Saverne, the natural border of Logres to the west, for example by the situation of a castle called Parens;[16] and another castle, Cairaire, is on the border of Norgales and Logres.[17]

In addition Norgales is said to have a border with a duchy, Cambenic, along a small, deep river which flows through the forests of Brequeham.[18] Since Brequeham is described as beyond the Severn from Logres and not far from

---

[14] Initial letter A added to personal names, examples: Ablechin for Blechin: Aganor for Ganor; Agornain for Gornain; Amador for Mador; and Ameraugis for Meraugis (from *Prose Index*, West); Adrian for Drian; Anates for Natanc; Aragre for Ragres (Index, *Vulgate*).

[15] *Vulgate*, III, p. 269.

[16] *Prose Index*, West.

[17] *Prose Index*, West.

[18] *Vulgate*, III, p. 310.

Leverzerp, it seems to lie in Wales south of Norgales and north of the mouth of the Severn. The position of Cambenic follows; it is contiguous with and to the south of Norgales. Once again, these conclusions will be confirmed in due course by other information, to be gleaned from an examination of itineraries.

Needless to say, the picture given by the romances is not completely consistent. Apart from apparent anomalies to be explained later, there was a tournament in the march of Sorelois and Northumberland, and the Severn is mentioned as the border of Norgales and Sorelois. These discrepancies (if that is what they are) are minor compared to the generally good fit between the information provided by the 'marches' with that from other sources.

## Itineraries

The earliest surviving geographical directions are in the form of a periplus, a narrative of the consecutive points reached on a sea voyage. The terrestrial equivalent, the road-book – merely a list of places passed through – continued in use until comparatively recent times. This format appears several times in the romances and associated material.

In *Sir Gawain and the Green Knight*, for instance, the unnamed English author has his hero travel from Camelot (perhaps conceived of in this work as Winchester) to somewhere in the north of England, in search of the 'green chapel' where he expects to meet his death. The author links the action to the landscape by talking of North Wales, Anglesey, and the fords by the foreland over at Holyhead leading to the Wilderness of Wirral. Compare this with a description of a rather similar journey, though with a very different objective, in an earlier French romance. King Lot and his sons, including Gawain, left the City of Logres[19] by the Bricoune Gate to go to Arestuel in Scotland via the Severn Valley. Their route was by the Chastel de la Sapine and by the Plains of Roestoc and by the Forests of l'Espinoe below Caranges, then by the river of Sauerne very close to the meadows of Cambenic, then skirting the city of Norgales, and so onwards toward Arestuel.[20] Between Roestoc and Cambenic they stopped at Leverzerp.[21]

The contrast between the two journeys is considerable. The English author talks only of recognizable places, the names of which were familiar to himself and to his audience. The French refers to places which apart from Severn are likely to have been unfamiliar to him, were probably not in use in Britain at the time he wrote (or some of them would have survived to the present day in local medieval manuscripts), and were known to his hearers only from other Arthurian tales. Yet the middle section of this sequence exactly fits the framework already built up from the 'marches'. From the south the first place to be

[19] The City of Logres was the principal city of Logres, probably Camelot but was occasionally confused for obvious reasons with Londres.
[20] *Vulgate*, II, p. 339.
[21] *Vulgate*, II, p. 365.

met, of those places which have previously been mentioned, is **Leverzerp**; then the **Severn** is followed to **Cambenic** and **Norgales** before the party travels on to the north. If the *Vulgate Merlin Continuation* was a work of the imagination, then the author shared his imaginary road-book with the author of another work, the *Book of Lancelot of the Lake*, or vice versa. This degree of organisation seems unlikely in the thirteenth century. A more probable reason for the consistency shown and the correspondence between the two authors is that they were both relying on the same tradition, in short, that in these Arthurian names we have a record of the pre-English names of places in the Severn valley, all of which except for the river itself have been otherwise completely forgotten.

Another journey undertaken by Gawain was from Norgales to Zorelois (as Sorelois is spelt in this account) which latter place was said to be 'at the end of Norgales, towards the west'. He was instructed as follows: 'Go straight through Norgales until you come to the Severn and then ask the way there, everyone will know. When you have followed the Severn a long way you will come to a high hill. It is called the Round Mountain by the locals. It is on the right, and you will know you are on the right road when you see a river going towards the mountain'. On top of the hill was a hermitage and from there the hermit's clerk took Gawain through the forests of Brequeham to within sight of Leverzerp. Sorelois, his destination, was on the same side of the river as Brequeham.[22] This route is a match to what has already been observed in five respects. Travelling south, it follows the **Severn** from **Norgales** past **Brequeham** and **Leverzerp** to **Sorelois**.

To complete the map of the west side of the Severn valley in Arthurian times, as it has so far been sketched out, it can be added that the forest of Brequeham or Brequeham was very large and overlapped the unidentified river between Norgales and Cambenic, stretching into both territories.[23]

This last journey by Gawain tells of a round mountain close to the Severn. It was on the right hand when going south and below it was the junction with another river which was called the 'Hombre'.[24] The City of Norgales was not far away, so the confluence of these two rivers may be supposed to have been towards the northern half of Wales. It is not possible to identify this mountain, but the journey continued came to the mouth of the Severn.

On the basis of this information some commentators, as mentioned above, have taken the view that Norgales was north of the estuary we know as the Humber today. To take this view on account of a single name-resemblance and to neglect all the links with the Severn in the rest of this passage is extremely unproductive. It would mean jettisoning the whole web of topographical links so far described (and with more to come) and offering nothing but confusion in their place. No wonder Arthurian geography is notorious for the difficulties

[22] *Vulgate*, III, p. 361.
[23] *Vulgate*, III, p. 310.
[24] *Prose Index*, West, under Hombre.

it presents when sweeping conclusions have been reached without scrutinizing the relative worth of different types of evidence.

Looking at the situation logically, to have the Hombre meet the Severn suggests three possibilities: either there was a lapse on the part of a narrator; or there was another Humber that did flow into the Severn; or the narrator got the Humber right and therefore the legendary Severn with all its appurtenances including North Wales has to be transferred to Northumbria. The third has nothing to offer in terms of providing locations for legendary places supported by topographical arguments. Either of the first two are compatible with the scheme so far advanced.

The Severn has now been followed to its tidal parts, from Norgales to Leverzerp. To continue this imaginary journey towards the west, along the north coast of the widening Severn estuary, it may be envisaged that at one time this part of the country was known as Sorelois. A place in Sorelois was Escalon,[25] if we may accept that the spelling Escaloine is a variant of that name. This is confirmed by a journey made by Morgan le Fay past Escalon to the forest of Sarpenic, where a cross road led to Sorelois in one direction and to the Valley of No Return and to the Dolorous Tower in others.[26]

Escavalon has a name that is reminiscent of Escalon. This name might have had its origin, it has been speculated, through the influence of the name Avalon on Escalon, or Escavalon might have been the original form of which Escalon is an eroded version. Whichever is the case, there is the same sort of link between Escavalon and South Wales as Escalon has. First, Escavalon was in Wales;[27] next, Lancelot travelled from Escavalon to the Castle of Dames on the Ocire/Ousque (Usk) via the forest of Sapinoie;[28] and finally Gawain rode from Carlion-on-Usk so far that he came to the kingdom of Escavalon and began to skirt the forest of Brequeham.[29] Within the limits of the oral tradition a picture of a cluster of named places located in South Wales seems to be emerging.

Still proceeding along the Severn estuary to the west the next landmark to be encountered after the mouth of the Severn is the river Usk, where the castles of Maidens and of Dames faced each other across this river.[30] The romances do not indicate how far Sorelois stretched along the coast of South Wales, but presumably much further to the west than the Usk was the forest of Darnantes, which marched with the realm of Sorelois and the Cornish Sea.[31] After Sorelois, the Severn estuary has been left behind and to the south is the

---

[25] *Prose Index*, West, under Escaloine.
[26] *Vulgate*, VII, pp. 135/136; IV, p. 108.
[27] Potvin, line 30798.
[28] *Vulgate*, IV, p. 227.
[29] *Vulgate*, VII, p. 84.
[30] As the castle of Maidens was on the Severn, *Vulgate*, VI, p. 34, they must have been at the mouth of the Usk.
[31] *Prose Index*, West.

open sea. To the west is the peninsula of Dyfed which has strong links with Merlin, whose mother was a princess of Dyfed and whose home is supposed to have been in Carmarthenshire. Merlin finally succumbed to the enchantments of the damsel of the Lake in a cave in Darnantes.[32] so perhaps Darnantes stretched right into Dyfed. There is a web of links between that part of the country and significant pagan activities and with deities important in the Arthurian story. The pagan sanctity of this south-west corner of Wales is vouched for by the episode of Bran's head on Grassholm; the siting of St David's at the seductive marsh (see Aroie in Gazetteer); the spring which gushed where Dunawd's throat was cut; the link between Boia and the forest of Aroie where the triple goddess was to be found beside the Adventurous Spring; the events at Glen Cuch (at the border of Pembrokeshire and Carmarthenshire) which led to Pwyll becoming ruler of the Otherworld; and the events at the magic mound at Arberth which so closely parallels the Perilous Seat at the Round Table.

Merlin's mother is said to have lived on the boundary of Ireland and Scotland,[33] and at the same time in West Wales, a seemingly impossible geographical puzzle. To add to the confusion some of the inhabitants of Ireland proper were originally called Scotti, a term later exported to Caledonia by conquest. Even when the romances were being committed to parchment, 'Scotus' still meant Irish. What one wonders, was the Celtic word represented in the romances which the narrator rendered as 'Irish'? Perhaps it was a word referring to language, perhaps meaning some version of Celtic speech; or it might have been a term relating to religion, since the name Ireland is derived from that of a goddess. Either way one can imagine an interface with Ireland, not so definite as a national boundary resulting from the establishment of a province, occurring in Wales or anywhere else. All we can be certain of is the importance of the 'Irish' presence in Dyfed. As well as the boundary just mentioned the King of 'Ireland' resisted the removal of the bluestones. He was based at St David's and was killed nearby. The association of 'Ireland' with events and personages of primarily religious significance tends to confirm the suggestion that it is likely to have been an enclave of a pagan system, perhaps one which was also practised in Ireland proper and which eventually gave that country its name.

An association between 'Ireland' and Dyfed can also be inferred from ancient Welsh literature, in which the word Ireland is used to represent the Otherworld. Two stations of the Otherworld have been localized in Dyfed: Annwfn at Glen Cuch in the *Mabinogion*, as already mentioned, and Caer Siddi at Grassholm in *The Spoils of Annwfn*. This disembodied 'Ireland' need not be thought of as an offshoot of Ireland proper. It is just as likely to have been, like the various rivers called Don, a relic left by a tide which at one time swept over a far wider area.

---

[32] In one version of this event: *Vulgate*, III, p. 21.
[33] *Vulgate*, III, p. 20.

This journey down the Severn and its estuary has shown how important this river was in the British tales underlying the romances, and there are still more places linked with it or with the adjacent realms already located. For instance, Estrangort, the realm of the King with the 100 Knights, was on the Severn.[34] It is also said to have marched with the realm of Norgales and with the Duchy of Cambenic.[35] Since these two territories are west of the Severn and their boundary is a river, Estrangort would have been at the confluence of the Severn with one of its Welsh tributaries. The Kingdom of Estroite Marche (the Narrow Boundary), in or near the forest of Brequeham, was bounded by Norgales, Cambenic and Estrangort so it would have been where those three territories meet. Another place not far away was Malehaut, on the boundary of the kingdom of the King with the Hundred Knights, that is, Estrangort. Near Malehaut was a great battle from which blood and battle wreckage[36] flowed down a stream into the Severn, staining the latter red for a day. Malehaut is said in another work to have been on the 'Hombre', no doubt the one which flowed into the Severn.

Other important places were on tributaries of the Severn. One of these was the Orguellouse Emprise, the Proud Ascendancy. This castle was in the strongest position in the whole land on a high rock below which ran a powerful river which fell into the Severn four 'lieues' away, a lieue being about a mile. Another stronghold was Dolorous Gard, later called Joyous Gard. Speaking of this latter place, the river is named as the Hombre, but Leverzerp was nearby, so this Hombre may be presumed to be the one which fell into the Severn. Dolorous Gard was situated on a native rock high above the river. From an arch at the foot of the tower ran another river, fed by forty springs.[37] Nearby on an island in the Hombre was the Dolorous Chartre, used by its owner Branduz of the Isles (Bran again) as a prison for Arthur's knights. Branduz was also Lord of Dolorous Gard. At the latter place Lancelot found the ancient pagan tomb in which he buried Galehot.[38] Yet another fortress on the Hombre was the Tor Perrine,[39] also known as the Dolorous Tower. Like Dolorous Gard it was captured by Lancelot and, again like Dolorous Gard, its name was afterwards changed from a sad to a happier one, Bele Garde. There is a good deal of overlap in these descriptions of strongholds on the 'Hombre' so one may suspect divergence from a common original.

So far, apart from Leverzerp, the places located by being linked to the Severn have been on the Welsh side. There are others on the eastern side, and therefore in Logres, which have not yet been examined in detail. For instance,

34 *Vulgate*, II, p. 172. Actually the Surne, but this may be presumed to be the Severn since Estrangort marched with two other countries which are on that river.
35 *Vulgate*, III, p. 176.
36 *Vulgate*, II, pp. 172/3; III, pp. 334–7 and VII, p. 202.
37 *Vulgate*, VII, p. 116 and III, p. 143.
38 See p. 180.
39 *Prose Index*, West.

a place called Taningues belonging to Duke Brandelis (Bran yet again) was on the Saverne not far from Roestoc but a long way from Norgales.[40] Roestoc itself was notable for its plains, and was not far from Leverzerp as well as being near Taningues. It is described as a beautiful city well sited and in a fine position. It was encircled all round with woods and waters, and the walls glowed with the reflected sunshine. There is not a lot to go on here, but Roestoc seems to have been on the south side of the Severn, near its mouth. Though we hear more about the Lady of Roestoc than of its castellan, her male counterpart, he was known as Helys and was brother to Mabonagrein (one of the manifestations of Mabon), a relationship suggesting that he too was a member of some half-forgotten pantheon.

We have now reached the end of the most obvious of these inferences to be made from topography which have enabled places mentioned in the romances to be located and in some instances have enabled their pagan characteristics to be compared with evidence from the wider field of Arthurian legend represented in the Welsh tradition. The time has come to review the results of the analysis.

First, it has been found that there were in what we now call Wales a number of smaller realms clustered along the Severn and round its estuary – Norgales, Cambenic, Estrangort, Estroite Marche, Malehaut, Terre Foraine, Sorelois, and, still to come, Carmelide, and Cardoel. In Logres east of the Welsh border and close to it were Taneborc, Taningues, Leverzerp and Roestoc. These small kingdoms sometimes have as their capital a city of the same name and in the story often play the part of a city-state. Then on a larger scale there are the important kingdoms. First Logres, with its capital Camelot, yet to be located. Then on a still wider scale there are identifiable countries stretching from far in the north to far in the south and more or less covering the coast of the north west of Europe. These are, from the north, Orcanie, thought to be centred on modern Orkney, whose King Lot was a brother of Bran (as Urien); then the largely maritime 'Ireland' and the Isles, clipping the coasts of Wales and Scotland and embracing the Far Away Isles or the Estranges Isles; then Cornwall, scene of Tristan's activities; next Gannes which has been argued for reasons to be discussed in the Gazetteer to have been centred on Vannes in the south of Brittany, whose king, Bors, was brother of Bran and a cult figure in his own right; and finally Benoic on the Loire, which was the kingdom of Ban (Bran, once again). The association of the so-called rulers of these countries with deities, particularly with Bran, shows how closely and consistently the topography of legend and the romances is bound up with mythology.

[40] *Vulgate*, III, pp. 296ff.

### The Location of Perrons and Temples

There are several places which seem to have been cult sites, since idols are said to have been destroyed there by the Grail missionaries under Joseph and Josephé, but these precede the Arthurian era and are not associated with main Arthurian characters like Uther and Merlin. The best defined perrons or temples which are sited at named places and play a role in the romances are at either Camelot, Cardoel, Sarras or on Salisbury Plain. Unfortunately the text with the most detailed descriptions of temples, *Perceforest*, gives no clues to the location of any of the temples mentioned in it except that one was surrounded by oak forest.

Sarras, an important pagan site since it is where Evalac, the Maimed King, had a sun-temple, a subterranean chamber and a goddess-dolly, is not easy to pin down, because narrators confused the British Sarrassins of the romances with the middle-Eastern Saracens, but let us see what is known about the others. Taking a wide perspective, Camelot is in Logres, that is, present-day England; Cardoel is always said to be in Wales; and no problems arise if we take Salisbury Plain to have its current meaning.

Many attempts have been made to identify Camelot culminating in extensive excavation at Cadbury in Somerset. However, Leslie Alcock describes 'the name, and the very concept of Camelot' as 'inventions of the French medieval poets.'[41] According to this view the place is not capable of being identified in the real world. The association which might have been supposed from the name Cadbury/Camelot on the spine of the book describing the excavations has thus less force than it otherwise might have had. However, we have been directed to the narrators of the romances as the principal source of information about Camelot. Let us then examine what they have to say about this intriguing place and the others on our list. Perhaps the links with standing stones and a temple will lead to a more positive identification than it has previously been possible to provide.

### Camelot

Without at this stage attempting to locate the place but merely to list what we know about it, Camelot was the richest city in Great Britain and of so great authority that the pagan king was crowned there. It was of greater religious significance to the Sarrassins (this is how the romances describe the earliest inhabitants of Britain) than any other city in the realm.[42] It had a pagan temple in the middle, which Joseph of Arimathea replaced by a minster dedicated to 'St Stephen' and 'Our Lady'. Arthur had a serpent painted in St Stephen's in

---

[41] *Arthur's Britain*, p. 163.
[42] *Vulgate*, I, p. 244.

remembrance of a dream.[43] The only other church mentioned was dedicated to 'St John'.[44] Courts were held there by Arthur at Christmas, Easter, Ascension Day, Pentecost, St John's Day,[45] mid-August,[46] and All Hallows. There were many 'adventures' and tournaments. It was to Camelot that the Round Table was brought with Guenever, as her dowry. Here the stone appeared from which Arthur drew the sword.[47] Here the stone floated from which Galahad drew a sword. Merlin's perron was a mile or two away.

There was a second Camelot, clearly distinguished in the romances, which belonged to the 'Lady of the Lonely Waste Forest' and was situated at the head of the most savage island of Wales, near the sea, towards the west. There was nothing there except the retreat itself and the forest and the water which surrounded it.

## Cardoel

Cardoel was on the sea in Wales.[48] It was, as has been mentioned, a haunt of the Children of Don[49] and so it was also of Uther Pendragon for it was his principal residence, and it was the scene of some significant constructions by Merlin – a perron[50] and the Round Table (specifically made for Uther);[51] and important activities took place there – the institution of the fundamental religious festivals of Christmas, Pentecost and All Hallows (again by Uther),[52] and

---

[43] *Vulgate*, V, p. 284 line 32.

[44] Huth *Merlin*, I, p. 263. And see Lot's grave p. 184.

[45] *Vulgate*, III, p. 118.

[46] *Vulgate*, II, p. 407.

[47] London in later versions is an intrusion. The Huth *Merlin* has Logres, implying by the context the city of Logres, that is Camelot.

[48] Cardoel is generally believed to be Carlisle. The name Carlisle consists of Caer- (Welsh for city) prefixed to an ancient name perhaps indicating the god Lugh. The latter element always begins with 'L' except in one instance where in 1092 the name was spelt Cardoel instead of the usual Carleoil, Karlioli (gen.), or in Latin versions, Luguvallum or Lugubalia. To have a 'd' in only one instance in stead of an 'l' is not enough to override the repeated description 'en Gales' which is backed up by links between Cardoel and other places which may reasonably be supposed to have been in Wales such as Caradigan.

[49] See p. 141 above.

[50] *Vulgate*, III, p. 275.

[51] *Vulgate*, II, p. 54. There is an alternative version provided by Layamon, an early source, in which the Round Table was constructed of wood by a Cornish carpenter, presumably in Cornwall. However, since this author describes the table as capable of holding 1600 knights – that is, it would have been over 300 yards in diameter – and readily portable as well, he stands convicted of at least very substantial exaggeration. Layamon's version seems to be embellishment of his precursor Wace's taut and enigmatic phrase 'all were seated within the table and no one was placed outside' (C. Foulon in *ALMA*, p. 99). Layamon does not seem to have influenced later writers. The authors of the French romances do not follow the Cornish origin nor the 1600 knights. Yet such varied texts as the Didot *Perceval*, the Huth *Merlin*, the *Vulgate*, *Perlesvaus* and the *Queste* present mutually compatible versions. To achieve unanimity, the narrators of these romances are likely to be following a different version from Layamon's but still with its origin firmly in tradition.

[52] *Vulgate*, II, p. 58.

the choice of a consort for the queen in *Perceforest*.[53] The drawing of the sword from the stone by Arthur took place there according to one version of that story,[54] and in *Perceforest* the sword which Arthur was later to withdraw was introduced into the stone at Cardoel.

The ritual of the Round Table at Cardoel was very different from that at Camelot. In Uther's time, knights were only allowed to take their places at the table if they were mutilated in the face. Knights were even allowed to bleed to death at the Table.[55] In later times, in the days of Lancelot and Hector, when the table had been moved to Camelot, admittance was only to be gained by having defeated a knight in single combat during the previous week.[56] On the other hand, the Perilous Seat operated in the same way as at Camelot, unauthorized sitters being burnt but authorized sitters accepted as candidates for achievement of the Grail. When Perceval, the prime example of the latter, sat in it the stone shrieked, the earth cried out in anguish and it thundered.

In that era, as they did in the Middle Ages, kings progressed round their country holding courts in various places. After he had succeeded Uther, Arthur held courts at Bedingran, Dinasdaron, Carlion, Pennevoiseuse, Carmelide and Caradigan as well as Cardoel and Camelot. Originally his main residence was Cardoel but later he transferred his seat to Camelot when there was a shortage of adventures at Cardoel,[57] a move, as already mentioned, very much influenced by dreams.

There are no direct indications of the location of Cardoel but, given that it was in Wales, there are some interesting links with the South West of that country.

(1) The Perilous Seat is paralleled by the Gorsedd at Arberth (modern Narberth 20 km S of the Preseli Mountains) where, according to Welsh tradition, a royal sitter could expect to receive blows and wounds or see a wonder.[58]

(2) Perceval first sat in the Perilous Seat at Cardoel. The 'Waste Land' motif, which provides Perceval's mother with her title, the Widow of the Waste Forest, is paralleled by the same effect at Arberth – when Pryderi and his companions sat on the mound all signs of life round them disappeared with a clap of thunder.[59]

(3) Merlin, also important at Cardoel (as an enchanter and constructor), was born in Dyfed and finally incarcerated in a cave in the forest of Darnantes in South West Wales.

(4) Uther, the original ruler at Cardoel, fought a battle at St David's.

53 See p. 171.
54 *The Romance of the Grail*, Bogdanow, p. 4.
55 *Vulgate*, V, pp. 130/1.
56 As note 55 above.
57 *Vulgate*, III, p. 199.
58 *Mabinogion*, Penguin, p. 52.
59 *Mabinogion*, Penguin, p. 86.

(5) There was a road from Cardoel to Caradigan, assumed to be present day Cardigan from the resemblance of the name.

## Salisbury Plain

### (a) The Battle with the Saxons

The fundamental importance of the Plain of 'Salesbieres' in the Arthurian tradition has never been given its true weight. First of all, before Arthur's reign, it was the site of a decisive battle between the Britons, led by the 'brothers' Uther and 'Pandragon', and the invading Sesnes (so-called Saxons). The Britons won, but Pandragon was killed. This is the version in the Huth *Merlin*[60] of the event which sparked off the bringing of the bluestones of Stonehenge as a memorial for Pendragon.

### (b) The Cemetery of Salisbury

The story of the carriage and erection of the bluestones, in the Historia of Geoffrey of Monmouth, has been described under the heading 'Graves' in the previous chapter. This draws attention to activities on the Plain, including the presence of graves, prior to the erection of the bluestones.

### (c) The Great Gathering

Much later, during the early part of Arthur's reign, Salisbury Plain was the scene of a great gathering which preceded the final defeat of the Sesnes. When first crowned, Arthur had failed to gain the allegiance of a group of rebel kings. However, under Merlin's guidance, a truce was arranged and the two parties met on the Plain to make common cause against the Sesnes. Peoples attended from all over the country, from Orkney to Cornwall. Merlin also fetched from Brittany the contingent of King Ban and King Bors, which seems to have had a decisive effect. The meeting took place on All Hallows. The rebel kings joined the Arthurian confederacy and the combined forces defeated the enemy. Merlin then prophesied that the final fatal battle between Arthur and Mordred would take place much later at the same site as the great gathering, but we are not told whereabouts on Salisbury Plain that was, except that it was marked by a tall, hard rock.[61]

Soon after the great gathering Arthur had a jousting place constructed on Salisbury Plain.

### (d) The Last Battle

Finally, when all the underlying discords of the court had come to the surface, when Gawain was dead and Lancelot driven out, Arthur faced his greatest enemy, Mordred, his own son by his sister, who had attempted to usurp the

---

[60] Vol. I, pp. 87/93; *Vulgate*, II, pp. 51/3.
[61] *Vulgate*, II, pp. 374ff. and 285.

crown in Arthur's absence by seizing and marrying Guenever. Arthur, returning from France, pursued him from Dover and the two armies met on
Salisbury Plain. Here they camped before the battle and in the evening Arthur
walked after supper on the Plain. He came upon the great, tall, hard rock with
the prophesy inscribed on it foretelling his own death. In spite of this, Arthur
went ahead against Mordred and his allies the 'Saxons', in doing so he lost all
the knightly complement of the Round Table and in killing Mordred was
mortally wounded himself.[62]

*(e)  After the last battle, Guenever was admitted to a nunnery at Amesbury*[63]

To recapitulate briefly, as the great gathering and the last battle were at the
same place, there are at most two sites referred to in the accounts mentioned
above of the events taking place on Salisbury Plain, one of them was marked
by the bluestone circle, the other by the great, tall hard rock.

**Where the Temples and Standing Stones of the Romances are to be found**

The brief sketches above of three places include most of the Arthurian perrons
and, to the extent that it can be considered Arthurian, the best defined temple
of all, the bluestone circle.[64] The presence of so-called Saxons in the stories can
be disregarded. The reason they have been substituted for the local Sarrassins
as the general enemy, because of a faulty historical perspective, has already
been described.[65] The significant features here are the major part played by
Merlin in all the stone erecting incidents and the general sense of transfer
between Cardoel, which is always the originating site, and Camelot, always
the recipient. The incidents linking Merlin with stones are as follows:

*Stones associated with Merlin*

(1) The Dance of the Giants: Uther and Merlin brought the stones of
Stonehenge, largely by water, and set them up on Salisbury Plain. The
young King of Ireland was killed in South-West Wales by Uther shortly
afterwards.

(2) Merlin's Perron (a): this stone was erected by Merlin to mark the site of his
defeat of two enchanters, near Cardoel.

(3) Merlin's Perron (b): this stone floated to Camelot after Balin's sword had
been inserted into it by Merlin. This was the perron from which Galahad
drew a sword.

(4) Merlin's Perron (c): this stone was erected by Merlin a mile or so from
Camelot. Balin killed the Prince of Ireland there.

(5) The Adventurous Perron: This seems to be Merlin's Perron under another

[62] *Vulgate*, VI, pp. 362ff.
[63] *Morte Darthur*, bk XXI, ch. 7.
[64] According to the romances, the 'Giants' Dance' was erected by Merlin for Arthur's uncle,
Ambrosius, as a memorial to Arthur's father, Uther.
[65] Above, Calendar of Arthurian Romance, p. 35.

name. It too was at Cardoel,[66] where a sword was inserted in it (in *Perce-forest*). It later appeared at Camelot, and Arthur withdrew the sword in the well known test.[67]

(6) The tall, hard rock on Salisbury Plain: this is only linked with Merlin by the prophesy which he made that it would be the site of Arthur's last battle.

## The relationship between Cardoel and Camelot

(7) The Arthurian story begins with Uther firmly established at Cardoel in Wales, where he had his court, had the Round Table made and instituted the major festivals of the Arthurian romances, and where he met Ygerne. Later Arthur had his favourite residence there, before he moved to Camelot in Logres.

(8) The Round Table, originally constructed by Merlin for Uther at Cardoel, passed into the ownership of Leodegrance and was later moved to Camelot as Guenever's dowry.

(9) Combining the individual motifs in (2) – (5) above, a standing stone originally erected at Cardoel had a symbolic sword inserted into it there which, when the stone was transferred to Camelot, conferred kingship on Arthur or any other authorized drawer.

This analysis shows a strong link between Merlin and standing stones, and also repeated transfers from Cardoel to Camelot. There are as well close links between Salisbury Plain and the Arthurian personages, Uther and Merlin. Leaving Arthur out of it for the moment, there is a consistent link between Merlin and stone erecting which, taken at its face value, seems to be set in the period of the late Neolithic/Bronze Age for that is the era of the erection of standing stones, a practice which was abandoned in the Iron Age. If that is the case, how is the sense of transfer from Cardoel to Camelot, including at least one perron, to be interpreted? Could it be an analogue of the bluestone move, putting Camelot on Salisbury Plain?

## Is there any link between Camelot and Salisbury Plain?

In considering factors which might lead to discovering the real location of Camelot, it should be remembered that all previous attempts to do this have had the home of the historical Arthur in mind. The Camelot of the romances is described as having been at one time the most pagan place in Britain and as being the site of a temple. The place we are looking for, even allowing for some degree of exaggeration, should therefore show traces of this pagan past. This may not be a significant pointer, since many places would fit, but might help to confirm a conclusion reached by other means. Unfortunately, except for an

---

[66] *Perceforest*, part VI, fol. LVIII recto, col. 1.
[67] *Prose Index*, West, under Perron de Merlin.

enigmatic comment that Camelot was contiguous with all its subject kingdoms and easily accessible by land and sea, there are no 'marches' or 'itineraries' to give any indication of position. The best that can be done is to
consider the associations of the individuals important there.

First it should be noted that the effect of the analysis above is to enhance the
pagan character of the Arthurian Camelot, not just its more obviously pagan
precursor, by drawing attention to the perrons there, those conspicuous blocks
of stone with magical properties and with many links with supernatural activities and personages. These Arthurian perrons are functioning in a magical
way at Arthur's court, indeed, for Arthur himself. Even if two or more of the
three perrons – the one from which Arthur drew a sword,[68] the one from
which Galahad drew a sword, and Merlin's Perron where Balin fought
Lanceor – are variations on a single original theme, Arthurian Camelot seems
to have been graced by a stone or stones at a period when such monuments
were considered potent. The effect of the sword drawn from the stone was to
give sovereignty, another correspondence in the romances with the description of Camelot as 'where the kings were crowned'.

Next, in the romances the personages associated with Camelot have strong
links with Salisbury Plain: Arthur's father and uncle were buried there;
Arthur's own power was consolidated there; and Arthur suffered his final
defeat and his fatal injury there.[69] The last two of these events are at the site of
a notable rock on the Plain. Since there are no natural outcrops on the Plain a
tall rock must have been a standing stone, yet another unexpected link between important events in the Arthurian story and standing stones.

Finally, it has been shown that there is a strong emphasis in the romances on
transfer from Cardoel, a place in Wales, to Camelot, a place in Logres. The
originating place has links with South-West Wales; the transfers include
among other items and people the transfer of stones; the transferors, Uther
and Merlin are firmly established at Cardoel and both individuals are linked
with Salisbury Plain. Thus there are links between Cardoel and South-West
Wales on the one hand and Camelot, or rather the personages associated with
it, and Salisbury Plain on the other. The strong sense of transfer in general and
the transfer of stones in particular is reflected closely in the story of the
removal of the bluestones by the same personages as are active at both
Cardoel and Camelot. When we look at the moving of the bluestones and of
the perrons as the work of Merlin, it looks as if a recollection of the stones he
moved has survived in tradition in two forms. In one he is said to have moved
the Dance of the Giants from South-West Wales to Salisbury Plain; in the other
to have moved the perrons from Cardoel to Camelot. It is a feature of the

---

[68] In the Didot *Perceval* Arthur drew the sword at Cardoel, indeed his court in that romance is
always at Cardoel. In view of the overlap between Cardoel and Camelot and the transfer of
power from Cardoel to Camelot, this presents no barrier to the arguments put forward here.
[69] E.g. *Morte Darthur*, bk XXI, ch. 3. Malory's only other reference to Salisbury is to say that the
records of the Grail Quest were preserved there.

legends that a motif or event can be described in different ways in different texts. If that is what has happened here, the transfer of a perron or perrons that has been described above is a distorted echo of the removal of the bluestones; in this alternative account the names at the time of the places of origin and reception have been remembered though forgotten by Geoffrey of Monmouth.[70]

This excursion into the topography of the romances has led, as far as the island of Britain is concerned, to a network of links between places in the Severn Valley, on both sides of the river; along the north coast of the Severn estuary and the Bristol Channel to the westernmost peninsulas of South Wales; and to the south-east to Salisbury Plain and Stonehenge. Whether on account of chance or some built in selective process in the method of oral transmission the places that can be located are, with the possible exception of Northumberland, all in the west and those on the mainland of Britain are grouped together in one corner of the country. Perhaps this distribution represents the boundaries of some cult whose pagan archives – some sort of pagan oral 'Old Testament' – were tapped by the earliest compilers of Arthurian romance; perhaps the stories just happened to be better remembered in those districts; or perhaps the presumed earliest compilers of Arthurian romance operated more freely there. For whatever cause, we have observed a scene which is largely complementary to that provided by the Welsh versions of the tales. Cornwall, in particular, is extremely poorly represented by places identified by the topographical method, in spite of its obvious importance in the Arthurian story. Another feature of this analysis is that it reveals only a few places in Logres, whereas smaller Wales is broken up into a relatively large number of small principalities whose rulers nevertheless play important parts in the romances. This, again, could due either to an aspect of the original situation or to a factor of transmission.

In one respect, the concentration of cult sites along the north coast of the Bristol Channel could be very significant. We have from the west St David's where the women danced naked in the river (see Gazetteer under Aroie); Solva Nine-Wells where maidens were burnt; Glen Cuch; Preseli; Escalon; the Castle of Dames and Castle of Maidens; the carted knight at Caerwent; a nemeton site at the mouth of the Wye;[71] Terre Foraine, in which was the Grail Castle, Corbenic; the castle of the Cart; and finally Gloucester with its nine witches who decapitated Peredur's cousin and which was the scene of

---

[70] There is an intriguing possibility that there is a third variation on the theme of the bluestone move. The Round Table followed the same route as the perrons, it is circular like the stone circle, it had pillars between the seats, and in *Perceforest*, a romance set in the pre-Roman era, it is said to be of stone. All phases of this monument are likely to have been conflated in tradition, so the Round Table of romance could be a recollection of Stonehenge in its Wessex culture heyday. This would give an entirely new significance to the Arthurian legend. It would provide a glorious setting in a heroic age for the Arthurian epic, and would give the stones their missing mythology.

[71] Metambala in Gazetteer, under Nemus place-names.

Mabon's imprisonment. This coast cluttered with cult sites[72] was the route of the bluestones, whether that took place by land or sea. Is there some connection, one wonders? Was the real reason for the bluestone move a propaganda exercise, designed to involve many important pagan systems in a concentration of power on Salisbury Plain?

The topographical method is by no means exhausted, but when it is applied further from the Severn becomes less reliable. There is also the problem of dealing with still more places, many unfamiliar to readers of Malory and Tennyson, without the narrative degenerating into a list. I have therefore consigned the remaining places to a Gazetteer. This is divided into two sections. In one, places where there is some indication of locality are listed, with the activities taking place at them. In the other, the places which cannot be located. The ratio of the two parts of this split gazetteer will show that a substantial proportion of the total number of Arthurian places is identifiable and, from what activities took place at them many can be recognized as cult sites.

---

[72] Carman, using different arguments, notes the importance of the Bristol Channel in *Perlesvaus. Research Studies*, Vol. 32, 1964, pp. 85–105,

# TIME AND PLACE

## A Recapitulation

The British pagan Celtic tradition, which has been to some extent preserved in the romances, is also recognizable in Geoffrey of Monmouth's *Historia* and, of course, in the Welsh legends. An important example in the *Historia* is an account of the removal of the bluestone circle of Stonehenge from the South West Wales to Salisbury Plain, which has been described as a remnant of Bronze Age oral literature.[1] It may not be generally known that this incident also appears in the romances, in a slightly different form, and that there are many other instances of stones being erected and moved, even floated; several important episodes in the Arthurian story take place on Salisbury Plain; and several important personages, Uther, for instance, and Arthur himself, are associated with the Plain. Here we may consider the extent to which the term Bronze Age tradition can be applied to those parts of the romances which describe events taking place at standing stones.

But first, can we even be sure that Geoffrey was talking about the bluestones? A recent theory has it that he had heard gossip about standing stones at Kildare in Ireland and imagined the rest. However, there is a piece of internal evidence, previously unnoticed, which suggests that that is not the case. Geoffrey's Latin text exists in two prose versions and a later one in verse. The latter, *Gesta Regum Britannie*, when it describes the ceremonies which accompanied the setting up of what has been generally supposed to be the bluestone circle, made an unexpected remark about the hospitality which Ambrosius, the King of Britain, offered to his distinguished guests on the occasion of his coronation and the celebration of the erection of the bluestone circle. Where the author of a romance might have been expected to indicate a

---

[1] A recent attempt to demonstrate that the stones were moved by glacial action relies heavily on a statement by an early geologist, de Luc, that the Plain was in his day scattered with blocks of granite and trap which has been interpreted as the two main kinds of bluestone. The authors have failed to notice that de Luc's comment includes the clause 'in the counties to which he refers'. When read as a whole, de Luc's statement puts the blocks of igneous rock in the Midlands, far away from Wiltshire. Details are published in a letter in *Current Archaeology*, 134, 1993, p. 78. There are other unresolved problems facing glacial transport.

considerable display of wealth – numerous great palaces, noble churches, rich halls – Geoffrey comments that Ambrosius's court was not decked with ivory and tortoiseshell but merely 'nemus et frondes',[2] that is, 'woods and leaves'. It is difficult to see why Geoffrey should play down the importance of the occasion. Of course, he did not understand the significance of the Giants Dance but its erection was clearly an important event and so was the coronation of Ambrosius,[3] The explanation might lie in the meaning of the word 'nemus'. As well as the general meaning of woodland, or at least a woodland clearing, nemus means a sacred precinct, as in Nemi itself and in the word nemeton. Has the word nemus been remembered as descriptive of Ambrosius's court until such time as its meaning of sacred enclosure had been forgotten, resulting in this odd remark? There may be an indication here that Geoffrey did have access to a tradition which long predates the Middle Ages, and his remark describing the court of Ambrosius as a 'nemus' may be a candidate for addition to our Bronze Age literature.

In the remnant of ancient oral tradition, events may sometimes cast a number of distorted shadows, no longer identified with the original. This may have happened with the removal of the bluestones. Merlin also set up several perrons, by which is meant pillars or blocks of stone, that is, in archaeological terms, standing stones. One stone with which he is closely linked is on Salisbury Plain; another in South-West Wales; a third is near Camelot; and one of them floats from Cardoel in South-West Wales to Camelot. The most important Arthurian personages start in Cardoel and finish at Camelot. In the case of Uther, he fought a battle where Stonehenge was later to be built, and he was buried in an adjacent barrow. On Salisbury Plain there took place the great gathering of peoples from all over the West, from Orkney to the mouth of the Loire, at which Arthur arranged the alliance which defeated the pre-Arthurian peoples, the Sarrassins. At the same place as the great gathering, Arthur fought Mordred at a place on the Plain marked by a tall, hard rock. The Arthurian standing stones are characterized by enchantment, in which they match our expectation of prehistoric cult sites, and even without the indication of date provided by the bluestone circle, standing stones can be dated as not later than the Bronze Age, so there is a good deal here which merits consideration for adding to our Bronze Age literature.

An interesting aspect of the situation revealed here is that the bluestone move provides a marker in time, at present regarded as the end of the Neolithic or Early Bronze Age. Whatever is previous to the marker, like the arrival of Joseph of Arimathea, or later, like Arthur's reign and the affairs of the Round Table, is given a place in the prehistorical record.

Not all the correspondences with archaeology are so early. The change to watery cult sites which may be discernible in the affairs of the Damsel of the

---

[2]   *Gesta Regum Britannie*, ed. Wright, lines 353–5.
[3]   A personage whose name is preserved in nearby Amesbury, originally Ambro's burg.

Lake, came during the Bronze Age and the deposition of offerings into water went on until well into the Roman occupation.

Most of the arguments which have been presented here refer to pagan activities which can be recognized by comparison with forms of paganism described in classical or Celtic sources, like the ritual at Nemi, but a fair number of features in the romances correspond to material finds by archaeologists.

They are as follows:

| Archaeological Feature | Correspondence in Romance |
| --- | --- |
| *Deposition in water* | |
| (1) Sword in pool | Excalibur, received by the spirit of the pool |
| (2) Cauldron in river | thrown by Perceval[4] |
| (3) Severed head in river | thrown by Perceval's sister[5] |
| (4) Severed head in spring | of King Lancelot[6] |
| (5) Severed head in pit | thrown in by Meleagant's sister after being severed by Lancelot[7] |
| *Cult sites* | |
| (6) Circular temples[8] | |
| (7) Stone temples[9] | |
| (8) Standing stones | Perrons,[10] numerous examples |
| (9) Idols in groves | Tristan |
| (10) Palisades around sites | Tertre Desvé etc. |
| (11) Heads on stakes | Isle d'Or, Joy of Court etc.. |
| (12) Boundaries | Marches, numerous examples |
| (13) Orientation of temple | to setting sun,[11] and possibly to rising sun at Tristan's Tomb |
| (14) Springs | Fountains, numerous examples |
| (15) River crossings | Fords, numerous examples |
| (16) Forest clearings | Landes, numerous examples |

---

4   In *Perlesvaus*.
5   In *Perlesvaus*.
6   Fontaine[27] in West, *Prose Index*.
7   *Vulgate*, IV, 197/8.
8   In *Perceforest*.
9   In *Perceforest*.
10  E.g. Perron Merlin at Cardoel, Perron[5] in *Prose Index*; the stone from which the sword was taken, perron[3] in *Prose Index*; and Merlin's perron near Camelot where Lanceor was killed by Balin (*Morte Darthur*, bk X, ch. 5).
11  In *Perceforest*; and see p. 184.

*Interments*

| | | |
|---|---|---|
| (17) | Lindow man | Triple death |
| (19) | Burial in boat | Arthur; Perceval's sister; the Damsel of Escalot; Brangemuer[12] |
| (20) | Pagan tomb reused | Urbaduc's, for Galehot and Lancelot.[13] |
| (21) | Body buried with arms | in Urbaduc's tomb. |
| (22) | Barrows | See pp. 48, 165, 184–5 and 238. |

*Miscellaneous*

| | | |
|---|---|---|
| (23) | Goddess in vehicle | Damsel of the Cart, Damsel of the Lake. |

Any single correspondence between myth and reality would be an unreliable guide on its own. However, when, as here, there are a number, and the mythological side is supported by the literary sources as having pagan links, they are likely to be significant. These correspondences might indicate co-ordinates in time and space. As far as date is concerned, they tend to support the views already expressed. Several features, notably 6, 7, 8 and 13 are to be found in the Bronze Age or earlier. As far as space is concerned, few of the pagan activities in the romances, except for those at perrons, can be located.

---

12 *First Continuation*, part VI.
13 *Prose Index* under Joieuse Garde; *Vulgate*, IV, 295.

# THE ONCE AND FUTURE KING

Either Arthur is a mythological personage in his own right or some unidentifiable figure has gathered round him a galaxy of pagan characters, acts and attitudes. Whichever of these is correct, the Arthurian court, as seen in the romances, presents an interesting glimpse of our pagan past since it was linked with Salisbury Plain and with perrons at a time when these stones were highly significant. Even if Arthur were merely a creation of a poet's imagination, there is a substantial chance that a good deal of the grouping of pagan motifs at a place of considerable pagan significance is a residue of Bronze Age tradition. The problem that has to be faced is that Arthur occupies such a prime position that one cannot trust narrators to have restricted their tales to the acts that were really his alone. Unimportant people and inconspicuous places in the romances are much easier to understand than those with higher profiles. Guenever, Gawain and Lancelot, to take but a few, have obviously attracted incidents from other heroes and heroines, now forgotten, and from other cycles. Having said that, it is nevertheless a fact that Arthur has few personal adventures. The severed head in St Augustine's Glade, the fight with Yder at the Chaucie Norgaloise, the defeat of a giant at Mont St Michel, and the fight with Gasozein are exceptions to the rule that Arthur is a somewhat distant king. Except perhaps for Arthur's struggle with Gasozein for Guenever, these incidents tell us little. To find the Arthur of the romances, his life will have to be examined, rather than his acts. Here is a brief sketch, which demonstrates many departures from normal human behaviour.

(1) His parents: his father is credited with a battle on Salisbury Plain and another in South-West Wales and he is said to have been buried at or near Stonehenge; his mother's daughters include Morgan le Fay, a goddess.

(2) His conception: there was a struggle for his mother; it was resolved by shape shifting and enchantment.

(3) His right to the throne was decided by drawing the sword from the stone.

(4) His wife was the daughter of a giant; she personifies Sovereignty.

(5) His son was buried in a tumulus at the source of a river.

(6) He consolidated his position at the great gathering on Salisbury Plain, attended by peoples from Orkney to the Loire. The site was marked by a tall, hard rock.

(7)  Many members of his court are recognizable as deities, or as heroic con-
     testants at Nemi-style combats, or as participants in the Grail cult.
(8)  His final battle against his last rival for the Queen, Mordred, was fought at
     the same tall rock on Salisbury Plain.
(9)  When fatally wounded he had his sword returned to the Damsel of the
     Lake, and he was taken in a boat by Morgan le Fay to the magic island of
     Avalon. Whether he actually died is disputed.

If narrators had magnified Arthur as a champion relative to the members of
his court their picture of Arthur would have been less easy to accept. Instead
they describe him by detail which to them may have seemed unimportant.
Only by analysis of its pagan meaning can we understand its significance;
looked at in this way, the portrayal rings true. The missing mythology of the
heroic culture that occupied the Plain in the Bronze Age has actually survived.
The resplendent fighting chieftains interred in the barrows, and their queens,
and their shamans, are to be met with in corresponding figures in the pages of
the romances. Only Arthur has no tumulus. He is to be sought among deities,
not ashes and bones.

# GAZETTEER

## I.  Places whose Location can be Roughly Established

ARESTUEL, a town in Escoce: *see* Roche as Sesnes.

AROIE, the Adventurous Forest:

This forest is vaguely said in the romances to be on the way to the kingdom of Norgales. However, it is one of the few places which is referred to in the *Mabinogion* as well as in the romances, and in the Welsh work its position is described in more detail. The forest d'Aroie of the romances has been identified by Rhys[1] as the wood Diarwya in the ancient Welsh story of *Pwyll, Lord of Dyfed*. It looks as if a French speaking scribe has mistakenly removed the initial 'D', thinking it was the French possessive 'd', leaving the residue Arwya as Aroie (the 'w' in these Welsh names has an 'oo' sound as in the word coombe or combe, from the Welsh cwm – a hollow on the flank of a hill). The place called the 'End of the Wood of Diarwya' was on the way from Arberth (that is, present day Narberth, the modern spelling being a corruption of the Welsh original) to Glen Cuch, on the border between the old counties of Pembrokeshire and Carmarthenshire. The same author, Rhys, points out[2] the resemblance of the second part of the name Diarwya to that of an 'Irish Pict' called Boia (alternatively Bwya or Boya) who gave his name to the fortified rock, Clegyr Voia, near St David's. The considerable pagan significance of this locality is demonstrated by the meeting of Pwyll and Arawn, King of the Otherworld, in this forest of Diarwya (or Aroie), an encounter which led to of Pwyll's year of kingship of the Otherworld, followed by the year-end combat at the ford against 'Summer-White'.

In the romances, Aroie was not called the Adventurous Forest for nothing. It has interesting mythological connotations, demonstrated by the occasion on which, searching this forest for 'adventures', three knights errant came to a fair fountain, with three damsels sitting thereby. The damsels were of 15, 30 and 70 years of age, an epitome of the Celtic triple goddess apparently showing three phases of womanhood.[3] Their sole purpose was to lead knights errant towards strange adventures. Each knight was to take one of the damsels and they were to return to the fountain at the end of a year.

Looking at the part of the country associated with Boia from another angle, this time from the Latin chronicles of the church, Boia's wife is said to have contended with St David himself in the sixth century. She provided a typical example of the severed head and well cult by cutting a girl's throat, at which a spring burst from the ground. Another incident connected with the Pictish Boia was his attempt to subvert the Christian evangelists who came with David to Dyfed, by getting his wife to send her female servants to the monks with orders to offer themselves to the passion of the saints in order to turn their

---

1  *Arthurian Legend*, p. 282.
2  *Arthurian Legend*, note to p. 283.
3  *Morte Darthur*, Malory, IV, p. 18.

minds from their holy purpose. 'Go to the river which is called Alun', she said and 'display your naked bodies in the sight of the saints and indulge in lewd talk'. The female slaves obeyed. They made shameless sport. They simulated coition. They displayed love's alluring embraces. The ploy nearly succeeded. The suggestive gestures enticed the minds of some of the monks and caused unrest in those of others The disciples, unable to endure this intolerable affront, said to holy David 'Let us fly from this place. We cannot dwell here on account of the molestation of these frightful sluts'. But David held his ground. He built his cathedral there in damp, boggy ground, over a spring which was still running in the 19th century, in a place notable also for its topographical disadvantages, being isolated from the more populous regions of Wales. No doubt he was constrained to do so 'from some particular attachment to the primitive sanctity of the spot',[4] that is, because of its original importance as a pagan cult site. The 'female slaves' of Boia's wife were, perhaps, priestesses engaged in their normal ritual. Its purpose would have been the exact opposite of its actual effect on the monks – not to alienate the missionaries but to persuade them to join in the orgiastic rites being performed.

We now have bearings on Boia's haunts in West Wales from three entirely distinct vantage points: from Welsh legend, from the French 'matter of Britain', and from the Latin *Life of St David*. They each describe pagan activities, and there is a good deal of overlap between them. There is the 'Waste' Land when Rhiannon and her companions sit on the gorsedd mound at Arberth; this is matched by the 'Waste' Forest of the Widow Lady of West Wales. Since, according to one view, Perceval in the romances corresponds to Pryderi, it follows that Perceval's mother, the Widow Lady, would correspond to Pryderi's mother, Rhiannon. It is interesting to find the same pagan concept of magical barrenness attributed to both. Then there are the fountains: that of Boia's wife with its severed head, of the triple goddess, and of St David's cathedral; and even the title 'Adventurous Forest' is to be taken as an indication of the pagan practices which abounded there and which are found ascribed to places of this name throughout the romances, though the other episodes are not specifically linked with West Wales. This unanimity presumably reflects the original pagan importance of the district, and also the stability of the tradition which has preserved a recollection of pagan activities in several different ways.

ARONDEL (not Arundel in Sussex): *see* Roche as Sesnes.

AVALON, an island at the end of the Adventurous Marshes:

Avalon, as everyone knows, was the 'magic island' to which Arthur was carried[5] in a barge by three black hooded queens to seek healing for his grievous wound. One of them was Morgan le Fay, who is described in the *Vita Merlini* (ed. Parry, lines 908ff.) as the first of the nine sisters who rule the island to which Arthur was taken after the battle of Camlann. She is skilled at healing, changing her shape and flying through the air like Daedalus. Avalon has already been mentioned in this book in the story of the dying raven which changed into a beautiful young woman and was carried off through the air by her raven comrades to recover in Avalon. Another motif linked with Avalon was that of human lovers of fays, who were kept there for long periods without realising that time was passing, but apart from this it looks at first sight as if the *raison d'être* of Avalon was to accept the dying and prolong their existence indefinitely. It was also, from the meaning of the word 'aval' in Welsh, an island of apples, with their Otherworld connotations,[6] and it was a fortunate isle, where the climate was always temperate and age took no toll. This all sounds very unreal, and corresponds to one version of the Celtic conception of the Otherworld. The other version is of a spirit world, inhabited entirely by divinities, which

---

[4] *Irish Heritage*, E. Estin Evans, p. 25; *Life of St David*, A. W. Wade-Evans, pp. 10ff. and p. 67.
[5] *Morte Darthur*, bk XXI, ch. 5.
[6] See index under apples.

occupied the same space as the real world but was invisible to the inhabitants of the latter. The Britons did not think that their Otherworld was, like heaven and hell, an abode of the spirits of the dead nor that it was, like some other 'heavens', an idealised continuation of the earthly life of dead heroes. As far as Avalon is concerned, it seems to have features of the delectable island type of otherworld but there is no question of it being a general meeting place for departed Arthurian heroes. The only individuals taken there apart from Arthur seem to have been his wife Guenever, and his son Lohot, or at least the severed head of the latter, which was sent for burial there in a chapel dedicated to 'Our Lady'.

Avalon thus seems to have every mark of being a creation of the imagination of priests or poets and, in spite of the pretensions of Glastonbury (largely vitiated by forgery), it would have seemed presumptuous to try to find a place for it in the real world if there had not been reports by Roman authors of places with very similar characteristics which were supposed really to exist at the time the reports were made. According to Pomponius Mela, the island of Sein, off the coast of Brittany, used to be the site of an oracular cult in the first century AD. It was occupied by nine priestesses, dedicated to virginity, who claimed to predict the future, to control the winds and the waves, to transform themselves into animal shape, and to heal. The same motif of an island occupied by priestesses is repeated by Posidonius[7] who tells of an island off the mouth of the Loire where priestesses performed the rites of Dionysus. The priestesses on this island used to visit men on the mainland, but no man dared set foot on the island. There was a temple on the island with a roof, presumably of thatch, which the priestesses had to remove once a year and replace that same day before the sun set. If any of them dropped her bundle of roofing material she was at once torn to pieces by her companions, who continued to carry the mangled remains round the temple until their tempers had cooled. Another island which might once have been a cult site is Oleron, a name which takes the place of Avalon in one version of the story of a certain Lanval and his fairy mistress. Since Morgan and her sister enchantresses at Avalon and the wounded bird-woman returning to Avalon could both very well be recollections of just such a cult site as Sein, it should be worth while after all to enquire where this place Avalon might have been in real life.

There is a close parallel to Sein in the ancient Welsh epic *Preiddeu Annwfn* which describes Arthur's raid on an Otherworld island, surmised to have been Grassholm, off the coast of Pembrokeshire, where there was a cauldron tended by nine virgins. The cauldron evidently had an oracular function, for it was warmed by their breaths to provide inspired utterances. Nine priestesses on an island is a feature common to Avalon, Sein and Grassholm, and there is a remarkable similarity in the situations of two of them, Sein and Grassholm. Both are some miles off extreme west-pointing peninsulas, and both are off-shore from megalithic holy places, in the case of Sein, from the south of Brittany, leading to Carnac in the east; and of Grassholm, not far from the source of the bluestones at nearby Preseli.

To have several recollections of this cult, again in three entirely different literatures, Latin, Welsh and French, gives some idea of its original power, but it does not lead directly to the location of Avalon. Glastonbury certainly fits, but at this stage only because it was once surrounded by water. On the other hand, the three recollections, of three different places of similar characteristics, two of them identifiable and far apart, indicate that Avalon was not unique. There were several cult sites of the same type, of which Avalon is merely a well publicized example.

The suggestion that Geoffrey of Monmouth knew of the classical account and merely relocated the details in an imaginary Avalon of his own choosing has been made by Prof. Piggott.[8] However, the presence of the nine-virgin-on-island motif in *Preiddeu Annwfn* and

---

[7] *Studies in the Fairy Mythology . . .*, Paton, p. 43 note 4.
[8] *Antiquity*, XV, p. 308.

the bird-transformation motif in the episode of the Perilous Ford shows that the characteristics of Avalon were present in traditions which appear to be uncontaminated by knowledge of classical authors.

Many pinnacles of rock which were originally cult sites had their pagan pretensions tamed by the erection on them of a chapel dedicated to St Michael; at Mt St Michel on the north coast of France the original deity is thought to have been Belenus, called 'the brilliant', from the original name of the island, Tombelaine; at Mount St Michael in Cornwall, the Celtic name was Din Sul, the Mount of the Sun; and at La Hougue Bie in Jersey, a chapel on top of a prehistoric mound over a chamber with entrance passage, the dedication was shared between St Michael and Our Lady, nicknamed 'of Brightness'. These examples give clues about the type of cult practised there, something to do with brightness. So there may then be something to be gleaned from the presence of a chapel dedicated to St Michael on Glastonbury Tor; at least we can be certain it was a cult site. If the dedication of the chapel at Glastonbury also carries with it the inference of worship of Belenus, there is an interesting correspondence with legend, for Belenus is an alternative form of Evalac (see Who's Who), of the sun temple at Sarras; and Evalac as a name is not to be distinguished from the Welsh Avallach; and Avallach sounds very like Avallo, the patron of Avalon. It seems possible that the cult site at Glastonbury could have generated traditions which resulted in the dedication to St Michael on the one hand and the tradition of Avallo on the other.

It would be interesting to see if the prehistoric archaeology of Sein matches that of pre-Christian Glastonbury; of Grassholm; and of Mont St Michel and the other St Michael's Mounts including Skellig Michael, an isolated islet lying off a westward pointing peninsula in Kerry, a very similar situation to Sein and Grassholm.

Nine priestesses is a motif by no means confined to islands. There were nine witches at Gloucester who clearly correspond in savagery to those of the Loire island for they were responsible for maiming the Maimed King in *Peredur* and also for cutting off Peredur's cousin's head and serving it on a dish. Savagery is a trait which was extremely persistent, for nine witches were still around to kill and devour an acolyte of St Samson of Dol in medieval times.[9] Mont Dol, rising abruptly from flat ground, is one of those hills mentioned by Bishop Germain[10] as having had an altar dedicated to Mercury, Belenus or some other Celtic deity, which was later replaced by a Christian church or oratory dedicated to St Michael. Here at Dol the name Belenus crops up again in conjunction with nine priestesses. It seems that the pattern of worship at the sites already mentioned may have been repeated yet again.

As previously mentioned, knights were sometimes carried away to Avalon by their fairy mistresses. This happened to Guingamor, with Morgan le Fay, and also to Sir Launval. Less otherworldly versions of a liaison with the lady of Avalon are given in the story of Gareth and Dame Lyonesse (sister in *Morte Darthur* of Sir Gringamour), in what is called in *Morte Darthur* the castle of Avilion; and in a close parallel in which the hero and heroine are Gawain and the King of Cavalon's sister. These stories overlap. In each case the love-making is interrupted by men with pole-axes, Gawain getting a wound in the thigh. This injury recalls the injury to the Maimed King, which was of the same nature, and also the injury to Evalac, who was himself a maimed king and whose name is thought to be the romance equivalent of Avallach/Avallo. Evidently the priestesses of this type of cult site were closely linked with the wound in the thigh.

The 'apple' motif suspected in the name Avalon crops up in Greek myth linked with Apollo (the sun again) and is also localized in the real world at both Emain Ablach,

---

[9]    *The Greek Myths*, R. Graves, vol. 1, p. 58.
[10]    *St Michel et le Mont St Michel*, Paris 1880, pp. 96f.

identified by Mac Cana as the island of Arran,[11] and at a cult site at the mouth of the Wye.[12]

Geoffrey of Monmouth tells us that the sword Excalibur was forged in Avalon. Unreliable though he is, there is a certain logic in ascribing to this watery haunt of priestesses the sword which was the gift of the Damsel of the Lake.

There is a corollary to the possible identification of Glastonbury as the Avalon in which a prehistoric Arthur met his end. In the reign of Henry II the monks of Glastonbury dug up an oak coffin from sixteen feet below the ground at a spot indicated as Arthur's grave by a Welsh bard. They faked a Latin inscription on a lead cross apparently for political reasons – so that an undying Arthur could not be used as a focus for revolt in Wales – and the story of this 'proof' of Arthur's death was widely disseminated. It is not impossible that they faked the truth. R. Graves in *The White Goddess* foreshadows the argument in this book by suggesting, among other possibilities, that they may really have found the body of a Bronze Age Arthur, buried in an oak coffin of a type used in that period.

BENOIC, a country:

Benoic was, with the neighbouring country Gannes, 'on the boundary of Gaul and Brittany'. It was on the plain between the rivers Loire and ARSIE,[13] the latter being not far from the forest of Broceliande. Since Gannes seems to have been Vannes, and the forest of Broceliande can be located because it contained the storm-raising fountain of Barenton (see below under Broceliande), Benoic is to be located to the south of Brittany or in Loire Atlantique, where the modern river ARZ flows from a few miles north of Vannes, passing within 30 km of the modern remnant of Broceliande, to Redon, which is 40 km north of the mouth of the Loire. Since they are river names, the close resemblance of Arz and Arsie is probably significant.

The King of Benoic was Ban. He and his brother, Bors of Gannes, were Arthur's staunchest allies at the time of the rebellion of the British kings. Their presence at the great gathering by the standing stone on Salisbury Plain was critical in obtaining the subjection of the rebel kings to Arthur.

Ban's heart broke and he died when he saw his capital city, Trebes, destroyed by King Claudas of the Desert (that is, of the Waste Land). A monastery was built on the site where Ban had fallen dead. At the same time as he died, his wife, Helaine, left her infant son Lancelot beside the Lake of Diana (q.v.), where he was abducted by the Damsel of the Lake and brought up by her.

BREQUEHAM, a forest:

The forest of Brequeham or Breskehan was on the Welsh bank of the Severn. It was 100 km long and 50 wide, stretching into Norgales to the north and Cambenic to the south. To the west it bordered on Escavalon. It contained an important cult site – a glade defended by a knight for his lady, the Glade of the Cross-roads, or of the Seven Ways.

BRIOSQUE, a forest near Diana's Lake.

BROCELIANDE, the enchanted forest:

As has already been noted, the position of Broceliande is indicated by the presence in it of the storm raising fountain of Barenton, said to be the scene of Arthur's vigil on Midsummer Eve and of the winning by Yvain/Owein of the *Lady of the Fountain*. This important cult site may nowadays, it is said, still be found to the north west of the Forest of Paimpont. Take the D 166 from Mauron to Ploermel. In about a mile a road to Trehorentuec leads to the left. Continue straight for two and a half miles then turn left for the

---

[11] *Celtic Mythology*, p. 69.
[12] See Metambala under Nemus in this Gazetteer.
[13] *Prose Index*, West.

village of Folle Pensee, bearing left at a fork marked 'to Barenton'. At the end of the village a lane to the left directs you to the fountain. The lane ends in a small car park. From here set off on foot along the wide track that leads into the woods. There are a number of paths in the forest. Stick to the broadest for several twists and turns. You will reach the fountain in about fifteen minutes, given a certain amount of good-will on the part of the *genii loci*. The presence of this well-authenticated cult site has led to various fanciful localizations in the district, such as Val sans Retour. Though daunting on a modern signpost, the latter can safely be disregarded. These Arthurian names seem to have been allocated in the nineteenth century, and the same suspicion falls on the tiny islet of Aval, near Isle Grande, said locally to have been the place of Arthur's burial, yet another possible Avalon.

It was in the forest of Broceliande that Merlin appeared as the giant herdsman, the Lord of the Animals. Since he was to be found sitting on a mound in a clearing, or alternatively on a bank by a ditch, it can be assumed that there was a sacred enclosure here not far from the spring. The name Barenton is a corruption of an earlier Belenton, which is also the name of a neighbouring hill, the highest spot in the surrounding countryside. Markale has suggested that the name Belenton derives from Beli Nemeton. To have a sacred enclosure, a nemeton, as part of this complex of cult sites reinforces this suggestion.

Being the principal magic forest in the Arthurian tradition, Broceliande has probably collected incidents which properly belong to other places. For instance, Merlin's mother Optima, who seems to have been a heroine or some minor supernatural personage in Dyfed in South West Wales, is reported to have slept alone in this forest, which resulted in the engendering of Merlin by a 'wild man of the woods'. Alternative versions of the story of Merlin's conception put this event in South West Wales.

Belief in the capability of the spring at Barenton to produce rain persisted well into modern times. In the late eighteenth century 'in times of drought the clergy of the parish of Concoret used to resort in procession with cross and banners to the fountain of Bellanton (as Barenton was known then) to ask for rain; and although Bellanton was situated in the parish of Paimpont, the religious [authorities, who were] curés of Paimpont, were reluctant to oppose it, doubtless because of the immemorial custom.'[14]

'Such a procession, followed by an immense crowd, took place in the exceptional drought of 1835, when the Rector of Concoret blessed the spring, plunged the foot of the cross into it [which has been described as an ingenious compromise between Christ and Merlin], sprinkled the *perron de Merlin* and the assistants standing nearby, "whereupon", we are assured, "a violent thunderstorm arose, and the rain fell with such violence that the crowd had to disperse" '. The last recorded official procession to the spring took place as late as 1925.

Not far from the spring, on the spot marked on the map as *Camp du Tournoi*, is a kind of enclosure bounded by fosses like a battle ground or tournament pitch, which tradition associates with the tournaments of the Knights of the Round Table. Is this, it could be asked, the nemeton that gave the place its name? If not, there may be some other structure lying undisturbed in the forest.

CAMBENIC, a dukedom:
Cambenic was on the Welsh side of the Severn, having a border with Norgales along a river to the north and reaching southwards towards the lower reaches of the Severn.

CAMELOT
The medieval editors of the 'matter of Britain' undoubtedly thought of Camelot as a city, Arthur's capital city. Indeed, in late versions of *Morte Darthur* they went to the length of substituting London for Camelot as the scene of the sword drawn from the stone. The reality is likely to have been somewhat different. Cities only became the norm in Roman

14 *Early Brittany*, Chadwick, N., p. 335.

times, and of the urban sites they left, none is seriously claimed nowadays as Camelot. The most likely site for a post-Roman Camelot at which a historical Arthur might have lived seems to be not a city but a hill-fort, Cadbury, one of hundreds scattered all over the country and each of no more than local significance. So we must discard the notion that Camelot, whenever it existed, was a city in the strict sense of the word, though it may have implied a centre of population of a more diffuse kind.

It is interesting to note that medieval editors, with the idea of a city in mind, chose Winchester and Caerleon as sites for Camelot. In the nineteenth century, place-names beginning with Cam-, such as Camulodunum (Colchester), Camelford, Camelon, Queen's Camel and so on were more popular. In the mid-twentieth century, by which time the 'historical' Arthur was in vogue, the obvious place to look was a post-Roman hill-fort. In this book, since Camelot first comes to notice in the romances, I suggest that the best way to find Camelot's original whereabouts is to examine its topographical links in the romances themselves.

The arguments for regarding Camelot to have been on Salisbury Plain, and to have been associated with standing stones, are to be found in the section on the location of Perrons and Temples in Geography above pp. 200ff.

One of the references to Camelot describes it as on the 'march' of all Arthur's subject kingdoms, which seems to be an impossibility when his dominions were widely scattered. The circumstances of the high kings of Ireland provide a possible parallel. The centre of power seems to have been where the individual kingdoms met, and territorial enclaves seem to have been provided round the throne almost as if there were corridors extending from the realms to the centre. The description 'on the march' of the other kingdoms may mean no more than 'with easy access to' – certainly true of Salisbury Plain, which is the hub of several long distance trackways and which is only a couple of days on foot from the English Channel and the Bristol Channel, linking it with major routes and with the Severn basin and estuary. In real terms, Wessex in its prehistoric heyday imported artifacts from or shared cultural styles with all the places that turn up in the romances from Brittany to Orkney.

CAMELOT, the home of the Widow Lady of the Lonely Waste Forest:

This second Camelot is always clearly distinguished from the one in Logres. It was situated in the most isolated and the wildest part of Wales, to the west near the sea. There was nothing there except the retreat itself and the forest and the water that surrounded it. This description would fit either Dyfed in the south of Wales or the Lleyn peninsula in the north, however, there are links between the Widow Lady's family and places in South Wales so the Dyfed alternative is to be preferred. The Widow Lady (Iglai) was so called because of the castration of her husband Julian (or Pellinor). Her son Perceval sat in the Perilous Seat at Cardoel and later attained the same title of Fisher King as his father and uncle.

Gawain became guardian of this Camelot for a year by defeating the Lord of the Marshes in single combat.

CARADIGAN, a residence of Arthur's:

Caradigan unfortunately is given no links with identified places except with the Lonely Waste Forest, which was in Dyfed. Present day Cardigan is not far to the north of Dyfed, so the obvious inference from the identity of the names may be correct. Arthur held a court here on Midsummer Day.

CARDOEL, a place in Wales:

Its name varies in different passages, being Cardoel, Cardoeil, Cardoiel, Carduel, Cardueil and so on. The reasons for believing Cardoel to have been in South-West Wales, not at Carlisle, are given in a footnote to p. 201 n. 48.

Though Malory barely mentions Cardoel it was one of the most important places in the

French Arthurian story. It was Arthur's home town. His father, Uther, lived there and met Ygerne there. And Arthur fought Gasozein, a rival for Guenever, at a ford there. The story of Guenever's earlier attachment and her abduction by Gasozein is in the *Diu Crône* of Heinrich von dem Türlin. A glimpse of the same affair may perhaps be found in the story of Gosengos in the romances.[15]

Cardoel was a place where things originated. Uther decreed that the major festivals should be held there; the Round Table with its Perilous Seat was made there; Merlin's Perron was erected there; and, in *Perceforest*, the sword was inserted in the stone there. The Round Table and Merlin's Perrons, with Arthur, later moved to Camelot.

Looked at from the angle of mythology, Cardoel was the home of several interesting personages. It was 'Caer' of Uther's 'master forester', Do, who was father of Girflet, the Arthurian version of the Welsh Gilfaethwy, one of the pantheon known as the Children of Don; and was also home of Lore, a fay in other contexts. Another link with the Children of Don is Yder, born at Cardoel and son of Nut or Nuada, one of their number. Since Do, when examined in detail is seen to be a person of mythological importance, the '-do-' of Cardoel (preceded by Car-, representing Welsh Caer- meaning castle, fort or city) is likely to be a significant element of the place-name, so the form Cardoel (given first of several variations in West's *Index*) is probably to be preferred to the alternative spelling, Carduel).

CARLION, a residence of Arthur's:

Carlion is generally supposed to be Caerleon (Caerleon means the fortress of the legion – Caer Legion – from the Roman garrison there). Apparently this name is easily confused with Cardoel as different manuscripts of the same episode sometimes give one instead of the other. However, Carlion is usually described as being a distinct place. For instance, Arthur spent a long time at Carlion when Cardoel was being rebuilt after a fire.[16] There are a couple clues to the position of Carlion in the romances. Lancelot made a journey through the forest of Gelde from Carlion to Sorelois (which was in south-east Wales);[17] and another journey from Carlion to Dolorous Gard (which was on a tributary of the Severn) was made by Gawain.[18] These links with the Usk (upon which Caerleon stands), South Wales and the Severn basin support the identification of Carlion as Caerleon. For what it is worth, Geoffrey of Monmouth records Caerusk, the Welsh name of Caerleon, as having been founded by Belinus.

CARMELIDE, a kingdom:

Its king was Leodegan, (alternatively Leodegrance) Guenever's father, a personage with Welsh antecedents as Ocuran Gawr, the giant Ocuran. He obtained possession of the Round Table from Uther. One of the important places in Carmelide was Carohaise which was Leodegan's principal residence. The knights of the Round Table who belonged to the table's first foundation at Cardoel migrated from there to Carohaise and became Leodegan's subjects. The church of St Stephen at Carohaise was the scene of Arthur's wedding to Guenever. In another version the wedding was at St Stephen's at Camelot, where the Round Table was taken as Guenever's dowry. It may be supposed that this important event was celebrated in both places, before and after Arthur's move to Camelot with the Round Table. The presence of a dedication to St Stephen at both Carmelide and Camelot is yet another instance of correspondence between the place of origin of the Round Table and its final resting place.

The location of Carmelide is indicated by the situation of Bedingran, which was on the marche of Ireland and Carmelide; and by the situation of the Castle of Charroie, on the

---

[15] *Vulgate*, VII, pp. 36f.
[16] *Vulgate*, VII, p. 74.
[17] *Vulgate*, III, p. 429 and IV, p. 5.
[18] *Vulgate*, VII, p. 120.

marche of Carmelide and Bedingran, towards King Ryons' country. These are rather tenuous links with the real world, but Ryons is associated with giants, with the West, with Ireland and with islands. The repetition of the link with Ireland here might indicate South-West Wales, where the 'Irish' presence seems to have been well established. The Round Table and Uther also belong to that part of Wales.

THE CASTLE OF THE BOUNDARY:

Chastel de la Marche belonged to King Brangoire, who has a name incorporating that of the god Bran. The anniversary of his coronation was celebrated by a tournament after which the winner was accorded royal honours and slept with the king's daughter, engendering a future Grail hero.

It has been commented that with the spread of Christianity among the Welsh, a people who at that time still relied on the oral transmission of their literature, the same stories continued to be told but with the gods demoted to kings. As no king could exist without a castle at the time the tales were being told, a god was automatically credited with possession of one. However, in the episode recorded briefly above the absence of a palatial fortified structure is quite obvious. The action is usually outdoors, but where it takes place under cover, it is in tents. Now that a search is being made for traces of this place in the ground, the presence of 'castle' in the name may prove a red herring.

As it happens there is a place on the Welsh border called Bran's Castle, in Welsh Dinas Bran, just north of Oswestry. The shattered ruins on a craggy peak are the epitome of a wild and romantic border fortification, but they are in fact mediaeval as well as being a castle and so doubly irrelevant to the argument. However, there is an unexpected correspondence of names. This castle was originally called the 'Old Marche', so there are two similarities with the original in the romances, an attribution to Bran and the name Marche. There is also an interesting legend attached to this more recent castle. In an Anglo-Norman romance called *Fouke FitzWarin* there is a nocturnal combat reminiscent of a similar event at the Grail castle, Corbenic. Although the latter is more often the home of the maimed King Pelles, this place can also be argued to have been the home of Bran[19] so there is a possible link here with Bran. In spite of having no topographical connection, there are three correspondences here – an association with Bran (though Bran also means raven), the name Marche, and the night combat.

It would perhaps have been expected from the name Brangoire, which has often been taken for a compound of Bran and the place-name Gorre, for Bran's castle to have been in a central position in Gorre, but in the context of primitive religion there could easily have been widely scattered centres of power. Also as Loomis has pointed out, the element 'goire' in Brangoire's name might very well be derived from the epithet '-gawr', meaning giant. Bran's sphere was an extremely wide one. His name as Brandalus is connected with Wales; as Brandelis with Taningues (on the Severn); as Branduz with the Isles; as Ryons with the Isles, with 'Ireland', and with 'Danemarche'; in Welsh legend with Harlech, with Aberffraw (in Anglesey), and with Grassholm; and on modern maps there is Gorsedd Bran, a cult site (from the meaning of Gorsedd) a mere ten mile from Dinas Bran, as the raven flies, and there are Bran's Lake and the Chair of Bronwen (Bran's sister) also in Wales. Even further afield there may once have been a Bran's Castle at Branodunum, now Brancaster, on the north coast of Norfolk.

THE CASTLE OF THE CART:

The Chastel de la Charrette was where Lancelot had his brush with the shameful cart and also experienced the sacrificial bed with its flaming lance. It was near the border between Logres and Terre Foraine (q.v.), a country which was perhaps somewhere between the Severn and the Wye.

---

[19] E.g. by Newstead.

THE CASTLE OF MAIDENS:

The only castle of Maidens which can be located was at the mouth of the river Usk, possibly where the eastern bank stretches out into a blunt westward-facing peninsula, a typical pagan choice for a cult site.

Though there is a reasonable location here, the name castle of Maidens is a generic one, and is likely to have been applied to any of the groups of priestesses which crop up in the Arthurian tradition. The other 'castles' of the same name may all have had their origin in this one on the Usk, or they may have been located at other sites. Two of them, Escalon and Escavalon are in the same neighbourhood as the Castle of Maidens.

The pagan system underlying these recollections of paganism will be dealt with under ESCAVALON after the castle of the Marvel has been described.

THE CASTLE OF THE MARVEL, a castle on a river:

This 'castle' was occupied by Pellinor who guarded the Grail in it with Ygerne,[20] who had been brought there by Merlin. As he was a 'fisher king' and, being 'maimed' was unable to walk, he spent a great deal of time fishing on the river, the same river as that which flowed past Pelles' castle of Corbenic and also Alain's castle of Edyope, thus connecting all three kings who had been maimed by the same lance as had maimed Joseph of Arimathea.

This castle is closely paralleled by the castle of the Severn Rock (actually Roche de Chanpguin, Canguin, Sabins etc, which Loomis equates with Severn, largely on account of the resemblance between the names Sabins and Sabrina). The Castle of the Severn Rock was occupied, like the Castle of the Marvel, by Ygerne, and also by her daughter and grand-daughter, Gawain's mother and sister. The castle of Chanpguin was an abode of many women and thus qualifies as a 'castle of Maidens' in the broadest sense. In Chrétien's account, Gawain became the lord of the castle, committed to its defence by single combat and not allowed to leave, by successfully enduring the adventure of the Bed of the Marvel in which he was assailed by a flaming lance. Mixed up with this adventure is the story of an encounter between Gawain and the Proud Damsel, who sent him to obtain the garland from the defended tree. One of Gawain's opponents in the series of single combats in which he engaged on her behalf was the defender of the Ports of Galvoie. Gawain's reward for success in single combat was bed with the Proud Damsel in the castle of the Marvel.

The castle of the Marvel is stated to have been in the city of Orquelenes in the country of Galvoie; and it was defended by the guardian of the Ports of Galvoie. There is a double link with Galvoie here, and it is also known that the territory of Galvoie (q.v.) was a dependency of King Pelles of Corbenic in Terre Foraine. And the river on which the castle of the Marvel stood connected it to Corbenic, so there is a double link between Galvoie and Terre Foraine – which latter country was Gloucester west of the Severn and perhaps part of Monmouth. By the name Severn Rock this castle is located where the river on which it stood met the Severn estuary, just like the rather similar castle of Maidens, which was at the mouth of the Usk. The two might very well be the same. But the Usk is not the only river flowing into the Severn from the general area of Terre Foraine. There is also the Wye. Here the Beachley peninsula ends in a rocky islet, the site of a chapel from the most ancient times, though unfortunately its dedication (now to St Tecla though in the Middle Ages to St Twrog or Tiriocus) is uninformative. There is a special reason why this islet could once have been a castle of maidens. A feature of the 'Castle of Maidens' in one of its descriptions was the beautiful maidens who would tempt passing knights to stay there for ever by offering them apples. The mouth of the Wye is mentioned in the *Ravenna Cosmography* and by Nennius as being what can nowadays be discerned from the meaning of its

---

[20] *Vulgate*, VII, p. 244.

Roman name as a cult site connected with apples.[21] So perhaps both the Usk and the Wye were the locations of cult sites characterized by virgin priestesses.

The style of paganism practised at these sites is discussed in more detail under Escavalon below.

CHANEVIERE, a port on the river 'Hombre':

Half a league from Branduz' castle of Dolorous Gard (q.v.) in the Severn Valley was a most commodious port called Chaneviere to which ships came from the sea carrying merchandise and victuals.

CLARENCE, a fine city:

Clarence marched with the kingdom of Sorgales, which is South Wales. Blood shed in a battle nearby stained the water of the river DRANCE, a tributary of the Severn.

CONSTANTINOPLE, the city of that name:

When a narrator introduced this name as a title in the phrase 'empress of Constantinople' he no doubt had the real Constantinople in mind but he may have jumped to an incorrect conclusion. In *Peredur*, for example, there is a typical native heroine whose residence is a pavilion, whose desire is for the bravest man, and for whom a great concourse has come to fight. Peredur was the victor, and he ruled with the unexpectedly named 'Empress of Constantinople' for fourteen years.[22] The exotic name looks like an importation into a local story, but why did the teller chose this particular name? One can make a guess here. The main British connection with Constantinople was in the person, tradition had it, of Helen, the supposedly British mother of the emperor Constantine. Perhaps the heroine of this story was, like so many other lovers of challenge knights, originally called Helen; then the title was added as a standard formula to emphasise her importance, and later the real name Helen forgotten.

The same process may have taken place more than once. Brangoire's daughter's son, who was called Helain, was later to be called 'Emperor of Constantinople' himself.

CORBENIC, the Grail Castle or the Adventurous Castle:

Corbenic was built in Terre Foraine (q.v.) by Kalafes to hold the Grail, when he had been converted to the Grail religion by Alain le Gros, the evangelizing Rich Fisher. Terre Foraine, on the boundary of Logres and Gorre, was west of the Severn and north of the Severn estuary.

Corbenic was a dangerous place for the devotees of the Grail religion. 'Many a knight wished to tarry there' at night, but 'without fail none tarried there but was found dead in the morning'.[23] Kalafes himself attempted the night vigil in the Adventurous Palace and, in the presence of the Grail, was wounded between the thighs by a spear thrust by a fiery man, from which he died. Later Corbenic was the residence of Pelles, another maimed Fisher King, who was the father of Galahad's mother, 'Elaine' who had the supremely important job of carrying the Grail in the Grail procession. Corbenic was the scene of various visits by heroes at which the ritual of the Grail procession was performed followed by a night vigil in which the hero was tested by a flaming lance in the Adventurous Bed. In the case of Gawain this was followed by exposure in the demeaning cart. Galahad is said to have cured the Maimed King at Corbenic by anointing him with blood from the Grail.

In the alternative version of events in which Perceval plays the major role instead of Galahad, Perceval became Fisher King at Corbenic in succession to his uncle who bore the same title of Fisher King.

---

[21] Nemus names in Gazetteer, under Metambala.
[22] *Mabinogion*, Penguin, pp. 246–8.
[23] *Vulgate*, I, pp. 289f.

Corbenic was on a river in which the Fisher King is said to have fished, since, being incapacitated, no more energetic occupation was open to him. His brothers Alain and Pellinor had residences on the same river, as already mentioned, an interesting development of the splitting of one original supernatural personage[24] into three Arthurian individuals with the same parentage and domicile.

In one description of a visit to the Grail Castle, Gawain rode out to sea along a narrow causeway for a long way before reaching the castle. Just such a situation occurs in the region already identified as Terre Foraine, at the mouth of the Wye. Here the Beachley peninsula juts out a mile or so into the Severn estuary. The flat area at the end of the causeway, no doubt once a numinous spot and just the sort of place which would have been chosen as a cult site, is now dominated by an enormous electricity pylon and overshadowed by the Severn road bridge. However, as mentioned under the castle of the Marvel, it does seem once to have been a sacred site, whether as Corbenic or as the Castle of Maidens.

After the death of the last Fisher King, the Grail Castle is said to have been left untouched in superstitious awe, surely an authentic account of the attitude of the unsophisticated people to a defunct temple.

CORNWALL:

Then a separate country from Logres with its own king, Cornwall occupied the whole of the south-western peninsula, not just the tip as it now does.

Cornwall gets a poor press in the French romances compared with its prominent position in the Welsh tradition, in which it was the location of Arthur's principal residence, Kelliwic (q.v.). However, it is the setting for the story of Tristan and Yseult. Though this romance was originally quite distinct from the other branches of the Arthurian legend, it displays much the same type of cult activity as has been found in the rest. There is Yseult, representing the sun and worshipped, with Branwen the moon, as a richly dressed wooden idol in an underground chamber. There is worship in groves. And there is the Sovereignty of 'Ireland', Yseult again, for whom Tristan fights what can be construed as a 'challenge' on an island, an event which is later celebrated at an annual festival linked to the summer solstice.

DANEBLAISE, a city in Carmelide.

DANEMARCHE, a kingdom:

There is no indication that modern Denmark is meant by Danemarche, nor is any guidance about its boundaries or neighbours given in the romances. From its royal family it appears to be entirely mythological. That is, it is a recollection of some ancient pagan cult rather than a political entity with specific boundaries. One of its kings was Ryons, one of the transformations of Bran and therefore a god. One of its princes, Oriols, was a typical red challenge knight, who was spurred on by his amie the countess Helaés to challenge Gawain. He lost, and Gawain and Helaés became lovers.[25] The unnamed Queen of Danemarche established an enchanted orchard, walled only by the air around, which contained a magic apple tree which bore bright red fruit all the year round. Any knight who ate an apple from this tree, proffered by a beautiful young woman, was constrained to remain there until such time as a champion would come and defeat the defenders of the orchard.[26] There were twenty of these defenders backed up by three cannibal giants. When they were eventually defeated the place became known as the Castle of Maidens

---

[24] Suggested here to be Belenus.
[25] Both Ryons and Oriols are sometimes called Sesne or Saxon, which is probably irrelevant unless this is a corruption of Sarrassin.
[26] *Vulgate*, VII, pp. 312ff.

from the hundred maidens who had lost their lovers there. The link between this Castle of Maidens and others of the same name, such as the one at the confluence of the Severn and the Usk, depends on the identification of Oriols as the same personage as Orguelleus, the Proud Knight of the Glade. The loss of Oriols' amie to Gawain is closely paralleled by the defeat of Orguelleus at the other Castle of Maidens.

The Queen of Danemarche schemed to make her son Oriols ruler of Logres with Guenever as his wife.[27] If Oriols was the Proud Knight his natural amie would be the Proud Damsel, who is, in fact, sometimes styled 'the Proud Damsel of Logres', suggesting that the Proud Damsel is another description of the Sovereignty. This incident is yet another instance of a union with Guenever thought of as conferring sovereignty on her consort.

Other mentions of Danemarche in the romances are as follows: a prince of Danemarche, Melian, was Galahad's squire at the outset of the quest for the Grail; and three men from Danemarche with three men of Gaul and three men of Logres were Galahad's sponsors in the initiation of that quest. My guess is that behind the first syllable of Danemarche lies the 'Dan-' of Danu or Danann, or, in Wales, Don. This would link Danemarche with Cardoel in Dyfed, and Galahad's sponsors from three different pantheons would seem to be a shadowy recollection of the confederation of deities which lay behind the success of the Arthurian era.

DARNANTES, an enchanted forest:

Since it is said to have boundaries with the Cornish Sea and Sorelois, Darnantes can be taken to have stretched along the north coast of the Bristol Channel from the western edge of Sorelois into Dyfed. Darnantes played an important part in the life of Merlin. His mother, called Optima, lived in the forest, and at the end of his life he was imprisoned here by the Lady of the Lake in an underground cell. As sometimes seems to happen, there is a Welsh version here of events which are otherwise supposed to have taken place in Brittany.

DISNADARON:

A place in Wales, in the vicinity of Caradigan, where Arthur held a plenary court.[28]

DOLOROUS GARD, the Sorrowful Keep:

Dolorous Gard is one of several places where knights were imprisoned under adverse conditions. The descriptions of these places have a considerable affinity with the Valley of No Return and might suggest an imaginary otherworld beyond the grave. If so, it must have been thought that Dolorous Gard coincided with the real world at a particular place, for its situation is described in detail. It was on the river 'Hombre' and it was near Leverzerp, which since this 'Hombre' flowed into the Severn and Leverzerp was on the Severn leads once again to the Severn valley, though in this instance apparently further south than in the version of the Hombre provided by the itinerary which includes the Round Mountain.[29] Half a league away was the port, Chaneviere, which received ships from the sea, and another prison, Dolereuse Chartre, was on an island in the 'Hombre'.

Dolorous Gard had a long history. Before the time of Joseph of Arimathea it had belonged to the pagan King Urbaduc whose tomb, which was surrounded by 'precious' stones, was much later reused for the burial of Galehot and later still of Lancelot. In the

---

[27] *Vulgate*, VII, p. 318.

[28] An alternative explanation is that that the correct form of this name is the form in the Verse Index, Dinasdaron, since Dinas is a common enough topographical term meaning stronghold. The name would then break down into Dinas d'Aron, that is Carlion, the home of Saints Aron and Julien.

[29] See p. 195.

times of Joseph (in *Guiron le Courtois*) the lord, a certain Paladés, used each May 1st to pay a tribute of six youths and six maids to the oppressive giant Asue, whose misdeeds continued until Tristan cut off his head.

In the times of Arthur, Dolorous Gard was in the possession of Branduz des Illes (Bran again). He was notable for his cruelty to his captives until defeated by Lancelot who released the castle from its enchantments, after which it became known as Joyous Gard. During Lancelot's war with Arthur over Guenever it was Lancelot's headquarters and successfully withstood a long siege by Arthur.

There is a particularly exact description of this 'castle'. Perhaps it will enable someone to locate the place somewhere in the Severn catchment area. It was situated high on a native rock. At its foot ran the river 'Hombre' on one side and on the other a large river which came from more than forty springs which poured through an arch at the base of the 'tower'. Within the 'keep' was what seems from the description to have been a chambered barrow later opened and reused.

DOLOROUS TOWER:

This prison was originally called Tor Perrine and was in the forest of Sarpenic, which seems from an itinerary to have been in South Wales, near the river Usk. Its owner was Karados, who was a brother of Terrican. Like the Dolorous Gard, it was on the 'Hombre' and it was captured by Lancelot who released its prisoners, after which its name was changed to la Bele Garde. There is obviously a great deal of overlap between the dolorous prisons, whether they are called keep, tower or prison.

ENTREE GALESCHE, a castle, also called Wandehenches:

The 'Welsh Entry', which led into the kingdom of Baudemagus. It was on the frontier between Gorre (or Terre Foraine) and Logres, not far from the Castle of the Cart, and thus in the south east of the original Wales which stretched to the Severn. Here the inhabitants jeered and threw mud at Lancelot when he was exposed in a cart.

ESCALON le Tenebreus, a castle:

Escalon is presumed to have been in South-East Wales. It was once strong and prosperous and was called 'the Joyful' until it became perpetually shrouded in darkness when, one Thursday of Easter week, the daughter of the lord of the place had intercourse with a knight in the church while the candles were extinguished during the *Kyrie Eleison*.[30] Or, in an alternative version, it was the lord of Escalon who had intercourse with a maiden on an Ash Wednesday. Much later Lancelot dispelled the darkness by successfully penetrating a dark cold underground cemetery and letting light into it. Not far away there was a pine tree round which many knights and damsels danced, bowing to Lancelot's shield as if it were a holy relic.[31] The episode in the church and the dance round the tree perhaps provide two unexpected glimpses of ritual acts from the remote past. Of the two versions of the event in the 'church', the former in which the woman plays the principal role is probably the original and the latter a later, male chauvinist, modification. Since Easter was originally a celebration of the vernal equinox, conception in this 'rite of spring' would have resulted in birth at about the winter solstice, that is, Christmas time.

The episode of the shield draws attention to the importance of so-called shields as cult objects. The insignia of a hero are several times referred to as being worshipped like holy relics.

ESCAVALON, a place where Arthur held court and a kingdom:

The position of Escavalon is suggested by links with Carlion and the Castle of Dames.[32]

---

30 *Vulgate*, VII, p. 136.
31 *Vulgate*, IV, p. 144.
32 *Vulgate*, VII, p. 84 and IV, p. 227.

Its king was Elinant, a brother of Alain le Gros, and after him his son Alain was king.[33] It was at Escavalon that Lancelot fought and killed Meleagant, in a typical 'challenge' in a glade by a fountain, with Guenever as the prize. It was also the home of Gawain's amie Florée, with all that name implies. It was the home of Giromelant, called Gramoflanz in the German tale in which he was the guardian of the tree from which Gawain and Perceval broke garlands to provoke combat.

It has been guessed that the name owes its shape to Avalon, indeed in one instance Avalon is used as an alternative for Escavalon, and also that Escalon is an eroded form of the same name. The discussion on Avalon suggests that that place was not necessarily unique but rather one of a number of sites where a group of priestesses offered oracular pronouncements. Just as Delphi was not the only oracle in the classical world, we may expect to find more than one oracular site in Wales. Previous commentators on the 'matter of Britain' have noted a resemblance between Avalon and the various versions of the Castle of Maidens. Escavalon is not the most typical of its kind, but since it is the last in this list it will be convenient to discuss the whole category here.

As the name 'of Maidens' implies, the essential feature of this type of cult site is the group of women, who can now be recognized as priestesses. But the use of the word Maidens here conveys a misleading impression, suggesting, like the word fay or fairy, sweetness and charm. The reality was just the opposite. It has been noted how priestesses would tear a colleague to pieces. Their bloodthirsty nature is particularly obvious in the nine at Gloucester who killed Peredur's cousin, whose severed head covered in blood was carried on a platter in the place normally occupied by the Grail;[34] and who were also responsible for the maiming of the Maimed King.[35] No wonder they are described with awe and loathing as hags.

At Avalon the goddess and her priestesses are Morgan and her bird-transforming sisters. Morgan is also resident, with many maidens, in the Castle of the Marvel, one of the equivalents of the castle of Maidens; and in another castle of Maidens the goddess is the Queen of Danemarche (otherwise Don?) who has many attendant maidens in her garden surrounded by a hedge of air.

The male elements of this system are on the same two levels of the divine and the human. There are gods to correspond with the goddesses and heroes to the maidens. On the level of the gods there are, in addition to Morgan, Belyas the Amorous of the Castle of Maidens, Pellinor, Elinant, Alain and Avallo/Avallach, all falling within the name scatter of Belenus (see Who's Who). On the human level, on the male side, heroes who enact the ritual of Nemi; on the female side it was the Proud Damsel under whose aegis the challenge was enacted. She it was who led Gawain to the castle. She had had the heads of many knights cut off at that port, and it was she who sent Gawain to get the garland from the defended tree. In her embraces we have a hint of the sexual nature of the ritual, which is made more explicit in the formal love-making of the princess of Escalon and her hero consort; and also by the embraces of Evalac (who can be taken to be a variant of Avallach) for the goddess-dolly in the underground chamber.

Belenus appears a number of times in this account of 'Avalons'. His worship included 'fire from heaven' in the shape of the lightning stroke which struck the sacred king between the thighs in the testing bed. This too was a feature of the castle of Maidens. Indeed, the lightning stroke in the testing bed was the 'marvel' which gave this castle one of its alternative names. However, as has been pointed out, the narrators could not afford to immobilize their errant heroes, so they allowed them to escape from the normally lethal

---

33 In *Prose Index*, West, Alain[4] and Alain[5] are both entitled 'of Escavalon'.
34 *Mabinogion*, Penguin, p. 226.
35 *Mabinogion*, Penguin, p. 256.

bed unharmed. At the castle of Maidens Gawain is said to have achieved great prestige from surviving the midnight flaming lance and to have been granted lordship of the castle on account of his success in this adventure. But the testing bed sounds more like the end than the beginning of a hero's period of office. His defeat of the Guardian of the Ports of Galvoie is given much less prominence in the story, but is the more likely reason for his advancement to the position of guardian of the castle of Maidens, the river-mouth cult site whose lord had been the rich and powerful ferryman of the place.[36]

The presence of forms of the god Belenus among the personages at Escavalon can be a link with the Usk, for Geoffrey of Monmouth reports that King Belinus (presumed here to be a euhemerized version of Belenus) was the founder of the city of Caerusk, as he calls Caerleon.

ESPLUMEOR MERLIN, Merlin's final refuge:

Merlin constructed the 'esplumeor' near Perceval's dwelling-place,[37] which suggests that it was near Corbenic in Terre Foraine. It seems to have been a tall, isolated rock far away in the mountains, on top of which were perched twelve prophetic damsels. Merlin retired into it and was never seen again.

West comments that the exact meaning of the expression 'l'Esplumeor Merlin' has not yet been satisfactorily decided, although there has been much discussion. Perhaps the most intriguing suggestion is that it refers to a shelter in which falcons retreated to moult, to emerge later in brilliant new plumage. This seems particularly appropriate for an ageing shaman who probably wore a feathered cloak, as Irish druids are reliably reported to have done. A similar sartorial effect would have been created by the perforated bone tassels found in a Bronze Age barrow on Salisbury Plain.[38]

As well as being near Perceval's dwelling-place, the Esplumeor was on a journey which ended in Escavalon, confirming the suggestion that it was in South-East Wales.

The usual story of Merlin's end is that he, in Malory's words, 'was assotted and doted on' the Damsel of the Lake. He 'always lay about the lady to have her maidenhood' but 'she was ever passing weary of him and fain would have been delivered of him. . . . And so on a time it happed that Merlin showed to her in a rock whereas was a great wonder, and wrought by enchantment, that went under a great stone. So by her subtle working she made Merlin to go under that stone to let her wit of the marvels there; but she wrought so there for him that he came never out for all the craft he could do.'[39] Though Malory puts it in Cornwall, this event is generally said in the romances to have taken place in the forest of Darnantes, or else in Broceliande, which is also the location of the parallel tale of the death of Faunus on the banks of the Lake of Diana. If Merlin had been an ordinary human being it would have been necessary to make a choice between Brittany, South Wales and Cornwall if one wished to search for his grave. But since he was a pagan cult figure he could live and die in many places. Diana and the Damsel of the Lake were not restricted to any particular location, and no doubt they displayed their superiority over the most accomplished male magicians in a great number of places, now all forgotten except these two or three. Either account of Merlin's end would bear the interpretation of dolmen burial already referred to.

---

[36] Since writing this I see that a Bronze Age ferry-boat has been dug up at this very place, the mouth of the Usk. I regard this as a mere coincidence, but by the association in the romances of the title 'ferryman' with a pagan figure, attention is drawn to the intriguing possibility that the priesthood may once have exercised control over the early stages of public transport by water, as it seems to have done over the first use of writing, wheeled vehicles, and, one may guess from the title Pontifex Maximus, bridges.

[37] *Prose Index*, West.

[38] *Pagan Religions . . .*, Hutton, p. 109.

[39] *Morte Darthur*, bk IV, ch. 1.

ESTRANGORT, the kingdom of the King with 100 knights:
On the west side of the Severn, between Norgales and Cambenic.

ESTROITE MARCHE, a kingdom:
'The Narrow Boundary' was contiguous with Estrangort, Norgales and Cambenic.

THE FORD PERILOUS, over which the Proud Damsel sent Gawain to get the garland from the defended tree:
This ford, unlike the one of the same name defended by Urbain can be roughly localized as it was over the river Sabins, which seems to have been the Severn/Sabrina.

FORESTS:
The descriptions 'Perilous' and 'Adventurous' are often applied to forests, however, they seem to have no particular geographical significance, being generic terms applicable to any forest. The Waste Forest, on the other hand, is spoken of as if it existed in the real world of South West Wales, since the Queen of the Lonely Waste Forest, Perceval's mother, had her residence there.

THE FOUNTAIN OF THE FÉES:
A spring in the forest of Camelot, that is, in Wessex or in West Wales. The name originated among the local inhabitants, who used to say that they had seen many beautiful women there and since they were unable to understand their true nature, they said they were fées.

THE FOUNTAIN OF THE LION:
A spring in Cornwall. Here the villainous King Mark disposed of his infant son, begotten on his niece, and also killed his own brother.

GAIHOM, the capital city of Gorre (q.v.):
After Guenever had been abducted by Meleagant she was held captive here, and it was to Gaihom that Lancelot crossed the sword bridge to rescue her. Gaihom was also known as Gohorru, from which Gorre took its name.

GALAFORT:
A castle belonging to the daughter of Baudemagus (i.e. Bran's daughter). On this account West presumes it to have been in Baudemagus' domains, that is, Gorre and Terre Foraine. This presumption is supported by an adventure Lancelot had in Terre Foraine. He was challenged by an unknown knight and fought and defeated him in a beautiful large glade. Baudemagus' daughter then came into the glade, as already mentioned, to ask for the loser's head and to throw it in a well. Baudemagus' daughter has been taken as playing on her home ground here, in her father's country of Terre Foraine.
Another pointer to the whereabouts of Galafort is that a river (called Agloride) was between Galafort and Baudemagus' court in Gorre.

GALEFORT:
A castle near the river 'Hombre'. There seems to be nothing to indicate if this place is the same as the Galafort just described, but it also (like other places whose names begin Gal-) has interesting pagan connections. Galefort was the headquarters of the Grail religion when it was first brought to Britain by 'Joseph of Arimathea'. Joseph's son Galahad, the future King of Wales, was born here. Missionaries set out from Galefort to convert the people of North Wales and the Sarrassins of Camelot. There was a church to Our Lady, founded on his conversion, by the pre-Grail king, Ganor,[40] and there was a church dedicated to St Stephen. Ganor owed allegiance to Crudel, King of North Wales. Galefort is said to have been on or near the Hombre, but since the 'Hombre' in the sense in which it

---

[40] *Vulgate*, I, p. 226.

appears in the 'matter of Britain' seems to have been a tributary of the Severn, a Welsh border site for Galefort is still a possibility.

Galafort has come first in alphabetical order, but the pagan activities taking place there were probably later than Joseph's pioneering visit to Galefort.

GALONNE, THE MARCHES OF, a kingdom:

This was the first place conquered by Galehot, the lord of the Far Away Isles. Since Galehot's conquests seem all to have been in Wales, it may be taken that Galonne was in Wales, quite apart from the tell-tale first syllable of the name.

GALOSCHE, an island:

Galosche is said to be in Norway in *Sone de Nausay*, the only romance in which it is mentioned. However, its name and the personages linked with it unmistakably indicate its Welsh origin. Its story is as follows: Joseph of Arimathea came to Norway and threw out the original inhabitants, the Sarrassins. He killed their king and married his daughter. For marrying a pagan he was punished by god with emasculation, which led to the comprehensive wasting of his country, Lorgres. After his death, by which time he was known as the Fisher King, his 'holy' body was taken to the island of Galosche, where an abbey was founded in his honour. There his body was displayed as a holy relic with the Grail. The island had earlier been in the possession of Baudemagus and Meleagant, in the latter's time many heads having been severed there. It was half a league from the shore and connected by a narrow causeway which led to a sword bridge.

There are several pagan themes in this description of Galosche, most of them repeated in other romances in slightly different forms. For instance, it has already been described how Joseph received the debilitating wound between the thighs from an angel with a countenance blazing like lightning, for disobeying god's will. We also find his talismanic corpse averting a famine by being taken to the abbey of Glay (alternatively Glannes or Urglay) in Escoce, perhaps an extremely distorted version of his body being taken to Galosche. The location of Galosche cannot be pinpointed, but the name is too close to the French word Galesche, meaning Welsh, and Joseph's country Lorgres sounds too close to Logres, for Norway to be favoured. The association with Baudemagus and Meleagant suggests South Wales, and the description of the site is reminiscent of that of Gaihom, where Meleagant took Guenever after he had abducted her and where he was challenged by Lancelot, who had to cross the sword bridge to get there.

GALVOIE, a kingdom:

The Lady of Galvoie was a liege of King Pelles of Corbenic in Terre Foraine. Galvoie included the castle of Maidens where Ygerne, her daughter and granddaughter lived, which has been identified as at the mouth of the Usk. Both suggest Galvoie was in South East Wales. The usual identifications as either Galway or Galloway are not secure because they are based entirely on name resemblance. Brandelis was count of Galvoie (West Verse). So we have Bran again, who in another disguise as Uther Pendragon was Ygerne's husband.

The knightly lover of the Proud Damsel, she who led Gawain to the Castle of Maidens, was the guardian of the Ports of Galvoie, that is he was its defender under the challenge system.

GANNES, or GAUNES, a kingdom:

Gannes was on the boundary between Gaul and Brittany and was near to Benoic, the position of which is fixed by the rivers Loire and Arz. The suggestion from the spelling of the name that Gannes was Vannes in southern Brittany makes good sense. A switch between native 'V' and romance 'G' is not uncommon.[41] The heroine Enid (of the romance *Erec*) seems to have been the territorial goddess of the tribe of the Veneti of Vannes.

---

[41] See footnote p. 110.

GARLOT, a city and kingdom:

Garlot was the kingdom of Neutre of Garlot, who was married to one of Arthur's sisters. Garlot was also the kingdom of Urien of Garlot who was married to another of Arthur's sisters. It looks as if Neutre is a scribal corruption of Urien.

GAUT DESTROIT, the Confined Wood:

The name Gaut Destroit usually appears as the title of a lady, Lore de Branlant, also called the Dame of Gaut Destroit. Her lands included the forest of Sarpenic, which was in Gorre.[42] Here Maduc the Black Knight of the Black Isle, who had an attachment to Lore, built a stronghold and founded a custom that passing knights must fight him. If he defeated any of Arthur's knights he impaled their severed heads on sharpened stakes.

Lore's title of Branlant reveals a link with Bran, the deity of the severed head.

THE GIANT'S HILL, Tertre al Jaiant:

The Giant's Hill was the scene of a ritual meal on a Friday. The principal participants were Josephé (the son of Joseph of Arimathea) and Bron (Bran), who sat on either side of the 'Perilous Seat' at the Grail Table on top of the hill. A certain Moys took his place in the seat but since he was not the foreordained rightful occupant he was seized by fiery hands and carried away through the air burning like a torch.[43]

The Giant's Hill was two days journey from Camelot. If the proposal here for the site of Camelot is accepted, it will be noted that Salisbury Plain is an area not notable for conspicuous hills. However, Markale has suggested that the word tertre, meaning strictly a mound or small hill, is often used in the romances for a tumulus. There are plenty of these artificial mounds in the neighbourhood, of which one stands out as by far the most substantial, Silbury Hill, surely to unsophisticated eyes the work of giants.

GORRE AND SORELOIS, and the entries into them:

The position of Sorelois has been established as in South East Wales. However, another kingdom, Gorre, has rather similar topographical links. Both are described as having only two 'entries', in each case difficult to cross; both are separated from Logres by the Severn.[44] The equation is not exact, because immediately inside the entry which might be expected to lead into Gorre,[45] the land is described as Terre Foraine.[46] It looks as if Gorre and Terre Foraine together occupied roughly the same area as Sorelois.

The position of Terre Foraine derives from Lancelot's journey undertaken in search of Guenever, who had been abducted by Meleagant, the son of King Baudemagus of Gorre. Lancelot entered Gorre at 'the Entree Galesche', not described as a bridge, where Terre Foraine began. After some time and sundry adventures he came to the Gaihom causeway which led to the Sword Bridge which crossed over to Gohorru/Gaihom, the 'master city' of Gorre. The Severn here was not able to be forded and had to be crossed by boat,[47] so this bridge seems to have been over the tributary which formed the eastern boundary of Gorre proper, between Gorre and Terre Foraine. The other notable 'bridge', the Lost Bridge or the Bridge under the Water, which sounds more like a ford, was five days travel away. This second crossing could, at a guess, have been the lowest ford over the Severn, which is likely to have been the one between the Arlingham peninsula and Newnham. This is only thirty miles as the crow flies from the Usk, but 'five days travel' may well be an exaggeration.

---

42 *Vulgate*, IV, p. 236.
43 *Vulgate*, I, pp. 247/8.
44 *Vulgate*, VII, pp. 144f. and III, p. 269.
45 *Vulgate*, IV, p. 40.
46 *Vulgate*, IV, p. 163.
47 *Vulgate*, VII, p. 145.

The entrance into Gorre consisted of a causeway and a terrifying narrow bridge, some-what similar to the entrance into Sorelois, next to be described.

Sorelois resembles Gorre in its location and in having two difficult entries, but as far as the latter are concerned, only in a general way. The entries into Sorelois are called the Welsh (or North-Welsh) Bridge or Causeway, and the Irish Bridge. Their founders are said to be different personages from the founder of the bridges into Gorre, and their locations do not exactly tally. But, like the bridge into Gorre, the Pont Norgalois was very high and made of wood, and was defended. This site provides two examples of 'guardianship'. In one, Gawain defeated Belinans (i.e. Belenus) there and took over command of the castle and its defence. In the other the attacker was Arthur who, as already mentioned, is said to have accepted liability to continue the defence of the site if victorious when he fought King Yder of Cornwall there.

Since Belinans was King of Sorgales, in at least this case the battle was not merely for a spring or a ford but for the whole country, and the sacred king defended it at its boundary at what sounds like an elaborately constructed cult-site.

GWALES, an island off South-West Wales, supposed to be Grassholm:

Gwales was the scene of the eighty year long hospitality of Bran's Head. It is possible that it may also have been the site of Arthur's expedition to obtain the cauldron tended by nine priestesses. A hurried excavation of the well on Grassholm in 1946 discovered high-grade Roman and possibly earlier pottery, unexpected in such an isolated and inaccessible place unless it was a cult site.[48]

HOSELICE, a country:

An earlier name for Wales. The first of the Galahads, who was the youngest son of Joseph of 'Arimathea', was crowned King of Hoselice at a place called Palagre at Pente-cost. Hoselice was then renamed Gales (i.e. Wales) in his honour.

Hoselice is a somewhat variable name. It appears as Haucelice, Hoceliche, Hoschelice, Cocelice, and Sorelice. Perhaps Hoselice in an even more eroded form even appears as LICES, a kingdom which stretches as far as the Waste Forest Adventurous, where the Maimed King lived – that is, on the basis of this analysis, it reaches as far west as Dyfed. It will be noted that the main associations of King Galahad of 'Wales' are in South Wales. The Gales of the romances may have a more restricted meaning than Wales has at the present day.

There are many examples of founding-fathers whose names are said to have been preserved like Galahad's in the names of countries. Most of them, like Brutus of Britain, Locrine of Logres, Camber of Cambria, Albanact of Albany (Scotland, before the Scots got there from Ireland), Corineus of Cornwall and Orcaus of Orkney, seem to be figments of the imagination, as if medieval historians felt compelled to explain the names of countries and responded in a standard way. We may therefore doubt if one particular individual gave his name to Gales, particularly as all the other countries with similar names – Gaul, Galicia and Galatia – reliably trace the origin of their names to the Galli, that is, the Celts under a well-known variation of their name. Though the story of King Galahad should therefore be treated with reserve, the renaming of Hoselice is not without interest. In Gal-icia and Gal-atia, the presence of Celts (Galli) is acknowledged because the names Nemetobriga in Galicia in North West Spain and Drunemeton in Galatia in Asia Minor contain the element Nemet, indicating a sacred enclosure. These reflect some form of worship in sacred groves – at Drunemeton it was an oak grove. This is a feature which corresponds to the Nemi type challenge system prevalent in Britain, of which the Galahads included notable exponents. Looking on Galahad as a name symbolic of the

---

[48] Personal communication.

religious system of the Gal- people (the Celts) makes the idea of him giving his name to Wales far more acceptable.

HUIDESANC, a port and city on the sea:

Huidesanc was in Gorre. It seems to have been not far from Dolorous Gard, as after Lancelot had defeated a red knight called Argondras at Huidesanc he travelled on to Dolorous Gard.

IRELAND:

In spite of sharing a name with the country called Ireland today, the 'Ireland' of the 'matter of Britain' is not given the same location in any respect at all. For instance, it has a border with Carmelide (West, under Bedigran) which was certainly not in Ireland, and it has a border with Scotland, since Merlin is said to have been born on the borders of Scotland and Ireland.[49] And, most specific of all, Ireland was the place of origin of the bluestones in the *Historia*. These last two localizations point in the same direction, towards South-West Wales. To have had a province called 'Ireland' in South-West Wales would probably not contradict the sense of any passage in the romances, but a closer look will indicate a wider spread of 'Ireland' with less formal boundaries than are implied by the term province.

Apart from geographical links, the most revealing feature of 'Ireland' is the way its royal family is closely linked with paganism. A queen of 'Ireland' was identified with the dawn and a princess with the sun; a princess was mother of the kings Ban and Bors; and a king of 'Ireland's' sister, Guenever, played the role of 'sovereignty'.

Further information about Ireland comes from its kings. Ryons was King of Ireland; or of Danemarche and Ireland; or of the land of Pastures and of Giants; or of the Isles; or of North Wales; and he was lord of the West. So, among other places, he is linked with Ireland, Wales and Denmark. Another king, Ammadus, was King of Ireland, Hoschelice (i.e. Wales) and of part of Danemarche.[50] This odd grouping of Ireland, Wales and Denmark suggests local links. At the time at which the stories originated the names of Ryons' realms may have had very different significance from that of those realms today. Narrators may have exaggerated the importance of the regions represented by the earlier names to correspond with the wider world of their own times. For the rest, there is a strong association between kings of Ireland and islands and the west. These last links correspond to Ryons King of Ireland's characteristics in one of his other incarnations, as Bran (see Who's Who).

Among other adventures of the royal family of 'Ireland', a prince was killed at St David's in Geoffrey of Monmouth's account of the moving of the bluestones, and another prince was killed by Balin (Belenus) at Merlin's Perron near Camelot.

The name Ireland is derived from that of a goddess, Eriu, one of three goddesses – the others being Fodla and Banba – from whom three of the ancient names of Ireland were derived. Name-giving founders seem rather more convincing when they are recognizable as deities.

THE ISLAND OF JOY:

An island not far from Corbenic in Terre Foraine. Having captured the island from a giant in a year-end single combat at Pelles' court, Lancelot lived there with Pelles' daughter and many damsels. It got its name from the joyfulness constantly expressed by Elaine and her maidens. Every day they used to carole round a pine tree on which Lancelot had hung his shield as an invitation to joust.

---

[49] *Vulgate*, III, p. 20.
[50] *Vulgate*, Index, under Maaglant.

THE ISLAND OF ST SANSON:

Where Tristan defeated Morholt in the battle for the truage (i.e. the sovereignty) of Cornwall. It is described as a little island in the sea on which only the two combatants were allowed to set foot. St Sanson's Island is sometimes said to be the island of the same name in the Scillies but according to the story it was a small island close to the coast of Cornwall (q.v.).

L'ISLE PERDUE, the lost island:

A castle of Galehot's on an island in the Severn.

LES ISLES LONTAINES, the Faraway Islands:

The Faraway Islands have a generally western location. It has been said on this account that they are what we now know as the Western Isles, that is, the Hebrides. However, their associations are all with Wales. For instance, King Galahad of Wales, the son of Joseph of Arimathea, married a princess from there and it was the title of Galehot, the conqueror of South Wales. There are in fact plenty of Welsh islands to fit the bill, and many of them have pagan or magical associations, such as: Grassholm, scene of the entertainment by Bran's severed head; Lundy, where Gwair was imprisoned; Bardsey, where Merlin withdrew with the Treasures of Britain; and Anglesey, where there was an important station of Bran.

There is, as it happens, a record from classical times of the British attitude to islands. A certain Demetrius, sent by the Roman emperor to reconnoitre the islands off the coast, found the nearest inhabited island 'occupied by few inhabitants, who were, however, sacrosanct and inviolable in the eyes of the Britons. Soon after his arrival a great disturbance took place, accompanied by many portents, by the wind bursting forth into hurricanes, and by fiery bolts falling. When it was over, the islanders said that some one of the mighty had passed away. For . . . with regard to great souls . . . the extinction and destruction of them frequently disturb the wind and surge as at present; oftentimes also do they infect the atmosphere with pestilential diseases. Moreover there is there, they said, an island in which Cronus is imprisoned with Briareus keeping guard over him as he sleeps; for, as they put it, sleep is the bond forged for Cronus. They add that around him are many deities, his henchmen and attendants.'[51] Here we have a description of an oracular cult site occupied in classical times. Its position off the coast is reminiscent of the Island of Sein in fact and the island of Gwales (Grassholm) in tradition. Also there is an association between an island and an important sleeping god. Commentators have invariably been reminded of Arthur and his men sleeping in a hollow hill until such time as the call of destiny brings them forth to save their country, and also of the maimed and bed-ridden or languishing Fisher King, sometimes Bran in the romances, though Belenus is also conspicuous in this role. Bran certainly has a close association with islands. He is Brandus des Illes, Brien des Illes, and, shorn of the initial letter 'B', Ryons des Illes. These associations of Bran with islands in French legends correspond with those in Welsh which link Bran with the islands of Anglesey and Grassholm.

Not all the associations of islands are with Bran. The prince of the Lontaines Islands was Belinor, a name which suggests an original link with Belenus. The link between Belenus and isolated peaks has already been mentioned.

On the face of it, off-shore islands had three sets of associations, perhaps in sequence. One set represented by Bran, a sleeping or languishing god, perhaps typified in classical times by Cronus; another set by Belenus, typified by brightness; and the third by the line of Galahads, prime figures in the Gallicization, that is to say the Celticization, of Wales.

The Welsh tradition treats the off-shore islands as potential entrances to the otherworld,

---

51 *Arthurian Legend*, Rhys, p. 368.

thus in one version of his ending, Merlin is supposed to have disappeared on Bardsey Island.

KELLIWIC:

Where Arthur held his court in Cornwall. 'Kelli' means a grove. The same word for grove occurs in the name of the tumulus on Anglesey called Bryn Celli Ddu, said to mean 'the mound of the dark grove'. The mound is superimposed on an earlier henge which included a ring of stones. Does the word Celli at Bryn Celli Ddu refer to the sacred enclosure represented by the henge? If so any attempt to locate Kelliwic should take into account the possibility that it was a henge

KINK KENADON, upon the sands that march nigh Wales:

Malory sets the scene at a Pentecost court here for his version of the story of le Bel Inconnu – *The Tale of Sir Gareth of Orkney that was called Beaumains by Sir Kay*. In it the hero, 'minded' by Lynet, defeats the knight of the Glade and wins the hand of dame Lyonesse, the sister of the lord of Avalon. Loomis proposes Sinadoun that is, Caer Seint (now Caernarfon) as an original, with an initial soft 'C' mistaken by Malory for a hard one.

LAC de DYANE:

Diana's lake was not far from Trebes in Brittany, and was reached on the third day when travelling from Gannes, that is Vannes, in the south of Brittany. It received its name in pagan times, but when Christianity became general, simple people said that Diana was a mortal queen whose passion for the chase led her to be called goddess of the chase and the woods.[52] Long before the time of Christ she is said to have hunted through the woods of France and Britain and to have chosen this lake to make her home, from which she used to hunt daily.[53] She cruelly murdered her lover Faunus, the son of the local king, in favour of another lover, Felix. The latter cut off her head and threw her body into the lake.

Much later, the Damsel of the Lake made her home in an underwater palace constructed for her by Merlin in Diana's Lake. At the moment when Ban's wife, Helaine, saw her husband die of grief at the loss of his lands, the Damsel of the Lake snatched up Helaine's baby son, Lancelot, and took him to bring him up in her invisible underwater home. The disconsolate Helaine set up a religious foundation in memory of her husband at the place where he died on top of a tertre, that is, a mound or knoll. Every morning immediately after hearing mass Helaine prayed for her husband in the minster then went down on to the lake and prayed for her son. Meanwhile, unknown to her, Lancelot was being brought up in a princely fashion in the waters below her feet. He spent a great deal of time hunting but was unaware of his mother's presence nearby. Later Helaine was joined by her sister Evaine; and Evaine's two sons, Lionel and Bors, went to join Lancelot in the lake but neither party seems to have had any inkling of the presence of the other.

This is a strange story in more ways than one, but departs furthest from reality in the underwater life of the Damsel of the Lake and her entourage. No one, as far as I know, has suggested any matter-of-fact antecedent from which such an end product might have been derived. It might, of course, be imagination. However, departures from the laws of nature sometimes reflect pagan thinking, like Bran's severed head, still talking after eighty years. The clues in this case are not far to seek. Diana is openly a goddess; her consort, Faunus, bears the name of a god; and her body thrown into the lake to give it her name has parallels which suggest a pagan observance. The second inhabitant of the lake, the Damsel of the Lake, is invariably spoken of in the romances as human, but her alternative title of Damsel 'Cacheresse', the Huntress, suggests she might have been following in the

---

[52] *Vulgate*, III, p. 8.
[53] Huth *Merlin*, II, p. 145.

tradition of Diana. Indeed, the close analogy between the deaths of Faunus and Merlin,[54] and between their characteristics, could be taken as indicating that the suggestion of a sequence in time is false, and that the stories of Diana and Faunus on the one hand, and of The Damsel of the Lake and Merlin on the other, are recollections of the same original by two different channels of oral transmission, in one of which they are called by the names of their classical equivalents.

There is good topographical evidence for the approximate location of the Lac de Dyane since it is linked with Benoic, a place identified by the names of two rivers. So it was in the south of Brittany. It was a large deep lake in a valley, surrounded by a small wood. Between the lake and Vannes was the river Charosche. Beside it were to be found a Perron and the tomb of Demophon, in which Diana had trapped Faunus under a stone slab, perhaps dolmen burial as seems a possible original for the parallel case of the death of Merlin. To take this line of argument a stage further, the other burial place beside the lake, Ban's chapel/tomb on a tertre, might be yet another recollection of barrow burial. In that case, Helaine would have been a religious figure whose devotions were divided between the grave and the lake. Lancelot would have been supposed to have been brought up under the protection of the divinity of the place, the spirit of the Lake.

THE LANDE OF SEVEN WAYS:

There are very many glades in the romances which are the scene of a challenge; this one is distinguished by being at a cross roads. It was guarded by a knight whose lover would accept him only if he could keep it for a month. Seven Ways is the only glade in the 'matter of Britain' which can be even vaguely located. It was in the forest of Brequeham close to the Severn, on the west side of the river.[55]

Diana's lake at Nemi was the historical site of a challenge in a glade. Here there is a tradition that exactly the same sort of ritual conflict was being carried out in the Severn valley. There are too many examples of the challenge theme in the romances for the localization of such a cult site in Britain to be disregarded. Like heads thrown in wells and swords thrown in pools, this episode is a distant memory of the real past.

Needless to say, no narrator could pass by this site without saying where the seven ways led, so a certain amount of imagination may have been brought into play. These places need not be taken too seriously. They are:

Turning Castle
The Castle of the Marvel
The Castle of Edyope, where King Alain of Ille en Listenois lived
The Castle of Maidens
Terre as Pastures, whose lord was Ryons or one of the Galahads
The Castle of Corbenic
The kingdom of Noargue

The places in this list which can be located are the castles of the Marvel and of Maidens, both on the Usk (and, indeed, argued here to be the same place); Corbenic, in Terre Foraine, and thus in the region of Gwent; and Edyope, on the same river as Corbenic. These, all west of the river Severn and north of the Severn estuary, are credible destinations for journeys from a place in the forest of Brequeham, which was itself to the west of the Severn and rather more to the north of the Severn estuary than Terre Foraine.

LEVERZERP:

A place on the Arlingham peninsula which is almost surrounded by a meander of the tidal Severn,[56] south-west of Gloucester. This area was once of much greater importance than it is now, for a ledge of rock in the bed of the river provides a low-water ford from Arlingham across to Newnham on the Welsh side of the river. A Roman road led to the ford, which is likely to have been the lowest crossing of the Severn, except by boat, in prehistoric times.

LISTENOIS, a country and kingdom:

Listenois was the scene of the Dolorous Stroke and other misfortunes suffered by sacred kings.

The Dolorous Stroke is not the only link between Listenois and the wound between the thighs. This injury also befell kings Kalafes and Pelles at Corbenic, which was in Terre Foraine, a constituent part of Listenois. The relationship between Listenois, Terre Foraine, the Lance Vengeresse and the various maimed and fisher kings is shown in the table below.

### Listenois, Terre Foraine and The Lance Vengeresse

| Name | Kingdom | Titles | |
|---|---|---|---|
| PELLEHAN of | Listenois, later Terre Foraine* | M.K. F.K. | wounded by L.V.[57] in thighs or wounded by sword[58] in thighs |
| PELLINOR of | Listenois | M.K. F.K. | wounded by L.V.[59] in thighs |
| PELLES of and of | Terre Foraine* Listenois | M.K. F.K. | wounded by sword[60] in thighs |
| LAMBOR of | Terre Foraine* | F.K. | killed by sword[61] |
| KALAFES of | Terre Foraine* | | wounded by L.V.[62] in thighs |
| ALAIN of the | Isle in Listenois | M.K. F.K. | wounded by L.V.[63] in thighs |

M.K. = Maimed King  F.K. = Fisher King  L.V. = Lance Vengeresse

* Listenois became known as Terre Foraine or Terre Gaste (the Waste Land) after the Dolorous Stroke. In the alternative version of this event, the neighbouring countries Terre Foraine and Gales both became known as Terre Gaste after the stroke.

To explain the extraordinary consistency of this group of traditions about Listenois from several sources, recourse may be had to a memory of the ritual emasculation of

[56] *Vulgate*, II, p. 213. Here the Saverne 'issoit de la mer et rechaoit en la mer . . .' One manuscript has Suret here, another Leverzerp.
[57] *The Romance of the Grail*, Bogdanow, pp. 241–9.
[58] *Vulgate*, V, p. 303. References to the *Vulgate* etc. here are supplemented by West's *Prose Index*.
[59] *Vulgate*, VII, p. 236.
[60] *Morte Darthur*, Malory, bk XVII, ch. 5.
[61] *Vulgate*, I, p. 290.
[62] *Vulgate*, I, p. 289.
[63] *Vulgate*, VII, p. 146.

sacred kings. The active agent is said to have been Balin[64] (the god Belenus the Brilliant) or else it was a fiery man. In similar incidents the lance is flaming or has a flaming pennon and there is generally a thunderstorm. From this it can be seen that the stroke represented lightning and that this was the symbol of Belenus. The lightning stroke maimed its victims in the sacrificial bed at the castle of the Marvel on the Usk as well as at Corbenic in Terre Foraine, and possibly also at Caerwent (where Bors was exposed in the cart) and at the castle of the Cart, on the border of Terre Foraine and Logres. Some of the victims, as much part of the system as the active participants, have names which fall within the name-scatter of the same god, Belenus.

LOENOIS, a country of which Tristan's father Meliadus was king:

Loenois had a border with Cornwall, on which the Castle of the Rock was situated. On this border with Cornwall, in a little wood called after Hercules who had once defeated a giant there, there was a temple of Venus. Pelias was a pagan King of Loenois; Luce, his son, succeeded him and was buried in this temple; and Apollo (a human being, grandson of Bron) followed Luce. Another king of Loenois was Lot of Orcanie. Since Luce probably means light; Lot was buried in a church dedicated to St John and his son Gawain's strength waxed with the sun; and Pelyas could be explained as a form of Belenus, it is perhaps not surprising that there was also a temple to the god Apollo in Loenois.[65]

There are no indications of the position of Loenois other than its contiguity with Cornwall, which country may, from the sense of the story, be presumed to be the Cornwall in Britain, not the one in Brittany. There is no hint as to whether we should look to any particular point of the compass from Cornwall to find Loenois. In ancient times Cornwall included the whole of the south western peninsula.

Loenois, also spelt Lyonois, seems to have been the original of Tennyson's Lyonesse.

LOGRES:

Logres, as already mentioned, was the country now known as England (or part of it), with the Severn as its boundary with Sorelois and with a border with Norgales. Although a similar word is now used in modern Welsh for England as a whole, Logres seems to have meant only the western part in the romances, except that Wales stretched further to the east than it now does.

The seat of power in Logres was Camelot, often referred to as the city of Logres. Remembering that the manuscripts were in French, the city of Logres, with the implied meaning of the capital of Britain, was inevitably sometimes misread as the city of Londres, that is, London. London is not an Arthurian location. As already mentioned, all the identifiable places in the romances, apart from the dubious Norhombellande, are in the western half of Britain and in Brittany and Orkney.

In the historical lore retailed in mangled form by Geoffrey of Monmouth, Britain had a name-giving first king called Brute or Brutus, from Troy. He brought with him to this country Corineus, the founder of Cornwall, and he had three sons who gave their names to his three kingdoms, Locrine to Logres and so on. It was of Locrine that the story of a secret mistress in an underground chamber was told.

Who is to say that no king worshipped a female idol in an underground chamber, or indeed that one of our earlier cultures did not stem from Anatolia, for which Geoffrey's Troy might be shorthand?

LOTHIAN, a district in Scotland:

Lothian is on the south side of the Firth of Forth with Edinburgh at its centre. It appears in the romances in three different ways. It is said be the kingdom of King Loth or Lot; it is

---

[64] It was he who struck the Dolorous Stroke.
[65] *Prose Index*, West, under Apolinus.

the title of the Lady of the Fountain, Laudine; and it is specifically the scene of a conflict for a 'fountain fay' in a late romance localized in Scotland.

Lot was primarily king of Orcanie. He was also king of Loenois, which was contiguous with Cornwall. In respect of Lothian, it looks as if Loth has got involved as a fictitious founding father because of a resemblance of name. As a result, his kingdom Loenois has become equated with Lothian in the minds of narrators and so for some commentators both Loenois and Cornwall have become unnecessarily transferred to Scotland.

In the second way in which Lothian appears, the name of the Lady of the Fountain was Laudine which is generally equated with Lodonensis, a Latinized form of Lothian. However, Chrétien places Yvain's battle for this lady at Barenton in Brittany, a far cry from Lothian.

It is difficult to draw satisfactory conclusions from names but there is a suggestion about the name Laudine which seems worth consideration. This name could really have been l'undine, meaning a water spirit, a change between 'n' and 'u' being common enough when Gothic script is copied. Laudine's title – of the spring – is exactly in line with the meaning of l'undine. Such a derivation would explain how a lady of Lothian came to be so far afield in Brittany. According to this view, the only link between Laudine and Lothian would be a chance resemblance between her name and Lodonensis.

As far as the third appearance of Lothian in the romances is concerned, to locate Laudine in Brittany does not by any means detract from other localizations in Scotland or anywhere else. There can be no objection to the notion that the combat for kingship of the Woodland Glade would have taken place at more than one site. The same applies to the combat at the fountain. To give a local 'lady of the Fountain' the title 'of Lothian' merely draws attention to the practice in Lothian of one aspect of the 'challenge' system which seems, according to the romances, to have been widespread in Britain.

Just how many such sites there were where kingship depended on a local spirit of sovereignty is little more than guess-work, but kingdoms are likely to have been small in comparison to those of modern times. The challenge knight seems to have been content with a simple life-style. His residence was generally a mere tent, though dignified by the name pavilion, and sometimes it was only a leafy bower; his true reward, apart from the person of the fountain fay, was not possessions but honour, the status of a temporary divinity. So there was no need for substantial capital expenditure on religious infrastructure requiring, like the construction of a massive barrow or a medieval cathedral, control of the surplus production from a large, well-populated area. The romances give two clues as to the size of realm in those pagan times when kings were selected for fighting ability. Sometimes the presence of all knights and ladies within a day or two's journey was required at a tournament, implying a catchment area comparable with a traditional county, of which there were ninety five in England, Scotland and Wales together. The other clue is that knights errant generally sent defeated defenders back to Camelot, where they usually became members of the Round Table. The Round Table can be looked at as a collection of challenge knights from the whole country, the result of muscular evangelism. The total number of 'knights' is said to have been one hundred and fifty,[66] which according to this view would be the number of 'Sovereignties' in Britain. Of course, no reliance can be placed on the accuracy of either figure, but each suggests that the realms of sacrificed sacred kings may have coexisted in considerable numbers.

Scottish tradition surviving into the middle ages has provided an insight into the longevity, as well as the spread, of the priestly order of the Arthurian system. N. Tolstoy argues in his persuasive *The Quest for Merlin* that a late representative of that distinguished line of priestly office holders, the Merlins, was still going strong a century or so after the times of the historical Arthur. He seems to have represented a tradition which

---

[66] An alternative number is 366, perhaps significant in a different way.

survived from the hunter fisher culture which preceded the first farmers. For many thousands of years the succession of shamans or medicine men continued. Apparently, adding astronomy to their priestly skills at one time enabled them for a period to enjoy a few centuries as the guiding spirits of a great culture. But they were eventually supplanted; the clear skies of the Bronze Age deserted them, and the last of them finished up as the hungry hanger-on of a barbarous petty king in a backwater in the sixth century AD.

MALEHAUT:

Malehaut scarcely appears in the romances except as the title of a certain lady of Malehaut, who was an important person, being the lover of Galehot and the confidante of Guenever. The place Malehaut shared a border with Estrangort, so it was in mid-Wales, near the Severn. After a battle three miles from the hill of Malehaut, blood flowed into a stream and thence into the Severn, making it red for a day.[67]

MALVERN:

The hero Yder in the romance of the same name killed two giants in single combat at their stronghold in the forest of Malvern (p. 48). It was surrounded by a palisade of sharp stakes with severed heads on them. The location is specifically stated to have been above the Val de Saverne, so once again a cult site is identified as having been in the Severn valley.

NEMUS PLACE-NAMES IN BRITAIN:

The word nemus has a specific meaning of 'woodland clearing'.[68] Its use in the context of Nemi implies a sacred enclosure. The sense of cult site is extended by Rivet and Smith to include constructed enclosures. In general use, the word means open woodland with grazing, or woodland in the broadest sense.

Aquae Arnemetiae:

A notable spring at Buxton in Derbyshire – a county known for well-dressing today.

Medionemeton:

On or near the Antonine Wall. Perhaps the henge at Carnpapple near Edinburgh.[69]

Metambala:

A cult site at the mouth of the river Wye.[70] Richmond and Crawford equate this place, which is mentioned only in the Ravenna Cosmography, with the site of a miraculous apple growing on an ash tree, recorded by Nennius. They suggest that the name is a corruption of Nemetabala, the Sacred Grove of Apple Trees, or else of Nemetambala, the Sacred Navel (of the World, implied).

Nametwihc:

Nantwich in Cheshire, a place where there are salt springs. (But Ekwall gives a different explanation of the derivation of this name.)

Nemetona:

The goddess of the grove worshipped at the hot spring at Bath.[71]

---

[67] *Vulgate*, VII, p. 202 line 1.
[68] *Golden Bough*, Part I, pp. 2f.
[69] *Place Names of Roman Britain*, Rivet and Smith, under Medionemeton. The authors quote Piggott for Carnpapple. Their own choice is Arthur's O'on, a Roman triumphal construction. The arguments here that nemetons are native ceremonial sites favour the choice of Carnpapple.
[70] *Archaeologia*, XCIII, under Metambala.
[71] *Gods of the Celts*, Miranda Green, p. 111.

Nemetostatio:
   By North Tawton in Devonshire.[72]

Nymet, Nympton etc.
   In Devonshire. They are named after rivers which originally bore the name Nymet, having the same derivation as the other Nemus-names.[73]

Nympsfield:
   In Gloucestershire, on the ancient route to the ford across the Severn from the Arlingham peninsula and about nine miles to the east of it. (Ekwall)

Rigonemetis:
   Not a place-name but part of a dedication found in Lincolnshire. It means 'to the King of the Sacred Grove'.[74]

Vernemeton:
   'the especially sacred grove' in Nottinghamshire.[75]

These names are all derived from classical sources or from the study of place names. There are no names in the romances or the Welsh tradition reminiscent of Nemi. Although the romances provide many examples of the custom of Nemi, and the Nemus names tend to confirm the practice, particularly Rigonemetis, the word nemus has not made much impression on the oral tradition. A possible exception is the use of the word 'nemus' to describe Aurelius's hall in a verse version of Geoffrey's *Historia*.

NORGALES, a kingdom:
   Literally, Norgales means North Wales. Logres was to the east, and to the south were several smaller principalities: Estrangort, Malehaut, Estroite Marche and Cambenic, the latter of which had a boundary with Norgales along a small river. The 'royal family' of Norgales plays a considerable part in the doings of Celtic divinities. Gawain and his kin were descended from one princess of Norgales and its queen was an associate of Morgan le Fay.

NORHOMBELLANDE, HUMBELLANDE, NORBELLANDE etc., a kingdom:
   The country which is north of the 'Hombre', which river is described in the romances as a tributary of the Severn. The Hombre, as already pointed out, is not to be thought of as the present day Humber, nor is Norhombellande as the present day Northumberland. As well as having a tributary of the Severn as its boundary, Northumberland has a boundary with Norgales.[76]
   Mythologically speaking, Norhombellande was the residence of Merlin's guide and mentor, Blaise. It was the birthplace of Balin and it was an important haunt of Merlin's, where he appeared as the Lord of the Animals, alternatively known as the Sergeant of Norhombellande.

ORCANIE, a kingdom:
   Orcanie was the kingdom of Lot. His wife was Arthur's sister, called Margawse by Malory and perhaps a pale shadow of Morgan. Their children include Gawain and other important heroes. West gives the Orkney Isles for Orcanie, though perhaps thought of as a kingdom in Britain.

ORGUELLOUSE EMPRISE, a stronghold:
   The Proud Enterprise was built by Galehot as a prison for Arthur, whom he originally

---

72 *Roman Place Names*, Rivet and Smith, under Nemetostatio.
73 Ekwall.
74 *Gods of the Celts*, Miranda Green, p. 111.
75 *Roman Place Names*, Rivet and Smith, under Vernemeton.
76 *Grimaud*, ed. Hucher, vol. III, p. 331.

intended to attack and make captive, before being dissuaded from doing so by Lancelot. The Proud Enterprise was the strongest place in the country, a rock washed by a rushing torrent which fell into the Severn four miles or so away. The other links of the Proud Enterprise, including its builder, are generally with Sorelois so it was on one of the rivers of South-East Wales or Monmouth running south into the Severn. This place is sometimes called Angarde, meaning lookout, instead of Emprise.

ROCEBORC:

Roxburgh in Scotland. The author of Fergus, the late romance in which this town appears, incorporated historical personages in his work and set it in a realistic landscape with contemporary place names. The motifs of the story are reminiscent of incidents in earlier romances such as the 'challenge' in *Yvain*.[77]

ROCHE AS SESNES, the Saxon (i.e. Sarrassin) Rock:

Roche as Sesnes was near Arestuel which was beyond Norgales on a journey which began at the mouth of the Severn; it was contiguous with Cambenic, which was on the Severn and had a border with Norgales; and it was near Estrangort, which had a boundary with Cambenic and also with Norgales. From these it seems that Roche as Sesnes was in Wales to the west of the group of realms which stretched along the Severn on the Welsh side and presumably, because of its links with Norgales, towards the north of the country.

Arestuel is always described as 'en Escoce', that is in Scotland. The reasons for not believing the Scotland of the romances to be present day Scotland are given in the Gazetteer, part 2 below, under Escoce.

The approximate location of Roche as Sesnes and Arestuel enables ARONDEL to be placed, since it was on the border of Cambenic and Arestuel. Commentators agree that Arundel in Sussex is not meant by the Arondel of the romances. Unfortunately it is impossible to be more precise than 'somewhere in mid-Wales', which is a pity, because the only clue to the whereabouts of the river DYANNE is that it was between Arondel and Bedingran. The position of the latter is by no means certain, but its links with Carmelide and 'Ireland' predominate so unless it means Igraine's Grave (see Bedingran in Gazetteer part two below), it may have been in the general area of South-West Wales, presumably to the north, but how far north it stretched is not known. Perhaps some Welsh river once bore the name of Diana or Don. The links described above are fairly tenuous and really only exclude South Wales and the Severn valley rather than pointing directly towards a possible site for the Dyanne.

ROCHE MABON:

Though mentioned only once in the whole of the romances, and without any apparent pagan significance, this rock has an interesting title, being named after the god Mabon. Since the name Mabon has survived the centuries attached to a real rock, the Lochmabenstane near Gretna Green, one cannot help wondering if this is the Roche Mabon in question.

ROCHE MARGOT:

A place on the Severn, not far from the forest of Brequeham, where there was a battle between the rebel kings and the 'Sesne'.

ROESTOC:

The plains of Roestoc and the city of the same name were between Camelot and the tidal part of the river Severn, perhaps nearer the latter. Its ruler was entitled the Dame de Roestoc. Her personal name is not revealed but her background is indicated, for she made two knights fight on an island. Her castellan was Helys, the brother of Mabonagrein.

---

[77] D. D. R. Owen on the Romance of Fergus, *Arthurian Literature VIII*, ed. R. W. Barber.

ROEVANT:

A place which was near the Val sans Retour. Arthur held a court here at mid-August, a date which roughly corresponds to the feast day of Diana. At this court Bors was driven past in the shameful cart, his legs tied to the shafts, and he was pelted with filth by the populace. Evidently a sacred king was so disposed of here in Wales, after he had served the goddess and engendered a son.

Although there are indications that the Val sans Retour was in Wales, it sounds much more like a notional place than a real one, so not much reliance can be placed on it as a guide to the location of Roevant. However, it is also said that the Castle of the Cart (which was where Lancelot of the Lake rode in the cart) was near the border between Logres and Gorre, and a manuscript variation of the name Roevant is Caravent. Caerwent in Gwent would neatly fit these two indications of place. It was a tribal centre before it became an important Roman town. The Roman name, Venta Silures, uses a word 'Venta' which occurs in the names of other tribal centres, Winchester was Venta Belgarum and Caister in Norfolk was Venta Icenorum. The word Venta seems to have the same implication as 'locus' does in the Ravenna cosmography – a folk meeting place which would have been of religious as well as political and social importance. This status might have persisted over many centuries, perhaps from the times when replaced heroes were exposed to the taunts of the crowd in four wheeled carts.

ROME, the Eternal City:

In the 'matter of Britain', Rome means Rome as a place, but the title 'Emperor of Rome' applied to Lucius Hiberius is a fiction.[78]

SALISBURY PLAIN:

To recapitulate briefly the analysis in the section on Location of Temples and Perrons in Geography above: before the Grail religion was brought to Logres the site of Camelot was the principal pagan site in the country and where the pagan kings of the Sarrassins were crowned. Before ever any stone was set up at Stonehenge, Uther fought and defeated the Sesnes at the site of the present monument. The fetching and erection of the bluestones resulted from this encounter. Uther was buried in the most conspicuous tomb in the (barrow?) cemetery on the Plain, and his brother Ambrosius at Stonehenge itself.

Much later in the story, to establish his ascendancy over the rebel kings, Arthur assembled the great gathering on Salisbury Plain at a tall rock, which was now where the commune of the people assembled.[79] The gathering included contingents from along the western seaboard from the Loire to Orkney.

The same tall rock was the site of Arthur's last battle against Mordred, the end of the Arthurian era. It is assumed here that the tall, hard rock is a megalithic monument on Salisbury Plain, probably Stonehenge.

Although the bluestone move is described in some detail, the much grander Sarsen circle is unrepresented in the romances, unless it is by a reference to the most beautiful hall in the world, with thirty tapering pillars as tall as lances, built by the high prince Galehot, but not given any location.

It is disappointing that the scene of so many important pagan edifices is unrepresented in Latin literature, unless it is the place meant by Hecateus, a Greek historian of the sixth century B.C. He is reported by Diodorus Siculus[80] as describing an island inhabited by Hyperboreans, not smaller than Sicily, situated in the north, opposite the coast of Celtic Gaul, in which Latona was born, for which reason the inhabitants worship Apollo (the son of Leto or Latona) more than any other god.

---

[78] P. 117.
[79] *Vulgate*, II, pp. 382f.
[80] Book II, 47, 1–5.

'And there is also on the island both a magnificent sacred precinct of Apollo and a notable temple which is adorned with many votive offerings and is spherical in shape. Furthermore, a city is there which is sacred to this god, and the majority of its inhabitants are players on the cithera: and they continually play on this instrument in the temple and sing hymns of praise to the god, glorifying his deeds.'

The account goes on to say that Greeks visited the island, and that the moon there appears near to the earth, so that eminences of a terrestrial form are plainly seen in it. Apollo visits the island once in a course of nineteen years, in which period the stars complete their revolutions, and for that reason the Greeks distinguish the cycle of nineteen years by the name of 'the Great Year of nineteen years'. During the season of his appearance the god plays upon the harp and dances every night from the vernal equinox to the rising of the Pleiades, pleased with his own successes. The supreme authority in that city and the sacred precinct is vested in those who are called Boreadae, being the descendants of Boreas, and their governments have been uninterruptedly transmitted in this line.

The main objection to identification of this island as Britain is that early geographers regarded the Hyperboreans as living much further to the north. Apart from that, the geographical description tallies in every respect; Mabon and his mother correspond to Apollo and Leto; the sacred precinct is a conspicuous strand of British paganism; and the interest in astronomy corresponds to the religion practised in Britain in the Bronze Age, which might well have been remembered in the time of Hecateus. The word 'spherical' used of the temple may imply 'astronomical function', rather than a somewhat improbable shape.

The possibility that the name Boreas corresponds to both the Arthurian King Bors and to Geoffrey's Ambrosius will be discussed in Who's Who?

SARPENIC, a forest:
Sarpenic was in Gorre.[81] It contained the Valley of No Return, the Dolorous Tower and the cult site with a ring of severed heads on stakes defended by Maduc.

SARRAS, a city with an important sun-temple:
Sarras was the scene of one of the most significant episodes in the Arthurian Legend, the year-long kingship of Galahad, followed by his death in association with the deadly lance, the blood-filled Grail and a blast of heat and light.

Given the medieval involvement with the Holy Land it is inevitable that there should have been confusion between the Sarrassins of Sarras and the Saracens of the middle East. This led narrators of the romances to put Sarras eleven miles from Jerusalem. However, it seems really to have been a place in Britain, for the earliest inhabitants of this country are always called Sarassins unless they are giants. Looked at closely, the romances do distinguish these local Sarassins from the Saracens of the Middle East. They are said to have taken their name from the city of Sarras, rather from the name of Sarah, Abraham's wife.

The links between Sarras and the rest of the British tradition are as follows: the King of Sarras was Evalac, a name which corresponds closely to that of the Welsh ancestor deity Avallach; Evalac and his goddess-dolly is a theme repeated in Geoffrey of Monmouth's native source, which has nothing to do with the Middle East, and also in the equally native Tristan legend; Evalac (at the end of his life, when he was known as Mordrain) was cured by blood from the Grail and is easily recognisable as a Maimed King of the type familiar at Corbenic in Wales; and the name of Evalac's queen, Sarracinte, which was repeated in a second generation, suggests sovereignty, a common motif in the native

81 *Vulgate*, IV, p. 236.

paganism. It is also said that the Sarrassins, the people of Sarras, were the inhabitants of the exclusively British Camelot.

Although there are enough links between Sarras and the British tradition to suggest that it was in Britain, it is not easy to locate it more accurately as there are two contradictory lines of approach.

The main clue is that Galahad became King of Sarras,[82] but he performed the ritual demonstrating kingship, drawing the sword from the stone, at Camelot. Camelot is described as the principal religious centre of the Sarrassins. What more natural than that the place called in one account the holy city of the Sarrassins should in another have been the holy city of Sarras? On the other hand it was at Corbenic that Galahad's forerunner Perceval, who may be supposed nearer to the Welsh original, became king. Here, like Pelles of Corbenic and all the other Grail kings who lived at the Grail Castle, he was entitled Fisher King. This would suggest that Sarras was equivalent to Corbenic in Terre Foraine in Wales.[83]

Perhaps, to take into account both the alternative locations, one in Wales and the other in Logres, the original scene of these cult activities was in Wales, where Perceval's maimed father lived and which was the location of the 'Perilous seat' at Arberth and of the Grail castle of Corbenic. Later, with the general shift from Cardoel to Camelot, the action may have shifted to Logres.

The affairs of Sarras and the Sarrassins are further complicated by the misunderstandings between Sarrasins and Saxons already mentioned, but, however central to the Arthurian story the Saxons may seem to be to readers of certain romances, they play a negligible part in the most famous exposition of all, Malory's *Morte Darthur*, and the story in no way suffers.

Where the Saxons do appear in the romances, their kings are named in detail. These so-called Saxon kings often have names incorporating Bran, such as Branmague, Brandalis, Brandon, Brangor and Hardagabran, and they are sometimes, like Newstead's Brans, giants. My guess is that the high proportion of Bran names among 'Saxon' kings is not due to a contrivance by which narrators filled in blank spaces with names picked up at random but represents an original association between Bran names, giants and the Sarrassins. This supposition is in conformity with other indications of the period to which Bran belongs, which put him in an early stratum, like the Sarrassins.

SINADOUN: *see* KINK KENADON.

SORELOIS, a country:
Sorelois stretched westward from the Severn along the south coast of Wales up to the forest of Darnantes. More details are provided under Gorre, q.v.

SORESTAN, a kingdom:
Sorestan was between Sorelois and Norgales. Its queen was one of a trio of enchantresses (that is, goddesses), the others being Morgan le Fay and Sebile.[84]

TANEBORC, a residence of Arthur's and site of a tournament, said to be at the entrance to Norgales:
Taneborc was perhaps in what is now Shropshire or Cheshire, but not to be more closely identified. In the *Lai of Doon* there is a place called Danebroc, whose mistress is married by the hero, Doon. This could be a recollection of the Do/Don system and so identify Taneborc/Danebroc as a cult site but does not help to locate it.

---

[82] *Morte Darthur*, bk XVII, chs 11 and 22.
[83] In Who's Who? it is argued that Pelles, of Corbenic, and Evalac, of Sarras, are the same personage.
[84] Thought by some to be Cybele, by others the Sybil.

TANINGUES:
The dukedom of Brandelis, situated to the east of the Severn. It was not far from Roestoc, and Gawain travelled thence across the Severn on his way to Norgales.[85]

TERRE FORAINE, a country linked with Gorre (q.v.):
Terre Foraine seems to have been between the river Severn and either the Wye or the Usk. It was the scene of an early evangelizing mission by the Grail cult, which led to the establishment of Corbenic, the Grail Castle, and the castration there of Kalafes by 'light-ning'. In the grip of this cult, it supposedly became waste as a result of the Dolorous Stroke.

The first Galahad, King of Wales, founded an 'abbey' at the burning tomb of Symeu in Terre Foraine.[86] This site became known as the Holy Cemetery, and King Galahad himself was eventually buried there in a tomb which consisted of a slab on top of four pillars.[87]

Terre Foraine was yet another of the places of 'no return', like the Val sans Retour, the Val de Servage and the various dolorous prisons – which generally required the defeat of their lord by a supreme champion to procure the release of the captives. The prisoners of Terre Foraine were deliberately trapped to replace the original population which had been wiped out in a war between Urien and Uther. Inhabitants of Logres were allowed to enter Terre Foraine, where they lived in unfortified towns, but they were prevented from leaving by castles at the exits.

When Meleagant abducted Guenever, and she thus became one of the captives, Lance-lot followed her trail, entering Terre Foraine at the Entree Galesche, near the castle of the Cart. On his way through the country he came across Galehot's and Moys' tombs in the Holy Cemetery. Finally, he crossed the Sword-bridge into the capital city of Gorre, de-feated Meleagant there, and released Guenever, the Exiles having been freed en route.

TERRE GASTE, the Waste Land:
The Waste Land is a generic term for places supposedly overwhelmed by having a castrated king. This fate is said to have fallen on part of South Wales, variously described as Listenois, Gales and Terre Foraine. Terre Deserte, in Brittany, is another example of the same kind, having been laid waste, like Terre Foraine, by Uther.

In the *Mabinogion* the Waste Land is associated with sitting on the throne mound at Arberth.

THAMISE, the river:
The Thames is scarcely ever mentioned in the romances, confirming the conclusion that London and the east of Britain were unimportant in the section of the Celtic oral tradition that was the foundation of the 'matter of Britain'.

TINTAGEL:
A castle by the sea belonging to duke Hoel of Cornwall. The spelling of this name is very variable. At Tinaguel Lancelot defeated two fencers, which sounds like a variation on the story of the defeat of four fencers at Pintagoel by Galeschin. Has 'P' changed to 'T' to match a real place-name or the reverse? It was a duke of Tyntaiuel who cut off King Lancelot's head, letting it fall in the fountain, and another duke of Tintaoel was Ygerne's first husband. Uther Pendragon slept with Ygerne at Tintagel in the guise of the duke, her husband, when Arthur was conceived. There is no topographical clue in the romances as to whether this place really was Tintagel on the north coast of Cornwall but it is generally accepted to have been so. The chapel there in the Middle Ages was dedicated to St Ulette, or Uliane, or Julian. The latter form is found as a corruption of Alain le Gross, who

85 *Vulgate*, III, p. 299.
86 *Prose Index*, West.
87 *Prose Lancelot . . .*, ed. Hutchings, p. 45A.

doubles up with Pellinor (and some others) as Perceval's father. There could be a slight ripple from past paganism here.

TREBES:
    King Ban's capital city in Benoic, q.v.

VAL DE SERVAGE:
    The country of Servage was at the extremity of Norgales opposite the isle of Giants. There was a castle there called Glat which dominated a plain, ringed by high mountains, through which ran a river called Marse.[88] Val de Servage resembles Val Sans Retour in some ways and Terre Foraine in others. Visitors were all held captive there and could only be released if the lord was defeated in single combat. The interest here is that the 'lord' was the giant Nabon the Black, Nabon being an alternative form of the name Mabon, the deity. It was Tristan who eventually killed him and released the prisoners.
    It is something of a puzzle that Mabon, the Celtic equivalent of Apollo, should sometimes be a *black* knight, yet this colour is applied also to Belenus, as Belyas le Noir, and to Bors, who fought as a black knight at Tertre Desvoyé. All three could be expected for various reasons to have the quality of brightness rather than darkness.
    Since the only substantial island off the coast of North Wales is Anglesey, Val de Servage might be thought of as the Caernarfon area. Loomis has identified Caernarfon as the site of the adventure of the Lady of Sinadoun who was turned into a serpent by the magicians Mabon and Yrain. Thus the god Mabon appears in the neighbourhood of Caernarfon in both localizations.

VAL SANS RETOUR, the Valley of No Return:
    The localization of the Val sans Retour in the forest of Paimpont in Brittany owes its existence to nineteenth century romanticists. Indeed the whole concept is so much in the realm of folklore that it might seem pointless to look for the location of what was a wholly imaginary site. For, of course, there never was a Valley of No Return, just as there never was a god Beli, except in people's minds. Yet Beli/Belenus is remembered at many cult sites, such as Barenton and Mont St Michel, already mentioned, and also perhaps at a place once called Kaer Belli, now Ashbury, in Cornwall. The god could be localized at places such as these, a spring or a perhaps a sacred grove, without leaving any permanent trace in the ground. Or there might have been some durable construction, such as a shaped stone block, or the boundary of a sacred enclosure or even a temple. Somewhere between the extremes of the wholly imaginary and the wholly real we may draw a line as to what can be localized by a name clinging to the spot and another line for what can not only be localized in this way but would have left tangible traces for a fortunate archaeologist to find. If it is possible to locate on a map the traces of so ephemeral a being as a deity, may not the same be said of the Valley of No Return? Perhaps the most obvious explanation of this place is that it was thought of as the abode of the spirits of the dead, though it seems that the Celtic Otherworld is an abode of the gods rather than of human souls. But even something so intangible could have been given an imaginary location. So at a certain cross-roads by a tertre in the forest of Sarpenic we are told that one road led to the Valley of No Return, and others led to Sorelois and to the Dolorous Tower.

THE VALLEYS OF CAMELOT:
    This was the realm of the castrated Julian le Gros,[89] otherwise Alain le Gros (or else Pellinor), and his wife, the Widow Lady, whose domain has already been described as the West Wales Camelot. The Grail cult seems to have been sea-borne. To a sea-faring man

---

[88] *Roman de Tristan*, Löseth, paras. 62f.
[89] *Prose Index*, West, under Iglai, Julian, Veve Dame and Veuve.

who had experienced the turbulent waters off the rocky peninsula of South West Wales, the most conspicuous feature of this area would have been the sheltered waters of the valleys whose rivers merge into Milford Haven. One of these leads up to Narberth, where there was a 'perilous seat' and it is also on the most likely route of the removal of the bluestones on their way to Salisbury Plain.

VANDEBERES, a fortified town:

It is unfortunate that the location of Vandeberes is somewhat vague, for it is described in greater detail than most places. It is said to have been very strong, in open ground with no hill or mountain within two miles or so. There were round the town great banks and ditches and large deep lakes amongst great marshes. Outside the water and the defences was a wall with stone towers not more than twelve feet apart. There were two entrances, heavily strengthened, and the marsh was as wide as an arbalister can shoot and fully four miles long.[90]

After a battle before Clarence (which had a boundary with South Wales), the losers dispersed towards Vandeberes, Arestuel and Roestoc. The most likely location for Vandeberes is therefore in mid-Wales.

WINCHESTER, the city of that name:

The one time importance of Winchester as capital city was well known to the narrators of the romances. Long before Alfred's time it had been Venta Belgarum, the tribal meeting place of the local Celtic people. The modern name consists of a first syllable 'Win' derived from 'venta' and a second meaning castle. However, the first syllable could easily be mistaken for a derivative of the Welsh 'guen' for white, so any similar sounding place-name meaning White Castle would probably have been assimilated to it.

WINDESORES:

A castle in the forest of Brequeham, so it is west of the Severn, and is therefore not Windsor in Berkshire. Sommer[91] regards Windesores as being a version of an entirely different place, Lindesores, assimilated to Windsor on account of the likeness between the names. Lindesores seems to have been in Broceliande, not Brequeham, showing how easily the magic forests of Britain and of Brittany could be confused.

90 *Vulgate*, II, p. 176.
91 *Vulgate*, index.

## II.  Unidentified Places

ATRE PERELOX, the Perilous Graveyard:

Gawain killed a devil here, and also a wicked knight called Escanor. The terrors of graveyards are a feature of the romances. The graveyard of Escalon the Shadowy has been located in a particular district, but not so the Atre Perelox nor the graveyard in the episode in which Perceval's sister obtained for a talisman a scrap of cloth from the shroud of a dead knight who had been buried in a tomb accessible only to people alone and on foot. A similar adventure was undertaken by Lore, Queen of Caradigan, who brought away from the Waste Chapel a scrap of cloth from a coat placed on the altar there by Ris, whose name is an eroded form of Ryons.

BEDINGRAN:

The principal city of Great Britain and of Carmelide. It is variously said to be on the borders of Ireland and Carmelide; in Ireland; and on the border of Cornwall. The latter appears to be incompatible with the rest. If Bedingan is to be given a single location, the link with Cornwall is better disregarded. This place seems more likely to have been in Wales, where such other indications of locality as there are place it. On the other hand, a Welsh name beginning with 'Bedd-' would convey the meaning 'grave'. Bedingan (Bedin-gran, Bedigan, Bendigran, Pedugrain etc.) might thus be a careless French narrator's recollection of Bedd Igran – the grave of Igraine or Ygerne. If I am right in believing Ygerne to be an early goddess her grave could be the style of barrow used by the cult, rather than a city of this world, and so be present in Cornwall and Carmelide and the 'Ireland' of the Arthurian tradition and anywhere else where the cult was practised.

BIAU REPAIRE, a castle surrounded by water and approached by a swinging bridge of osiers:

Biau Repaire comes from an early stratum of the romances, before the Grail hero was saddled with a chastity untypical of the heroes of romance. A certain Blancheflor lived here and was besieged in the castle until rescued by her lover Perceval. It was also the residence of Morcades,[92] one of Ygerne's daughters. Although said to be on the river Lombres (is this the 'river of Shadows' or the 'Hombre'?) Biau Repaire sounds as if it were yet another distorted reflection of the Castle of Maidens complex. But since the Castle of Maidens is not a unique location, this does not locate Biau Repaire.

Blancheflor's name is reminiscent of the flower maidens who regularly attracted the attention of heroes. The original of these 'Florées' was a heathen princess and on conversion to the Grail religion became known as Sarracinte, after the eponymous goddess of Sarras whose husband was Evalac. Another Florée was princess of Escavalon; she was the mistress of Gawain, and bore Guinglain to him. Unlike this second Florée who has a link with the South-East Wales, what is known of Blancheflor does not provide any topographical aid to location.

THE BURNING CITY:

Here Lancelot declined an election to annual kingship which would have ended in death by fire.

THE CASTLE OF TEN KNIGHTS:

A 'challenge' site at which a victorious challenger must take the lord's place if successful and take over the defence of the site himself. Lamorat of Gales won such a combat,

---

[92] *Verse Index*, West.

having first defeated the ten supporting knights, and was thus obliged (the story has it) to marry the damsel of the place.

Lamorat was one of Pellinor's sons. Once again the god Belenus (see Who's Who?) is associated with challenge sites.

CHASTEL ORGUELLOUS :

There was a jousting place here where Bran de Lis did well, and Girflet son of Do was imprisoned here. At noon on Saturday the inhabitants of Chastel Orguellous broke off jousting to a peal of bells, to honour the Mother of God, until nine o'clock on Monday. In that country the Mother of God was more honoured than elsewhere in Christendom.[93] The veneer of Christianity fails to conceal that this was a cult site.

The Proud Knight did not in fact live in the Proud Castle at all but with the Proud Damsel in a tent in a woodland glade at many different locations.

CHALLENGE SITES, UNIDENTIFIED:

(a) sites with pavilions:

(1) Urbain, son of the Queen of the Blackthorn, was requested by his fairy amie to set up a pavilion beside the Adventurous Ford and to defend it against any knight wishing to cross it. They lived in splendour in a castle but this was invisible to all except themselves. To the rest of the world they lived in a tent. A successful challenger was expected to take over the defence. Urbain's selection by the fay, involving a chase on horseback, is reminiscent of a similar incident in the *Mabinogion* in which the prime mover was Rhiannon, wife of Pwyll King of the Otherworld, who is suspected herself to have been a goddess.[94] The outcome of Urbain's adventure involved the transference of the fay and her maids to Avalon in the form of black birds.[95]

(2) Belyas, alternatively Helyas, a black knight, guarded the Fountain the Two Sycamores with his brother Briadan (thought by Loomis to be Beli and Bran). They lived in two pavilions.[96]

(3) Malgiers le Gris, defender of the Isle d'Or, lived in a pavilion at the head of the causeway he defended, next to a row of stakes with heads on them. At this site the damsel of the place expected a winning challenger to take over the defence.[97]

(4) An unnamed knight lived in a pavilion in a grassy clearing which was surrounded by barriers. At the entrance a maiden of great beauty sat under an oak. She told Gawain that the knight of the pavilion guarded the passage against errant knights. To cross the barrier constituted a challenge.[98]

(5) Orilus de Lalander (argued here to be Orguelleus de la Lande, the Proud Knight of the Glade, the embodiment of the defender in the 'challenge' system) had a fine pavilion in a meadow by a ford.[99]

(6) Orguelleus de la Lande in Chrétien and the 'Pride of the Clearing'[100] in *Peredur* both lived with their lovers in tents.

(7) Oriols, a red knight, was defeated by Gawain at a Lande where there was a pavilion, near a spring under an olive tree. Helaés, whom he wished to marry, sat there in the shade of a sycamore.[101]

93  *First Continuation*, lines 11725–9.
94  E.g. *Celtic Heritage*, Rees and Rees, p. 45.
95  Didot *Perceval*, ed. Roach, pp. 195ff.
96  *Vulgate*, V, pp. 252f.
97  *Le Bel Inconnu*, ed. G. Perrie Williams, pp. 56–9 and 66.
98  *Vulgate*, VII, p. 295.
99  *Parzival*, tr. Hatto, pp. 76–8.
100  *Mabinogion*, Penguin, p. 220.
101  *Vulgate*, VII, pp. 265/6.

(8) Baruc, a black knight of the people of Fairyland, wished to marry a pagan queen called Sebile who had her tent in a lande full of tents and people. Sagremor fought in the glade first to possess her and then as her champion, defeating Baruc. Sagremor and Sebile became lovers.[102]

(9) Sephar li Rous guarded the Pont Perdu. When a dwarf blew a horn, the knight came from his pavilion and prepared to defend the bridge against Gawain, but he was defeated because Gawain's strength doubled as midday approached.[103]

(10) Perceval's sister had a black tent pitched in the middle of an island, with a spear and a shield hanging before it, in order to show that jousters could always be found there.[104]

(11) Clochidés guarded the Tertre Desvé, where a challenging knight had to swear to take the place of the defender if he should win. At the top of the hillock there was a castle and a pavilion. Nearby was a most beautiful sycamore and also an oak with a horn hanging from it. By blowing the horn a challenge could be made. Clochidés was defeated by Bors, who took his place as defender.[105]

(12) An unnamed red knight fought Sagremor at a very rich pavilion under an oak, where blowing a horn was the signal of a challenge.[106]

(13) King Arthur, with a black shield, defended a ford where there was a pavilion. Arthur was guarding the passage after having 'liberated' it.[107]

(14) Guiron fell in love with the lady of the Isle Desvé. To please her he set up a pavilion for them both, by a spring at the entry of the plain. Here he challenged all comers.[108]

(15) Perceval came upon a red tent with a girl in it, in a prairie above a fountain. Her attendants were four damsels with chaplets of primroses and violets. A knight called Gauliien carried off the girl, but Perceval defeated him and took the girl back to the pavilion.[109]

(16) Perceval killed a lion and then a knight in a beautiful meadow surrounded by a high wall. In the middle was a tref (an elaborate tent) above a fountain. In front of the tref was a cypress tree, and inside it a beautiful fair girl.[110]

(17) Perceval came upon a lande in the forest in which was a tall leafy tree with a very rich tent below it and two loges galesches (leafy arbours). There was a girl under the tree, which had a stag's head hanging from a branch. Perceval took the head and fought a knight called Garsalas, whom he defeated and sent to Arthur's court as a prisoner.[111]

(18) Gawain defeated Brun de la Lande in a lande in which there was a tree with a pavilion underneath it containing a beautiful damsel richly dressed wearing a chaplet of flowers and leaves.[112]

(19) Perceval came upon the Amorous Ford, which was guarded by a white knight who had a rich tent in a meadow across the water. They fought and Perceval sent his defeated opponent to Arthur. Here the winning challenger was obliged to remain as defender.[113]

(20) A knight with a pavilion in a grassy place enclosed by 'brokes' had a shield hung from a bush. Girflet knocked it down to provoke a fight, but he lost.[114]

102 *Vulgate*, VII, pp. 280f.
103 *Vulgate*, IV, pp. 194/5.
104 *Folie Lancelot*, Bogdanow, p. 95.
105 *Vulgate*, V, pp. 235–40.
106 *Vulgate*, IV, pp. 306f.
107 *Guiron le Courtois*, Lathuillère, para. 21.
108 *Guiron le Courtois*, para. 231.
109 Potvin, vol. VI, lines 41110f. and line 41312.
110 Potvin, vol. IV, lines 23314f. and 23378.
111 Potvin, vol. IV, lines 27007–27055.
112 *Second Continuation*, Potvin, lines 33218–33276.
113 Potvin, vol. IV, lines 24191f.
114 Huth *Merlin*, Paris and Ulrich, vol. I, pp. 175 and 181/2.

(21) Gawain came upon a pavilion beside a fountain in a clearing, and made love to the damsel in it. This provoked a battle with her father, Ider of Lis, who was killed. A second combat with Ider's son Bran de Lis followed.[115] The child born as a result of this encounter was Le Bel Inconnu.

**(b) Sites where damsels sit under trees:**

Arthur's adventure in the glade, with which this enquiry began, includes a typical motif, the damsel sitting under a tree, often presiding over a challenge. The title of this tree, 'the Oak of the Glade', might suggest that the oak would be a significant species of tree in this respect. Analysis shows this not to be the case.

(1) The damsel who sits under the 'Chesne de la lande'[116] at the entrance to St Augustine's glade.

(2) The damsel who sits under an oak by the barrier of stakes which Gawain merely had to cross to challenge the knight of the pavilion in the glade.[117]

(3) A damsel who sits under an oak is Perceval's cousin; she holds the headless corpse of her lover.[118]

(4) The damsel who sits under an oak holding her unconscious lover who has been severely wounded at the Bourne (i.e. boundary) of Galvoie.[119]

(5) Orguelleuse de Logres, who sits under an elm, wearing a circlet of gold.[120]

(6) Mabonagrein's lover, who reclines under a sycamore in the Joy of the Court episode in *Erec*.

(7) A veiled damsel, Saraide, sits under a pine on top of a tertre where there is single combat after a challenge.[121]

(8) A veiled damsel, Helaés, sits under a sycamore where a red defender fights in a glade where there is a spring, pavilion and olive tree.[122]

(9) A damsel sits under an elm where Hector fights a red knight in an open space surrounded by sharp stakes.[123]

(10) A girl sits under an unidentified tree in a glade with a pavilion, where Perceval takes down a stag's head and provokes a fight with Garsalas.[124]

(11) The Damsel of the Harp lies under a pine while Gawain fights Rous de la Falaise.[125]

(12) Greomar's amie sits under a sycamore by a fountain. Sagremor killed him there.[126]

ESCOCE, apparently the country of Scotland:

The modern name Scotland is derived from the name of an element of the Irish population who migrated there. These Irish 'Scotti' did not subdue Scotland until after the period of the 'historical' Arthur so the use of the word Escoce may be misleading. The term Scottish continued for some centuries after that to have the alternative meaning of Irish, and since there are no topographical indications that the Escoce of the romances is the Scotland of today, the 'Escoce' and the 'Ireland' of the romances cannot be distinguished

---

115 *Sir Gawain and the Lady of Lys,* tr. Weston, pp. 34/9.
116 *Perlesvaus,* ed. Nitze and Jenkins, note to line 433 on p. 41.
117 *Vulgate,* VII, pp. 294/5.
118 *Li Contes del Graal,* ed. Hilka, line 3431.
119 *Li Contes del Graal,* ed. Hilka, line 6540. Original for 'bourne' is 'bosne'. Luttrell gives marche for this.
120 *Li Contes del Graal,* ed. Hilka, line 6676.
121 *Vulgate,* IV, pp. 248 and 251.
122 *Vulgate,* VII, pp. 265/6.
123 *Vulgate,* IV, pp. 349f.
124 Potvin, IV, lines 27007–27055.
125 *Vulgate,* VII, pp. 178f.
126 *Vulgate,* VII, p. 194.

from each other. Escoce seems to be contiguous with or synonymous with 'Ireland' on the west coast, including a station in Wales (see Roche as Sesnes). The equivalence of Escoce and Ireland has previously been commented on, for instance by Loomis in discussing the attribution of the Irish saint, Brandon, to Escoce. The lack of a firm location for Scotland was evidently realized by a narrator who, having said a place was in 'Escoce', went on to explain that it was so called because it belonged to the King of Scotland, not because it was in the country of Scotland.[127] So the description 'in Escoce' does not necessarily lead north of the present border.

In the romances places said to be in Escoce, such as Roche as Sesnes and Arestuel, have links with Cambenic, Norgales and Malehaut which are all close to the river Severn on the Welsh side.

FLOUDEHOUG, a seaport:

Floudehoug was the landing place in southern England for travellers from Brittany. There are several sheltered landing places which it might be but no indications, apart from the vaguest name-resemblances, as to which is to be preferred.

The FORD of the QUEEN:

This was across the river 'Hombre' near Dolorous Gard and led towards Carlion. Carlion is a name which often has alternative Car- names in different versions of the manuscript, so it is not on its own a basis for identification. There are too many imponderables here to justify an exact location but there is general support for a site in Wales.

The FORD of MABON:

This crossed the river of Mabon and, though neither can be identified, the last place mentioned in the story was Carlion.

THE FORD PERILOUS OR AMOROUS:

This was the ford defended by Urbain for the love of a fay.[128] There is no indication of where it was.

LA FORÉT DE L'ESPINE, the Thorny Forest:

There are several forests with rather similar names – l'Espine, Espinoie, Sapinoie, Sapine and Sarpenic. Some of them have the appearance of being localized, the last two in Gorre. However, the possibility must be envisaged that they do not represent real places, but are a sort of purgatory – that Whinnymoor to which we come at last, where the thorns will lacerate the ungenerous to the bare bone.

THE FORESTS PERILOUS AND ADVENTUROUS:

These are best regarded as descriptive of forests in general and not as defining specific places. Thus, though an identifiable forest, Aroie, may be called 'the adventurous forest', not all the events taking place in adventurous forests necessarily happened in Aroie.

THE FOUNTAIN OF GALABES:

When Ambrosius wished to commemorate his fallen countrymen with a suitable monument (which turned out to be the bluestone circle of Stonehenge), he was advised to consult Merlin, who was 'wont to haunt' the spring called Fons Galabes in the land of the Gewissae. The land of the Gewissae has been described as a sort of enlarged Wessex stretching as far as the Bristol Channel, but it is also rendered as Gwent (i.e. to the south-east of Wales) in the Everyman edition of Geoffrey of Monmouth, and both Wace and Layamon put this fountain in Wales. The name Galabes is indistinguishable from that

---

[127] Hucher, vol. III, p. 229. 'Si n'estoit mie issi apielés pour con fust Ecosse mais pour cou que le roys avoit issi non.'
[128] Didot *Perceval*, pp. 195ff.

of Galaphes/Kalafes, the castrated sacred king of Corbenic in Terre Foraine, which also seems to have been in Gwent. The link of this fountain with Kalafes and Merlin indicate very great original importance.

N. Tolstoy in *The Quest for Merlin* suggests that the name Galabes is synonymous with a basic word meaning 'iron' (cf. Greek Khalups for steel). This would identify Fons Galabes as a chalybeate spring, one displaying the red rust marks of contamination by iron. Such a spring occurs in an area associated with Merlin in Scotland. There are thus three pointers towards a location for Fons Galabes – in an enlarged Wessex, in Gwent or in Scotland – none of which on its own is certain enough to take precedence over the others.

THE FOUNTAIN OF GALAHAD:

This was in the Perilous Forest, which is no help in finding a location for it. At this spring King Lancelot, who was married to the King of Ireland's daughter and who was father of Ban (that is, Bran) of Benoic and grandfather of the well-known Sir Lancelot, met his death. He went to drink from the fountain on Easter Day and had his head cut off by a jealous cousin. The fountain thereupon began to boil. Much later in the story the fountain is described as gushing from a silver pipe beside an old, low house which had next to it a tomb between two stones. The bleached head was still in the spring. Finally, Galahad visited the place and stopped the fountain from boiling.

THE FOUNTAIN OF TWO SYCAMORES:

A spring at the end of the Perilous Forest,[129] towards the Waste Land. This is a rather vague description, since the Waste Land could be anywhere subject to magical barrenness, and forests in general seem to have been perilous. The spring was defended by Belyas le Noir. A challenger approaching this 'fountain' found a large clearing in the middle of the forest. In it there was a strong castle with walls and ditches but no water. Below the castle was a valley with two conspicuously large and mature sycamores growing in it, below which a spring gushed from a silver tube. Nearby there were two pavilions. When the challenger announced his intention to fight, a dwarf blew loudly on a horn. Many ladies and damsels, hearing the signal to joust, came from the castle to watch. The defender who lived in one of the pavilions came out to fight clad all in black. Eventually he was defeated by Lancelot and his captives were released.

GLAY, an abbey in Escoce:

Alternatively Glannes or Urglay. When Josephé (son of Joseph of 'Arimathea') died, his talismanic body was taken to this place in Escoce, where it averted a famine.[130]

ISLE MERLIN:

The Isle Merlin was the scene of the celebrated combat between the brothers Balin and Balan. There are no indications of the location of this island but it has several similarities to the castle of Maidens and to Gaihom. It is situated at the junction of a river with the sea; there are many rejoicing women; it is the scene of a combat for the person of the Sovereignty; Merlin later made a very narrow and difficult bridge to the island, reminiscent of the sword bridge at Gaihom; and Merlin also made a testing bed which gave its users complete forgetfulness, different from but reminiscent of the testing bed in the castle of the Marvel. Once again fundamental themes have survived in more than one version, producing in their various combinations episodes and descriptions of sites which the narrators considered to be both real and distinct.

ISLE D'OR:

The Isle of Gold was surrounded by an arm of the sea. It was the scene of the battle between le Bel Inconnu and Maugis.

---

[129] *Prose Index*, West.
[130] *Vulgate*, I, p. 285.

MARES, a castle surrounded by marshes (marais):

The lord of the castle, Agravadain the Black, had a beautiful daughter or niece who had a child by King Ban (Bran) under the influence of Merlin's magic.[131] This child, Lancelot's half-brother, was to become an important hero as Sir Hector of the Marshes. This sounds like a variation on the stories of Lancelot and Bors. The daughter (or niece) was related to the ladies of Roestoc, of Malehaut and of Nohaut, the latter being a sister of King Lot of Orcanie. This group of 'dames' show traces of having once been divinities – they were lovers and mothers of heroes; they were fought over; and they were related to deities. At a guess, the Damsel of the Marshes is a minor divinity, the spirit of the marshes, who, much like the Damsel of the Lake, would be represented by a real woman for ceremonial purposes. As far as location is concerned, she could be found wherever such natural features exist. No doubt she would have had certain favoured places, but there are no clues in the romances as to where they were.

MONT DOLOROUS:

The Sorrowful Mound had a magic pillar on top, erected by Merlin, to which only the most valiant could tether their horses. Merlin's unnamed daughter was entitled 'of Mont Dolorous'.[132] In *Peredur* the Sorrowful Mound is a tumulus, from which a black serpent appeared, fought the hero and was defeated by him. Considering its lack of importance, this place is remarkable for the variety of modern localizations, such as Stirling, Dollar, Edinburgh, Melrose Abbey and the Roman fort of Trimontium.

MONTESCLAIRE:

The Sword of the Strange Hangings was kept here. This sword was used by Varlan to kill Lambor in the version of the Dolorous Stroke in which the King of Gales kills the King of Terre Foraine. The 'strange hangings' were originally of hemp and were said to have been made by Solomon's wife. They were replaced by new ones made by Perceval's sister from her own hair before the sword came into Galahad's possession. Montesclaire has no links with other places which might indicate its position.

NOHAUT:

A place-name which most often appears as the title of a lady, the dame of Nohaut. She played a standard role in the romances, sending to Arthur's court for the help of a champion and offering herself in marriage to the big knight of a pavilion if he would do battle for her and defeat the Arthurian knight. There was a temple of the god Apollo at Nohaut. Jupiter, Mars and Saturn were also worshipped at altars in the temple.[133] An unidentified cult site.

TERTRE DESVÉ, the deceiving hill:

This Tertre, also called Desvoyé, was defended by Clochidés, as described in *Challenge*, pp. 55f.

The Tertre Desvoyé was about a days journey from the Fountain of the Two Sycamores, which itself was at the end of the Perilous Forest, towards the Waste Land. These are generic terms, able to be applied to any forest or country, and so are unsuitable as the basis of a localization.

TURNING ISLAND, a large island in the western ocean with a circumference of eighty miles:

Turning Island was between Ornagrine and Port Astriges,[134] neither of which can be

---

131 *Vulgate*, II, pp. 402f.
132 *Verse Index*, West.
133 *Prose Index*, West, under Apolinus.
134 *Prose Index*, West, under Isle Torneant.

identified. It had been set up as a cult site by Merlin in the time of Uther and was defended by the lover of the damsel of the place and four other knights. It was approached from the mainland by a causeway and a bridge. At the base of the causeway was a sort of abbey, described as a 'house of converts'. At this place the natives of the country had built beautiful gardens long before Merlin brought the damsel to the island. In due course the passage was forced by Arthur and Gawain and the damsel and her companions were 'freed'.

Turning Island must be consigned to the unreal from its rotary motion. However, it conforms to a standard pattern of defended islands in being approached by a causeway and a bridge made by Merlin and notable for its narrowness;[135] in being defended by the lover of the lady of the place; in the presence of many women; and in the expression of great joy that the enchantment had been removed.[136]

THE WASTE CITY:

Here Lancelot beheaded a young lord wearing a great gold cap, one of a long sequence of annual beheadings, and he was obliged to return on the same day a year later to be beheaded in his turn by the victim's brother. His observance of this promise brought renewed prosperity to the city, without (as the story has survived) himself suffering the appropriate fate. There are no clues to its whereabouts.

[135] *Vulgate*, VII, pp. 302/3.
[136] *Vulgate*, VII, pp. 309 and 311.

# APPENDIX

# WHO'S WHO IN THE ROMANCES?

## Distant Echoes of Divinity

Tennyson warned his readers that they must not expect to find in his Arthurian verses:

> that gray king whose name, a ghost,
> Streams like a cloud, man shaped, from mountain peak
> And cleaves to cairn and cromlech still . . .'[1]

This analysis of the romances unrepresented in Tennyson shows that certain names other than Arthur's are closely associated with tumuli and standing stones, and although traditional material of the kind discussed here can never be precise, there is a possibility that the names of deities and some of their relationships may have been remembered from the times when such monuments were objects of veneration. During that period the names of deities will have been repeated countless times and translated several times. Changes will have taken place in them, to the extent that one original deity may be represented by several apparently distinct personages in the tradition that was finally stabilized in written form.

The extent to which such changes may have taken place can be guessed at, but there is no way of checking if the guesses are right. Too much depends on the slippery evidence of names alone. The kind of guesses thought invalid in dealing with topography cannot be relied on when it comes to deities. Such doubtful procedures must be excluded from the body of the book, hence this appendix. However, some fairly obvious arguments do explain a statistical aspect of the romances, the large numbers of names beginning Bran-, Bel-, Gal-, and Pel-,[2] so the effort may not be wasted.

A deity can be remembered in many ways. It is not for nothing that the devil in popular imagination has horns and a tail, features which match the pagan images carved in stone some two thousand years ago. But the picture given in this way is generalized. There were horned and tailed gods derived from various animals; without writing, their names are forgotten. In some cases, of which Mabon is a notable example, the missing link has been provided by our literate conquerors and enables the name of a deity to be traced in spoken tradition, a far more ephemeral medium than written characters. Perhaps, if the appearances in tradition of this personage widely accepted as a deity are examined in detail, it will help us recognize other deities in that medium.

---

[1] *King Arthur in History and Legend*, W. Lewis Jones, p. 133.
[2] There are about five times as many in the *Prose Index*, West, in proportion to the total number of items indexed, as in a one volume edition of *The Diary of Samuel Pepys*, chosen for comparison because its subject is people and places.

### The Celtic God Mabon

**Romano-British inscriptions** show Mabon, in the latinized form Maponus, to have been equated with Apollo, the sun god of both Greeks and Romans. Altars bearing this name have been found in the region of Hadrian's Wall and in North Lancashire. One of them also depicts Apollo as a harper with the goddess Diana as a Huntress.

The name Mabon crops up in several other contexts, in some cases with associations which fit the proposition that it is the god Mabon who is meant. Within the area in which the inscribed altars are found, **topographical features** carry the name Mabon at the stone called the Lochmabenstane, just north of the Solway Firth near Gretna Green, and at the loch called Lochmaben, about 28 km to the north-west. The Lochmabenstane is a rounded boulder about 3.3 m tall which is nearly all that remains of a Bronze Age stone-circle.[3] It was the great traditional meeting-place of early medieval folk on the west of the Border. The name of this stone when it first appeared in modern written records, in 1398, was 'Clochmaben', that is 'Maben's stone'. The element 'cloch' has the meaning 'stone' in Gaelic, so the later addition of the Anglo-Saxon 'stane' is unnecessary. The name has no connection with any 'loch' but in its modern form with the 'C' missing has been assimilated to that of Lochmaben.

A much earlier reference to a place-name incorporating the element 'Mabon' occurs in a **Roman geographical work**, *The Ravenna Cosmography*, a list of places in the Roman Empire and on its borders which, as far as Britain is concerned, describes the situation toward the end of the Roman occupation. The *Cosmography* refers to several places described as 'locus'. One of these is Locus Maponi which could have been either Lochmaben or the Lochmabenstane. The latter is probably to be preferred because another standing stone, which gives its name to the place Clackmannan, is called after one of the other 'locus' names, Manavi. The Manau[4] were a British tribe, so it seems as if standing stones were tribal gathering points of sufficient importance to have been recorded by the Romans. It is interesting to find at the Lochmabenstane a degree of continuity unmatched in the British Isles except in Ireland. The Bronze Age setting of stones of before 1000 BC was still in use 2500 years later for what may be presumed to have been its original purpose of an assembly point[5] since the 'Wardens of the Marches', appointed by the English and Scottish kings, were obliged on occasion to show their commissions there; laws were proclaimed; there were appointed days of truce; cases were judged; prisoners were ransomed; and there was a market.[6] Within the setting of stones, which still existed in the Middle Ages, wearing arms was prohibited. The Wardens met at other places as well, and at irregular intervals, but on an occasion when they were obliged to display their commissions at the Lochmabenstane, it was on the first day of truce after Midsummer Day and within four days of that date.[7] Is this link between Mabon's Stone and midsummer a recollection of the time when he was acknowledged to be an equivalent of Apollo?

The Lochmabenstane is noteworthy in two ways; it demonstrates the importance that standing stones could still have, at the time the romances were composed, so lends point to the significance they still have in the romances; and it is one of the few instances of a prehistoric monument (as opposed to a natural feature) to which the name of a recogniz-

---

[3]  Actually an oval, enclosing about 0.2 hectares (half an acre) of ground. Apart from the Lochmabenstane only one other stone about a metre high survives. It is 23 m to the north-east of the main stone.

[4]  Manavi is the genitive of the Latin form of Manau, Mannan of the Gaelic.

[5]  *Transactions of Dumfries & Galloway etc.*, XXXI, p. 40.

[6]  *Annals of the Solway until 1307*, p. 15. G. Neilson, Glasgow, 1899.

[7]  Nicholson's *Leges Marchiorum*, p. 152, quoted by R. B. Armstrong.

able native deity is still attached under circumstances which suggest the link may be original.[8]

An eleventh century **Gaulish charter** refers to Mabono Fonte, Mabon's Spring, in France. There are also several place-names in Wales which incorporate the name Mabon. Lewis in the eighteenth century records the following: Llanvabon in Glamorgan, Rhiwfabon (Ruabon) in Denbigh, and Bodfafon in Creuthin. It would be interesting to know if any of these places retains traces in the ground of prehistoric pagan activity.

**Ancient welsh tradition** refers to Mabon in association with his mother, Modron. Since 'Mab' means 'son' and 'Modron' means 'Mother', Mabon son of Modron means literally 'Son, son of Mother' but implied is 'the Divine Son of the Goddess Mother' (not to be confused with Mother Goddess, a rather different concept). Another Welsh character with the name Mabon is Mabon son of Mellt, where Mellt means lightning. These two are by some supposed to be the same person, for the following reasons. In the *Mabinogion*, one of the Mabons is required to hunt the Chief Boar Ysgithrwyn, the other the magic boar Trwch; perhaps these two stories are developments of the same boar hunting theme. And if Mabon son of Modron corresponds to Apollo, his father would correspond to Apollo's father, that is Zeus, the wielder of lightning and thunder, an appropriate father for Mabon son of Lightning.

Mabon was stolen from his mother at three days old and kept prisoner at Gloucester until rescued by Arthur and his men, in an expedition undertaken because Mabon's presence was essential for the success of the hunt of the supernatural boar.

**The French Arthurian romances** speak of several Mabons, or characters such as Mabonagrein whose name incorporates the element Mabon, or whose name like Nabon or Mabuz is generally recognized to be a variant of it. Only one episode concerning one of these Mabons has been repeated by Malory, the greatest popularizer of the Arthurian romances in English. In this story a certain Nabon was a black giant, lord of the Valley of Bondage in which he kept all visiting knights captive. He was killed by Sir Tristan at a tournament attended by all the people of his realm.[9] This episode does not convey any aura of paganism, neither is the name Nabon in this case obviously a variant of Mabon, so no hint of the deity Mabon has been passed on by Malory to his English-speaking readers.

Half a dozen other episodes centred on Mabon were not chosen by Malory for inclusion in *Morte Darthur*. In them Mabon (or Nabon, the name is variously spelt), plays several roles:

(1) He was a sorcerer who learned his trade from Merlin, and he was the brother of Branduz, the latter being the god Bran lightly disguised.
(2) As Mabon le Noir he fought Gawain over a fairy called Marsique.
(3) While he was incarcerated in a tower,[10] Mabon provided a magic boat to take Tristan and Yseult to challenge another couple, he in strength and she in beauty. The severed heads of the losers were sent back to Mabon.
(4) As Mabonagrein he was a gigantic red knight who defended a garden which was encircled with an impenetrable wall of air and was furnished with a row of heads on stakes. The place was called Brandigan, the castle of King Eurain.
(5) Mabon and Eurain were two enchanters who turned the Queen of Wales into a

---

[8]  The names of Arthur and Merlin, like that of the Devil, seem to be scattered at random over the countryside. To have a stone circle called, say, 'King Arthur's Round Table' is probably irrelevant except in so far as the spread of Arthurian names indicates some local interest in the tradition at the time the names were formed.

[9]  *Morte Darthur*, Malory, bk VIII, ch. 39.

[10] *Prose Tristan*, Löseth, p. 251.

serpent and laid waste by magic her city of Sinadoun. After her nameless rescuer, le Bel Inconnu, had killed one of the enchanters and wounded the other, she appeared as a winged serpent with a woman's face; she twined round his neck, kissed him on the mouth and then turned into a most beautiful woman who presented him with her person and her possessions.

(6)  Mabuz, lord of Death Castle, is another of the recognized disguises of Mabon. He was the son of the water-fay who fostered Lancelot.

It is easy enough to see why Malory chose only the episode of the Val de Servage to include in *Morte Darthur*. The favours of a fairy would not have been considered an adequate reason for a fight in the fifteenth century, and a heavy tinge of the unreal was sufficient to exclude the other stories related of Mabon. Fortunately, some Arthurian enchantment, like the sword in the stone and the sword returned to the lake, did survive the rational Malory's selection procedure, or else almost all trace of the magic which pervades the romances would have been lost to later readers.

The Mabon not featured by Malory is characterized in all his appearances by magic. That is not surprising, for it is not to be expected that residues of paganism should conform to the laws of nature as we understand them now. But the type of magic is not the harmless unreality of an imagined tale intended only to entertain. The wall of air which enclosed the garden was a 'psychologically impassable barrier'. It is perhaps not an accident that it coincides here with the row of severed heads. The significant site defended by an armed man ready for single combat is an echo of the rite of Nemi. These and the association with another god, Bran,[11] and with a water-spirit all speak of a pagan origin. So does the woman transformed into a serpent who, like the king transformed into a boar in a Welsh story, is not an aimless flight of fancy but a survival from the times when deities could easily slip into the shapes of animals, as their surviving images testify. The serpent, a queen transformed, represents the principle of sovereignty in this story.

Even Malory's low-key episode in the Valley of Servage (i.e. Bondage) can readily be discerned as having a pagan origin when compared with other situations in the romances in which large numbers of captives are retained. The cruel captor is invariably a deity, and the hero who releases the captives, generally by killing the captor in single combat, is human. One can only speculate on what lies behind this type of story, but its origin clearly lies in religion.

To sum up, although not all the characteristic features of the Welsh Mabon are to be found in the romances, the mother and son link, for instance, is missing, a less obvious feature, the status of captive, is included and there are many links with paganism. In all, there are enough indications to suggest that the Latin, Welsh and French versions are descended form a common original, from which all three diverge through error, omission and corruption, but which when combined provide a substantial portrait of a native British god.

## Other Deities in the Romances

The full extent to which the French versions of the Arthurian legend conceal the names and attributes of deities has been obscured by the inevitably destructive effects of continual repetition. However, a detailed analysis of the material will enable us to observe specific tendencies within the oral tradition. Once the effects of repetition are understood, original forms of can be recognized and it will be possible to show that the romances have a considerably greater contribution to make to our knowledge of native paganism than has so far been revealed.

---

11  Bran, in Branduz, Brandigan, king Eurain and Eurain the enchanter (see below).

It has been a major theme of this book that in the course of repetition the descriptions of events become eroded and garbled until the different versions are almost unrecognizable. More or less the same thing happens with the names of places and persons. Thus it can be argued, for instance, that Bran and Urien are derived from the same original name, and so are Balin and Pellinor from another (see below). The arguments in favour of this sort of equation are of two kinds. One is that the characteristics, behaviour and personal relationships of the two personages thought to have diverged from a common original should tally. The other is that the nature of the change from one form of the name to the other should follow one of the general rules under which letters change their phonetic value at language boundaries, or else should follow a course of erosion or distortion which can be paralleled in other examples.

Over much of the period during which the Arthurian tradition developed it is possible to obtain practical guidance from the changes which have actually taken place in names which were recorded in classical times. Take for example the name of Britain. This country was known to the Greeks as Prettania, perhaps as early as 500 B.C., and to the Romans a few centuries later as Britannia. This leaves us guessing as to how the inhabitants pronounced the name of their island, but the Welsh today retain in Prydain the 'P' of the Greek form and the English the 'B' of the Roman. Evidently confusion between b and p in a Welsh context has always been a commonplace.

Turning next to Ireland, that country was called Iverna by the Greeks, or else Ierne, a slightly eroded form of the same word. Iverna in turn became Latin Hibernia and later, again by erosion, the poetic Erin and the modern Eire and Ireland. Although Ireland proper is not linked with the Arthurian legend, there are two lessons to be learned here, that different ears listening to a particular sound may hear it as a 'b' or a 'v';[12] and that letters may disappear completely from a word, particularly, as it happens, 'v'.

Finally, to complete this short survey of documented examples from early times there is York, which started off as Eboracum (possibly from a native personal name, Ebrauc) and changed to its present form through Eferwic, Eforwicceaster, Iorwic and Iork. And there are the examples already mentioned, the river Usk, which was first recorded as Isca and is derived from the same root as Exe, Axe and Esk; and the river Severn, which the Romans called Sabrina and the Welsh, at different times, Haffren or Habren.

**Local Linguistics**

At first sight the changes in these names are bewildering and may seem without rhyme or reason, but in spite of this there are certain characteristics of the groups above which can be rationalized. Perhaps the most obvious feature is the extraordinary variability of the vowels. No one has difficulty today in distinguishing between 'pat', 'pet', 'pit', 'pot' and 'put', nor between similar words using the long form of the vowels. How strange that the initial vowel of one well-documented river name can diverge from the 'I' of Isca to all the other vowels.[13] Set against this there is obviously a relatively constant structure of consonants, which only change in a limited range of ways. The latter follow certain specific routes according to the empirical rules governing consonant shift which have been formulated for the languages concerned. The corresponding changes of the vowels are more complex and are of no help in the present investigation.

To demonstrate what is happening it will be helpful to set out in tabular form the names which have already been mentioned:

[12] See footnote to p. 190.
[13] Axe, Esk or Exe; Ocire or Ousque in the romances; and the modern form, Usk.

| (1) | (2) | (3) | (4) | (5) |
|-----|-----|-----|-----|-----|
| Pretta nia | Iver na | Eb rauc | I sca | Sab ri na |
| Bri tan nia | I er ne | Ebo ra cum | U sk | Hab re n |
| Prydai n | Hiber nia | Efo rwic | E xe | Haff re n |
| | Erin | Io rwic | Axe | Sever n |
| | | Io  r  k | E sk | |
| | | | (Oscire) | |

This table shows that there is more consistency than might have been thought from a casual reading of the names in sequence. Looking first at the consonants, it is at once apparent that 'n' and 'r' and 'k' (or hard 'c') retain their values and so does 't' apart from a minor change to the rather similar sound 'd'. But 's' is not constant because of the use of 'h' instead of 's' in a group of languages including Welsh. This is not a phenomenon likely to affect the discussion which follows. Among the variable consonants, 'b' alternates with 'p' in column one and 'b' with 'v' (or 'f' itself scarcely to be distinguished from 'v') in columns two, three and five, according to standard form. The tendency for this last pair of letters to disappear altogether is confirmed by columns two and three. This is a factor not unknown in common speech, where o'er has been used in the past for over, e'er for ever and e'en for even. In contrast, though 'e' is constant in the names of Ireland and 'o' more or less so in York, the vowels are more erratic and it is difficult to express the changes by simple rules.

At this stage some comment should be made about the initial and final letters of words in languages other than present day English. The intrusive 'h' will be familiar to an older generation of readers who will remember the time when a majority of the population, at least in the north of England, inserted an 'h' before all vowels and, conversely, dropped the 'h' of words like 'have' in which the 'h' was retained in educated speech when standard English prevailed. This volatility of initial 'h' means that Helaines and Helains are indistinguishable from Elaines and Alains. Turning now to the end of the word, there is of course a general habit for this to indicate gender or case. The final 'e' of Helaine indicating feminine gender is an example. The use of case endings had almost died out in 12th century French but was retained in the masculine nominative singular 's' (roughly corresponding to the Latin termination '-us'). This is not rigorously used, so the same personage may have his name spelt with or without an 's'; Urien or Uriens; Ryon or Ryons; and so on.

There is also an unusual grammatical quirk in Welsh that the initial consonant is sometimes modified by the gender of the previous word, but that need not concern us for the moment.

The changes in spelling so far mentioned more or less conform to general rules, but there are others which are the result of accident or faulty memory. Reversed syllables and accidental anagrams occasionally crop up, and miscopying of Gothic script gives rise to a long list of standard errors.

### Variations on a Theme

This foray into linguistics will enable some variations in the names of personages in the Arthurian tradition to be recognized, which would otherwise have gone unnoticed. Fortunately we do not need to begin at the beginning. A great deal of the work has already been done by Helaine Newstead in *Bran the Blessed in Arthurian Romance*. It has often been commented that there is an extraordinarily large number of Arthurian characters whose names begin with Bran or who incorporate Bran as an element in a compound name. Newstead points out that a large proportion of them can be related back to the personage in the *Mabinogion* called Bran 'the Blessed', though there is nothing particularly saintly about his behaviour, rather the reverse. In doing this she does not take Bran's divine status into account nor does she call linguistics in aid. Her approach is entirely literary and is therefore not in any way biased towards the theme of this book. A list now follows of the personages Newstead regards as derived from the Welsh Bran, starting off with Bran himself and adding to Newstead's list Bran's sister, who also seems to be of divine status according to the criteria used here:

BRAN:

In Welsh legend, a giant King of Britain; the son of Llyr, a sea god; also described as son of the (presumably female) Iwerit (that is, Ireland); grandson of Beli (the god Belenus); or in another context, brother of Beli. His severed head was a talisman and was taken first to Harlech, then to the island of Grassholm and finally to London, where it was buried to protect the realm from invasion and infection.

BRANWEN, alternatively BRONWEN (the Brangain of the romances):

The sister of Bran. Married to a King of Ireland. Said to be buried in a four sided grave[14] on the bank of the river Alaw in Anglesey. Her name still clings to the spot, where there is a tumulus which contained a rectangular cist of flagstones enclosing a Bronze Age urn containing ashes.

BRENNIUS (or Brenne):

King of Britain, the equivalent, in Geoffrey of Monmouth, of the Welsh Bran. Brother of Belinus.

BRANDALUS:

Entitled of Wales. Brother of Julian le Gros and of Elinant of Escavalon.

BRANDELIS:

A huge wounded knight in a tent in which there are grails holding severed heads.

BRANDUZ:

Entitled des Illes. Lord of Dolorous Gard. Brother of Mabon.

BRANGEMUER:

Lord of the Isles of the Sea. Son of lord of the Isle of Avalon.

BRANGOIRE:

Lord of the Castle of the Boundary.

BRON:

The first Fisher King. Guardian of the Grail. Dwelt in the Isles of Ireland. Father of Alain le Gros.

BALAN:

A challenge knight. Brother of Balin. Defended an island.

BAN:

King of Benoic in Brittany. Son of a princess of Ireland. Father of Lancelot.

BAUDEMAGUS or Bandemagus:

King of Gorre and of Terre Foraine.

BRIEN:

Tall brother of the dwarf king Billis of the Antipodes, i.e. the Otherworld.

BRIEN:

Entitled des Illes. According to West, perhaps a double of Branduz.

14 *Mabinogion*, Penguin, p. 80. For details and references see *The Real Camelot*, pp. 146/7.

URIEN:
   King of Gorre. Husband of Morgan, the goddess. Father of Yvain, who was the victor at the lightning fountain.

EURAIN:
   King of BRANdigan where MABONagrein defended a magic garden surrounded by a hedge of mist where there were severed heads on stakes.

EURAIN:
   Mabon and Eurain were a pair of enchanters who turned the lady of Sinadoun into a winged serpent.

Treating these personages entirely in a literary framework and never mentioning deities nor stirring up the muddy waters of linguistics, Newstead shows that those listed above each possess some of the following characteristic features of Bran: he is associated with abundance; he is wounded or languishing; he is connected with islands or water; he is a giant, or, if represented as a mere human being, of more than human stature; he is connected with severed heads, corpses and the drinking of blood; his companions are untouched by age; and he often has a brother called Beli or some similar name. As I pointed out in *The Real Camelot* (p. 74), this list, though not so intended by Newstead, is a compendium of paganism. The links with known deities, Belenus/Beli, Morgan and Mabon tend to confirm this conclusion.

A factor scarcely less prominent than some of those enumerated by Newstead is a link with Ireland. Bran is essentially a supernatural being. It is probably Ireland's meaning of 'the Otherworld' rather than the geographical Ireland that is meant in this context of paganism.

The other test is that any variations in spelling should be readily explained according to the shifts already encountered. Looking at the names on the list, it is clear that the consonants in the names on this list prepared by Newstead conform to the types of change noted above. Apart from the obvious compounds containing 'Bran-', there is the same variability of vowels in the B-r-n structure with a consonant occasionally missing. There is also a switch from 'b' to 'v'[15] in Urien and Eurain as in the cases of Hibernia – Ivernia and Sabrina – Severn.[16] ('u' and 'v' are indistinguishable in medieval French, in which the letter 'u' generally does duty for both).

In conformity with the general rule that a personage who is described in some detail will tend also to appear in a declining series of distorted and eroded images, there are plenty of other 'Brans' who are omitted by Newstead from the list above because they are not linked to the original Bran by any of the characteristics mentioned above. West, for instance, lists three other individuals called Brandelis and one called Brandilias, and there are five or six so-called 'Saxon' kings whose names begin with Bran. Newstead also leaves out some rather better contenders for a place on her list, largely because she deliberately restricted the range of her enquiries, excluding the *Vulgate Arthurian Romances*. By including this extra material and with the assistance of Loomis and Squire[17] it is possible to extend Newstead's list to include several more personages, some of them of the greatest importance in the Arthurian story.

First an example of erosion[18] in which the initial letter 'B' or 'V' has been lost from Brien, Urien or Bron:

---

15 From 'b' to 'v' only because 'b' is predominant in surviving Bran- type names, but this begs the question of which was the original. It might have been the 'v' form.
16 See footnote to p. 190.
17 *Celtic Myth and Legend*, C. Squire, pp. 356/7.
18 *The Grail, from Celtic Myth to Christian Symbol*, p. 234. Loomis reports that Bruce and other

R Y O N S or R I O N:
    Entitled des Illes. King of Ireland, or of Ireland and Danemarche, or of the land of Pastures and of Giants. Lord of the West.

Ryons conforms to the pattern by links with Islands, Giants and Ireland. Eroded by the loss of the initial letter for a second time Ryon becomes:

Y O N:
    King of Ireland, or of 'Ireland the Less'.

Next, a form in which the first letter of the name derived from Bran is 'u' or 'v' instead of 'b' but in which '-vran' comes at the end of the word. In the section that follows the significant consonants of each name have been enhanced to display the structure more clearly:

O C-U R A N or
G O G-V R A N   Two versions of the Welsh name of the same person, the father of Guenever, who was herself sister (West, *Verse Index*) of the King of Ireland.

L E O D E-G R A N C E   Malory's version of the name of the same individual, Guenever's father, in which 'g' has replaced the 'v' of the last two examples.[19]

Replacement of 'v' by 'g' gives rise to other derivatives of Bran:

M A B O N A-G R E I N   This is a compound name derived from those of two gods, Mabon and Eurain, the latter being one of the forms of Bran recognized by Newstead. Mabon and Eurain function as separate enchanters in *Le Bel Inconnu*.

Ocuran and Mabonagrein follow the 'Bran' pattern by being giants; and the association with a god, Mabon, and description, Enchanter, tend to confirm that in Eurain we are dealing with a supernatural being.

For different reasons, Arthur's father shows traces of derivation from Bran. His name

U T H E R   B E N   or Uther
U T H E R   P E N D R A G O N

carries the meaning 'head' in the word Ben or Pen. 'Dragon' is generally assumed to be some honorific epithet added to a basic Uther Ben, in which Uther is an adjective meaning cruel or wonderful - perhaps with reference to Bran's severed head. Uther also has the other characteristic of Bran, that he was wounded or languishing, for he is described in Geoffrey of Monmouth as the half-dead king, carried on a litter.

Finally there are alternatives in the romances to Bran's sister Branwen:

B R A N W E N   corresponds to
B R A N G A I N

who was the accomplice of Tristan and Yseult

and to

B R O N W E N   an alternative spelling of Branwen corresponds to the princess
R O N W E N   (a Saxon) better known under a later misspelling of her name, Rowena, with whom Vortigern fell in love.

Brangain[20] and Ronwen both proffered a cup, a motif representing the gift of

scholars have pointed out that proper names in manuscript transmission sometimes lose their initial letter.
[19] See footnote to p. 110.
[20] Ewert, in Beroul's *Tristan*, p. 197, mentions the instances in which it is Brangain who proffers the cup. Another is the image of Brangain in the cave, which represents her holding a cup.

sovereignty. In Tristan's case it turns up in romance as a 'love philtre' which bound him to the goddess Yseult (princess of Ireland); but in the other instance Ronwen seems to act herself in the capacity of the 'sovereignty'.

That goddesses can sometimes be demoted to organizing damsels has already been mentioned.

### Links between Bran in his various forms and Ireland

| | | |
|---|---|---|
| Br | an | son of Ireland |
| Br | on | dwelt in the Isles of Ireland |
| Br | anwen | married to King of Ireland |
| B | an | son of a princess of Ireland |
| | Ry on | King of Ireland |
| | Yon | King of Ireland the Less |
| Ocvr | an | his daughter was sister to the King of Ireland |

The many links between Bran and Ireland suggest that there is a general correspondence in the background, between Bran and 'Ireland'. This is not to be thought of as an exact equation, but there are several hints that a single deity lies behind Bran and his congeners on the one hand and the various manifestations of 'Ireland' on the other. Perhaps 'Ireland' has acquired slightly different name-forms in different tribes or national language groups and has left a fall-out of territorial names and god names. For the territorial names: Ivernia and so on in Ireland and the manifestations of 'Ireland' in West Wales. And for the names of supernatural personages: Bran, Branwen, Urien, and the various kings, queens, princes and princesses of Ireland who play such a prominent part in the romances. A possible explanation of the importance of the royal family of Ireland is the ubiquity of the motif of sovereignty, exemplified by Guenever, a sister of the King of Ireland, and perhaps Ygerne, whose name is alternatively spelt as Yverne, an early form of the name of Ireland.

One of the most obvious characteristics of the members of the group of Bran names is their link with islands. It has already been remarked (Gaz. Isles Lontaines) that the sleeping Cronus on an off-shore island has been likened to Bran, and several instances of his other links with islands have been given. The names Bran and Cronus (or Cronos) both mean crow or raven in their respective languages (mythology does not seem to distinguish between the different species of large black birds), and Bran's resemblance to Cronus is emphasised by a link with castration, for the latter so treated his father Uranus. But as far as name is concerned, the similarity is entirely with Uranus, whose name is scarcely to be distinguished from Uriens, one of the forms of Bran.

Some of the 'individuals' whose names are derived from Bran can be recognised by their behaviour even when they are unnamed, as Newstead pointed out, and there is one personage with an entirely different name who also fits into this category. He is Joseph 'of Arimathea' – firmly identified as a Fisher King in *Sone de Nausay* and having the characteristic wound between the thighs. Joseph's reputation as the founder of the first Christian church in Britain and as the bringer of the 'holy' Grail corresponds to Bran's title 'the blessed' – given by Christian scholars in the Middle Ages, ironically, to as savage a god as ever terrified his believers into accepting severe mutilation.

### The Sanctity of Bran's Sepulchres

In a paper entitled *Perceval's Father in Welsh Tradition*, Prof. Newstead in 1945[21] drew attention to many points of correspondence between several characters from very different

---

[21] *Romanic Review*, XXXVI.

backgrounds. From the French Arthurian romances there are Perceval's father, also King Ban and the Fisher King; from Geoffrey of Monmouth's *Historia Regum Britannie* there is Brennius, King of Britain; and from the Welsh *Mabinogion* there is the supernatural ruler, Bran. The extent of the correspondence is indicated by the phrase 'derived from the same reservoir of tradition'. One of the most interesting points of correspondence is the sanctity of the burial places of many of the persons concerned. Thus:

Perceval's father in Wolfram von Eschenbach's *Parzival* was buried in a splendid tomb in a distant place, where the heathen worshipped him as if he were a god; and his bloodstained shift and the spear which caused his fatal wound were reverently buried in a minster in his own land.

Perceval's father in *Perlesvaus* was buried in a chapel/tomb on an island, the richest of a group of twelve, where a religious office was later celebrated. The sarcophagi in these chapels were against the altars.

Where King Ban died a chapel was erected on a tertre (a small hill) overlooking the lake where the Damsel of the Lake brought up Lancelot. Here his widow set up the 'custom' of holding a daily mass for her husband in the minster and prayers for Lancelot (her son) on the lake.

The 'holy' body of the Fisher King (in this instance called Joseph of Arimathea) was enshrined in the island monastery of Galosche, with two venerated relics: the Grail and the head of the spear with which he had been pierced.[22]

Bran's head was buried in the White Mount in London as a protection against invasion and infection.

Newstead comments on the last of these that; 'The burial place was therefore a hallowed spot with supernatural powers. No great effort of the imagination is needed to see how such a legend, translated into Christian terms, would develop into the tradition of a tomb in a chapel or a minster, a place of sacred associations.' Newstead is generally chary of any comment which might indicated a link with paganism. However, for once, the 'translation into Christian terms' of a 'spot with supernatural powers' implies a pagan original. And when the analogues of Bran are examined, so does the worship by the heathen at the burial place of Perceval's father; so do the two sets of relics not hallowed by any link with Christianity; and so does the wound between the thighs, implying castration, which was suffered by Perceval's father and by the Fisher King, and which is said to have caused the comprehensive wasting of their respective kingdoms.

Newstead looks on the interment of the Welsh Bran's head as the direct original of the other burial places of Bran, apparently regarding the chapel or minster as a Christian rationalization of the pagan buried-head motif. In that case all that could ever be known of the pagan cult in question would be the limited information from the surviving ancient Welsh tradition: that he possessed a horn of plenty which provided whatever food or drink was desired; that his followers enjoyed perpetual youth and lived joyful lives; and that he was a giant whom no house could hold. However, it would be equally legitimate to regard the Welsh material as 'derived from the same reservoir of tradition' rather than being the whole story in a pure and unalloyed form. The surviving Welsh tales are generally acknowledged to be a fragment of an immense oral literature. Some of what has been lost may have been picked up by the French romance writers. Perhaps the chapel/tombs, with their pagan relics and their association with the castrated sacred king, are to be taken at face value. That is, that the various burial places of Bran really were a number of pagan shrines in different places, or else that the recollection of a single shrine has survived in several distorted forms. The wide variation in the type of site at which

---

[22] *Sone de Nausay*, ed. Goldschmidt, lines 4906ff.

Bran is said to have been buried – a splendid tomb in a distant place, on a hillock near a lake, and in an island monastery – might suggest that the first of these alternatives is more likely.

Since so many of Bran's characteristics transcend the boundaries of humanity, he cannot be thought of as a mere mortal, dying and being buried in the ordinary way. But that does not rule out the possibility that his burial was celebrated at the site or sites of his imagined death, or even that the real tombs of his human representatives could have been regarded as shrines. Whether one shrine or many, the argument put forward by Newstead that the sanctity of Bran's burial places has an origin in Welsh tradition is unaffected. It is yet another indication of a pagan feature in the Arthurian romances being derived from a Welsh original.

Just as Bran's buried severed head, with its supposed protective value, can be seen as suggesting an explanation for real buried heads in the archaeological record, so there is a possibility here of a correspondence with certain real burial places. The point that the burial places were places of worship as well as tombs is interesting, for that is a feature of the Neolithic Age, already mentioned in connection with Bran's talismanic head.

Another chapel/tomb tended by Perceval's mother, though not stated to contain the body of Perceval's father, held 'one who had helped take Christ down from the cross',[23] that is, in terms of the early French romances, Joseph of Arimathea, one of Newstead's analogues of Perceval's father. For what it worth, this building is described as a chapel standing on four columns of marble with inside it a beautiful tomb, open to view since the chapel had no sides.[24] It was 'situated at the end of the most savage island of Wales, near the sea, towards the West', and it is a place which has other links with south west of that country.

This analysis of Bran- names leaves no doubt that he has his origin in Welsh tradition and that he is an important god in that tradition. It is possible that the same process which has produced many characters as the end product of traditional tales recorded in the romances has also operated on the Welsh tradition. The consonant sequence U-R-N crops up there in a modified form in the personages Wrnach, Awrnach and Diwrnach.[25] These are all of a mythological nature and have Arthurian links. They represent the survival in Welsh tradition of themes which produced the 'matter of Britain' in the French. Wrnach was a giant who could only be killed by his own sword, Kei (Kay) killed him with it by a subterfuge; it was in Awarnach's hall that Arthur cut a hag in half; and the raid by Arthur on Diwrnach to obtain a cauldron, in which Caledvwlch (Excalibur) saw action for the only time in the whole of the *Mabinogion*, sounds like Arthur's raid on the Otherworld in *Preiddeu Annwfn*, which also features a bright sword and a cauldron. For the Wrnach trio to represent the Head of the Otherworld seen from three angles and also to be a survival of the nucleus from which Bran emerged is not beyond the bounds of possibility.

[23] *Perlesvaus*, tr. N. Bryant, p. 147.
[24] *Perlesvaus*, tr. N. Bryant, p. 44.
[25] *Mabinogion*, Everyman, tr. Jones and Jones, pp. xxiv, xxv, 121–3, 130. The names of these three personages include the consonant sequence w-r-n. Not much detail is preserved, but what there is – two are described as 'giant' and one as 'Irishman' – conforms to the pattern of the group of names to which they are compared here. Diwrnach and Wrnach are generally thought of as imported from Irish tradition but, like some other references to 'Ireland' could equally well be considered to be survivors from a wider spread at one time of motifs now restricted to Ireland proper.

## Belenus the Brilliant

When Professor Newstead was preparing to write *Bran the Blessed in Arthurian Romance* she deliberately restricted the scope of her researches, excluding the Grail kings in the *Continuations* and in the *Vulgate*, to avoid confusion with the Pelles tradition. The problem she faced is that the characteristics used to identify the derivatives of Bran are to be found associated with other personages, notably a group with names beginning 'Pell-'. To say this is not in any way to decry Newstead's notable book. There is no reason whatever why any characteristic should be restricted to a particular group of personages. But it is certainly surprising that tradition should have thrown up two entirely distinct groups, those with Bran names and those with Pell- names, with so many overlapping features, even such uniquely distinguishing characteristics as being a wounded or languishing king who has to be carried on a litter, and of being father of Perceval. How this came about need not concern us for the moment. First the material should be examined.

To the French authors who first committed the romances to parchment, there would have seemed to be half a dozen characters in the group which form the core of the Pelles tradition. Their names are as follows: one called Pellehan or Pelleans, two called Pelles and two or three called Pellinor. The dominant features of this group are that they tend to be kings of Listenois, Fisher Kings, guardians of the Grail, Maimed Kings and 'fathers' of Perceval. Though only a couple on the list possess all these characteristics, it can easily be seen from the vantage point of knowledge of the workings of the oral tradition that this scatter of names and attributes is typical of a much told tale. One narrator has made an error in a name, a later, repeating the same tale, an error in a description. In the early stages the personages may have had overlapping attributes, like the two Pellinors, who have much in common; finally two seemingly separate individuals emerged, like Pellinor and Pelles who, though they have lost their original identity, logic requires to be brothers or cousins since they have the same degree of kinship with other members of their 'families'.

Once the method by which the characters became separated is understood, no problem arises if we suppose all these 'fathers' of Perceval whose names begin with Pell- to be derived from the same original.

There is yet another 'father' of Perceval who conforms to the pattern of being a Fisher King and a guardian of the Grail. He is Alain le Gros. To complicate matters he is also known as Julian, an error, and as Helain, a standard phonological variant, but we can disregard these as incidental. The presence in the group of Pelles, Pelleans, Pellinor and Alain gives a clue as to the linguistic process which has produced these slightly varying names – the same as we have already seen at work in the development of many characters from an original Bran.

```
P    l    n        is the basic consonant structure
P e l l e  s
P e l l i  n o r
P e l l ea n s
A l a i  n
```

Looking at the members of the group together, the first and last can be seen to be eroded versions of the middle ones. In Pelles the last consonant (excluding of course the nominative 's') has been lost, in Alain, the first. It is easy enough to see how a slight slovenliness in repetition could have split two or more characters from one original. And since there seems to be no reason to suppose the initial 'P' or the final 'n' to have been accidental additions, it may be presumed that the original form was something like the middle examples, that is it had the basic structure P-l-n.

At this stage the definitive characteristics for the 'Pell-' names are almost the same as the principal ones for the 'Brans': the title Fisher King; being incapacitated by wounds;

being a father of Perceval; and being a guardian of the Grail. These characteristics are not linked to every member of the group, but are possessed by two or more. The only distinguishing feature so far is that one of the two characters called Pelles is 'King of the Little People'. Here is a notable contrast with Bran, who is always regarded as above average size. The presence of this particular personage called Pelles in the group is also a clue to the character of the group as a whole. For this Pelles is identified by Loomis with the Welsh Beli, the brother of Bran. This illuminates the 'Pell-' group in three ways. First, it suggests that the initial 'P' is a phonological equivalent to initial 'B' in other names; second, it indicates another distinguishing characteristic for the 'Pell-' group – that of being a brother of Bran (in this respect the mirror image of the Bran group, in which the characteristic was having a brother called something like Beli); and finally it provides a raison d'etre for the existence of the group, since Beli was a deity, the Welsh equivalent of the Belenus of continental inscriptions or its British form Belinus.[26]

The relationships between the 'Pell-' group and its congeners which begin with an initial letter 'B' can now be demonstrated as follows:

|  |  |  |
|---|---|---|
|  | Pellinor |  |
| Pelles | Pelleans | Alain* |
|  | Belenus |  |
| Beli* | Belinus* |  |
| Billis* | Balin* |  |
|  | Belinant | Elinant* |
|  | (Belinor) |  |

In this table, forms beginning with 'B' are placed below forms beginning with 'P'; the left hand column shows forms with end consonant lost (excluding nominative 's'); and the right hand column, forms with the initial consonant lost. A star* indicates a brother in the Bran group, and underlining, dwarf stature. The 'fathers' of Perceval are Pellinor, Pellehan and Alain le Gross.[27] Belinor has been put in brackets because he has only a tenuous connection with the group, but his existence might indicate the possibility of an intermediate form between Belinus and Pellinor.

Analysis of this table shows an extraordinary parallelism between the derivatives of Belinus and those of Bran in that in both cases the name and the characteristics of a god have provided (by standard modifications of the initial letter of the name, for which there are analogies outside the group) the basis for a dozen or more characters who appear in traditional tales to be human beings. The main distinguishing feature is that the Belinus group includes dwarfs while the Bran group tends towards giants.

In other ways such as being wounded, Fisher kings, Grail guardians, fathers of Perceval and a link with islands, the two groups have much in common. And just as in the case of the Bran group, the characteristics of the Belinus group can be used to identify as members of the group other personages, in addition to those already mentioned, who have names like Beli. Examples are included in the list which follows.

BELENUS the Brilliant:
A Celtic god first glimpsed in written histories under the name Bolgios in about 300 BC and still popular at the time of the Roman occupation of Britain. The cult sites of Belenus might be attributed to Mercury by the Romans and were in one or two instances replaced by churches dedicated to St Michael in Christian times.

---

26 *Pagan Celtic Britain*, Ross, p. 472.
27 See *Prose Index*, West, under these names.

BELINUS or (Belin):

The equivalent of Belenus in Geoffrey of Monmouth, where he is king of southern Britain and brother of Brennus, king of the North. Belinus was renowned as a builder of roads from one end of the country to the other: from Cornwall to Caithness, from St David's to Southampton, and two others slantwise across the island. He is also said to have founded the city of Caerleon. His name is translated in Welsh versions of *Historia Regum Britannie* as Beli.

BELINANS or Belinant:

Entitled 'des Isles'. He was King of Sorgales and guardian of the entry into South Wales called the Chaucie Norgalois.

BELINOR:

A dwarf prince of the Estrange Islands.

BALIN:

A challenge knight. He struck the Dolorous Stroke with the Lance Vengeresse, wounding Pellehan (q.v. below) between the thighs. He was brother of Balan, a form of Bran.

BELI:

An ultimate ancestor of a Welsh royal dynasty. He is presumed on this account to have been a god.

BILLIS:

Dwarf King of the Antipodes. Brother of Brien.

BELYAS:

A black challenge knight, who was guardian of the Fountain of the Two Sycamores. His brother Briadan is thought by Loomis to be a form of Bran.[28]

BELYAS:

The amorous knight of the Castle of Maidens.

PELLINOR:

King of the Waste Land and also of the Grail Castle, of the Savage Forest, and of Listenois. He was entitled Fisher King and Maimed King, and was struck between the thighs by the Lance Vengeresse. Said to be father of Perceval. West sees two kings of Listenois of this name with 'several attributes in common,' representing 'a form of duplication'.

PELLEHAN or Pelleans:

King of Listenois. He was wounded by Balin with the Lance Vengeresse. He was entitled Fisher King and Maimed King. He was father of Pelles. Said also to be father of Perceval.

PELLES:

King of Listenois and of Terre Foraine. He was guardian of the Grail at Corbenic, and was entitled Fisher King and Maimed King. He was father of 'Elaine', Galahad's mother.

PELLES:

King of the Little People.

ALAIN le Gros:

The second Rich Fisher or Fisher King. He was guardian of the Grail after his father Bron. Said to be father of Perceval.

---

[28] See *Prose Index*, West, under these names.

JULIAN le Gros:
Of the other Camelot in West Wales. He was the maimed husband of the Widow Lady of the Lonely Waste Forest. The name is an error for Alain (West). Said to be father of Perceval.

ALAIN of the Isle in Listenois and of Terre Foraine:
He was the 'brother' of Pelles and Pellinor. Entitled Fisher King and Maimed King.

HELAINS li Gros:
The grandfather of Lancelot.

HELAIN the White:
Son of Brangoire's daughter by the winner of a tournament, Bors. It was foretold that he would become an important Grail knight.

ELINANT of Escavalon:
Brother of Brandalus. Uncle of Perceval and father of the Alain who next follows.

ALAIN of Escavalon:
He was the father of Florée, who was Gawain's mistress and mother of le Bel Inconnu.

ABALLAC:
Son of, and probably a duplicate of, Beli. His position towards the top of ancestor lists suggests that he was a deity.

EVALAC:
As in the case of Bran there are some names in the Belinus name-scatter in which 'v' replaces 'b'. Evalac conforms to other characteristics of the group by being a maimed king, and he was healed by Galahad with blood from the Grail in exactly the same way as Pelles.

AVALLACH:
The name Evalac has inevitably called to mind Avallach, the patron of Avalon[29] but always previously without the equation being supported by a convergence of behaviour. However, as pointed out in the Gazetteer under Avalon, the chapel to St Michael on Glastonbury Tor might link the site with Belenus or the sun. Either would be appropriate to Evalac, with his association with sun-worship at Sarras and with his presence within the name-scatter of Belinus. These links, though tenuous, tend to support previous identifications made on name-resemblance alone.

Just as some of the names in the Bran- group are reminiscent of Uranus, some of the forms of the Bel- group are not unlike Apollo, who being a sun god has the same style of worship as Evalac.

The personages so far listed have all been male. They are accompanied in the romances by a considerable number of females with equivalent name forms. These now follow. Those in inverted commas have had names bestowed on them by Malory which do not seem to be preserved in extant French texts, though, who knows, they may once have existed since he is known to have followed his sources carefully, if not completely. This list largely duplicates the list on p. 146 under the heading of the 'British Helen'. These names are repeated here to show their links with the rest of the 'Bel-' group and to explore further their relationships among themselves.

---

[29] E.g. Ashe, *King Arthur's Avalon*, p. 23. Evalake is 'Avallach transformed into a heathen prince'.

BALIENNE:
   The mother by Galehot, lord of the Far Away Isles, of Galehodin, King of Sorelois.

BELE IAIANDE:
   The mother of Galehot.

'ELAINE', Pelles' daughter:
   In surviving romances called Helizabel or Amite. She was bearer of the Grail in the Grail procession at Corbenic until she became Galahad's mother. The Grail bearer, with her arm in a sling, came to Arthur's court on Midsummer Day with the cart containing 150 heads.

ELAINE,[30] one of the names of the Damsel of the Lake:
   She provided Arthur with Excalibur and received it back at the end of his life; she is recorded as driving in the cart.

'ELAINE', a daughter of Ygerne:
   She married King Neutre of Garlot (a variant of Urien, thus Bran).

ELAINNE, a grand-daughter of Ygerne:
   Gawain's sister (or in another version, his cousin). She fell in love with Perceval and encouraged him to win the battles which led to his selection as an occupant of the Perilous Seat.

'ELAINE' the White, the Fair Maid of Astolat:
   Died of love for Lancelot. Her body drifted in a boat to Camelot, where it was buried.

'ELEINE', King Pellinor's daughter:
   Her mother was the Lady of the 'Rule' (does this mean the Sovereignty?). Her severed head was found by the spring which her lover, the Knight of the Glade had defended.

LEONE:
   Who killed herself at Merlin's Perron near Camelot, where her lover Lanceor had been killed by Balin.

ELENE, messenger of the lady of Sinadoun:
   The 'minder' of le Bel Inconnu. In this capacity she is the equivalent of

LUNETE in *Yvain*.

HELAINE or ELAINE, the Queen of Great Sorrows:
   Wife of Ban and mother of the Galahad later known as Lancelot.

HELIENE without Equal:
   Wife of Persidés the Red of Corbenic (Sommer Index). Perhaps the same as Elainne, Perceval's lover, whose original position as wife of the red knight Perceval of Corbenic would have been suppressed by the twelfth century concept of the desirability of male virginity in the ultimate hero.

HELAINE, killed by a giant:
   Her tomb was said to be still visible in the twelfth century at the French Mt St Michel, then called Tombelaine, whether for Elaine or Belinus cannot be discovered. Perhaps there is no distinction except in the gender.

   The members of this group are mothers or lovers of heroes, or otherwise linked with the pagan themes described in this book. In addition to those listed there are, as usual, a number of personages with similar names who do not have the pagan attributes which

---

[30] Sommer, *Vulgate*, index.

would have justified inclusion. That this should be so is to be expected. Characters will inevitably have become separated from their attributes in the course of many repetitions.

Perhaps the last gleam from Belinus, almost extinguished by a deliberate attempt to Christianize, is in the description in Wace's *Roman de Brut* of Arthur's second coronation at Caerleon.[31] At this place two saints were worshipped, Julius the Martyr, whose church held a convent of nuns, and his companion Aaron, whose priests were skilled in astronomy and foretelling the future. Although we have already met Belenus in the form Julian, I would hesitate to identify Julius as Belenus (and hence Aaron as Bran) if it were not for the unexpected comment that the knights at the wedding festival went from church to church, at one enjoying the singing of the clerks and at the other delighting their eyes with the loveliness of the damsels – the latter a compliment more likely to have been paid to the entourage of Belyas the Amorous of the Castle of Maidens (which was, of course, on the Usk) than to the demure nuns of the fifth/sixth century church. And though the name Aaron (companion now rather than brother) is not much like Bran, except in the debased form Ron noted above, the activities of his priests, particularly astronomy, match quite well those of the cult figures of the romances. Belenus/Belinus was also linked with Caerleon by Geoffrey of Monmouth, who records him as founding that city.

There is now in the Bel- and Elaine groups a substantial portrait of two important figures from the distant past, surfacing in various disguises according to the whim of narrators but nevertheless providing clues about their original circumstances. The idea of Beli and Elaine as divinities has already received attention. Now one of the principal attributes of Elaine can be seen to have been that she was the mistress or mother of heroes, the latter status as mother naturally following from the former of lover.

It has already been noted that the characteristics of the group of personages with Bran-names and the group with Beli- names overlap considerably. As well as 'brotherhood' with Beli, Bran even has a sister who has some resemblances to Elaine. The main distinction between the two groups which has so far emerged is that between giant and dwarf, though it may be suspected that Bran's name, meaning raven, is in contrast with that of Belenus, which signifies brightness. Perhaps, since they are closely linked deities, the members of this group originally formed part of a pantheon, with considerable polarity between the two principal male deities – a dark giant and a bright dwarf.

Many personages linked with the earth-bound challenge theme are mentioned in the lists of Beli names and Elaine names, and intermingled with divinities there are, as has been shown, some characters who seem to display human behaviour. For instance, in the case of Pelles' daughter there is motherhood by a challenge knight, a motif repeated by Balienne and also by Bele Iaiande. In the case of the last two there is an unexpected repetition of names in successive generations, which parallels the situation of the Galahads and Elaines already mentioned in The Real Camelot.

| Brunor and | Bel'Iaiande[32] | had a child called | Galahad,[33] who |
| by | Balienne | had a child called | Galehodin |
| Ban and | Elaine | had a child called | Galahad,[34] who |
| by | Elaine | had a child called | Galahad.[35] |

---

[31] *Wace and Layamon – Arthurian Chronicles*, tr. E. Mason, Everyman (paperback), p. 67.
[32] The pronunciation of Balienne and Bel'Iaiande is so similar that the narrator probably derived the latter seemingly sensible title, Beautiful Giantess, from the former.
[33] I have used Malory's spelling here as it is familiar. The French originals often use Galaad, Galahas, Galehos, Galehot or Galehaut for the members of this group of personages.
[34] This is Lancelot, who was christened Galahad.
[35] The well known Galahad, achiever of the Holy Grail.

We have already seen Elaine/Helen to have been some sort of divinity, remembered as 'empress' and in Welsh legend as the mighty Helen of the Hosts, patroness of ancient tracks and Roman roads, described by Bromwich as 'in origin a character of early Welsh mythology who was renowned as an ancestor deity'.[36] In the group of personages with names like Elaine she can be seen to have a more human face. She loves, she bears children, she dies. Yet she is far from seeming an individual. Those repetitions of names in successive generations suggest that what we can see is the name of an office. The goddess has descended to earth and, in the shape of her priestess, performs the normal functions of her sex in an unending sequence of generations, assisted by the heroes who likewise carry the same name from father to son.

### The Galahads

This last analysis has thrown up several characters with the name Galahad or something very similar. There is in the romances a surprisingly large number of names of individuals and places beginning with 'Gal-',[37] roughly as many as there are with 'Bel-', 'Bal-' and 'Bran-' put together. Of these the 'Galahads' are a core of important personages. They are as follows:

GALAHAD[1]:

Son of Joseph of Arimathea; born at Galafort; King of Gales, to which he gave its name; married to a princess of the Far Away Islands buried originally in the 'Holy Cemetery' of Gorre; later his body was carried away to be buried in Wales.

GALAHAD[2]:

Galahad was the name given in baptism to Lancelot. He was the son of Ban (Bran) and Helaine, and he was brought up by the Damsel of the Lake. He wore red for his initiation to the Round Table on Midsummer Day. He is best known as the paramount champion of the Round Table. In this capacity he defeated defenders of fountains, he severed a head for throwing into a well, he endured the lightning spear in the testing bed, and he was lover of the cruel goddess in several of her guises, most notably, as Guenever. Galahad[2] was buried in the same tomb as Galehot.

GALAHAD[3]:

Son of Galahad[2] and Elaine, who herself was descended from a long line of Fisher Kings and Maimed Kings. He drew the sword of Balin from the floated stone. He wore red like his father for his initiation to the Perilous Seat at the Round Table at the spring festival, Pentecost. He became an annual king at the sun-worshipping 'holy' city of Sarras, where Perceval's sister had already been buried in a boat after dying from bleeding a sacrificial dish of blood. On the last day of his year's reign, Galahad died 'achieving' the Grail, a vessel normally used to hold the blood of sacrificial victims. He was buried in the Spiritual Palace of the Holy City of Sarras.

GALEHOT:

Lord of the Far Away Islands. Son of a giantess, father of Galehodin. Buried in the reused pagan tomb at Joyous Gard.[38]

GALEHODIN:

Succeeded to Galehot's possessions on his death and so became King of Sorelois.

---

[36] *Trioedd Ynys Prydein*, p. 341.
[37] Over forty in *Prose Index*, West.
[38] Galehot or Galehaut is an important character in the romances. He occupies as much space in West's *Prose Index* as Galahad.

As usual when the recollection of an important traditional figure is being examined, there is a considerable scatter of other names beginning 'Gal-' including several which are, as far as spelling goes, scarcely to be distinguished from Galahad. This is an effect which we have seen in the case of a couple of important gods and a goddess. The 'Gal-' names are the only others, apart from the two gods to which reference has already been made, Bran and Beli, which look as if they came into being as a result of 'name scatter'. Perhaps enquiries should be made to see if the original of these personages with names beginning with 'Gal-' was also a divinity.

That is not so obvious as in the other cases because there are not the same convergences of behaviour among the members of the group. There are among them an example of the name-giving founding father, a dubious motif; there is an interesting challenge knight called Galeschalain, alternatively Galeschin, (which seem to be Welsh Alain), prince of Escalon (or Escavalon); and there is the principal Welsh champion, Gawain - for the earlier versions of this name contain an 'l', Galvain and so on. But it is the Galahads that most attract our attention. They, or at least the later of them, clearly come from the same more earth-bound background as the human personifications among the Elaines. They are a 'generation' after the obvious deities, Bran and Beli, and they partake of human delights and sufferings. They are conceived and born, they die and are buried, in a more realistic way than is generally found in the affairs of deities. The severed head thrown into the well, the election to annual kingship, the ritual bleeding to death, all give an impression of actuality. We are witnessing the roles played by people in a complex system under which the rituals described were enacted in real life in Britain at particular times and in particular places.

It is pointless to speculate on the frame of mind of a sacrificial victim, but there is no doubt that men and women have always been found who have been prepared to give up their lives for their gods, whether in a Roman amphitheatre or under the wheels of a juggernaut. And historical evidence for ritual castration, even self-inflicted, is equally compelling. There may indeed have been a substantial number of men who would put their lives on the line, win or lose, in the often vain hope of attaining the honour of being supreme champion of their people. As such they would enjoy the glory of being a god for a period, however brief, and the ecstasy of believing that their union with the goddess was pumping prosperity into the affairs of the whole community.

Predominant among the places where this cult was practised would have been Camelot, the 'holy city' which had been taken over by the Grail religion, where Galahad assumed the perilous throne; and Sarras, where he was king for a year before perishing, the story has it, in a flash of light from the sky.

Chance has preserved in the 'matter of Britain' two groups of characters deriving from the gods Bran and Belenus. In each case, the members seem to have become differentiated by much the same consonant shift. A list of representative members of each form might look something like this:

| Derived from: | | **Bran** | **Belenus** |
|---|---|---|---|
| Form with U/V | | Urien | Avalon |
| Form with B | | Bran | Balin |
| Form with P | | | Pellinor |
| Form with G | Leode | grance. | |

There are two gaps in this listing. First, there is no form of Bran beginning with P (except that in a German story King Ban of Benoic crops up as Pant of Genewis, but this is likely to have been an idiosyncrasy of that particular language boundary rather than a recollection of an original form beginning with 'P'). To give a positive reason for this, the stories of Belenus, but not those of Bran, may have been picked up by an English speaking folk-tale collector in the twelfth century, who like a present day English speaker would interpret the Welsh pronunciation of B as P. Second, there is also at first glance no representative in the Balin group beginning with G. I suggest that this gap should be filled with the Gal-names.

In this scheme it is not necessary to suppose, as philologists sometimes do, a hypothetical antecedent, now lost, but to suppose that the original form has survived as well as the variant. Thus if the original form of the Bran group was something like Uriens or Wrnach, that may have been modified into a B form and a G form as well as surviving; and exactly the same pattern might have evolved from an original Aval- form in the other group. This can be shown diagrammatically, using representative members of each form, as follows:

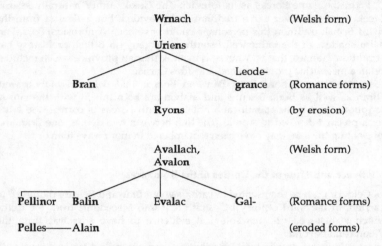

The same changes in letters applied to this second group show how apparently diverse individuals like Evalac and Pelles share the same phonological make-up as well as several similarities in behaviour.

## Ambrosius/Bors

King Bors of Gannes, a place in the south of Brittany, played one of the more important parts in British prehistory though there is little to show for it in Malory. In the romances there are indications of pagan status as a god, for he is the brother of a god, Ban (that is, Bran), and he is the father of a hero, Bors (who was brought up by the Damsel of the Lake with Lancelot, and was the lover of Brangoire's daughter). This is not very substantial, but Rhys, a century ago, made an illuminating observation to the effect that the name Bors is an eroded form of Geoffrey's Ambrosius, which is rendered Emrys or Embreis in Welsh versions of the *Historia*. It is now possible to substantiate Rhys's philological guess by comparing the relationships and behaviour of the two to see if they have resemblances apart from a vague similarity of name. As far as relationship is concerned, they each have brothers with whom, in their respective stories, they act in concert. It will be seen from the following comparison that there is a strong resemblance between the careers of two sets of brothers.

The **'brothers' Bors and Ban** (a form of Bran) who **came from Brittany** were instrumental in establishing the Arthurian regime at the great gathering on **Salisbury Plain**.

The **'brothers' Ambrosius and Uther** (also a form of Bran – see Who's Who? above) who in Geoffrey of Monmouth's *Historia* **came from Brittany** and later set up the blue-stone circle on **Salisbury Plain**.

There is a possibility that these two sets of circumstances could be considered as derived from a recollection of the same original event. As far as Ambrosius is concerned, there are several links with Stonehenge: this name is the title of Aurelius who as king of Britain commissioned the move of the bluestones and who was buried there; it is the title of Merlin who moved and re-erected the stones; and it is preserved in the place-name, Amesbury. Bors only has a link with Salisbury Plain in his presence at the great gathering which took place there at the tall rock, but there is a possibility of a more direct link with Stonehenge in his name. The classical account which seems most likely to refer to Stonehenge[39] gives the name Boreas as its founder. The Greek author naturally assimilated to a Greek word whatever name tradition had provided, but looked at from the point of view of British tradition this personage could have been Ambrosius/Bors. Perhaps some faint shadow of the influence of southern Brittany on British prehistory has persisted in tradition. Gannes, that is, Vannes, is in an Arthurian province which includes Barenton, and in a megalithic province which includes Carnac.

Another aspect of the relationship of Ban and Bors is that Beli and Mabon were brothers of Bran as well as Bors. Belenus and Mabon are both linked with the sun in classical inscriptions, and if the identification of Bors with Boreas is correct, the latter presided over a precinct devoted to Apollo. The link between two deities, one Bran and the other representing the sun, may have been remembered in more ways than one.

### The Spread in Space and Time of the Deities of the Romances

The spread of Celticism can be represented in various ways: Bran and Beli are thought[40] to have been carried, in the third century BC, south east into Macedonia from the Celtic heartland which is believed on archaeological evidence to have stretched from the Atlantic to Vienna and beyond.

The Gal- names have an equally wide distribution, and are indeed synonymous with Celticism, since Galli was the title used for the Celts by the Romans and, it is supposed, represented to classical ears the name they used for themselves. As mentioned above, members of this group of names crop up in Gaul, which is now France; Galicia, a province occupying the north west corner of Spain; and Galatia in central Anatolia.

A third set of names linked with Celticism, and with a somewhat similar distribution, is to be found in the place names which include the element Nemet. A group of these from England and Wales has been mentioned in the Gazetteer under Nemus. To these may be added Nemi itself, south of Rome; Nemetodurum, now Nanterre (Hautes-de-Seine); Nemeton in Vaison (Vaucluse); Nemetacetum in north east Gaul; Nemtobriga in Galicia; and Drunemeton in Galatia. As well as these there should probably be added the Irish 'invader' called Nemed, from whom the Fir Bolg (the men of Beli) and the Tuatha De Danann are said to have been descended.

The presence of Drunemeton in Galatia is particularly informative in several ways. The first element in the name, Dru- means oak, and the rest of the word, sacred enclosure; this is reminiscent of the oak-king who reigned at the nemeton at Nemi. The names of the three tribes for whom this place was a ceremonial centre are known, so Galatia is not a tribal name but has a much more all-embracing significance. Finally, the date on which this system was carried into Anatolia with an invading force was in the second century B.C., which shows that it was very much a going concern at that time.

---

[39] See Gazetteer, Salisbury Plain.
[40] *Pagan Celtic Britain*, Ross, p. 221.

Though Brennos and Bolgios (probably Bran and Beli) may have been demoted by classical authors to human status, the presence of pagan elements casts light on what is going on here. Bran and Belinus are known to have been gods, a nemeton is a sacred enclosure, and there is more than a hint from the romances that the Gal-names are linked with the pagan cults of watery places and of the challenge at the glade.

These religious features which correspond in their geographical range to the spread of Celticism demonstrate the spread of a package of deities but they do not represent the whole of the Celtic tradition. The Rees brothers suggest that the Dan- or Don- names of the Children of Don and the Tuatha De Danann share a common Indo-European root with many rivers and with the goddess Danu, who features in the Rig Veda.[41] If that is the case the spread far exceeds that of Celticism. The inference is that this element of the tradition of the west of Europe existed in the phase when expansion of the Indo-European languages took place both to the east and to the west. Don and Danu and their families therefore have more ancient origins than the Celts. This is in line with the view that Celticism was the last fling of Indo-Europeanization. That Don and Danu seem to be typical of Celticism is no bar to this proposition. As already remarked, tradition is short of historical perspective, and there is nothing to prevent deities like the Lord of the Animals or the Fisher King – who sound as if they have a footing in an era before even the agricultural age – sharing the pagan stage with a divinity of the Iron Age.

The sequence of deities can be further refined by reference to the suggestions of dating provided in this book. Here Bran and Beli are shown by their association with standing stones and tumuli to have been long-lived deities, surviving from a period not later than the Bronze Age. The Gal- names with their links with watery cult sites and their prominence in the last stages of Celticization may well correspond with the change to the watery cult sites which were favoured in the late Bronze and the Iron Age. So there is a sequence of deities from the times of hunter-gatherers onwards, but all appearing to exist together in the oral tradition. To what extent their worship continued into historical times cannot exactly be determined. Many strands have contributed to the paganism revealed in the first few centuries BC and AD, when classical records and masonry inscriptions first provide evidence for named deities. New forms of worship did not entirely replace the old. For instance, there is evidence for the worship of Faunus at Thetford in the late fourth century AD.[42] Faunus has characteristics in common with Sylvanus and Pan,[43] among the most primitive of gods. But by then Christianity was a force in the land. No doubt as time went on belief in the original dogmas became blunted. They were more than half-forgotten in the twelfth century when the Welsh folk-tales that were the originals of the 'matter of Britain' were collected. The lord of the Animals was still spoken of but by now no longer recognized as a god; and by the time of universal education in this century little remained but recollection among a superstitious peasantry of the healing power of wells[44] and the ritual fires appropriate to Beltaine, Midsummer Day and Hallowe'en.

---

[41] *Celtic Heritage*, A. Rees and B. Rees, p. 53.
[42] *Pagan Gods and Shrines of the Roman Empire*, ed. Henig and King, p. 93.
[43] *The Greek Myths*, Graves, vol. I, p. 193.
[44] In the Isle of Man I was myself, when a child, sent to fetch healing water from a saint's well in about 1936. It had no beneficial effect on the invalid.

# BIBLIOGRAPHY

Adams, A. (ed. and tr.), *The Romance of Yder*, Cambridge, 1983

Alcock, L., *Arthur's Britain*, Harmondsworth, 1971

Anon., *Perceforest: les anciennes croniques Dangleterre* etc., Paris 1528 (and see Lods, J., Roussineau, G. and Taylor, J.)

Armstrong, R. B., *The History of Liddesdale*, Edinburgh and London, 1883

Atkinson, R. J. C., *Stonehenge, Archaeology and Interpretation*, Penguin, 1979. Reprinted

Bain, J. (ed.), *Calendar of Letters and Papers relating to the Borders*, Edinburgh 1894 etc.

Barber, R. W., *The Figure of Arthur*, London, 1972

Barber, R. W., *King Arthur in Legend and History*, Ipswich 1973

Baring-Gould, S. and Fisher, J., *The Lives of the British Saints*, London, 1913

Blaess, M., 'Arthur's Sisters', *Bibliographical Bulletin of the International Arthurian Society*, 8, 1956, pp 69–77

Blakeslee, M. R., *Love's Masks*, Cambridge, 1989

Bogdanow, F. (ed.), *La Folie Lancelot*, Tübingen, 1965

Bogdanow, F., *The Romance of the Grail: a study* etc., Manchester 1966

Bowen, D. Q., Pleistocene Scenario for Paleolithic Wales, *British Archaeoligical Reports*, 76, 1980

Bradley, R., *The Dorset Cursus: the archaeology of the enigmatic*. Council for British Archaeology Group, 1986

Bradley, R., *The Passage of Arms*, Cambridge, 1990

Brereton, G., *Des granz geanz*, Oxford, 1937

Bromwich, R., *Trioedd Ynys Prydein*, Cardiff, 1961

Bryant, N., *The high book of the Grail: a translation of the 13th century romance of 'Perlesvaus'*, Ipswich, 1978

Burgess, C., *The age of Stonehenge*, London, 1980

Burl, A., *Rites of the Gods*, London, 1981

Burl, A., *Prehistoric Astronomy and Ritual*, Aylesbury, 1983

Burl, A., *The Stonehenge People*, London, 1987

Burrow, J. A., *A Reading of Sir Gawaine and the Green Knight*, London, 1965

Carman, J. N., 'The Perlesvaus and the Bristol Channel', *Research Studies*, vol. 32, 1964, pp. 85–105

Carroll, C. W. (ed. and tr.), *Erec et Enide*, New York and London, 1987

Cavendish, R., *King Arthur and the Grail: the Arthurian legends and their meaning*, London, 1987

Chippindale, C., *Stonehenge Complete*, London 1983

Chrétien de Troyes, see Comfort, Roques, Linker etc.

Christie, P. M. L., 'The Excavation of an Iron Age Souterrain and Settlement at Carn Euny', *Proc. Prehistory Soc*, 44, 1978

Clark, J. G. D., *Archaeology and Society*, London, 1968

Comfort, W. W. (tr.), Chrétien's *Erec et Enide*, *Yvain* and *Lancelot*, London and New York 1914

Crawford, O. G. S. and Richmond, I. A., 'The Ravenna Cosmography', *Archaeologia*, XCIII

Cunliffe, B., *The Celtic World*, London, 1979

Cunnington, B. H., 'The "Blue Stone" from Boles Barrow', *Wiltshire Archaeological and Natural History Magazine*, 42, 431–437
Darrah, J. H., *The Real Camelot, London*, 1981
Darvill, T. C., *Prehistoric Gloucester*, Gloucester, 1987
Davidson, H. R. E., *Scandinavian Mythology*, London, 1982
de Luc, J. A., *Geological Travels*, London, 1811
Dumville, D. N., 'Sub-Roman Britain: History and Legend', *History*, no. 62, 173–192, 1977
Ekwall, E., *The Oxford Dictionary of English Place-Names*, 4th edn, 1960
Estyn Evans, E., *Irish Heritage*, Dundalk, 1942
Evans, S. (tr.), *Perceval le Gallois. The High History of the Holy Graal*, Everyman, 1969
Ewert, A., *The romance of Tristan/Beroul*, Oxford, 1939
Frappier, J., *Étude sur la mort le roi Artu. Roman du XIIIe siècle*, Paris and Geneva, 1961
Fraser, R., *The Making of the Golden Bough*, London, 1990
Frazer, Sir J. G., *The Golden Bough*, London, 1907–1915
Ganz, J. (tr.), *The Mabinogion*, Penguin 1976
Gelling, P. and Davidson, H. E., *The Chariot of the Sun and other rites and symbols of the northern bronze age*, London, rev. 1982
Gelzer, H. (ed.), *Der altfranzöische Yderroman*, Dresden, 1913
Germain, A. A., *St Michel et le Mont St Michel*, Paris 1880
Gimbutas, M., *The Goddesses and Gods of Old Europe*, London, 1982
Glob, P. V., *The Bog People: Iron-Age Man Preserved*, (tr.) London, 1969
Glob, P. V., *The mound people: Danish Bronze-Age man preserved*, London, 1983
Goetinck, G., *Peredur: a study of the Welsh tradition in the Grail Legends*, Cardiff, 1975
Goldschmidt, M. (ed.), *Sone de Nausay*, Tübingen, 1899
Graesse, J. G. T., *Orbis Latinus*, Dresden, 1861
Graves, R., *The Greek Myths*, Harmondsworth, rep. 1966
Green, M. J., *Gods of the Celts*, Gloucester, 1986
Grinsell, L. V., *Folklore of Prehistoric Sites in Britain*, 1976
Harward, V. J., *The Dwarfs of Arthurian Romance and Celtic Tradition*, Leiden, 1958
Hatto, A. T. (tr.), *Tristan*, London, 1974
Hatto, A. T. (tr.), *Parzival*, Penguin, 1980
Henig, M. and King, A. (ed.), *Pagan Gods and Shrines of the Roman Empire*, Oxford, 1986
Hilka, A. (ed.), *Li contes del Graal*, Halle, 1932
Hole, C., *Saints in Folklore*, London, 1965
Hucher, E. F. F. (ed.), *Le Saint Graal, ou le Joseph d'Arimathie etc.*, Le Mans-Paris, 1875
Hutchings, G. (ed.), *Le roman en prose de Lancelot du Lac: le conte de la Charrette*, Paris, 1938
Hutton, R., *The Pagan Religions of the Ancient British Isles*, Oxford and Cambridge (USA), 1991
Jackson, K. H., *The International Popular Tale and Early Welsh Tradition*, Cardiff, 1961
Jillings, L., *Diu Crone of Heinrich von dem Türlein: the attempted emancipation of secular narrative*, Göppingen, 1980
Jones, F., *The Holy Wells of Wales*, Cardiff, 1954
Jones, G. and Jones, T. (tr.), *The Mabinogion*, Everyman, 1949
Jung, E. and von Franz, M.L., *The Grail Legend*, London, 1971
Kendrick, T. D., *The Druids. A study in Keltic prehistory*, London, 1927
Kershaw (later Chadwick), N., *Early Brittany*, Cardiff, 1969
Lacy, N. J. (ed.), *The Arthurian Encyclopedia*, N.Y. and London, 1986
Lathuillère, R., *Guiron le Courtois*, Geneva, 1966
Legge, M. D., *Le Roman de Balain*, Manchester, 1942
Linker, R. W. (tr.), *The Story of the Grail*, Chapel Hill, 1952
Lods, J., *Le Roman de Perceforest: origines, composition, caractères, valeur et influence*, Geneva, 1951
Loomis, R. S., *Celtic Myth and Arthurian Romance*, New York, 1927

Loomis, R. S., *Wales and the Arthurian Legend*, Cardiff, 1956
Loomis, R. S., *The Grail: From Celtic Myth to Christian Symbol*, New York, 1963
Loomis, R. S. (ed.), *Arthurian Literature in the Middle Ages*, Oxford, 1959
Loomis, R. S. (tr.), *Trystram and Ysolt, by Thomas the Troubadour*, New York, 1951
Löseth, E., *Le Roman de Tristan etc.*, Paris, 1891
de Luc, J. A., *Geological Travels*, London, 1811
Luttrell, C., *The Creation of the First Arthurian Romance. A Quest*, London, 1974
Mac Cana, P., *Branwen, Daughter of Llyr*, Cardiff, 1958
Mac Cana, P., *Celtic Mythology*, Feltham, rev. 1983
Marco Polo, *The Travels of Marco Polo*, Everyman, 1908
Markale, J., *Le roi Arthur et la société celtique*, Paris, 1983
Markale, J., *Le Druidisme: traditions et dieux des Celtes*, Paris, 1985
Mason, E. (tr.), *Wace's Roman de Brut* and *Layamon's Brut*, London, 1962
Mason, E. J., *The Wye Valley: from river mouth to Hereford*, London, 1987
Matarasso, P. M. (tr.), *Queste del Saint Graal*, Penguin, 1969
Matthews, W. H., *Mazes and Labyrinths*, London, 1922
Maxwell, Sir H., *A history of Dumfries and Galloway*, Edinburgh and London, 1896
Morris, Lewis, (fl. 1701–1765) 'Celtic Remains', *Cambrian Archaeological Association*, 1878
Morris, R., *The Character of King Arthur in Medieval Literature*, Cambridge, 1982
Neilson, G., *Annals of the Solway until 1307*, Glasgow 1899
Newstead, H., *Bran the Blessed in Arthurian Romance*, New York, 1939
Newstead, H., 'Perceval's Father in Welsh Tradition', *Romanic Review* XXXVI, 3–29, 1945
Nicolaisen, W. F. H., *Scottish Place-names*, London, 1976
Nilsson, N. M. P., *A History of Greek Religion*, Oxford, 1949
Nillson, N. M. P., *Greek Popular Religion*, New York, 1961
Nitze, W. A., *Le Roman de l'Estoire dou Graal of Robert de Boron*, Paris, 1927
Nitze, W. A. and Jenkins, T. A., *Le haut livre du Graal, Perlesvaus*, Chicago, 1932
O'Meara, J. J., *Giraldus Cambrensis: The First Version of the Topography of Ireland*, Dundalk, 1951
O'Rahilly, T. F., *Early Irish History and Mythology*, Dublin, 1946
Owen, D. D. R., 'The Romance of Fergus', in *Arthurian Literature VIII*, ed. R. W. Barber, 1989
Paton, L. A., *Studies in the Fairy Mythology of Arthurian Romance*, Camb. Mass, 1903
de Paor, L., *The peoples of Ireland: from prehistory to modern times*, London, 1986
Pare, C., 'Use of the wagon in later prehistory', *Antiquity*, 63, 1989
Paris, G. and Ulrich, J., *Merlin, roman . . . publie avec la mise en prose du poème de Merlin de Robert de Boron*, Paris, 1886
Parry, J. J. (ed. and tr.), *The Vita Merlini*, Illinois, 1925
Pearce, R. T., *Stones, bones and gods: discovering the beliefs of primitive man in Britain*, London, 1982
Pei, M. A., *The Families of Words*, New York, 1962
Pennant, T., *A Tour in Scotland, Mdcclxix*, facsimile, Perth, 1979
Pennant, T., *A Tour in Wales, MDCCLXXIII*, Dublin, 1779
*Perceforest*, N. Cousteau pour Galiot du Pre, Paris, 1528
Perret, M. and Weill, I. *Le bel inconnu . . .* tr. into modern French, Paris, 1990
Pickford, C. E. (ed.), *Erec: roman arthurien en prose*, Geneva, 1968
Piggott, Prof S., 'The Sources of Geoffrey of Monmouth', *Antiquity*, XV, 1941, pp. 305–319
Potvin, C., *Perceval le Gallois, ou le conte du Graal*, Soc. des Bibiolphiles Belges, 1866
Renfrew, C., *Archaeology and Language. the puzzle of Indo-European origins*, London 1987
Rees, A. and Rees, B., *Celtic Heritage*, London, 1961
Rhys, Sir J., *Studies in the Arthurian Legend*, Oxford, 1891
Rhys, Sir J., *et al.*, *Pembrokeshire Antiquities*, Solva, 1897
Richmond, I. A. and Crawford, O. G. S., 'The Ravenna Cosmography', *Archaeologia* XCIII, 1–50, 1949

Rivet, A. L. F. and Smith, C., *The Place-Names of Roman Britain*, Princeton, 1979

Roach, W. (ed.), *The Continuations of the Old French 'Perceval' of Chrétien de Troyes*, Philadelphia, 1949–1983

Roach, W. (ed.), *The Didot Perceval according to the Manuscripts of Modena and Paris*, Philadelphia, 1955

Roques, M. L. G. (ed.), *Les Romans de Chrétien de Troyes: Erec et Enide, le Chevalier de la charrette*, and *le Chevalier au lion* (*Yvain*), Paris, 1952–1960

Ross, A., *Pagan Celtic Britain*, London, rep. 1974

Roussineau G. (ed.), *Perceforest pt. IV; Édition critique avec introduction, notes et glossaire*, Geneva, 1987

Ruggles, C. N. L. and Whittle, A. W. R., 'Astronomy and Society in Britain during the period 4000–1500 B.C.', *B A R British Series 88*, Oxford, 1981

Saintyves, P. (pseud. for Emile Nourry), *Les Saints successeurs des dieux*, Paris, 1907

Schmolke-Hasselman, B., *Arthurian Literature II*, ed. R. W. Barber, Cambridge, 1982

Scott, Sir W., *Minstrelsy of the Scottish Border*, fifth edn. Edinburgh, 1821

Service, A. and Bradbery, J., *A Guide to the Megaliths of Europe*, St Albans, 1981

Sommer, H. O. (ed.), *The Vulgate Version of the Arthurian Romances*, (7 vols) Washington, D.C., 1909

Sommer, H. O. (ed.), *The Adventure of Gawain, Yvain and le Morholt with the three Maidens. . . .*, Beihefte zur Zeitschrift für Romanische Philologie, 47 Heft, 1913

Spencer Jones, H., *General Astronomy*, London, 1934

Stead, I. M., *et al.*, *Lindow Man: the body in the bog*, London, 1986

Stokes, W. and Windisch, W. O. E., *Irische Texte etc.*, 1880

Taylor, J. H. M., *Le Roman de Perceforest* (pt. I), Geneva, 1979

Taylour, Lord W., *The Mycenaeans*, London, 1983

Thomas, H. H., 'The Sources of the Stones of Stonehenge', *Antiquaries Journal*, III, 239–260, 1923

Thompson, A. W. (ed.), *The Elucidation: A Prologue to the Conte du Graal*, New York, 1931

Thorpe, R. S., *et. al.*, *Proceedings of the Prehistoric Society*, 57 pt. 2, 1991

Tolkien, J. R. R. and Gordon, E. V., *Sir Gawain and the Green Knight*, Oxford, 1930

Tolstoy, N., *The Quest for Merlin*, London, 1985

Wade Evans, A. W. (ed.), *Life of St David*, 1923

Webster, K. G. T., *Guinevere: A Study of her Abductions*, Milton, Mass, 1951

Webster, K. G. T. (tr.), *Lanzelet: A Romance of Lancelot*, New York, 1951

Wait, G. A., 'Ritual and Religion in Iron Age Britain', *British Archaeology Group, British Series 149 (i)*, Oxford, 1985

West, G. D., *An Index of Proper Names in French Arthurian Verse Romances*, Toronto, 1969

West, G. D., *An Index of Proper Names in French Arthurian Prose Romances*, Toronto, 1978

Weston, J. L. (tr.), *Sir Gawain and the Lady of Lys*, London, 1907

Weston, J. L. (tr.), *The Legend of Sir Lancelot du Lac*, London, 1901

Weston, J. L., *From Ritual to Romance*, Cambridge, 1920

Weston, J. L., (tr.), *The Story of Tristan and Iseult*, London, 1899

Williams, G. Perrie (ed.), *Renaut de Beaujeu: Le Bel Inconnu*, Paris, 1929

Williams, Mary (ed.), *Gerbert de Montreuil. La Continuation de Perceval*, Paris, 1922 etc.

Wolfgang, L. D. (ed.), *Bliocadran: A Prologue to the Perceval of Chrétien de Troyes*, Tübingen, 1976

Womack, J., *Well-dressing in Derbyshire*, Clapham, 1977

Wright, N., *The Historia Regum Britannie of Geoffrey of Monmouth:*
   *I Bern Burger-bibliothek Ms 568*, Cambridge, 1985
   *II The First Variant Version: a critical edition*, Cambridge, 1988
   *V Gesta Regum Britannie*, Cambridge, 1991

Zenker, R. (ed.), Lai de l'Espine, *Zeitschrift Für Romanische Philologie*, XVII, 1893

# INDEX

THE ORIGINS of Arthurian romance will always be a hotly disputed subject. The great moments of the legends belong partly to dimly-remembered history, partly to the poets' imagination down the ages, whether Welsh, Breton, French or German. Yet there is another element behind the stories which goes back deeper and further, and which is even more difficult to pinpoint, the traces of ancient pagan religion.

We know so little for certain about Celtic religion that any attempt to document these recollections of prehistoric and mythological material is a hazardous undertaking. However, John Darrah makes a persuasive case for the existence of these underlying themes, both in terms of heroes who have inherited the attributes of gods, and of episodes which reflect ancient religious rituals. His careful study of the thematic relationships of many little-known episodes of the romances and his unravelling of the relative geography of Arthurian Britain as portrayed in the romances will be valuable even to readers who may beg to differ with his final conclusions.

His most original contribution to an unravelling of a pagan Arthurian past lies in his appropriation of the fascinating evidence of standing stones and pagan cultic sites. The magical attributes of stones are exemplified in prehistoric standing stones, the real counterparts of the *perrons* of the French romances. This is dark and difficult territory, but certain events in the Arthurian cycle, which take place on and around Salisbury Plain, have correspondences with known prehistoric events. Building on these elusive clues, and tracing a range of sites around the river Severn and south Wales, John Darrah has added a significant new dimension to the search for the sources of England's great epic, the legends of Arthur and his court.